GENDER POLITICS IN GLOBAL GOVERNANCE

Edited by Mary K. Meyer and Elisabeth Prügl

ROWMAN & LITTLEFIELD PUBLISHERS, INC.
Lanham • Boulder • New York • Oxford

ROWMAN & LITTLEFIELD PUBLISHERS, INC.

Published in the United States of America
by Rowman & Littlefield Publishers, Inc.
4720 Boston Way, Lanham, Maryland 20706

12 Hid's Copse Road
Cumnor Hill, Oxford OX2 9JJ, England

British Library Cataloguing in Publication Information Available

Library of Congress Cataloging-in-Publication Data

Gender politics in global governance / edited by Mary K. Meyer and
    Elisabeth Prügl.
      p. cm.
    Includes bibliographical references and index.
    ISBN 0–8476–9160–8 (cloth : alk. paper). — ISBN 0-8476-9161-6
(paper : alk. paper)
      1. Women in politics.   2. International relations.
3. International agencies.   4. International organization.
5. Feminist theory.   I. Meyer, Mary K., 1957– . II. Prügl,
Elisabeth.
HQ1236.G4617   1999
305.42—dc21   98–39357
                                                CIP

Printed in the United States of America

♾ ™ The paper used in this publication meets the minimum requirements of
American National Standard for Information Sciences—Permanence of Paper for
Printed Library Materials, ANSI Z39.48–1984.

Contents

Part III. Contesting Language: Gendered Rules in Global Governance

Illustrations

Tables

Preface

The 1990s have seen unprecedented international activism not only on security issues but also on social and economic issues. The proliferation of United Nations peacekeeping missions after the end of the cold war, the series of United Nations conferences on a diverse set of topics, and the strengthening of the European Union all attest to an intensification of politics beyond the nation-state. Such politics are not confined to deliberations between states but have increasingly included the contentious activities of internationally oriented social movements and nongovernmental organizations. A mature feminist movement has contributed extensively to global debates in the 1990s, and feminist researchers have analyzed and documented its activism.

In this book we have compiled empirical work documenting the intersection of feminist activism and international politics. The project grew out of discussions at the 1995 meetings of the International Studies Association (ISA) and of ISA/South. Several contributors and the editors presented papers at these meetings. Together we realized that international organizations and the various UN conferences of the 1990s provided a wealth of information about women's activism and gender politics. We found it important to document this activism not only because it constituted a significant aspect of globally oriented feminist politics but also because it provided materials for current reconceptualizations of the international that reach beyond the interstate arena.

We owe thanks for the idea for this volume to Cynthia Enloe, who suggested sometime ago that this was a collection that needed compiling. She was right, and her vision proved unfailing. We would also like to thank our contributors for their responsiveness to our queries and for their patience as the project drew on. The Department of International Relations at Florida International University and the Department of Political Science at Eckerd College provided diverse office support in the preparation of the manuscript and funding for our travel to conferences, where we discussed conceptual issues and developed the outline for the volume. Mary K. Meyer would like to thank the National University of Ireland, Galway, and its Women's Studies Center for office space and technological support during an important phase of this project. Elisabeth Prügl also would like to thank Peter and Rosalie for providing backup on housework and child-care duties when the demands of the project spilled into weekends and long evenings. Little Helen, of course, supplied all the inspiration.

Acknowledgments

Chapter 3 appeared in an earlier, longer form as "Peacekeeping and Peace Research: Men's and Women's Work" in *Women & Politics* 18, no. 1 (1997): 27–51. Reprinted by permission of Haworth Press.

Chapter 4 originally appeared in *Aggressive Behavior* 24, no. 2 (1998): 135–46. © 1998 John Wiley & Sons. Reprinted by permission.

Chapter 13 originally appeared as "Women and the Neoliberal Agenda of the North" in *Women in Development: Trade Aspects of Women in the Development Process,* edited by Eva Haxton and Claes Olsson (Uppsala, Sweden: United Nations Youth and Student Association of Sweden, 1995), 104–17. Reprinted by permission.

Abbreviations

Alt-WID	Alternative Women in Development
ANGOC	Asian Non-Governmental Organization Coalition
APWLD	Asia Pacific Women Law and Development
ASG	Assistant Secretary-General
CARICOM	Caribbean Common Market
CCPP	Permanent Commission of the Representatives of the Refugees
CEDAW	Convention/Committee on the Elimination of All Forms of Discrimination against Women
CEEC	Central and Eastern European Countries
CEPIA	Citizenship, Studies, Information, Action
CIAM	Women's Center for Research and Action
CIERFCA	International Conference on Central American Refugees
CIM	Inter-American Commission of Women (Comisión Interamericana de Mujeres)
CIS	Commonwealth of Independent States (former Soviet Union)
CONGO	Council of Non-Governmental Organizations
CREW	Centre for Research on European Women
CRIAW	Canadian Research Institute for the Advancement of Women
CSW	Commission on the Status of Women (UN)
CWPE	Committee on Women, Population, and the Environment
DAW	Division for the Advancement of Women (secretariat of the CSW)
DAWN	Development Alternatives for Women in a New Era
DPCSD	Department for Policy Coordination and Sustainable Development
EC	European Community
ECE	Economic Commission for Europe
ECJ	European Court of Justice
ECOSOC	Economic and Social Council (UN)
EP	European Parliament
EU	European Union

FAO	Food and Agricultural Organization
FINNRRAGE	Feminist International Network for Resistance to Reproductive and Genetic Engineering
FoReFem	Regional Forum of Refugee and Repatriated Women
FWCW	Fourth World Conference on Women (Beijing conference)
GATT	General Agreement on Tariffs and Trade
GNP	gross national product
GROOTS	Grassroots Organizations Operating Together in Sisterhood
GS	General Service
IAEA	International Atomic Energy Agency
IAW	International Alliance of Women
IBRD	International Bank for Reconstruction and Development (World Bank)
ICAO	International Civil Aviation Organization
ICJ	International Court of Justice
ICPD	International Conference on Population and Development
ICW	International Council of Women
ICWPP	International Committee of Women for Permanent Peace
IDA	International Development Association
IFAD	International Fund for Agricultural Development
IFC	International Finance Corporation
IFI	international financial institution
IGC	intergovernmental conference
IGO	international governmental organization, or intergovernmental organization
ILO	International Labor Organization
IMF	International Monetary Fund
IMO	International Maritime Organization
INGO	international nongovernmental organization
INSTRAW	International Research and Training Institute for the Advancement of Women
IO	international organization
IOM	International Organization for Migration
IR	International Relations
Isis	International Women's Information and Communication Service
ITC	International Trade Centre, UNCTAD/WTO
ITU	International Telecommunication Union
IWHC	International Women's Health Coalition
IWHM	international women's health movement
IWRAW	International Women's Rights Action Watch

IWY	International Women's Year
JUSCANZ	Japan, the United States, Canada, Australia, and New Zealand
MAI	Multilateral Agreement on Investment
MEP	Member of the European Parliament
MIGA	Multilateral Investment Guarantee Agency
NAACP	National Association for the Advancement of Colored People
NAC	National Action Committee on the Status of Women
NGO	nongovernmental organization
NIC	newly industrializing country
OAS	Organization of American States
OECD	Organization for Economic Cooperation and Development
PCIJ	Permanent Court of International Justice
RG	Reflection Group
SANE	Sustainable Agriculture Network
SEWA	Self-Employed Women's Association
STOP	Sexual Trafficking of Persons
TEU	Treaty on European Union
TNC	transnational corporation
UNAMIC	United Nations Advance Mission in Cambodia
UNCED	United Nations Conference on Environment and Development
UNCHR	United Nations Commission on Human Rights
UNCHS	United Nations Centre for Human Settlements (Habitat)
UNCTAD	United Nations Conference on Trade and Development
UNDP	United Nations Development Programme
UNEP	United Nations Environment Programme
UNESCO	United Nations Educational, Scientific, and Cultural Organization
UNFPA	United Nations Population Fund (formerly United Nations Fund for Population Activities)
UNHCR	United Nations High Commissioner for Refugees
UNICEF	United Nations Children's Fund
UNIDCP	United Nations International Drug Control Programme
UNIDO	United Nations Industrial Development Organization
UNIFEM	United Nations Development Fund for Women
UNITAR	United Nations Institute for Training and Research
UNO	United Nations Organization
UNOMSA	United Nations Observer Mission in South Africa
UNPF	United Nations Population Fund

UNTAC	United Nations Transition Authority in Cambodia
UNTAG	United Nations Transition Assistance Group (Namibia)
UNU	United Nations University
UNV	United Nations volunteer
UPU	Universal Postal Union
USG	under-secretary-general
WEDO	Women's Environment and Development Organization
WFP	World Food Programme
WGNRR	Women's Global Network for Resistance to Reproductive Rights
WHO	World Health Organization
WID	women in development
WIDE	Women in Development Europe
WIDE	Women in Development and Environment
WILDAF	Women in Law and Development Africa
WILPF	Women's International League for Peace and Freedom
WINGO	women's international nongovernmental organization
WIPO	World Intellectual Property Organization
WLDI	Women, Law, and Development International
WMO	World Meteorological Organization
WRAP	Women's Rights Advocacy Program (of the International Human Rights Law Group)
WTO	World Trade Organization

INTRODUCTION

1

Gender Politics in Global Governance

Elisabeth Prügl and Mary K. Meyer

Women in many countries have organized to fight male supremacy and to advance interests that arise from their unique life experiences. With the rise of multilateral institutions in the twentieth century, there emerged in addition a form of feminism with an internationalist orientation that sought to shape the agendas of international organizations and the normative practices of global governance. The United Nations' Fourth World Conference on Women held in Beijing in September 1995 and the parallel Non-Governmental Women's Forum fifty miles away drew renewed attention to the international women's movement and the issues it has placed on the global political agenda. International women's activism earlier in the twentieth century was part of the political struggles of middle- and upper-class women in Europe, North America, and Latin America for suffrage, equal rights, and peace. Such activism in the latter part of the century has broadened to embrace the economic and social struggles of women burdened with various forms of oppression throughout the world and includes the voices of women from diverse social classes. The series of United Nations women's conferences punctuating the United Nations Decade for Women (1975–1985) and culminating in the 1995 Beijing conference became both a catalyst and a focus for women's organizing from the grass roots to the global level. The result today is a global women's movement characterized by diverse organizational structures, political strategies, and feminist voices focused on one common goal: the empowerment and advancement of the world's women.

This volume draws together new research that explores gender politics in global governance. It is attentive to historical and contemporary modes of women's organizing from the local to the global levels to effect change in the governance structures and practices that oppress women. It employs a variety of approaches to study the mainstreaming, disengaging, and networking strategies of women's organizations operating in global spaces. It also identifies

3

conceptual and political debates within global feminist movements. Above all, it focuses on the gendered nature of the institutions, practices, and discourses of global governance and the ways in which women have struggled to change them.

Defining Gender in Global Governance

This collection employs two expressions with contested meanings, *gender* and *global governance*. Both terms emerge from specific political debates that have characterized the latter part of the twentieth century; namely, the debates about the role of women in society and about political authority in a world that increasingly connects agents from different continents, states, regions, cities, and neighborhoods. Our use of the term *global governance* signals a movement beyond the narrow study of international organizations. We are concerned not only with women's roles in the United Nations and other intergovernmental organizations but also with the political processes that engage nongovernmental organizations (NGOs) and agents as well as with norms and rules that emerge from global economic practices. This is in line with a general broadening of the field of international organization from a preoccupation with describing the output of intergovernmental organizations, their formal attributes, and processes of decision making to a concern with structures of governance (Kratochwil and Ruggie 1986).

Because the attention to gender in international organizations is relatively new, we have not imposed unitary definitions nor asked contributors to employ our own understandings of global governance. Their diverse interpretations enable comparisons of historical fact, conceptual frameworks, and theoretical approaches and allow creative insights to emerge. To facilitate debate, we have organized the collection according to the assumptions that contributors bring to the terms of our inquiry.

These converge around three different approaches. First, some contributors approach gender in global governance as involving institutional structures in which women have found or carved out niches for themselves and their interests as women. International organizations, including the United Nations Organization as well as regional organizations such as the European Union (EU) and the Organization of American States (OAS), define or contain these spaces, allowing women to become diplomatic or political agents as members of women's commissions or as staff in bureaucracies. In the past three decades the institutions of "global civil society," including NGOs based in broader social movements, have become more visible and enlarged these spaces of global governance. As political agents in governmental and nongovernmental organizations, women introduce into global governance women-centered ways of framing issues, and they advance feminist agendas. The chapters in part I of this collection share this approach.

The second way in which contributors approach gender politics in global governance is by exploring the purposive, goal-oriented activities and strate- 2.) gies of influential actors that propel diverse policy processes in the interstate arena. These processes involve the interchange between intergovernmental organizations and states on the one hand and forces in the international women's movement on the other. Analyses from this perspective focus on social-movement strategies to influence the United Nations in particular. They also include accounts of the ways in which states, bureaucracies, or forces of civil society have facilitated or obstructed the agendas of women's movements. The chapters in part II of this collection focus on these processes.

Finally, contributors approach gender politics in global governance as con- 3.) testations of rules and discursive practices in different issue areas. Global rules include those codified by intergovernmental organizations as well as informal rules with a global reach—for example, those embodied in global economics. Feminist critique and practice reveal that such rules are gendered, that is, they construct and reproduce notions of masculinity and femininity and associated power differentials. The chapters in part III of this collection explore global governance from this perspective.

These approaches are not mutually exclusive, but they shed light on different aspects of gender politics in global governance. For example, a focus on political spaces often suggests a belief that the creation or opening of such spaces for women signals feminist politics. A focus on goal-oriented strategies and struggles implies a belief that feminist organizing can bring about changes in the politics of international organizations, thus advancing feminist agendas. A focus on norms and rules is more likely to highlight structural impediments to women's advancement and to view international organizations as implicated in the reproduction of gendered hierarchies. Authors we place in one category often share insights and understandings from others. Yet the chapters in different parts do illustrate particular meanings, highlighting the contested character of the field.

Like the term global governance, the term *gender* is politically loaded. In including "gender" rather than "women" in our title, we follow prevailing practice among feminist scholars today, but we do so with an awareness of the theoretical commitments the term implies. Gender emerged as a crucial concept of the women's movement, originally replacing the term *sex* (which social scientists had used to describe differences between women and men) but increasingly replacing as well the term *woman*. Feminists insisted that sex differences were not natural and biologically given. Instead, they argued that gender identities were the result of pervasive social construction processes ranging from early childhood socialization to gender images in the media and practices in the workplace. Joan Scott argued further that gender was "a primary way of signifying relationships of power" (1986, 1067). Gender divided the world in a binary fashion that provided the means for the articulation and legitimation of power. Like power, gender inhabited social relations including symbols, norms, organizations, institutions, and subjective identities.

As feminists increasingly understood gender as a social construct, "women's studies" increasingly became "gender studies," focusing on the construction of binary relationships that mapped onto gender. Yet, some feminists have warned about the political implications of this shift (e.g., Zalewski 1998). They argue that it moves attention from women's subordination to gender constructions, from the politics and choices of agents (including the women's movement) to gendered structures that passively envelop both women and men. The shift makes it more difficult to determine ways of emancipating women.

This debate has particularly severe implications for internationalist feminists who claim to speak for the women of the world. Leila J. Rupp (1994) documents how internationalist feminists during the first wave of the women's movement early in the twentieth century reproduced global power relations in the process of creating a collective identity. In the second wave of the feminist movement, which was closely linked with the UN Decade for Women, women of color, "Third World women," lesbians, and other previously marginalized groups fiercely criticized language that assumed that all women were the same and were oppressed in the same way. They insisted that it was important to recognize differences arising from identifications based on race, ethnicity, culture, class, sexual orientation or national location (hooks 1981; Spelman 1988; Mohanty 1991).

The retreat to analyzing gender, a social construction emerging from particular geographical and historical contexts, provided an alternative approach that took seriously this critique. The result has been a proliferation of descriptions of women's local experiences, gender constructions, and feminisms in diverse contexts as well as a retreat from claims to commonality, including those of common oppression and even common sisterhood that had rallied women at the beginning of the UN Decade. Two recent collections focusing on women's movements from an international perspective (Basu 1995; Scott, Kaplan, and Keates 1997) describe movements in different countries but are silent on the encounters between these movements in international spaces. An internationalist "we" has become unspeakable, the internationalist woman has been silenced before she was ever heard (Zalewski 1998).

The writings in this collection reflect the tensions within contemporary feminist scholarship that arise from efforts to avoid totalizing judgments about "women" on the one hand while retaining a focus on women's agency on the other. Chapters in parts I and II locate women and treat them as active agents effecting change. However, they rarely problematize diversity among women or the historical meaning of woman, risking the charge of obscuring differences. In contrast, chapters in part III employ gender as an analytical category, illustrating the ways in which masculinity and femininity are codified in global norms and practices. However, this approach risks the charge that it silences women by placing less emphasis on strategies and political choices. Yet, any of our chapters clearly attempt to focus on both women and gender, on women's emancipatory strategies and the power consequences of linguistic frames.

Locating Women in Global Governance

Internationalist women's activism has succeeded in finding or opening important—if circumscribed—spaces for women inside multilateral institutions. International governmental organizations like the League of Nations, the United Nations, the Organization of American States, and the European Union have responded, albeit reluctantly, to activist women's demands for representation and participation inside their political and bureaucratic structures. In the 1920s, the activists from across the Americas deliberately turned to inter-American diplomatic conferences to pressure their own governments to improve the rights and status of women at the national level. The diplomats responded by creating the Inter-American Commission of Women (Comisíon Interamericana de Mujeres, CIM) to study the laws and constitutions of the Americas, thus opening an important new diplomatic space for feminist politics in the inter-American system. The CIM women went beyond the technical studies they were assigned and became a crucial feminist force in various multilateral spaces. The League of Nations noticed their path-breaking work for women's rights in the Americas as an important model (Meyer on CIM this volume). The CIM women, along with individual women activists on governmental delegations, also played an influential role in the negotiations to establish the United Nations and incorporate women and women's rights into its charter and organizational structure. They secured the establishment of the nuclear Subcommission on the Status of Women, which was raised to the status of a commission of the Economic and Social Council in 1947 (Stienstra 1994, 78-84; Reanda 1992, 266, 272; see D'Amico this volume).

After their early successes in including and codifying women's political and civil rights in international conventions, the CIM and the UN Commission on the Status of Women (CSW) became ghettos for "women's issues" in the OAS and the UN in subsequent decades, lacking sufficient funding, staff, and political clout to carry out their missions fully. Nevertheless, they did maintain some space to conduct important work, including gathering international data on women, preparing technical reports, drafting conventions or treaty language relating to women and children, keeping certain women's issues on the multilateral agenda, and helping to translate new issues into official policies such as "women in development" (see Reanda 1992; Meyer on CIM this volume; D'Amico this volume). Yet, because the political decision-making bodies of these commissions are made up of women diplomats representing their governments, and because their governments have continued to resist improving women's status, these commissions have been seriously limited in their scope and their ability to be leaders in women's emancipation from oppression in all its forms. In this sense, official women's commissions depend on the activism of women's movements to break new ground, place new issues on the international agenda, and force governments and multilateral institutions to respond.

The official diplomatic spaces for women in multilateral institutions are complemented or supported by certain bureaucratic spaces in which women have been able to develop technical expertise and bureaucratic machinery to track or mainstream "women's issues" inside those institutions. For example, in response to the verbal commitments of governments to improve the status of women through the four UN women's conferences, the UN created two new bodies dedicated exclusively to—and primarily staffed by—women: UNIFEM (United Nations Development Fund for Women) and INSTRAW (International Research and Training Institute for the Advancement of Women). The 1979 Convention on the Elimination of All Forms of Discrimination against Women (CEDAW) also led to the creation of a new specialized commission known by the same acronym to oversee the implementation of the convention. Likewise, as the UN has begun to take account of gender issues in recent years, new official posts in the UN Secretariat and new offices in the specialized agencies such as the World Bank have been created as defined spaces where certain kinds of feminist politics can take place (see D'Amico this volume).

Internationalist women did not confine themselves to creating spaces inside international governmental organizations. They also explored new political terrain outside multilateral institutions to carry out feminist politics. Women's NGOs, both earlier in the twentieth century and since the UN Decade for Women, constitute such alternative political spaces at the international level. Some women's international NGOs (or WINGOs), particularly the older ones, are more formally organized and seek to influence more directly the political agendas of multilateral institutions. Other WINGOs, particularly those founded since the 1970s, eschew this formality and its related hierarchy and bureaucracy, preferring instead to mobilize and organize women at the grassroots and national levels around global feminist issues like development, population, women's human rights, violence against women, environment, and so on (see Tinker, Higer, Miller, Joachim, West, all this volume; Stephenson 1995).

International events such as UN conferences and WINGO-sponsored conferences have been focal points for internationally oriented feminist activism. These conferences have increasingly linked international, national, and local women's groups through transnational issue networks (Sikkink 1993) that can exchange information, ideas, and political support. Through such networks, WINGOs have begun to provide national and grassroots women's groups with information, training, financial resources, and political support as the latter work to hold their governments accountable for promises made in multilateral institutions, particularly in the area of women's human rights. In exchange, national and grassroots women's organizations from all parts of the world are making their perspectives and local realities known in ways and in places previously closed to them (see Miller this volume).

To the extent that connections exist between international and grassroots activists, it is possible to identify today the outlines of a global women's movement. The transnational women's networks linking individual activists and women's organizations of all types define and drive this movement. It extends into the spaces internationalist feminists have carved out in multilateral institutions, and it encompasses local and international NGOs as well as transnational issue networks. It often enacts a counterpolitics that values horizontal communication streams over vertical aggregations of interest, unstructured networks over hierarchical organizations (West this volume; Tinker this volume). It also strives toward realizing democracy as a transparent, participatory, and nonexclusionary practice (Hoskyns this volume).

Shaping International Agendas

From spaces they have carved out in the institutions of global governance, women and their movements have sought to introduce an awareness of gender and women's concerns into the international political agenda and into policy-making processes. What issues have they raised and what strategies have they employed? How have women gained influence and made a difference in global governance?

Two waves of women's movements have swept the twentieth century, both including a significant international component. In the first two decades of the century women fought for suffrage, peace, and labor protection through a variety of organizations that exchanged information, lobbied governments, monitored or sought to shape the activities of newly established international organizations, and worked to mobilize women at the national and local levels. The second wave of the movement, which began to build in the 1970s, was especially concerned with women's equal rights in the workplace and in civil space, the role of women in economic development, and gender-based violence. During both waves activist women employed "mainstreaming" and "disengaging" organizing strategies; that is, some worked for change "within the context of existing institutions and propose[d] adaptations that would allow for change without transformation" while others sought to "remain separate from existing societal institutions and provide critiques of and alternatives to these institutions" (Stienstra 1994, 32, following Adamson, Briskin, and McPhail 1988).

First-wave feminists used both strategies. We have seen how they used mainstreaming strategies within the OAS and the UN. One of the most memorable occasions of a disengaging strategy was the 1915 Women's International Peace Congress at The Hague, which brought together leading activists from Europe (from both sides of the conflict) and North America to denounce World War I and propose peaceful alternatives to the settlement of international conflicts (Meyer on WILPF this volume). Another early example of a disengaging feminist strategy occurred at the time of the Versailles peace conference. Internationalist women invited German women (who could not get visas to travel to France) to an alternative peace conference in Zurich, where they protested the harsh terms of the Versailles negotiations, especially reparations.

But the agitations of a vigorous internationalist women's movement also employed mainstreaming strategies during the negotiations of the Versailles peace treaties. Feminists lobbied national delegates and made "deputations" to official negotiating commissions. As a result of their interventions, the Versailles treaties codified such principles as the representation of women in the new League of Nations, the International Labor Organization (ILO), and government delegations, as well as "equal remuneration for work of equal value"; they also placed on the agenda of the new international organizations such issues as the protection of women's, children's, and young persons' labor as well as traffic in women and children (D'Amico this volume; Stienstra 1994, 55-56; Lubin and Winslow 1990, 1).

By the late 1940s the first-wave internationalist women's movement was clearly in decline. While the Cold War helped mobilize some First World women on antinuclear issues, and while national liberation movements and decolonization mobilized Third World women in new ways, the 1950s and 1960s also marked a lull in international feminist politics.

The second wave of the movement reintroduced strategies of disengagement, which fed the vitality of the movement (Higer this volume; Joachim this volume; Tinker this volume). The mainstreamed groups from the early part of the century, many now with consultative status to the UN, instigated the declaration of an International Women's Year in 1975, which extended to become the Women's Decade. Significantly, the four UN women's conferences since 1975 focused the second wave of internationalist feminism. In addition, and to an unprecedented degree, feminist organizations, including now many from Africa, Asia, and the Middle East, entered the corridors of the UN and began to make their imprint on international agendas.

The second wave of the women's movement can claim a remarkable set of international accomplishments. Women were able to imprint distinctive agendas on population policy at the Cairo conference (Higer this volume) and on human rights policy at the Vienna conference (Joachim this volume); they also introduced gender issues into the development and environment agendas (Tinker this volume; Johnson this volume). Furthermore, they can claim credit for getting governments to agree on a women's rights treaty (CEDAW) and on the Declaration on the Elimination of Violence against Women.

Scholars have asked how these successes were possible. They have identified an improvement in resources and propitious circumstances as crucial explanatory variables. First, the series of UN conferences in the 1970s, 1980s, and 1990s allowed for a learning process that improved the lobbying skills of women's organizations. According to Marty Chen, international activists learned that they needed to make a deliberate and concerted effort to get women onto government delegations and become knowledgeable about UN procedures. They also learned that the preparatory process to conferences was more important than the conferences themselves. They came to understand the importance of forming consensus and coalitions among movement participants (Chen 1996; also Tinker this volume; Higer this volume).

Second, a crucial innovation was the Women's Caucus. Introduced at the 1992 Conference on Environment and Development, it became a fixture at subsequent UN conferences, coordinating lobbying efforts among women's NGOs while also disseminating information (Chen 1996; also Higer this volume; Tinker this volume). Third, the communications revolution enabled the broadening of global networks, facilitated the coordination of strategies and the exchange of ideas, and drew into a global discussion women previously excluded (West this volume). These new resources together enhanced capabilities and increased the effectiveness of the women's lobby at the UN.

Propitious circumstances also provided a fertile backdrop for the effectiveness of the internationalist women's movement. Joachim (this volume) argues that the end of the Cold War constituted an opportunity for the movement. As governments were less concerned with security issues, they freed up "agenda space" and paid attention to UN conferencing. The end of the Cold War allowed progress on conflicts, such as those in the Middle East, Central America, and South Africa, that previously seemed insurmountable. Calls to condemn Zionism and racism, which almost derailed government negotiations during the 1980 Mid-Decade Women's Conference in Copenhagen (see West this volume), were notably absent at the 1990s UN conferences. In the case of the 1994 Cairo population conference, a change in U.S. policy under the Clinton administration, along with careful preconference preparation and consensus-building by the international women's health movement, resulted in a women-centered approach to population policy at the conference (Higer this volume). Opportunity structures and feminist strategies thus coalesced in the 1990s to advance the international causes of feminists who were able to shape the political agendas of multilateral institutions in effective ways.

Perhaps the most significant outcome of international conferencing for women has been that governments and international organizations have begun to take steps to mainstream, or integrate, a gender perspective into various policies, programs, and bureaucratic procedures. Mainstreaming has been discussed most extensively in agencies concerned with economic development. Such agencies, including the World Bank and the United Nationals Development Programme (UNDP), have instituted policies and programs addressing the role of women in development (WID), albeit to varying degrees depending on structural factors such as organizational goals, ideologies, procedures, and the presence of "WID policy entrepreneurs."

For example, WID policies were only weakly institutionalized at UNDP, a decentralized organization that defers to recipient governments and whose organizational ideology emphasizes self-determination and self-reliance as crucial goals of development. Because recipient governments were rarely interested in gender issues, UNDP hesitated to force them to include a focus on gender. An absence of leadership or commitment among high-level staff members, mostly male government appointees, further inhibited the integration of a gender perspective. In contrast, WID has received more attention at the World Bank, a highly centralized organization. The World Bank's organizational ideology, which stresses economic rationality, allowed for the mainstreaming of gender concerns if it raised project efficiency and furthered economic growth. However, because of pressures on staff time and the emphasis on "feeding the project pipeline" (as opposed to judging the success of projects), gender analysis was less widely integrated than Bank ideology would have permitted (Kardam 1991).

While it thus appears that centralization and hierarchical bureaucratic structures can facilitate the integration of a gender perspective, there is considerable debate over the desirability of integrating gender policies and programs into bureaucracies. Some have argued that bureaucracies by definition cannot empower local communities because they style themselves, not the communities, as the locus of power and knowledge (Ferguson 1990). Bureaucratic language makes women into objects of planning interventions and negates them as subjects who have a stake in their own emancipation. It disempowers because it frames women as having problems and needs, but never choices and agency (Hale 1989). Furthermore, feminists working inside development bureaucracies often discover that projects with emancipatory objectives become distorted when forced into standard blueprints that never challenge dominant development paradigms (Goetz 1991).

Others are less pessimistic and find that the way in which WID policies are implemented can destabilize the core commitments of development agencies. For example, Ann Therese Lotherington and Anne Britt Flemmen (1991) find that the efforts to mainstream women—that is, to revalue existing policies according to their impact on women—touch the "Near Core" (policy statements and plans of action that realize an organization's basic philosophy) and begin to "shake the foundations of current policy" (283). Thus it is possible, albeit very difficult, to change an organization's "Deep Core,"that is, "the fundamental normative and ontological axioms which define . . . an organization's underlying philosophy" (274; see also Prügl this volume). Lotherington and Flemmen go on to detail successful strategies for feminist innovators in organizations.

Despite the successes, it is difficult to measure the impact that various policy achievements for women at the international level have had at national levels. Some cite as positive the fact that governments produced reports and made available, often for the first time, data on women's status in their countries. Yet, follow-up reports produced in the aftermath of conferences constituted often-dubious demonstrations of government commitments (West this volume). Overall, governments did little to fulfill their pledges (Stienstra 1994, 134–35, 141). In its 1990 report on the implementation of the Nairobi "Forward-Looking Strategies," the Commission on the Status of Women found, not progress, but that "the situation of women had deteriorated in many parts of the world" (United Nations 1991b). The Secretary-General's 1995 report was a bit more optimistic but still noted continued disproportionate growth in the number of women living in poverty, little progress in women's attaining power in the political systems of their home countries, and continued lack of commitment to women's human rights (United Nations 1995b).

On the other hand, the significance of international documents is not that governments will automatically implement them but that national and local groups can use them to hold their governments accountable. In this sense, what appears as universal standards can be adapted and used in local contexts to further specific emancipatory agendas (Elshtain 1995). In the field of human rights, where international norms are highly institutionalized, women's international NGOs work with national NGOs to provide access to international machineries and make them useful for local purposes (Miller this volume; Baines this volume).

In sum, feminists and women's movements have influenced global governance through strategies ranging from disengagement to changing policies and bureaucratic procedures. They have honed their skills, built networks, improved their resources, and taken advantage of historical opportunities that arose at the end of the two world wars and the Cold War, thus helping to construct new gender orders within the framework of new hegemonic orders. Inside international bureaucracies they have institutionalized, to varying degrees, gender perspectives and concerns for women's issues. They are using international norms to further their local agendas.

Contesting Language

New policies and bureaucratic procedures may be just one expression of a broader change in global rules and norms. International encounters, including the interventions of women's movements, have produced or inhibited transformations by employing certain linguistic conventions, framing questions in certain ways, and constructing gendered identities of a diverse set of agents. Changing oppressive conventions, in addition to government policies, has always been a crucial goal of women's movements. Possibly their greatest achievement has been precisely to change the way in which women are talked about and in this way to alter values and practices at many levels of analysis (Tinker this volume).

One of the most widely noted changes in the course of this century involves a shift in international debates towards emphasizing women's equality with men. At the beginning of the twentieth century, arguments about women often emphasized their different needs, capabilities, and virtues arising from the fact that they bear children. Equal rights arguments nevertheless appeared in certain contexts. The Covenant of the League of Nations included the principle of equal pay for work of equal value, but the principle did not guide the work of League institutions. Indeed, the 1928 ILO Convention on Minimum Wage Fixing failed to require governments to set the same minimum wages for women and men, and unequal minimum wage rates were the norm. Internationalist feminist demands for equal treatment were most contentious in the area of protective labor legislation. The ILO, in the interwar period, passed a number of conventions limiting women's right to work, including their right to work at night, underground, or with dangerous substances. In the late 1920s, feminists formed international NGOs to crusade against ILO standards designed to provide differential protection for women workers. The rally for an equal rights treaty was associated with the fight against protective legislation and met considerable opposition from women affiliated with, and sympathetic to, unions (Prügl forthcoming; Whitworth 1994).

But feminists were united in demanding equality in other areas. They attacked the practice by which states subsumed married women under the nationality of their husbands and demanded a nationality treaty that made no difference between women and men in laws and practices relating to nationality (see Meyer on CIM this volume). They united in their condemnation of government practices, which became prevalent during the Great Depression, restricting women's right to work. After the Second World War, the UN Charter and the UN Declaration of Human Rights affirmed the equal rights of men and women. Equal rights language also informed UN policies and international agreements of the Women's Decade. The language of equality today is dominant in UN debates about women (Miller 1994; D'Amico this volume).

However, there is considerable diversity in the way in which rights language has appeared in various issue areas and the effects that rights language has had for women. Ucarer (this volume) points out that the language of international migration often substituted for rights language in debates about trafficking in women, shifting states' attention away from safeguarding the victims to policing borders. Feminist human rights advocates argue that the distinction between public and private implied in liberal notions of rights has been detrimental to recognizing women's rights to bodily security. International human rights law has constructed an identity of families as naturally and fundamentally harmonious, thus obscuring violence in the family and reifying existing gender inequalities (Rao 1996). Similar legacies inhere in the international legal definition of a refugee, which considers persecution based on race, religion, nationality, or membership in a particular social group but is silent on gender-related persecution, often construed as a "private" matter (Baines this volume).

Likewise, the rules of the global economy limit what policies can accomplish in specific issue areas. With the rise of capitalism, the rules of economic growth and profit devalued feminine subsistence practices. Combined with the language of control that informs modern scientific ways of thinking, these rules have functioned to exploit both women and nature (Johnson this volume). In the contemporary world economy, Stienstra (this volume) identifies liberalization and globalization as hegemonic "comprehensive norms" that severely limit women's advancement. "The neoliberal frame," to use Anne Sisson Runyan's expression, favors corporations and big business at the expense of public services and redistributive policies, which are so crucial to women and others at the bottom of the economic hierarchy. It takes globalization and liberalization as given processes that cannot be contravened, only managed; the fates of people become secondary (Runyan this volume). In the end, it may very well be that global business rules, while governments and international organizations are left to manage people and soften the harshest consequences of globalization, especially for marginalized groups, including women.

The regulatory structure of a global economy contributes to constructions of identities, forcefully realizing power hierarchies not only between workers and capitalists but also between geographical regions, ethnic groups, and genders. With regard to gender, for example, development practices seeking modernization and industrialization often constructed women in Asia, Africa, and Latin America as housewives (Rogers 1980). The economic restructuring of the 1970s and 1980s made this construction problematic as flexible production required flexible labor and found that labor in women. But the destabilization of gender constructions also opened space for feminist interventions. Thus, in contemporary debates about regulating informal-sector work, mostly female home-based workers appear not only as the ideal flexible workers in an economy thriving on new communications technologies but also as heroines securing family survival, thus revealing that the opposition between housewife and breadwinner is a myth (Prügl this volume).

It appears that international economic and political crises destabilize entrenched institutions, including institutions of gender, thus opening up opportunities for emancipatory politics. The end of the Cold War constitutes such an opportunity for change, as did the rebuilding of global governance structures after the two world wars. While extraordinary circumstances provide unique opportunities, only the widespread and persistent interventions of an active movement can make the most of such opportunities. Indeed, the everyday successes of the women's movement often have been unspectacular or gone unnoticed, but they have worked to effect structures of global governance in which women can no longer be ignored.

PART I

LOCATING WOMEN: ORGANIZATIONAL SPACES IN GLOBAL GOVERNANCE

2

Women Workers in the United Nations: From Margin to Mainstream?

Francine D'Amico

In her 1990 book on gender and international relations, Cynthia Enloe asks, "Where are the women?" (7). If we examine the United Nations with Enloe's question in mind, we find that women workers at the UN are concentrated in gender-traditional, junior-grade jobs. That is, women are overrepresented in the lower echelons of staff personnel in administrative and clerical positions and underrepresented in upper-level managerial positions. Further, the few women who do rise to higher ranks within the international civil service are concentrated in what the UN refers to as the economic and social fields rather than the political and security fields. Similarly, women are underrepresented among the highest-ranking diplomats in national delegations to the UN, and they may be more or less well represented among the lower ranks of diplomatic missions, depending upon the practices of the sending country.

Progress on increasing the number of women personnel across the UN system and efforts to improve the conditions of work for women at the UN have been slow in coming. For example, the UN relied on explicitly gendered promotion criteria until the late 1970s and has just begun to address sexual harassment seriously in the 1990s. But change has been occurring for several reasons. First, women workers at the UN have organized against the most invidious practices. Second, leaders of influential member states have pressed for change. Third, concerned and compassionate allies within the UN's ranks have signaled their commitment to women's rights with actions, not just words, such as appointing women to prominent diplomatic and non-gender-traditional positions. Fourth, nongovernmental organizations (NGOs) have pressed the UN from the outside to keep its promises (Timothy 1995a, 1995b; Galey 1995b; Stienstra 1994). However, much remains to be done. The UN has not achieved the gender equality promised in its charter (1945), the Universal Declaration of Human Rights (1948), and subsequent human rights documents.

Promises, Promises

The precursor to the United Nations was the League of Nations, established after World War I at the Versailles Peace Conference. The League operated from 1920 to April 1946, and the structure of the League formed the foundation for the new United Nations Organization (UNO) after World War II. While the drafters of the UN Charter took the League as their model, they sought to correct its perceived shortcomings by encouraging universal participation and empowering the UN to enforce the peace.

The four principal organs of the League of Nations were the Assembly, the Council, the Secretariat, and the Permanent Court of International Justice (PCIJ), also known as the World Court. At the insistence of women's rights activists, the League's Covenant had provided that women could serve as delegates and as staff in the Secretariat, yet few did during its twenty-six-year history. Only about a dozen of the 250 delegates in each session of the League Assembly were women, and no woman ever served on the League Council or sat as a judge on the World Court. Women delegates to the Assembly were assigned to committees dealing with so-called women's questions, such as traffic in women (international prostitution) or child welfare. Only two women held high positions in the League Secretariat, and those were in the Social Section and the Information Section; most other women in the Secretariat were clerks and secretarial staff (Galey 1995a, 4–5; Stienstra 1994, 55–58). Just as the League of Nations formed the foundation for the new United Nations Organization, so, too, did this pattern of women's participation at the margins of the League carry over to the new international organization.

From 25 April to 26 June 1945, representatives of fifty countries met in San Francisco to draft the charter of the United Nations, a new international organization for cooperation, peace, and security to replace the failed League of Nations. Among the women at the San Francisco conference were delegates Minerva Bernardino (Dominican Republic), Cora T. Casselman (Canada), Virginia Gildersleeve (United States), Berta Lutz (Brazil), Jessie Street (Australia), Isabel P. de Vidal (Uruguay), and Wu Yi-Fang (China). Other women present included Ellen Wilkinson and Florence Horsburgh, assistant delegates from the United Kingdom, and Lucila L. de Perez Diaz and Isabel Sanchez de Urdaneta, counselors for the Venezuelan delegation. In addition, Dorothy Fosdick, Majorie Whiteman, Esther Brunauer, and Alice McDiarmid served as technical experts in the American delegation (Stienstra 1994, 77–78; Galey 1995a, 7).

Women delegates to the San Francisco conference were assigned by their governments to address mainly nonmilitary issue areas, especially those dealing with social issues, such as war refugees and women's rights and status. The single exception was Casselman, a member of the Canadian Parliament, who was the only woman delegate with credentials to attend meetings of the Commission on the Security Council (Stienstra 1994, 78). This pattern of women's participation on social rather than security issues continues today, with only a few women involved in security decision making or implementation.

The women delegates did not speak with one voice. At the time, Bernardino was president of the Inter-American Commission of Women, Lutz was President of the Brazilian Federation of Women, and Street was chair of the Australian Women's Charter Conference. These women actively supported the establishment of a commission on the status of women within the UN framework. They were opposed, among others, by Gildersleeve, dean of Barnard College, who represented the United States's view that women's rights were not to be considered as separate or "special rights" but instead subsumed under the auspices of the soon-to-be-established Commission on Human Rights (Stienstra 1994, 77–78).

In addition to government representatives, NGOs were present at the San Francisco conference. Attending with the official U.S. delegation were representatives of forty-two NGOs, including the National Association for the Advancement of Colored People (NAACP), for which Mary McLeod Bethune served as an adviser. However, the State Department excluded others from the official delegation, such as four other African American women (Dorothy Ferebee, Eunice Hunton Carter, Sue Bailey Thurman, and Anne Arnold Hedgemen) who composed an unofficial delegation from the 800,000-member National Council of Negro Women, along with other women's groups, such as the National Council of Jewish Women and the National Council of Catholic Women (Walton 1995, 47–49; Lewis 1995, 16–23). The State Department argued that these women's concerns were adequately represented by "umbrella" groups.

The San Francisco delegates, both women and men, who supported equal political and participatory rights for women helped shape the language of the UN Charter. The preamble affirms "faith . . . in the equal rights of men and women and of nations large and small" (full text in Roberts and Kingsbury, 499–529). Four other articles pledge to promote and protect human rights without distinction as to race, sex, nationality, or religion: Article 1.3 on the general principles of the organization; Article 13.1b on General Assembly representation; Article 55c on Economic and Social Council (ECOSOC) representation; and Article 76c on the trusteeship system. Further, Article 8 of the Charter states that the United Nations "shall place no restrictions on the eligibility of men and women to participate in any capacity and under conditions of equality in its principal and subsidiary organs." While this provision echoes the language of Article 7 of the League of Nations' Covenant, the proposal encountered much opposition at the conference but was ultimately adopted.

However, the proposal to establish an autonomous commission on the status of women was initially derailed (Galey 1995a, 7; Stienstra 1994, 56–57, 79–80). This left responsibility for attention to gender equality with the Economic and Social Council, which the Charter empowered to act on issues concerning human rights. In its resolution of 16 February 1946, ECOSOC created the UN Commission on Human Rights and the Subcommission on the Status of Women. Shortly thereafter, ECOSOC elevated the Subcommission to the Commission on the Status of Women (CSW) (ECOSOC 1946b). Eleanor Roosevelt (United States) became the chairperson of the Commission on Human Rights, and Bodil Begtrup (Denmark) became the chairperson of the Subcommission on the Status of Women (ECOSOC 1946a; Reanda 1992).

The first task of the Commission on Human Rights was to draft the Universal Declaration of Human Rights, the text of which was adopted by the General Assembly on 10 December 1948. The Universal Declaration states in Article 1 that "All human beings are born free and equal in dignity and rights" and in Article 2 that "Everyone is entitled to all the rights and freedoms set forth in this Declaration, without distinction of any kind, such as race, colour, sex, language, religion, political or other opinion, national or social origin, property, birth, or other status."

For its time, the Universal Declaration was a progressive document on gender relations, thanks to the efforts of Roosevelt, Begtrup, Bernardino, and others. Article 16 declares equal rights for men and women in marriage "and its dissolution" (divorce), Article 21 calls for "universal and equal suffrage" (right to vote), Article 23 requires "equal pay for equal work," and Article 26(3) asserts parental (rather than paternal) rights in decisions regarding the education of children. But the initial gender-neutral language of the declaration lapses beginning in Article 8, as "everyone" is specified as "him" or "his," which becomes especially problematic in the gendered construction of men as the head of the family in Articles 23.3 and 25.1.

The Universal Declaration was a nonbinding resolution that sought to outline future goals rather than delineate legal rules for state behavior; thus, gender equality was something to aim for rather than a requirement for participation in the organization. The goals outlined in the Universal Declaration were subsequently codified, or made legally binding upon signatory states, through the International Covenant on Civil and Political Rights and the International Covenant on Economic, Social, and Cultural Rights, which were drafted in 1966 and entered into force in 1976. Although these treaties were initially binding only upon states that signed them, many international jurists argue that fundamental human rights have acquired a universally binding character even against nonsignatories (Singh 1993, 392–401; Farer and Gaer 1993, 242–96). While these documents, along with the Charter, provided a legal basis for the United Nations to ask its member states to promote gender equality within their diplomatic missions to the UN, the lack of an enforcement mechanism and the UN's failure to meet equitable gender representation goals within its own staff make the UN a doubtful champion of women's rights.

Women's Representation inside the UN Structure

The United Nations System consists of the various principal and subsidiary organs of the United Nations Organization as well as an array of specialized agencies, some of which, like the International Labor Organization, existed before the UNO came into being (see appendix). There are six principal organs of the UNO proper: the Secretariat, the General Assembly, the Security Council, the now-defunct Trusteeship Council, the International Court of Justice (ICJ)—like its predecessor, also known as the World Court—and the Economic and Social Council. Among the subsidiary organs in the UN system are the United Nations Development Programme (UNDP), the United Nations Environment Programme (UNEP), the United Nations Fund for Population Activities (UNFPA), and the United Nations Children's Fund (UNICEF). Specialized agencies, such as the World Health Organization, the International Bank for Reconstruction and Development (IBRD, or World Bank), the International Monetary Fund, and the World Trade Organization, are affiliated with the United Nations Organization through liaison agreements and report to the UNO on their activities. Because the specialized agencies remain autonomous in terms of personnel selection, women's participation in these agencies will not be considered at length here. We will focus on women's participation in the UN's principal and subsidiary organs.

Women Workers in the Secretariat

Of the six principal organs of the UN, women are most visible in the Secretariat. Much progress has been made in bringing women workers into the Secretariat in staff and administrative positions, and much of this has come in the past two decades. The two basic categories of Secretariat employees are the Professional category and General and Related Services. Employees within each category are ranked by grades that indicate level of seniority, responsibility, and, of course, salary. From the top of the organizational pyramid, the grades in the Professional category are: Secretary-General; Under-Secretary-General; Assistant Secretary-General; D-2 and D-1 (D = Director); and P-5 through P-1 (P = Professional), with P-2 and P-1 grades usually referred to as "junior professional." The grades in the General Service category are G-7 through G-1.

In response to a request by the Commission on the Status of Women, the Secretary-General issued a report on the participation of women in the work of the United Nations on 16 March 1950. The report noted that as of 30 November 1949, of the total 3,916 Secretariat staff at UN headquarters, the Geneva offices, and the information centers, 1,737, or 44 percent, were women. While this seems fairly equitable, women employees were concentrated in the lower-level positions. No woman was in any of the highest-level positions of Assistant Secretary-General or above, and only 1 woman was among the 87 employees in the next three ranks. Women comprised 16 percent of the 1,055 employees in the intermediate ranks and 57 percent of the 2,765 employees in the secretarial, clerical, and nonprofessional positions. Women were disadvantaged by staff rules that allowed men automatic status as "head of family" for receiving dependent benefits, while women had to be single heads of families or prove their husband was incapacitated or fully financially dependent to be eligible for these benefits, which included a children's allowance, education grant, and higher expatriation, rental, and installation allowances (United Nations Office of the Secretary-General 1950). At the General Assembly's request, the Secretary-General revised some of the most egregious of these discriminatory practices the following year (United Nations Office of the Secretary-General 1951), but differential treatment of male and female employees in other areas, such as pensions, continued (Timothy 1995a, 125–30).

In the first three decades of the UNO, efforts to improve the status of women in the Secretariat continued to focus upon ending overtly discriminatory rules rather than on actively enabling women's participation. This approach proved ineffective, as evidenced by the continued low numbers and proportions of women in the Secretariat until the 1970s, when demands for proactive programs to redress the continued gender imbalance among UN employees grew out of organizing by UN workers themselves and the successive world conferences on the status of women. The Ad Hoc Group on Equal Rights for Women at the UN was formed in 1971 and worked to change personnel policy to improve working conditions for women. For example, the group sought to change promotion criteria to cumulative seniority, whereby an employee who interrupted her career—as women tend to do when having and raising children—might return to work without losing seniority previously accrued (Timothy 1995a, 120–25; 1995b). With the support of key member states and continued pressure from NGOs and women employees, proactive initiatives such as this have succeeded in slowly increasing the presence of women in the ranks of UN personnel, especially over the past decade.

Between 30 June 1987 and 30 June 1997, the proportion of women in positions subject to geographic distribution requirements[1] in the Secretariat staff rose from 25.67 percent to 36.61 percent (see table 2.1). The number of women workers increased from 666 to 901 while the number of men workers fell from 1,928 to 1,560, as many senior male employees opted for early retirement offered as part of the UN's staff-cutting reform efforts or, like Secretary-General Kofi Annan, moved on to higher positions within the UN (United Nations Office of the Secretary-General 1997a, 6–21). By 1 January 1998, the percentage of women at the professional level in posts subject to geographic distribution had risen to 36.8 percent (United Nations Office of the Secretary-General 1998c). The proportion of women staff in technical cooperation posts is also increasing, but slowly, as for professional staff. From 31 December 1987 to 31 December 1997, the proportion and number of women technical workers increased as the number of male workers fluctuated (see table 2.2).

Table 2.1
Gender Distribution of the United Nations Secretariat Staff in Posts Subject to Geographic Distribution (30 June)

	Men	Women	Total	% Women
1987	1,928	666	2,594	25.67
1988	1,858	663	2,521	26.30
1989	1,844	679	2,523	26.91
1990	1,836	725	2,561	28.31
1991	1,841	759	2,600	29.19
1992	1,811	797	2,608	30.56
1993	1,769	804	2,573	31.25
1994	1,720	830	2,550	32.55
1995	1,658	857	2,515	34.08
1996	1,632	882	2,514	35.08
1997	1,560	901	2,461	36.61

Source: United Nations, *Advancement of Women: Improvement of the Status of Women in the Secretariat: Report of the Secretary-General* (New York: United Nations, 30 September 1997) (A/52/408).

Table 2.2
Gender Distribution of the United Nations Secretariat Staff in Technical Cooperation
Posts (31 December)

	Men	Women	Total	% Women
1987	881	87	968	8.99
1988	898	102	1,000	10.20
1989	911	109	1,020	10.69
1990	947	130	1,077	12.07
1991	916	125	1,041	12.01
1992	805	122	927	13.16
1993	726	136	862	15.78
1994	616	131	747	17.54
1995	476	106	582	18.21
1996	481	109	590	18.47
1997	582	177	759	23.32

Source: United Nations, *Advancement of Women: Improvement of the Status of Women in the Secretariat: Report of the Secretary-General* (New York: United Nations, 30 September 1997)
(A/52/408).

These increases were the result of a concerted effort by the Secretariat,
sanctioned by the General Assembly, to increase the recruitment and retention
of women personnel. After decades of hoping that the representation of
women among the ranks of UN workers might improve, the organization
began to take concrete steps to make that goal possible. In the strategic action
plan for 1991 to 1995, the General Assembly had called for the proportion of
women in the Secretariat professional staff to reach 35 percent by 1995 (United Nations General Assembly 1990). In the strategic action plan for 1995 to
2000, the Secretary-General set an overall target goal for women at the professional level at 50 percent. As of 1 January 1998, only four UN depart-
ments/offices had reached the goal of 50 percent female employees in posts
subject to geographic distribution; ten departments/offices had achieved the
35 percent mark and twelve remained below this mark (United Nations Office
of the Secretary-General 1998c). The vast majority of women workers were
still employed in the General Service (GS) category and concentrated in the
lower grades and gender-traditional occupations, such as secretary or administrative aide. In 1997, the Secretary-General reported that women comprised
54 percent of workers overall in the General and Related Services, but only
4.1 percent (8 of 195) of Security Service personnel and 3 percent (6 of 196)

of Trades/Crafts personnel (United Nations Office of the Secretary-General 1997a).

The Secretary-General's report further noted that mobility between departments and offices was limited because of low staff turnover. This low turnover has been due in part to low promotion rates from the G-5 through the G-7 level and from the General Service to the Professional category, despite the introduction in 1979 of a merit examination to advance GS employees into professional-grade positions (Timothy 1995a, 123). Low promotion rates disproportionately affected women employees concentrated in the lower grades of the Secretariat. To redress the gender imbalance in promotion rates, the Secretariat issued proactive administrative instructions in 1993 and in 1996 that are beginning to increase the pool of women eligible for promotion to the Professional category.

Kristin Timothy has noted that women in the international civil service system of the UN are concentrated at the lower staff levels, and she argues that women seem unable to break through the glass ceiling into upper management, except in token numbers (Timothy 1995a, 117–32; 1995b, 85–94). The chief administrative officer and representative of the United Nations Organization as a whole is the Secretary-General; of the seven Secretaries-General to date in the organization, none has been a woman. The next highest political staff level in the Secretariat is that of under-secretary-general (USG); there are currently eighteen of these positions. As of 30 June 1997, only one woman was serving at this level: Under-Secretary-General Elizabeth Dowdeswell of the United Nations Environment Programme.

Of the fourteen positions at the next-highest level of assistant secretary-general (ASG), only 2 women were serving as of 30 June 1997: Angela King (Jamaica) as special adviser to the Secretary-General on gender issues in the Department for Policy Coordination and Sustainable Development (DPCSD), and Gillian Martin Sorenson (United States) as assistant secretary-general for external relations. Data from 1 January 1998 list 3 women in ASG positions: King and Sorenson were joined by Rafiah Salim (Malaysia), who was appointed assistant secretary-general for human resources management effective 15 October 1997 (United Nations Office of the Secretary-General 1998c and 1997b). As of that date, the proportion of women in the top two levels of the UNO Secretariat, USG and ASG, was 16.67 percent.

As of 30 June 1997, 12 of 63 staff members at the D-2 level were women (19.05 percent) and 47 of 214 staff members at the D-1 level were women (21.96 percent). Overall, 62 of 309 staff members at the director level were women, for an average across the ranks of 20.1 percent (United Nations Office of the Secretary-General 1997a). This figure had risen slightly, to 22.6 percent, by 1 January 1998 (United Nations Office of the Secretary-General 1998c and

1997b). The goal set by the Secretary-General in 1985 and supported by the General Assembly (United Nations General Assembly 1985) was for the proportion of women at the D-1 level and above—UN senior management—to reach 25 percent by 1995, yet that goal had not been reached as of this writing (1998). In 1998 only one department (Human Resources) had met the 50 percent goal at the D-1 level (57.1 percent); in two departments (International Drug Control Programme and Office of the Coordinator for Humanitarian Affairs), women were still absent from senior positions (United Nations Office of the Secretary-General 1998c).

In order to "mainstream a gender perspective" in all aspects of UN policy/decision making effectively—that is, to ensure that issues of concern to women are addressed in the work of all UN organs, committees, and agencies—women personnel must be mainstreamed as well. One step in this direction immediately after the Fourth World Conference on Women, held in Beijing, China, 4–15 September 1995, was the transfer of Rosario Green (Mexico), then assistant secretary-general for political affairs, to the cabinet of the Secretary-General to serve as a special adviser on gender, effective 1 January 1996. The position was created by the Secretary-General, with the approval of the General Assembly, to ensure that the promises of the Beijing conference were implemented (United Nations General Assembly 1996).

Green left the United Nations in late 1997 to accept a cabinet position in the Mexican government, where she is currently minister of foreign affairs. Subsequently, Angela King of Jamaica was appointed special adviser on gender issues and the advancement of women to ensure that a gender perspective would continue to be formally represented in the highest political levels of the UN decision-making hierarchy. King, a career UN diplomat, had been serving as director of the UN Division for the Advancement of Women.

In December 1997, the General Assembly created the position of deputy secretary-general, whose duties include standing in while the Secretary-General is away and coordinating the activities of the UN's numerous departments, programs, funds, and specialized agencies. Louise Fréchette (Canada) was appointed to this position, effective 28 February 1998. Fréchette had previously served as Canada's ambassador and permanent representative to the UN from 1992 to 1994—one of only a handful of women, never numbering more than eight at one time, to hold this position within the UN in the 1990s.

Some regions have a better track record than others in promoting women into the UN Secretariat. As of 30 June 1997, the proportion of women in the professional staff category and above was 51.38 percent for North America and the Caribbean, 44.57 percent for Asia and the Pacific, 37 percent each for Western Europe and Latin America, 32.5 percent for the Middle East, 23.45 percent for Africa, and 11.72 percent for Eastern Europe (see table 2.3).

Table 2.3
Staff in the Professional Category and Above in Posts Subject to Geographic
Distribution, by Region and Gender (30 June 1997)

	Men	Women	Total	% Women
Africa	284	87	371	23.45
Asia/Pacific	240	193	433	44.57
Europe (East)	211	28	239	11.72
Europe (West)	358	214	572	37.41
Latin America	129	76	205	37.07
North America/ Caribbean	261	247	508	51.38
Others	10	3	13	23.08

Source: United Nations, *Advancement of Women: Improvement of the Status of Women in the Secretariat: Report of the Secretary-General* New York, 30 September 1997 (A/52/408).

This regional pattern of gender representation in the UN Secretariat can be explained in part by the fact that both the structure of gender relations and the level of economic development of different communities shape women's level of education and involvement in the professions, including law, politics, and diplomacy. Moreover, political transitions seem to have had an important—and problematic—impact on women's representation inside the UN. With the decolonization movement in the post–World War II era, especially in the 1960s and 1970s, the leaders of many developing states sought to balance what they perceived as the overrepresentation of the developed states in the United Nations Organization by increasing the representation of un- and underrepresented states. Their focus was on geographic distribution and nationality rather than on gender. One of the achievements of the UN Decade for Women was a shift toward an effort to strike a more equitable balance in representation between considerations of geographic distribution and other factors. Unfortunately, the recent political transformations in Eastern Europe have discredited the previous regimes' commitment to gender equality, resulting in a decline in the numbers of women in legislative and other public offices. This may explain the small numbers of women in these states' UN delegations.

Despite the organization's paper commitment to gender equality, working at the United Nations is not nirvana for female employees, as evidenced by the UN's handling of incidents of sexual harassment. Consider the case of a high-ranking UN diplomat who sexually assaulted an administrative aide on 2 March 1988. Fearing retaliation and certain that diplomatic immunity would protect the harasser, the woman kept silent for a time, until the following year when the diplomat resumed his harassment by threatening to block her promotion. She then took her case to an internal UN tribunal—her only legal option, given his immunity from criminal and civil prosecution. Several witnesses testified that the woman was shaken and bruised following the assault, which occurred in a UN office, and other women testified that the diplomat had similarly assaulted or harassed them. The case took several years to conclude; on 24 January 1994 the tribunal ruled that the woman had indeed been assaulted. Then-Secretary-General Boutros Boutros-Ghali ordered the decision sealed and told the woman she would face disciplinary action if she disclosed its contents.

Someone at the UN leaked information about the ruling to the media, and Boutros-Ghali took the highly unusual step of appointing an "independent" group to review the case. In the meantime, the diplomat—who had been undersecretary-general of the UN Development Programme—resigned with a pension of $137,000 a year. He was rehired shortly thereafter as a consultant to the UN, so that he was receiving both his pension and a new salary. When the woman's lawyers tried to file suit against him in a New York civil court, the diplomat argued that he still had diplomatic immunity, but he left the United States to return to his home country. Seven years after the assault, the UN finally agreed to compensate the woman for her legal fees and the damage to her career, which marked the first time the UN had publicly settled a sexual harassment case (*Finger Lakes Times* [Geneva, N.Y.], 24 January 1995). The UN now has an explicitly stated policy on sexual harassment and provides training on what constitutes harassment and how managers ought to address harassment complaints, but many women workers have found these initiatives inadequate or pro forma.

Continued resistance to the goal of gender equality in the United Nations personnel system is evident in a recent discussion of UN reform by the General Assembly's Fifth Committee (Administrative and Budgetary). Nazareth Incera of Costa Rica, speaking on behalf of the Group of 77 and China, expressed concern that staff cuts and hiring freezes would affect representation of developing countries and women in the ranks of UN employees; she urged that efforts be made to safeguard the gains women had made in the Secretariat. Sheila Sealy Monteith (Jamaica), speaking on behalf of CARICOM (Caribbean Common Market), shared this concern, as did Mahamane Maiga (Mali) and Liu Yanguo (China). However, two other speakers, Carlos Riva (Argentina) and Yevgeny Deineko (Russian Federation), raised reverse-discrimination criticisms. Riva "did not support actions to recruit staff outside the context of the national competitive examinations," as he said had been done in hiring seven women recently recruited to P-2 positions. Deineko cautioned that "achievement of women's representation should be in keeping with the principles of competence, integrity, and efficiency" that govern the international civil service, implying that this had not been the case with recent appointments (United Nations General Assembly 1996). However, far more men than women have been appointed in this "exceptional" manner, and women's performance on the competitive merit exams, not exceptional appointments, has helped women advance by depoliticizing and degendering the promotion process (Timothy 1995a, 125–26).

On the occasion of the appointment of Louise Fréchette as deputy secretary-general, members of the UN press corps asked whether other candidates had been considered for the post and whether any of the candidates were men. Fred Eckhard, spokesman for the Secretary-General, replied that Secretary-General Kofi Annan had "cast a wide net" and "considered a number of candidates" and selected, in Annan's own words, "not the best woman, but the best person" for the job (United Nations Office of the Secretary-General 1998a). Given the still abysmally low proportion of women in the upper echelons of the organization despite their experience, cumulative seniority, and qualifications, the implication that women candidates were getting special preferences on appointments appears absurd.

Women's Representation in States' Diplomatic Missions to the UN

Women and the General Assembly. Each United Nations member state is allowed a delegation of up to ten persons, with five ambassadors and five alternates to represent the country in the organization. All member countries are represented in the UN General Assembly. The head of each country's delegation is designated "ambassador extraordinary and plenipotentiary" or "permanent representative" of that country to the United Nations. Since the UN's founding, few women have served as permanent representative. Only four women's names appear among the government representatives who addressed the first session of the General Assembly in 1946: Eleanor Roosevelt (United States), Minerva Bernardino (Dominican Republic), Frieda Dalen (Norway), and H. Verwey (Netherlands). This prompted the French ambassador to call for greater participation by women in subsequent Assembly sessions (United Nations General Assembly 1946). Yet by 1949 there were still only four women among the then-fifty-nine permanent representatives to the Assembly, only nine women alternate representatives, and eleven women advisers, experts, and consultants to delegations (United Nations Office of the Secretary-General 1950). This pattern of the near invisibility of women in the General Assembly has continued, with some fluctuation from session to session over the ensuing years. In 1997, women headed the delegations of only 7 of the

185 member countries; women's rate of representation at this level was thus a mere 3.78 percent. The permanent representatives in 1997 were Ambassador Penelope Anne (Penny) Wensley of Australia, Ambassador M. Patricia Durrant of Jamaica, Ambassador Cristina Augiar from the Dominican Republic, Ambassador Annette des Iles from Trinidad and Tobago, Ambassador Akmaral Kh. Arystanbekova of Kazahkstan, Ambassador Zamkira B. Eshmambetova of Kyrgyzstan, Ambassador Aksoltan T. Ataeva of Turkmenistan, Ambassador Bangoura Mahawa Camara from Guinea, and Ambassador Claudia Fritsche of Liechtenstein, whom some refer to as the "dean" of women UN ambassadors because of her long tenure—since 1990—in the organization (*Christian Science Monitor,* 24 June 1991; UNIFEM press briefing, 24 October 1997).

Each year, the General Assembly elects a presiding officer for its session, which runs from late September to December. In the fifty-two sessions of the Assembly, only two women have served as its president: Vijaya Lakshimi Pandit (India) in the eighth session (1953) and Angie Brooks-Randolph (Liberia) in the twenty-fourth session (1969) (United Nations Office of the Secretary-General 1995). Similarly, each year the General Assembly selects officers to chair its standing and ad hoc committees; few women have served in these positions. The first woman to do so, Ana Figueroa of Chile, chaired the Social, Humanitarian, and Cultural Committee in 1951; in 1957 she also became the first woman to serve on (but not preside over) the Security Committee. Women's representation as members of these committees and other commissions associated with the General Assembly, such as the International Law Commission, has varied greatly, depending upon the committee or commission's area of responsibility. Women from national delegations tend to be elected or appointed to General Assembly committees and commissions perceived as gender appropriate or gender specific (United Nations Office of the Secretary-General 1950).

Although not many of the UN's permanent representatives are or have been women, women are more frequently found among the other members of the ambassadorial delegation from a given country at the level of deputy permanent representative or alternate representative. Women are also sometimes well represented on the country's UN mission support staff, serving, for example, as legal counsel or secretaries who advise and prepare documents for the permanent representatives for meetings of the various organs, commissions, committees, and agencies of the UNO. In 1994, 22 percent of diplomatic personnel in permanent missions were women, up from 20 percent in 1989. But the number of states with no women on their delegations increased as well, from fifty-seven in 1989 to sixty-seven in 1994 (United Nations Office of the Secretary-General 1995).

Women and the Security Council. The permanent representative or another regular member of a country's UN mission represents that country if it holds a seat on the UN Security Council, the chief decision-making body in the United Nations system on matters of international peace and security. The Security Council is composed of fifteen member states, five of which—the People's Republic of China, France, the Russian Federation, the United Kingdom, and the United States—have permanent seats and veto powers. Of the ten nonpermanent seats, five are selected every two years, apportioned to represent geographic regions. Among other things, the Charter gives the Security Council the ability to impose sanctions, up to and including the use of military force, in response to breaches of the international peace or acts of aggression.

The presidency of the Security Council rotates on a monthly basis among the fifteen seats. The first woman to preside over a meeting of the Security Council was Ambassador Jeanne Martin Cisse, who served as permanent representative of Guinea from 1972 to 1976. Most recently, Madeleine Albright served as Security Council president in 1996. Because so few women have sat on the Security Council, women's voices and perspectives have been virtually excluded from the central decisions made by the organization—that is, from the major political and security decisions of the past fifty years, such as how to deal with the Korean, Middle East, and other conflicts, apartheid South Africa, and the Iraqi invasion of Kuwait. The lack of women on the Security Council has also excluded them from key personnel matters, since the Security Council "recommends" (nominates) top UN officials, such as the Secretary-General and judges to the World Court.

Further, women have been absent not only from the making of Security Council decisions but also from their enforcement. As Judith Hicks Stiehm discusses in this collection, few of the personnel who wear blue berets or blue helmets are women. Only two women have served as civilian commanders of UN peacekeeping missions: Margaret Anstee (United Kingdom), who served as chief of mission in Angola in 1992, and Angela King (Jamaica), who served as chief of mission for the United Nations Observer Mission in South Africa (UNOMSA) from 1992 to 1994 (D'Amico and Beckman 1995, 94–102). In addition to peace enforcement, women are also beginning to find a place at the peace table. In his first year in office, Secretary-General Kofi Annan appointed Elisabeth Rehn of Finland as special representative for Bosnia and Herzegovina and Heidi Tagliavini of Switzerland as deputy special representative for Georgia (United Nations Office of the Secretary-General 1998c).

Women and the Trusteeship Council. During its years in operation, the Trusteeship Council was made up of the permanent members of the Security

Council, with additional members elected by the General Assembly in proportion to the number of territories in the trusteeship system. Former colonies of countries defeated during World War II were designated "trust territories" to be administered by UN trustees until such time as the people of those territories were prepared to exercise their right of self-determination. As with the Security Council, few women participated on the Trusteeship Council during its years of operation. For example, in its first six sessions, no woman served as either a representative or an alternate; in the fifth session (1949), two women served as advisers; and in the sixth session (1950), one woman served as adviser (United Nations Office of the Secretary-General 1950). One notable exception was Angie Brooks-Randolph of Liberia, who served as Trusteeship Council vice president in 1966 (Galey 1995b, 25, n. 30). The council suspended operation after the people of the last trust territory, Palau, voted in 1992 to establish a semi-autonomous relationship with the United States.

Women and the World Court. Records of the International Court of Justice indicate that no woman served on the bench during its affiliation with the United Nations from 1945 to 1995. Rosalyn Higgins (United Kingdom) was appointed 12 July 1995 to fill a vacancy left by the resignation of Robert Yewdall Jennings (United Kingdom); her term expires in 2000. While Judge Higgins has been the only woman to serve on the World Court, other women jurists are moving into high-level positions in the international legal system. For example, Judge Gabrielle Kirk McDonald (United States) became president of the UN's Ad Hoc War Crimes Tribunal for the former Yugoslavia and Rwanda in November 1997 and had served as a judge for the tribunal since its inception in 1993 (*Washington Post,* 12 April 1998). The International Law Commission's proposal to establish a permanent international criminal court with the power to try individuals accused of crimes—rather than only states, as with the World Court—will, if adopted, present another opportunity for the United Nations to practice what it preaches with regard to gender equality.

Women and ECOSOC. While women's participation in the Economic and Social Council itself has been marginal, it has been comparatively less so than in the other principal organs of the UN. Many women have served in the subsidiary organs and satellite agencies that ECOSOC governs, in particular those that address women's political rights and economic situation. However, on the council itself, women continue to be vastly underrepresented. For example, the 1950 report of the Secretary-General to the Commission on the Status of Women on women's participation in the UN's principal organs indicated that during the eighth and tenth sessions of ECOSOC, no women were among the then-eighteen chief representatives on the council, though a handful served as alternate representatives or advisers (United Nations Office of the Secretary-General 1950). The number of seats on the ECOSOC increased from eighteen in 1946 to twenty-seven in 1965 and to fifty-four in 1973 in response to the growth in UN membership as decolonized states joined and demanded a greater voice in the organization. I have found no data to indicate that the growth of the ECOSOC increased the participation of women in that forum; geographic distribution, rather than gender, appears to have been the main basis for increased representation on the ECOSOC.

The highest concentration of women diplomats within ECOSOC is found in the Commission on the Status of Women, which is one of six functional commissions under the authority of ECOSOC. Women have predominated as members of the CSW, whose size steadily grew from fifteen to forty-five members between 1946 and 1990. It had an all-female membership until 1966, when one male representative was included. Since then, never have more than a handful of men at any one time served on the commission (Reanda 1992, 268 n. 13, 269 n. 16). The members of the CSW are appointed by their governments and confirmed (elected) by ECOSOC according to a geographic pattern. Thus the members of the CSW sit as representatives of their governments, whose instructions and interests they serve. Consequently, and despite its promising beginnings, the CSW became both a marginalized and limited body for advancing "women's issues" within the UNO. The Commission was only tangentially involved with the UN Decade for Women (1975–1985), and there was even a proposal to abolish the Commission in 1980 (Reanda 1992, 293–95). However, the mainstreaming of a gender perspective in the UN system and the Commission's own efforts to participate in such a strategy may help to revitalize its role in the future.

If most governments seem to have been able to find women diplomats to represent their interests on the CSW, why have there been so few women leading their national delegations and representing their countries in the principal organs of the United Nations? Either women have historically been (and in some cases, continue to be) excluded from the study or practice of law, politics, and diplomacy or they simply have not been encouraged to enter these fields. Moreover, most states continue to employ gender preferences that limit the career possibilities of women diplomats through gendered selection, retention, and promotion criteria (see, e.g., McGlen and Reid Sarkees 1993; Olmstead et al. 1984; Morin 1995). These practices severely limit the number of women who reach the top ranks of their national diplomatic corps. Some women have come to top diplomatic posts as replacements for deceased spouses. For example, among the African American women appointees to the U.S. General Assembly delegations are two widows of slain civil rights leaders. This illustrates that, as in national politics, the "widow's walk," or what I have elsewhere called political surrogacy, has been one avenue for women's access to international diplomacy (D'Amico 1995, 15–30). This example also illustrates that a woman's appointment to her country's UN mission may signal a commitment to some other political cause relevant to national politics or national interest rather than to women's equality.

Women in Subsidiary UN Organs and Specialized Agencies

Women who rise to the highest levels in the United Nations system tend to do so in areas where they have responsibility for social services or care-taking activities the UN performs rather than in the core political areas of diplomacy, peace, and security. Sadako Ogata of Japan is High Commissioner for Refugees; Dr. Nafis Sadik of Pakistan is executive director of the United Nations Fund for Population Activities; Carol Bellamy of the United States is executive director of the United Nations Children's Fund. The former president of Ireland, Mary Bourke Robinson, was appointed head of the Commission on Human Rights in 1997 (United Nations Office of the Secretary-General 1998b). Incumbents in these positions carry the rank of under-secretary-general.

In UN subsidiary organs, women predominate in positions that deal with women or women's issues. Women direct and staff the International Research and Training Institute for the Advancement of Women (INSTRAW) and the United Nations Development Fund for Women (UNIFEM). Typically, the director of the Women's Office has been a woman; the former location of this office in Vienna illustrated its marginality to the UN core. Many women in the UN staff avoid this "woman track," as some perceive it to be a dead-end for anyone who seeks to rise higher in the organization, while others argue that all areas of UN work deal with issues that affect women.

As with the Commission on the Status of Women, women predominate in the affiliated committees that explicitly address women's issues and status. For example, the majority of the personnel of the twenty-three-member Committee on the Elimination of Discrimination against Women (CEDAW), which monitors implementation of the convention (treaty) by the same name (CEDAW), have been women since its inception eighteen years ago. In 1998 the chair and vice chair were Salma Khan (Bangladesh) and Carlota Bustelo Garcia de Real (Mexico).

Similarly, women have directed few major UN conferences on global issues authorized by the General Assembly, most notably the four conferences on the status of women. Helvi Sipila of Finland, who at the time was an assistant secretary-general for the UNO, was secretary-general of the first Women's Conference, which was held at Mexico City in 1975. Lucille Mair of Jamaica was secretary-general of the second conference at Copenhagen in 1980. Letitia Shahani of the Philippines was secretary-general of the third conference at Nairobi in 1985, and Gertrude Mongella of Tanzania served as secretary-general of the fourth World Conference at Beijing in 1995.

In the UN specialized agencies, women have also remained at the margin, but their numbers and proportions have increased as a result of the initiatives of the Decade for Women (Winslow 1995a, 155–75). In 1949, women were absent from the meetings of seven of ten extant specialized agencies, including the International Monetary Fund, the International Bank for Reconstruction and Development (World Bank), and the International Telecommunication Union. Nine women—only 2 of whom were principal representatives—were among the 230 representatives, alternates, and advisers to the World Health Organization Assembly in Rome, and just 3 of the 185 representatives and advisers at the fourth conference of the UN Educational, Scientific, and Cultural Organization (UNESCO) in Paris that same year were women.

Women's representation was somewhat better at the International Labor Organization's conference in 1949, where 17 of 244 government representatives, 1 of 143 employers' representatives, and 4 of 156 workers' representatives were women (United Nations Office of the Secretary-General 1950). At the ILO's 1993 conference, 300 women were among the 2,200 participants. Of these 300 women, 51 were delegates, comprising 16.9 percent of government representatives, 9.1 percent of employers' representatives, and 12.5 percent of workers' representatives (Winslow 1995a, 161).

In 1984, the proportion of women in all ranks at specialized agencies stood at 13.9 percent, with more than a third of those women in entry-level positions and just over 1 percent in senior management positions. By 1988, the proportion of women in all ranks had climbed to 16.3 percent and the proportion of women in senior management had risen to 2.7 percent—but more than a third of women employees were still concentrated in entry-level positions (United Nations Office of the Secretary-General 1989). Only UNFPA had met the goal of 50 percent women at the professional level in 1997. Three other agencies had achieved or come close to the 35 percent mark: the Office of the UN High Commissioner for Refugees (38.5 percent), UNESCO (37.1 percent), and UNDP (33.5 percent). The World Food Programme doubled its number of women staff between 1992 and 1997 (United Nations Office of the Secretary-General (1997a). According to Winslow, the World Health Organization (WHO) has had the best record on recruiting and retaining women staff and promoting women to the managerial level as well as addressing the needs and concerns of women in its field programs (Winslow 1995a, 170–71).

Conclusion

Most women, as well as indigenous peoples and nation-peoples without a state, have little or no formal representation in the United Nations. Those who obtain consultative status, through nongovernmental organizations, to the various committees or working groups of the UN have a voice in, but no vote on, the UN's final decisions and policies. While the number of NGOs with consultative status continues to grow, groups that lack resources remain excluded, and those with meager resources remain at the furthest margins of the UN system. Within these groups, women often have the fewest resources and therefore the least access.

We need to pay attention not only to countries that are un- or underrepresented in the UN system but also to the variety of perspectives that are un- or underrepresented, including those of women and men from excluded or marginalized groups. We must recognize that different perspectives and life experiences are valuable, and we must include the perspectives and voices of women and men who are differently situated with regard to class/caste, race/nationality, and sexuality. We must also recognize that different perspectives lead to different priorities. For example, women in developing countries prioritize issues differently from women in developed countries, as debates over agendas for the four world conferences on women have shown. Women of color may have different priorities from white women, while poor women, middle-class women, and wealthy women within the same community will have different needs and concerns. Their voices and those of other excluded groups deserve to be heard within the current structure of the UN system, not just at its margins in commissions, working groups, or NGOs, where their views are mediated by state representatives or by community elites.

While the UN now pledges to "mainstream *a* gender perspective" (emphasis added), this pledge suggests an essentialized womanhood—that is, a singular gender perspective as the voice for all women. Opening the door to only a singular gender perspective neglects the diversity of women's life experiences; just as no one man is capable of representing the concerns and interests of all men, no one woman can represent all women. "Shuffling the deck" by shifting women who have already risen in one area of the United Nations system into other areas, so that individual women accrue impressive credentials as the "first this" and the "first that" while many other women's voices go unheard, does not provide adequate representation for women's diversity.

Part of the burden of achieving gender equity lies with the UNO itself, and part lies with the member states. Implementation of policies designed to establish gender balance has been delayed both by recalcitrant UN managers and by conditions brought on by the UN's financial crisis, such as the staff hiring freeze. While the Secretary-General's report of 1998 says that the current retirement pattern will provide a "window of opportunity" for women to advance in the Secretariat in the next decade (United Nations Office of the Secretary-General 1998c), this window must be open to more women. For example, staff training opportunities must be provided, as recommended in the Secretary-General's 1997 report, but must be scheduled in a flexible way to accommodate women's different employment and life patterns. Issues such as recruitment policy, employment of spouses, child care, and sexual harassment still need attention. The establishment of the Task Force on Harassment in January 1995 and gathering of more reliable data on the incidence of sexual harassment provided by the 1997 staff survey are steps in the right direction. Managers must be held accountable for the underrepresentation of women through performance appraisals. Member states must pay their "dues" (assessed annual contributions) to open hiring and promotion opportunities and must commit to offering qualified women for posts subject to geographic distribution.

While the United Nations system reflects the gender politics of its constituent member states, it also has the ability to make its own rules. It can say no to a country like Afghanistan that rebuffs UN women staff and curtails the rights of women nationals. Through the opportunity for international exchange that the organization presents in many venues, the UN can also pursue an agenda for change and provide a model'for how state leaders might behave. With continued pressure from within and outside the organization, the United Nations can meet the goal of gender equality. As Secretary-General Kofi Annan pointed out on the occasion of International Women's Day, 8 March 1998, the United Nations must get its own house in order:

> If we accept that in any society, gender equality is more than a goal in itself; if we believe that the empowerment of women is a vital means to meeting the challenge of sustainable development; if we argue that the participation of women is a requirement in building good governance; if we insist that the rights of women are a precondition for the effectiveness of humanitarian assistance; if we are convinced of all these things in relation to all the societies we are trying to help in this world—then how can we fail to apply this conviction to our own society in our own house? (United Nations Office of the Secretary-General 1998b)

Note

1. The concept of geographic distribution of UN personnel positions is stated in Article 101.3 of the UN Charter. The purpose of this distribution is to ensure that perspectives and values of the peoples of the different UN member states are reflected in

the staff. A quota system for this geographic distribution, based roughly on a member state's contribution to the UN budget, was introduced (Timothy 1995b, 89). Posts not subject to geographic distribution are those that are earmarked to be filled, for example, as part of a host government's lease agreement with the United Nations. Positions in the "Professional" category are subject to geographic distribution and for this reason are sometimes called the "political" level of the Secretariat staff.

3

United Nations Peacekeeping: Men's and Women's Work

Judith Hicks Stiehm

Peacekeeping is a new approach to conflict management that seeks to combine the military's emphasis on strength as the way to obtain or maintain peace with peace activists' focus on justice, reconciliation, and cooperation. The United Nations has been experimenting with a variety of approaches to peacekeeping, but the common denominator has been that it is done by military personnel who have all but forsworn the use of violence and work closely with a variety of civilian humanitarian, relief, and development organizations. Women need to consider when and how peacekeeping is effective and whether it should continue to be dominated by the military—and, consequently, by men. To date, women have played a very limited role as peacekeepers, but, as will be argued below, it may be that women's mere presence has a variety of positive results, such as better contact with the female half of the served population, a reduction in interpersonal tension, and more appropriate sexual behavior on the part of peacekeeping men.

Since 1948 the United Nations has authorized more than forty peacekeeping operations. These operations have involved more than 650,000 personnel from seventy countries and have cost more than a thousand peacekeepers' lives and more than $9 billion (United Nations Department of Public Information 1994). Traditionally, the "Blue Helmets" have been guided by three principles. They are (1) that the parties in conflict consent to the peacekeepers' presence (usually as observers and/or buffers); (2) that the peacekeepers observe strict neutrality between all parties; and (3) that peacekeepers use force only for self-defense and only as a last resort (Evans 1993, 104). The Blue Helmets themselves are military personnel, but many civilians work directly for the UN in peacekeeping, and civilians are numerous in the nongovernmental organizations (NGOs) that are now integral to most peacekeeping operations. Most missions have been to small countries, and most peacekeepers have come from small countries (e.g., the Scandinavian countries, Ghana, and Fiji).

There were fifteen UN peacekeeping operations prior to 1989. From 1989 to 1997 the UN launched almost twice as many missions as it had in the previous forty years. Since 1989 the complexity and expense of peacekeeping operations have also increased tremendously.[1] Peacekeeping has expanded to include institution building, economic development, human rights monitoring, relief, and the monitoring of elections. Something new has also been added: peace enforcement. It is essential that women play a central role in all these activities.

This essay reviews women's participation in peacekeeping, assesses their special contributions, and discusses the prospects for their future participation. It is based on a month of both extensive and intensive interviewing of UN staff who had worked in the field in peacekeeping missions. More than forty interviews were conducted; most of them were with women, most of whom did not want to be identified by name.

Women's Participation in Peacekeeping

Women's potential for an expanded role in peacekeeping is largely the result of the expanded role of peacekeeping missions. While women are a significant proportion of some militaries (e.g., 12 percent of the U.S. and Canadian militaries), and while some have been deployed in member-state units that are seconded to serve as peacekeepers, the number of military women who have been peacekeepers is low.

A recent UN report on women's role in peacekeeping provides data on all missions in operation in 1993 (United Nations Statistical Division 1994). This means the report includes the oldest mission, UNTSO (to Jerusalem) but does not include some recent, but completed missions, such as UNTAG (Namibia). As table 3.1 shows, approximately ninety thousand individuals seconded from their countries served in peacekeeping missions in 1993. Only 1.75 percent were women. This average was exceeded only in UNOSOM II (Somalia), UNIFIL (Lebanon), UNDOF (Golan Heights), UNMIH (Haiti), UNIKOM (Kuwait/Iraq), and MINURSO (Western Sahara), which had the highest percentage of women's participation—9.4 percent. UNOSOM II (Somalia) had the largest number of women, some 625 from twelve countries; however, 75 percent of them were from the United States, and a substantial number of the women were medical personnel.

Canada and the United States have the highest percentage of women in national armies (12 percent); in comparison, they contribute a low percentage of female military personnel to UN peacekeeping missions (8 and 5 percent respectively.)[2] Women represented an even smaller percentage of the civilian police sent to participate in peacekeeping, less than 1 percent. Overall the data

Table 3.1

Member-State-Contributed Personnel to UN Peacekeeping Missions, by Mission (1993)

	All contributed personnel		Military[a]		Civilian police	
	Total	% Female	Total	% Female	Total	% Female
UNOSOM II (Somalia)	29,703	2.1	29,703	2.1	0	—
UNTAC (Cambodia)[b]	19,232	..[c]	15,684	..	3,548	0.2
UNPROFOR (Yugoslavia)	24,853	1.6	24,200	1.6	653	2.1
ONUMOZ (Mozambique)	6,501	0.1	6,501	0.1	0	—
UNIFIL (Lebanon)	5,247	2.3	5,247	2.3	0	—
UNFICYP (Cyprus)	1,237	1.1	1,201	0.7	36	16.7
UNDOF (Golan Heights)	1,103	4.0	1,103	4.0	0	—
ONUSAL (El Salvador)[d]	706	0.3	161	0.6	545	0.2
UNIKOM (Kuwait/Iraq)[e]	369	1.9	369	1.9	0	—
MINURSO (W. Sahara)[e]	350	9.4	324	10.2	26	0.0
UNAVEM II (Angola)	316	1.0	256	0.0	60	5.0
UNAMIR (Rwanda)	512	0.0	510	0.0	2	0.0
UNTSO (Jerusalem)	220	0.0	220	0.0	0	—
UNOMIL (Liberia)	246	0.0	246	0.0	0	—
MICIVIH (Haiti)	113	2.7	62	0.0	51	5.9
UNMOGIP (India/Pakistan)	38	0.0	38	0.0	0	—
UNOMIG (Georgia)	12	0.0	12	0.0	0	—
TOTAL	90,758	1.7[f]	85,837	1.7[f]	4,921	0.7

Source: United Nations Statistical Division, Report of Statistical Compilation on Women in Peace-keeping for the Second Issue of The World's Women: Trend and Statistics. New York, 29 March 1994 (DESIPA STAT 321[a]).

[a]Including all military personnel (e.g., officers, enlisted personnel, military observers), excluding civilian police
[b]Figures reflect staffing levels at second quarter 1993.
[c]Data not available
[d]Figures reflect deployment of personnel during the entire period of 1993.
[e]Military figures based on field communiqués and lengths of rotations among member state contributors.
[f]Excluding UNTAC

suggest that for the first forty years almost no women participated in peace-keeping. Thus, the 1993 figure of 1.75 percent does represent a change. Practice has moved from exclusion to no prohibition; however, inclusion has certainly not become policy.

The picture is somewhat different when international and locally recruited civilian staff are considered. These fall into one of three categories: Field Service, General Service, and Professionals. Field Service (FS) personnel are ranked 1–7. They perform a wide variety of tasks that include both technical and administrative duties. They need to be highly mobile. Women constitute 6 percent of these personnel (see table 3.2).

General Service (GS) personnel serve primarily in clerical and administrative positions. They are predominantly women. This suggests that women are available for deployment, are willing to accept the challenges of working in the field, and are not restrained because of danger, family, and/or uncertainty.

Professional (P) staff hold grades 1–5. Because P-5s may have high-level and decision-making responsibilities, they are sometimes clustered with directors (D-1 and D-2) and with Under-Secretaries-General (USGs) rather than with Professionals 1–4. A USG is an appointive position. UN staff, then, have something equivalent to civil or foreign service career ladders, but their work, like that of the civil and foreign service, is directed by an appointed official, in this case, by an under-secretary-general.

Among professionals ranked P-1 through P-4 the representation of women stands at 30 percent, but there is great variability by mission. Some missions, for example, El Salvador and South Africa, reach almost 50 percent; others, such as Lebanon and Cambodia, are much lower. Large numbers of women are correlated with newer missions and with those having a mandate that extends beyond military observation.

At the decision-making level (USGs, directors, and P-5s), the shrinkage in the number of women is striking. It falls to 6 percent. Although the proportion of women in D-1 and higher positions in the UN Secretariat as a whole is 12.8 percent, in peacekeeping it is only 4 percent. In the P-4 and P-5 categories, it is 27 percent in the Secretariat, but only 17 percent in peacekeeping. In P-1 through P-3, it is 42 percent and 35 percent, respectively (United Nations Statistical Division 1994, 11). Often women find opportunities in new fields. This seems not to be the case in peacekeeping, where women are much more poorly represented than in the UN in general.

Locally recruited staff are civilians under contract and typically hold the equivalent of GS positions. Here, too, there is great variability as far as women are concerned (see Table 3.3). In El Salvador and the former Yugoslavia close to half the locally recruited staff were women. In another five missions a quarter were women. However, in the two largest missions, Cambodia and Somalia, only some 15 percent were women, and in Liberia, India/Pakistan, and Georgia, women were less than 10 percent. This probably reflects two things: (a) the percentage of women in the local work force; and (b) the attitudes and leadership of UN staff making hiring decisions.

An attempt to reconstruct the distribution of UN civilian men and women in peacekeeping operations from the period 1957–1991 yields some interesting results (see table 3.4). Overall, the percentage of women ranged from 5 to 23 percent, with highs in 1989 (primarily because of the Namibia operation) and in 1961. The numbers for 1990 and 1991 are only about 14 percent, but in 1957 and in 1964 they were 12 percent. Thus, there has not been anything like a steady increase over the thirty-five-year period, and it is very possible that any recent high numbers for women may eventually appear only as blips, as did those from 1961. No new policy or commitment accounts for the recent data. It will be very easy to backslide.

Field Service staff show a small positive change from 0 percent to about 6 percent. The percentage of women in levels P-1 through P-4 shows a noticeable dip after 1965 (to 0 percent in 1970, 1975, and 1980) and improved but variable numbers since 1986. Women showed up only twice in the fifteen sample years at the policymaking level of P-5 and above. In General Service staff, however, their proportion dropped from over half to about 20 percent of slots.

While the percentages of women who participate in UN peacekeeping missions remains low, women's roles and experiences in recent missions suggest that they can make positive contributions to peacekeeping. The cases of women's participation in UN peacekeeping missions to Namibia, South Africa, and Cambodia provide useful illustrations.

Women's Participation in Namibia, South Africa, and Cambodia

Namibia

Namibia (UNTAG 1989–1990) was a mission that went as planned. Nestled between South Africa, the Atlantic Ocean, and Angola, Namibia had been the scene of a war of liberation led by SWAPO (South-West Africa People's Organization) against South Africa, which was the trustee for the territory known as Southwest Africa. In just under a year UNTAG (United Nations Transition Assistance Group) was able to supervise the disarmament and repatriation of armed groups, monitor the return of some forty-three thousand refugees and the release of political prisoners, observe the activities of local police, and monitor voter education, voter registration, and the election of a constituent assembly. That assembly then drafted a constitution, and UNTAG left behind a newly independent and functioning country (United Nations 1991c).

Table 3.2
International UN Civilian Staff in Peacekeeping Missions, by Category and Mission (December 1993)

	All categories[a]		P-5–USG		
	Total	% Female	M	F	% Female
UNOMSA (South Africa)	56	46.4	3	1	25.0
ONUSAL (El Salvador)	140	42.1	16	1	5.9
UNPROFOR (Yugoslavia)	314	41.4	17	3	15.0
MICIVIH (Haiti)	144	40.3	5	0	0.0
UNTAC (Cambodia)	338	39.9	6	0	0.0
ONUMOZ (Mozambique)	167	35.3	9	1	10.0
UNOMIL (Liberia)	22	31.8	0	0	0.0
UNAMIR (Rwanda)	48	29.2	3	0	0.0
UNAVEM II (Angola)	50	28.0	5	0	0.0
UNOSOM II (Somalia)	373	27.0	18	0	0.0
UNOMIG (Georgia)	4	25.0	1	0	0.0
MINURSO (W. Sahara)	100	25.0	5	0	0.0
UNFICYP (Cyprus)	31	22.6	4	0	0.0
UNIFIL (Lebanon)	163	21.5	3	0	0.0
UNMOT (Tadjikistan)	5	20.0	1	0	0.0
UNIKOM (Iraq/Kuwait)	78	17.9	3	1	25.0
UNTSO (Jerusalem)	141	13.5	3	0	0.0
UNMOGIP (India/Pakistan)	24	12.5	1	0	0.0
UNDOF (Golan Heights)	30	6.7	2	0	0.0
TOTAL	2,228	31.8	105	7	6.3

	P-1–P-4			GS-1–GS-7			FS-1–FS-7		
	M	F	%F	M	F	%F	M	F	%F
UNOMSA (South Africa)	23	16	41.0	0	6	100.0	4	3	42.9
ONUSAL (El Salvador)	42	40	48.8	9	17	65.4	15	1	6.3
UNPROFOR (Yugoslavia)	68	15	18.1	50	109	65.6	49	3	5.8
MICIVIH (Haiti)	63	48	43.2	10	10	50.0	9	0	0.0
UNTAC (Cambodia)	38	7	15.6	88	121	57.9	71	7	9.0
ONUMOZ (Mozambique)	27	14	34.1	28	40	58.8	45	4	8.2
UNOMIL (Liberia)	2	0	0.0	5	6	54.5	8	1	11.1
UNAMIR (Rwanda)	3	1	25.0	8	13	61.9	20	0	0.0
UNAVEM II (Angola)	6	1	14.3	9	13	59.1	16	0	0.0
UNOSOM II (Somalia)	91	17	15.7	69	81	54.0	94	3	3.1
UNOMIG (Georgia)	0	0	0.0	1	0	0.0	1	1	50.0
MINURSO (W. Sahara)	17	6	26.1	28	19	40.4	27	0	0.0
UNFICYP (Cyprus)	1	1	50.0	2	4	66.7	17	2	10.5
UNIFIL (Lebanon)	14	1	6.7	13	31	70.5	98	3	3.0
UNMOT (Tadjikistan)	0	0	0.0	1	1	50.0	2	0	0.0
UNIKOM (Iraq/Kuwait)	5	0	0.0	14	12	46.2	42	1	2.3
UNTSO (Jerusalem)	0	0	0.0	3	13	81.3	116	6	4.9
UNMOGIP (India/Pakistan)	0	0	0.0	0	0	0.0	20	3	13.0
UNDOF (Golan Heights)	0	0	0.0	0	0	0.0	26	2	7.1
TOTAL	400	167	29.5	338	496	59.5	680	40	5.6

Source: United Nations Statistical Division, *Report of Statistical Compilation on Women in Peace-keeping for the Second Issue of The World's Women: Trend and Statistics.* New York, 29 March 1994 (DESIPA STAT 321[a]).

[a]Exluding locally recruited staff

Table 3.3
Locally Recruited Staff in In Peacekeeping Missions, by Mission (December 1993)

	Total	% Women
ONUSAL (El Salvador)[a]	224	47.3
UNPROFOR (Yugoslavia)	1,161	45.7
ONUMOZ (Mozambique)	296	29.1
UNFICYP (Cyprus)	368	25.8
UNDOF (Golan Heights)	84	25.0
MINURSO (W. Sahara)[b]	49	24.5
MICIVIH (Haiti)	152	24.3
UNIKOM (Iraq/Kuwait)[b]	113	21.2
UNTAC (Cambodia)[c]	9,666	16.0
UNAVEM II (Angola)	71	15.5
UNOSOM II (Somalia)	1,116	14.0
UNFIL (Lebanon)	352	13.6
UNTSO (Jerusalem)	160	10.6
UNOMIL (Liberia)	74	9.5
UNMOGIP (India/Pakistan)	49	0.0
UNOMIG (Georgia)	3	0.0
TOTAL	13,938	19.3

Source: United Nations Statistical Division, *Report of Statistical Compilation on Women in Peace-keeping for the Second Issue of The World's Women: Trend and Statistics*. New York, 29 March 1994 (DESIPA STAT 321[a]).

[a]Figures reflect deployment of personnel during the entire period of 1993.
[b]Military figures based on field communiqué and lengths of rotations among contributors.
[c]Figures reflect staffing levels at second quarter 1993.

Because the process was long delayed (until after Cuban troops left Angola), planning was extensive. Special Representative Martti Ahtisaari (later the president of Finland) was able to recruit just the team he wanted, often after extensive interviewing, to provide training and meet several principles, including the use of large numbers of women personnel (60 percent of the professional staff). In particular he recruited women for decision-making positions. Nevertheless, the special representative, the deputy special representative, the three directors, and the police adviser, and the force commander were all men. Also, 90 percent of the short-term staff were men. There were more than eight thousand UN men and women from a hundred countries in the Namibian mission scattered at two hundred locations over a large and arid country. Forty-two political centers were organized under ten regions. A satellite communications network and a radio/vehicle network made the organization of Namibia's first election possible.

Table 3.4
International UN Civilian Staff in Peacekeeping Missions, by Selected Years (1957–1991)

	All categories[a]		P-5-USG		P-1-P-4		GS-1-GS-7		FS-1-FS-7	
	Total	% F	Total	%F	Total	%F	Total	%F	Total	%F
1957	266	11.7	8	0.0	17	11.8	45	64.4	196	0.0
1961	783	22.2	24	0.0	116	11.2	328	49.1	315	0.0
1964	460	12.0	29	3.4	37	5.4	104	50.0	290	0.0
1965	356	11.2	22	0.0	17	17.6	53	69.8	264	0.0
1970	264	5.3	9	0.0	4	0.0	15	86.7	236	0.4
1975	669	8.7	16	0.0	13	0.0	310	18.1	330	0.6
1980	956	12.6	12	0.0	16	0.0	503	19.7	425	4.9
1985	958	13.4	10	0.0	20	15.0	487	15.0	441	11.8
1986	1,166	12.5	9	0.0	17	35.3	698	16.6	442	5.4
1987	1,127	12.2	11	0.0	10	10.0	678	17.0	428	4.9
1988	1,099	12.7	15	0.0	12	25.0	729	16.5	343	5.0
1989	1,590	23.0	59	10.2	158	38.6	902	29.8	471	6.2
1990	1,506	14.2	23	0.0	23	13.0	875	20.3	585	5.6
1991	1,449	14.5	20	0.0	28	25.0	894	19.1	507	6.3

Source: United Nations Statistical Division, Report of Statistical Compilation on Women in Peace-keeping for the Second Issue of The World's Women: Trend and Statistics. New York, 29 March 1994 (DESIPA STAT 321[a]).

[a]Excluding locally recruited staff

Working in the field can be exhilarating. There are a variety of logistical problems to solve. Tasks almost always require innovation and initiative. Individuals may hold temporary appointments that are higher than their regular appointments; for example, a P-5 may hold a D-1 post. The field especially demonstrates that "hardly anyone is trained for what needs to be done." Women especially seemed to enjoy the responsibility they were given and the diminution of hierarchy that is a part of field work. In fact, many women described their Namibian experience as the first they had where they were given real challenges. Five persons who held director rank (D-1 and D-2) and three of the ten regional directors were women, including one who was assigned a post on the northern border, where fighting had been routine. She had eight hundred troops assigned to her.

One woman took her children to the field with her. Another described Namibia as "the best year of my life." Other phrases used were "a breakthrough," "visibility and hardship but responsibility," "it took them two months to figure out I was really in charge," "shock—they celebrated Hitler's birthday in the town I was stationed in," "exciting," "a thrill," "we did what needed to be done—mediation, education—it was impossible to be just an observer." Civilian men were described as sometimes helpless; women and military men were seen by a number of women as "more resourceful and resilient." One woman in her fifties had never been on a field mission and was so pleased with the work that she has been "going ever since." Another noted that women's practical competence made them valuable in the field but that being accommodating, which made them effective there, could also work against them, because they were then seen as "not a leader."

One woman assigned to Namibia said that it was the first mission really to "give women a chance" and that, while it now seems to have been easy, at the time it was "startling, heretical." She added that there was resistance to Ahtisaari's efforts to bring so many women into responsible positions. Arguments were made that women could not be effective working with the military and police, that the patriarchal culture in which they would have to work would be pained by the presence of foreign authority, and that having that authority rest with women would be "adding insult to injury."

Namibia, with its large numbers of women, may have been the first mission where the conduct of UN staff vis-à-vis local women was called into question. Apparently, some male peacekeepers moved local women into their quarters, UN official vehicles were parked in front of brothels, and even high-ranking officials were believed to exploit local women hired by the UN. The presence of religious NGOs may also help to explain the voice given to complaints about the relationships between male UN personnel and local women. This does not suggest that UN women were celibate or that local women were unconsenting. It is just that this may have been the first mission in which the issue and its effect on the mission were raised.

One woman noted that because Namibia was a success, it should not be assumed that it was easy. Fighting broke out not long after the UN arrived, a political leader was assassinated, and the violence in nearby Mozambique, Angola, and South Africa did not suggest Namibia would be immune. Further, what is often thought of as an electoral exercise involved a great deal of political reconciliation and mediation related to human rights. Different people in different regions agreed that "the turning point" was getting representatives from each of the different parties into one room to meet face-to-face (most for the first time), and then getting them to agree to an electoral code of conduct. This often took a great deal of time, persistence, and cajolery. UN women were extremely active in this process and felt exceptionally effective. An analogy might be made to certain police work. At least in the United States, going to the scene of a domestic dispute is considered a hazardous assignment. As more women joined U.S. police forces, it was found that giving them this assignment was very effective; they seemed to have a higher potential for calming rather than inflaming a volatile situation (Martin 1980).

It was also noted that women UN personnel reached groups that men might have found difficult to reach and participated in different community groups and projects. In a voter education and registration mission, this probably meant that local women's political participation was affected positively.

More than one individual who reported a successful and fulfilling field experience that permitted her to "blossom" also noted that high performance did not "pay off" on return to New York. Some women were not even able to return to previous jobs that had been filled in their absence. The rules are not different for women, but women may have had different expectations about the rewards for merit and may not have been as careful or as well informed about providing for their futures. One woman remarked that three of the five women D-1s she knew were wives of senior executives. (It is possible that they are better informed than other women about both the opportunities and the realities.) On her return from Namibia one woman was told point-blank that she could not go to Western Sahara because women could not go to Arab societies. Ironically, Western Sahara had the highest percentage of women of any mission active in 1993!

South Africa

South Africa (UNOMSA 1993) seems to have been similarly successful in valuing women's participation. This mission was led not by a Finnish man but by a woman from Jamaica, Angela King, who has recently been appointed an under-secretary-general. Originally, UNOMSA (United Nations Observer Mission in South Africa) was an observer mission of about fifty people intended to promote negotiation and reconciliation and to monitor compliance with the terms of the rules for procedure for a governmental transition in South Africa. It then expanded into a mission for monitoring elections. This was a civilian operation. The UN staff was roughly fifty-fifty men and women. The three hundred UN volunteers (UNVs) trained and recruited in Geneva were also approximately half male and half female. However, for the two weeks prior to the election, the mission expanded again as some twelve hundred monitors selected by their governments arrived; these were mostly male. Thus, when the mission became visible at the time of the election, the proportions had shifted to male predominance.

Interestingly, South African women, who had long participated in the struggle for freedom, had insisted that, because the purpose of the peace process was national reconciliation, one of the three members representing each political party in the negotiating forum must be a woman. South African women from all groups were (and are) involved in a wide range of peace, church, and political groups and had published a women's-rights charter even before the UN arrived. They were familiar faces on TV, and when the elections were held, they insisted that 30 percent of the seats be given to women. This suggests that one must be wise, indeed, to sort out what are "Western values," what are "UN principles" (of nondiscrimination), what are "traditional values," and what are the views and values of women as well as men in a host country.

When the UN mission quadrupled in size just prior to the 1994 election, a man was appointed over King, and men were appointed to the major administrative posts. A large number of short-term, mostly male, election monitors were also added to the group. The new mission head was a non-UN-staff, political appointee who came in with a number of other non-UN diplomats to preside over the professionals who had been directing the mission up to that point. One of the professionals said the culture created by the new head of mission had the spirit of "it is a favor that you are getting your salary." Another observer, who had "survived Ian Smith," noted that she and other staff survived the new boss too.

Briefings for the South African elections tried to prepare (and, probably, overprepare) staff for danger and hardships that included "sharing water with animals" as well as possible political violence. Commenting on such hazards, one staff person noted: "Women are not fearful; men and their fears and rules are what limit us. They are afraid of our competence. The question is not, do women contribute something special, but in what ways is men's work limited?" The UN's implicit messages are of great importance. When there are victims, women are always among them. Doesn't the UN then have an obligation to see that women are among those providing relief and, equally important, making decisions about peace?

Cambodia

The mission in Cambodia (UNAMIC and UNTAC 1991–1993) followed the one in Namibia and may be usefully compared to it. It was larger (twenty-two thousand) and included fifty-five fatalities, but its fully integrated mandate specified seven components: human rights, electoral, military, civil administration, civilian police, repatriation, and rehabilitation. Its primary objective, or at least the one most fully realized, was to hold elections. It did not just supervise the elections; it actually conducted them. However, it carried out its work in the face of noncooperation by one of the four parties to the Paris agreements. Further, few of the other components worked as planned; for example, the different armies were not cantonmented and then disarmed.

The head of UNTAC was Yasushi Akashi of Japan. Even though the Namibian mission had been seen as a great success and women had been an integral part of it, no special efforts were made to learn lessons from it or to recruit women for the Cambodian mission. Women held no high-level decision-making positions, even though many civilians were involved and several components of the mission were of great and direct importance to women—for example, human rights and rehabilitation. The seven D-2s selected were all men, although some women were recommended for those positions, and the thirteen regional directors (D-1s and P-5s) were also all men. Several thousand police were brought in to monitor the local police, especially for human rights violations. All were men.

On the other hand, there were more than four hundred United Nations volunteers, a third of whom were women. The UNVs played an important role in organizing the election. They worked under very difficult conditions in areas where fighting could erupt at any time, in isolation, and in situations where there was no one else to make decisions, regardless of what policy was. Some felt women were not even considered for important jobs. Possibly this was not just oversight but also a failure in leadership; one woman professional flatly said, "I would not work with Akashi." Another senior woman noted that "grassroots women always play a crucial role in conflict resolution—they are always cleaning up men's mess. How can they be ignored in something called peacekeeping?" Another woman said, "We always say 'it's an emergency,' 'can't take the time' to find women—but we never have trouble finding GS women—lots of them. It's only professional women who don't get found." Indeed, the data show no women at the policymaking level, 16 percent women in P-1–P4, and 58 percent women in the GS series.

The abuse of local women, and children, by UN troops and civilian police was brought to public attention, not just by UN women, but also by those working in NGOs. Apparently, the fear of AIDS made "virgins" highly desirable, and younger and younger girls were being recruited for prostitution. A letter signed by more than 180 women was sent to Akashi charging sexual harassment of staff by UNTAC personnel and harassment of women on the street and asserting that there was no channel for redressing this behavior. UN troops were in a foreign country with money to spend, and some women were anxious to have it spent on them. However, the image of the UN and its capacity to fulfill its mission were negatively affected by sexual misconduct.

Akashi was quoted as responding that "boys will be boys." Still, there were other responses to the bad publicity. First, a code of conduct was prepared that is part of an elaborate training program that has recently been developed but not institutionalized. Second, a young Asian woman information officer was given the assignment of troubleshooter. In that position she learned what personnel officers already knew: some people have no common sense, others lose it while abroad, some countries send troops to serve abroad as a form of exile, other people come for a vacation and a cash bonanza, and some police officers do not drive and cannot speak the language. The information officer also found that blame for AIDS was being attached to UN troops and that ignorance about the disease was rampant. She ended up preparing brochures in six languages on the use of condoms and urged troop and police training at home and in native languages, including training on cultural differences related to gender— for example,when a Cambodian woman smiles and laughs, she is not delighted but angry or embarrassed. Many Westerners did not understand this or the need to save and give face. One woman noted that in New York there was at least consciousness about gender issues and that, in UNDP, gender-sensitivity training was required of all staff. Many women saw Cambodia as a setback.

Prospects for Women in Peacekeeping

Peacekeeping is an important way that women can participate in international peace efforts. Their participation is particularly necessary when human rights, humanitarian relief, elections, police training, and economic development are an integral part of those efforts. When peace is understood to result only or primarily from military strength, however, women and civilians (except at the highest level) can expect to be shut out.

Not all recent peacekeeping has been successful. Operations are expensive, and some have no endpoint; the UN has suffered significant fatalities; and sometimes antagonists have not, in fact, accepted the terms of peace. Therefore, there has been a drawing back, and a new emphasis is being given to peacekeeping's original format, one where international troops are positioned between enemies who consent to their presence in order to serve as a buffer and to observe both sides for possible violations of agreed terms. This has the effect of remilitarizing, and therefore remasculinizing, peacekeeping, even though there is every reason to believe women could be highly effective peacekeepers. Further, with the end of the Cold War, existing militaries and military strategists are seeking new roles. Some are choosing to become peacekeepers and peace experts rather than go out of business. Also, militaries are ready, organized, equipped, competent, and often unemployed. Therefore, the tendency will be to call upon them rather than to recruit and train civilian peacekeepers. Thus, one must expect a remilitarization of peacekeeping, if only as a matter of convenience.

In discussions of peacekeeping one often hears two assumptions about the "trickle effect." Even though women suffer extensively from war and more civilians die than soldiers (after all, soldiers have weapons to defend themselves), it is assumed that peace will "trickle down" to women from all-male, high-level deliberations. When women ask for a place at the peace table, though, a counterflow is assumed—that is, that women may now be admitted to the lowest levels of the military, diplomacy, and government and that over the years they will "trickle up" until all is resolved a generation from now. The problem is that "trickle down" ignores too many issues, and "trickle up" still has not happened several generations after the UN was founded. In assessing the participation of women, it may be important to compare the ages of women and men at different levels. It may be that women are admitted to different career opportunities but at a rather early stage are either passed over or promoted so slowly that their careers end before they reach positions of responsibility. Fast-charging men, then, are the only ones able to rise to the top.

It is important to ask whether women have any special contribution to make to peacekeeping and whether they create any special difficulties and also to consider how they are perceived as peacekeepers. At present, even though there has been excellent experience in Namibia and South Africa, answers to these questions remain tentative and are drawn from analogies and perceptions that sound suspiciously like stereotypes. Still, whether or not they are accurate, perceptions are important because people act on them.

Among the special contributions women are perceived to make to peacekeeping are:

1. Their presence, especially in decision-making roles, can demonstrate a fundamental UN principle: no discrimination against women.

Conversely, their absence is a nonverbal denial of this principle. The UN also looks bad if women are employed only in low-level positions.

2. Women's presence puts new items on the agenda—for example, the sexual conduct of UN personnel.

3. Women are perceived as more empathetic, which enhances their reconciliation and political work.

4. Women may have better and important access to host-country women. For example, in Afghanistan they have been useful in demining operations, which have to be conducted in fields worked primarily by Muslim women.

5. Their outreach may be essential to women's participation in elections and other programs.

6. They are seen as defusing tension rather than trying to control events. The other side of this coin is a perceived vulnerability or unwillingness to apply force.

7. When there is a critical mass of UN women, women in the host country tend to be mobilized too; also, UN men tend to behave more as they would at home rather than with the license some take in a foreign country.

8. When UN peacekeepers are by definition unarmed, or when they may use a weapon only in self-defense, women's presence seems to reinforce the commitment to that principle.

Conclusion

Important lessons can be learned from the variety of peacekeeping operations conducted by the UN in recent years. First, there is a significant potential for forging a partnership between those who wield society's legitimate force and those committed to nonviolent resolution of conflict, between high-level negotiators/mediators and grassroots organizers, and between interested and disinterested parties. Second, because they are available, trained, equipped, and ready, military forces will be called upon to do most of the peacekeeping even though others—for instance, UNVs—might be more effective in particular situations. Third, there is every reason for women to insist that legitimacy requires that they be full partners in all peace processes, but the militarization of that process will constrain their contribution. Cases like Namibia, where a concerted effort was made to integrate women into the peace process, have resulted in a sustained peace. Maybe it is time to create an international, civilian, women's peacekeeping corps, or at least one that is half men and half women.

Notes

1. For current information, see the UN peacekeeping operations Web site (http://www.un.org:80/depts/dpko.html).

2. This is because women are underrepresented in combat units and countries tend to send their combat troops to peacekeeping operations. This is true even if it would be more logical to send public affairs officers, logisticians, and military police. Many troops are given special training in peacekeeping skills such as negotiation, and the UN has developed training manuals and videos for peacekeepers. The materials have not, however, been systematically used.

4

Negotiating International Norms: The Inter-American Commission of Women and the Convention on Violence against Women

Mary K. Meyer

The Inter-American Convention on Violence against Women is the first of its kind and deserves attention by scholars, governments, and citizens. The convention breaks new ground by defining violence against women as a violation of women's human rights and by identifying the duties of states to address this endemic social problem. Moreover, the work of the Inter-American Commission of Women since 1988 in bringing this convention to life is an important contemporary example of how women in the Americas have been able to negotiate international norms aimed at defining and securing women's rights. Indeed, since the 1920s, the Inter-American Commission of Women has been working to shape international norms concerning women's rights in the Western Hemisphere and press the region's governments to bring their laws and policies into compliance with these new norms.

The work of the Inter-American Commission of Women—also known by its Spanish acronym, CIM (Comisión Interamericana de Mujeres)—over the past seven decades provides important if often invisible examples of gender politics in global governance. Here we have an autonomous commission of the Organization of American States (OAS), which is a regional intergovernmental organization made up of many states with long-standing authoritarian political traditions, of many societies with deeply embedded cultural values of machismo, and families where women's subordination to men is considered natural and right. Here within the structure of the OAS is a commission that gives diplomatic space and status to women and focuses on improving the status of women at the regional, national, and local levels. In its seventy-year history, the CIM has played an important role in pressing national governments from above—that is, from the international level—to extend suffrage to women in the 1930s, 1940s, and 1950s and in urging—from above—that women and gender issues be taken into account in regional, national, and local development strategies in the 1960s, 1970s, and 1980s.

Yet despite its work "from above," the CIM has also been connected to the national and local levels in a variety of ways. CIM's origins are rooted in suffragist organizations from the United States to the Southern Cone. Its founders were women activists from across the Americas who turned to the international level in the 1920s to pressure their governments for the vote and equal rights. After the CIM was created and institutionalized, it worked with women's groups and feminist organizations to implement its programs in promoting women's education, development, and political equality. While some diplomatic appointments to the CIM were merely a ceremonial distinction for a dictator's or president's wife, in most of its history, CIM's diplomatic members have been distinguished professional or political women playing leading political roles in their nations. Thus, the CIM has connected women at the local and national levels to the international level, where some diplomatic space was opened to address women's issues that were significant to the nations of the Americas.

Nevertheless, in the context of the recent expansion of the women's movement and the explosion of the number of women's organizations in the Americas, the CIM remains obscure, and one senses that the states of the hemisphere have only paid lip service to women's issues. Apparently they placated earlier women's organizations by creating the CIM and then largely ignored it. During the 1980s, the CIM was besieged by budget cuts, staff cutbacks, and even the loss of space for its library. Yet the CIM's dedicated secretariat and executive committee moved to reassert its relevance and mobilized hemispheric expertise in its most recent campaign to draft an Inter-American Convention on Violence against Women.

CIM's historic mission and its recent work on the Convention on Violence against Women present a number of insights into the role that women have played in addressing feminist issues within international organizations and influencing gender politics at the international and national levels, albeit in a regional context. In this chapter, I trace the historical and contemporary role of the CIM in defining new international norms aimed at securing women's rights in the Americas. I argue that, despite problems of public obscurity and state resistance to change, the CIM has been able to open an important international space for feminist politics in the Americas and to bring together a women's network aimed at pressing governments from above to improve women's rights and status. Moreover, in the 1980s and 1990s, the governments of the Americas have also been pressed by a growing number of women's organizations working from below—that is, at the grassroots and national levels—to address women's issues (Sternbach et al. 1992; Miller 1991). Thus, pressed from above and below, the states of the Americas are now being held accountable for taking steps to combat the widespread problem of violence against women.

International Norms and Violence against Women

Before examining the CIM and its recent work on the Inter-American Convention on Violence against Women, it is helpful to ask why such a convention would be necessary in the first place. Feminist legal scholars, theorists, and activists have questioned the marginalization of women-specific abuses from the international human rights regime. Issues such as domestic violence, rape, female feticide and infanticide, patterned malnutrition, female mutilation, bride burning, entrenched discrimination in education and health care, and demeaning images of women in the media have not been framed as human rights violations in the present international human rights regime. At best these manifestations of violence against women are considered unfortunate cultural practices outside of the state's or the international system's responsibilities.

Feminist legal scholars have begun to examine the deeply gendered nature of international law and have shown how both the organizational structures and the normative structures shaping the international human rights regime are biased against women (Charlesworth, Chinkin, and Wright 1996; see also Miller this volume). Organizationally, the absence of women in powerful or influential positions in international bodies specializing in the development of international law has been an important source of gender bias. There have never been any women members of the United Nations International Law Commission, and only one woman was ever appointed to the International Court of Justice. Women are still "vastly underrepresented" on UN human rights bodies (Charlesworth, Chinkin, and Wright 1996, 264; see also D'Amico this volume), although the appointment of former Irish President Mary Robinson as the UN commissioner for human rights in 1997 is a notable step forward.[1] The institutional lack of representation of women also exists in regional organizations like the OAS. This gender bias in the organizational structures of the UN and the OAS

> means that issues traditionally of concern to men become seen as general human concerns, while "women's concerns" are relegated to a special, limited category. Because men generally are not the victims of sex discrimination, domestic violence, and sexual degradation and violence, for example, these matters can be consigned to a separate sphere and tend to be ignored. (Charlesworth, Chinkin, and Wright 1996, 264)

The UN's Commission on the Status of Women and the OAS's Inter-American Commission of Women thus become the principal but marginalized sites for addressing "women's issues."

In addition, such issues lack political or legal salience because the normative structures of international law—the content of the rules and norms—marginalize or ignore altogether women's experiences, interests, and rights. Indeed, a number of conceptual or discursive practices in legal thinking have worked to define women out of international human rights norms altogether. The most obvious example is the universalizing language (e.g., "man," "mankind") of international human rights conventions that obscures or omits the specific experiences of women. More important, the distinction between "public" and "private" at the national level is reproduced and reinforced at the international level in a number of ways, with detrimental effects for women's human rights (Charlesworth, Chinkin, and Wright 1996).

First, the principle of state sovereignty distinguishes between "domestic" space (i.e., internal to the state) and "international" space (i.e., external to and between states). Sovereignty precludes intervention into another state's domestic affairs in most cases, thus creating a space of "privacy" in which the state is the preeminent authority and from which the international legal regime is usually excluded. Second, the present international human rights regime consists primarily of agreements between states (hence, it is public international law) that posit the state's responsibility to guarantee certain rights of people living within its borders and that hold the state accountable if it violates those rights. Legally, the state occupies a central—and problematic—role as both the chief protector and the principal (potential) violator of human rights within its borders.

Third, in the present international human rights regime, states have given greater importance to political and civil rights, which are associated with the public sphere, than to economic, social, and cultural rights, which are associated with the private sphere and are seen as lying beyond state responsibility (Rao 1996; Charlesworth, Chinkin, and Wright 1996). International human rights law, as well as mainstream human rights nongovernmental organizations (NGOs), focuses its attention on the state's protections/violations of political and civil rights in the domestic public sphere, largely ignoring violations taking place in the domestic private sphere of the family, the market, and culture. But in most parts of the world today, women continue to be excluded from, or marginal to, the former, while it is in relation to the latter that women's oppression is the greatest (Rao 1996, 243). The effect of this double privatization by states through international legal norms has been to ignore women's experiences of gender-specific violence, abuse, or discrimination and exclude such experiences from the very definition of "human" rights and state responsibility.

Feminist critics have called for the expansion of state responsibility and accountability to redress these gender biases in international human rights law. Slow and piecemeal steps have been taken at the international level through the 1979 Convention on the Elimination of All Forms of Discrimination against Women (CEDAW) and the 1993 United Nations Declaration on the Elimination of Violence against Women. While these create "soft law" by positing new principles, definitions, and norms regarding the rights of women, neither goes very far in creating "hard law" requiring immediate state action and establishing mechanisms to enforce compliance, particularly in the area of violence against women. In 1988, the Inter-American Commission of Women took up this task through its work on the Inter-American Treaty on Violence against Women. This was not the first time the CIM broke new ground in defining the rights of women.

CIM: Seven Decades of Work on Women's Rights as Human Rights

From its beginnings, the CIM has concerned itself with improving the legal and civil rights of women in this hemisphere. In the 1920s and 1930s, suffragists across the Americas organized to pressure governments to improve women's legal status by turning to the international level and asking diplomats assembling at inter-American conferences to define women's rights through legally binding conventions. As early as 1923, a number of women activists traveled to Santiago, Chile, to lobby the diplomats meeting at the Fifth International Conference of American States for attention to women's rights in the hemisphere. In response, a resolution was passed recommending the inclusion on the program of future conferences the study of the means to abolish the constitutional and legal incapacities of women in the hemisphere, the promotion of women's education, the study by each country of the status of its women, and the integration of women into each country's diplomatic delegations (Organization of American States 1992, 3; Miller 1991, 95).

While this resolution was subsequently ignored by governments, the next International Conference of American States in Havana (1928) attracted a similar gathering of women activists from Cuba and throughout the hemisphere to press the diplomats for attention to the rights of women and fulfillment of the 1923 resolution. Led by U.S. suffragists like Doris Stevens, who was invited to address the conference in a special extra-official plenary session, these women specifically sought an equal rights treaty (drafted by U.S. equal rights advocate Alice Paul) consisting of just one article: "The contracting parties agree that with the ratification of this Treaty men and women have equal rights in the territories subject to their respective jurisdictions" (Organization of American States 1992, 4; translation mine). While most of the diplomats were reluctant to approve such a bold treaty,[2] they responded to the women's lobbying effort by creating the Inter-American Commission of Women, or the CIM, which was charged with "preparing juridical and any other kind of information that can be considered useful" so that the next inter-American conference (in 1933) might draft a study on the civil and political equality of women on the continent (Organization of American States 1992, 4; translation mine).

The CIM soon set to work at its first formal conference in 1930 by calling on its fifteen delegates to compile a report on laws relating to women in their respective countries, creating a subcommittee to develop a plan of action for the commission and an executive committee to speak for the commission between formal meetings, and urging the cooperation of the women of the Americas and especially of organizations working for equal rights. The main focus of its first meeting, however, was the question of the nationality of women. Without clearly defined constitutional and legal rights, a married woman had difficulty securing her own passport. Like children, a wife was forced to travel on her husband's passport. A married woman's nationality was especially ambiguous if she and her husband were from different countries. Did she acquire her husband's nationality at marriage, or did she retain her own? What happens if she is then widowed or divorced?

These legal questions led the CIM to draft the Inter-American Convention on the Nationality of Women, which it presented to the Seventh International Conference of American States held in Montevideo, Uruguay, in December 1933, along with its report on the civil and political equality of women and a careful comparative study of the laws relating to women of each country (Organization of American States 1992, 6–9). The commission also recommended passage of the Equal Rights Treaty of 1928. The diplomats voiced their fears of threatening the sovereignty of member states by "legislating" such a treaty; however they found the Convention on the Nationality of Women a bit more palatable. The convention was signed by nineteen of the twenty countries represented at the conference, although a number of states attached reservations. However, few states bothered to ratify the convention until much later (Organization of American States 1992, 11–12).

Despite the ambiguous legal status of these treaties given their lacking, delayed, or reserved ratifications, the Equal Rights Treaty (1928) and especially the Convention on the Nationality of Women (1933) were pathbreaking international human rights documents written by women and aimed at taking women's rights to the international level through the intermediary of the CIM. They were also clever vehicles designed to force governments to bring national laws into compliance with what were intended to be new, progressive international commitments. Rather than placating women's demands, the CIM was focusing them through international legal documents, which seemed to catch statesmen off guard. A controversy soon developed about appointments to the

CIM and whether its members were private persons willing to look into questions of little interest to statesmen, functionaries of the Pan American Union, or official governmental representatives—hence diplomats. The issue was temporarily resolved by naming two classes of members to the CIM: seven appointed by the Pan American Union and seven appointed by the commission but named by their governments (Stevens n.d.).

The CIM was clearly a new kind of organization, and it soon gained the attention of the League of Nations as a pathbreaker for women's rights. As the CIM gained attention and diplomatic status, it also sought to replicate itself at a more global level. The CIM was the mother of the United Nations Commission on the Status of Women (CSW). Delegates to the UN from the CIM pressed for the CSW's creation in 1946, and many of the CSW's first members were the CIM's founding members as well. Opening spaces for women and women's rights in international organizations has been the historic mission of the CIM.

With the reconstitution of inter-American institutions through the Organization of American States in 1948, the CIM's organic structure was reformed and the CIM became an autonomous specialized commission of the OAS. As such, the CIM continued its work in the legal sphere with the drafting and signing of two more pathbreaking conventions in 1948. The Inter-American Convention on the Granting of Political Rights to Women and the Inter-American Convention on the Granting of Civil Rights to Women spelled out women's political and civil rights more precisely than the earlier Equal Rights Treaty and undoubtedly served as important catalysts to get many more governments to extend the vote to women. By 1948, fifteen countries in the hemisphere had recognized women's suffrage. In the ten years before that date, only eight countries had done so; in the ten years after 1948, seventeen countries recognized women's suffrage. The impact of the CIM and the two conventions on the political and civil rights of women was significant. Moreover, these conventions served as models for similar conventions at the UN years later. The CIM is clearly proud of its historic role "in pushing for the debate of the issue of female suffrage at the national and international levels" and the gradual winning of the rights to vote and stand for office throughout the Americas (Organization of American States 1995, 6–7).

In the 1950s and 1960s, CIM moved away from civil rights issues and into promoting women's education and women's roles in development. The CIM played an active role in the UN Decade of Women (1975–1985) and implemented the Regional Plan of Action for the Decade of Women in the Americas that focused on a wide variety of projects seeking to improve the economic and social life of women. Now in its seventh decade, the CIM has evolved to meet the demands of the day.

Since 1988, the CIM has reinvigorated its historical attention to pressing governments for progress on the rights of women through its (once again) pathbreaking work on a new convention, the Inter-American Convention on the Prevention, Punishment, and Eradication of Violence against Women (referred to hereinafter as the Convention on Violence against Women). The text of the convention was adopted by acclamation by the twenty-fourth regular session of the General Assembly of the Organization of American States on 9 June 1994 in Belem Do Para, Brazil. Defining violence against women and specifying states' responsibilities to end it, the treaty officially entered into force in March 1995 with two ratifications. As of March 1997, it has been signed and ratified by twenty-six of the OAS's thirty-two member states (Kremenetzky 1997). The process that brought the Convention on Violence against Women into being and the new norms it defines are important examples of gender politics in global governance.

The Convention on Violence against Women

International and Regional Context

The issue of violence against women has been gaining attention at the international level in recent years owing to the work of growing numbers of international women's and feminist organizations, human rights groups, and international conferences focusing on women. Media attention to atrocities in Bosnia, Rwanda, and other war-torn areas where rape was used as a strategy of warfare has also helped to raise the question of violence against women at the international level.

In Latin America, reports and denunciations of rape as a tool of war or torture by state officials in El Salvador, Peru, Haiti, and elsewhere during the 1980s gained public attention, and the once taboo subject of domestic violence also began to enter the public discourse. This new attention to public and private violence against women followed the development of a growing women's movement throughout the region rooted in a proliferation of local and national women's groups as well as regionwide meetings (*encuentros*) uniting such groups from across the Americas during the 1980s and 1990s (Sternbach et al. 1992; Miller 1991). Significantly, these groups have seized the democratic opening in many Latin American countries after years of military dictatorships to pressure civilian governments to respond to the issue of violence against women. For example, in Brazil, Chile, and Mexico the emergence of women's groups and the democratic openings have combined to create government agencies devoted to addressing domestic violence through specialized police forces (the Delegacias in Brazil), public information and education programs to prevent family violence (such as the programs sponsored by Chile's Servicio Nacional de la Mujer), and the compilation of some official statistics on the problem (e.g., Mexico's Center for Attention to Intra-Family Violence, an agency of the justice ministry) (Government of Chile 1992a; Torres Jimenez 1993, 10). Other countries have seen recent progress on modernizing family and divorce laws while also moving to address domestic violence through public information programs and the provision of legal services and psychological counseling in cooperation with local NGOs (e.g., Costa Rica).

While some governments have only begun to respond to the problem through legislation and appropriate services, and while social attitudes remain resistant to change, the demands of many new grassroots and regional women's organizations throughout Latin America during the 1980s clearly put the issue of violence against women on the regional political agenda. In fact, 379 separate women's organizations were working on gender violence issues alone in the region in 1990 (Heise 1994, 30). The election of more and more women to national parliaments also appeared to be related to the public discussion and slow but growing criminalization of violence against women. It is within this context that the CIM took up the question in 1988 and began to explore what its role might be in combating violence against women in the hemisphere. Following its traditional strategy of pressing governments to bring national laws into compliance with new international norms in the area of women's rights, the CIM decided to draft an inter-American convention focusing on violence against women that the governments of the Americas might accept, respect, and enforce.

Negotiating New International Norms

The process of drafting and ratifying the Convention on Violence against Women illustrates the CIM's careful and determined diplomatic work. The project for the convention progressed through four stages in a relatively short period of time. In the first stage, beginning in 1988, the CIM Executive Committee[3] identified domestic violence and the lack of adequate national laws about it as serious problems for women in the Americas. The executive committee called for action by placing the issue on the agenda of the CIM's Assembly of Delegates, which led to the second stage of the process. The CIM Assembly held a special Meeting of Consultation in 1990 to study the nature of the problem and to consider the need for an inter-American convention on violence against women.

The Inter-American Consultation on Women and Violence was the first of its kind and opened new diplomatic space to this closeted topic. To facilitate the Meeting of Consultation, the CIM Executive Committee called for national reports on existing and model legislation, national measures to eliminate violence against women or to support its victims, and statistical information on the incidence of such violence. The conclusions and recommendations of the Meeting of Consultation defined violence against women as going beyond domestic violence traditionally located in the private sphere. Significantly, it also included institutionalized violence perpetrated or tolerated by the state, such as the lack of adequate health services to women, political and occupational discrimination against women, and rape and sexual abuse as forms of repression or torture. Violence against women was also defined to include pornography and demeaning images of women in the media as well as forms of public sexual abuse like prostitution (Organization of American States 1990, 4–5).

The Meeting of Consultation recommended a number of actions in the fields of awareness and education, legislation and law enforcement, and support services for victims and perpetrators. The meeting concluded that there was a need to draft an international convention on violence against women. It reasoned that

> an international convention specifically devoted to the topic could establish violence as the most serious, severe and persistent form of discrimination against women which, due to its erroneous perception as a private problem, constitutes a violation of human rights with special characteristics. (Organization of American States 1990, 18)

Embracing CIM's traditional strategy, the Meeting of Consultation argued further that a convention was appropriate to set the stage for "States to take legislative, legal or administrative measures for the investigation, prevention, and punishment of violence against women," and *"to establish effective measures as a means of international denunciation of States for their shortcomings in this regard"* (Organization of American States 1990, 18, emphasis added).

In its response to these recommendations to create hard law in this area, the CIM gathered more information from member states on the topic and guided the process into its third stage. The CIM convoked two Meetings of Experts to make presentations, find common ground, and begin to draft the text for the convention. The Meetings of Experts included jurists, diplomats, lawmakers, educators, police officers, doctors, sociologists, and psychologists specializing in the relevant issues—thus drawing together a network of experts to draft the text of the convention. The government of Canada provided financial assistance for the first Meeting of Experts, which was held in August 1991 in Caracas, Venezuela. Ten legal experts from across the hemisphere participated.

They suggested a structure for the convention (six sections) and drafted a proposed text that was then sent by the CIM to member governments for consideration and comment (Organization of American States 1993, 1–3). The second Meeting of Experts was held in October 1993 at CIM headquarters in Washington, D.C., to refine the text (Organization of American States 1994, 1). A final draft was submitted to the OAS General Assembly meeting in Belem do Para. Its language was adopted by acclamation on 9 June 1994. The process then entered its fourth stage as the convention was open for signing and ratification by member governments (Murfitt-Eller 1995; Kremenetzky 1995).

The Terms of the Convention

The Inter-American Convention on Violence against Women has a preamble that situates the convention within the international and regional human rights regimes (Organization of American States 1994). Chapter I defines violence against women to include "any act or conduct, based on gender, which causes death or physical, sexual, or psychological harm or suffering to women, whether in the public or the private sphere" (Art. 1, emphasis added). The scope of violence defined in Chapter I reaches from the family or domestic level to the community level (e.g., the workplace, educational institutions, health facilities) and up to the state level insofar as such violence is "perpetuated or condoned by the state or its agents" (Art. 2). Chapter II specifies the rights protected, including the right of every woman "to be free from violence in both the public and private spheres" and the right of every woman to enjoy the exercise and protection of all internationally recognized human rights. "The States Parties recognize that violence against women prevents and nullifies the exercise of these rights" (Art. 5). Article 6 equates the right to be free of violence with the right to be free of all forms of discrimination as well as "stereotyped patterns of behavior and social and cultural practices based on concepts of inferiority or subordination." These articles thus present an important erosion of the public-private distinction that, both legally and culturally, has allowed states to tolerate violence against women.

Chapter III defines the duties of states both to condemn all forms of violence against women and "to pursue policies to prevent, punish, and eradicate such violence" (Art. 7). States must ensure that their authorities, officials, and agents act in conformity with the obligation to "refrain from engaging in any act or practice of violence against women." States must also undertake legislative and administrative measures to bring national laws and regulations into conformity with the convention and "establish fair and effective legal procedures for women" subjected to violence. The duties of states also include the development of a variety of social programs to help raise public awareness and prevent such violence. The specificity of the measures named in Article 8 is remarkable; the measures include such steps as supporting educational and training programs throughout society to change attitudes that contribute to violence against women; providing specialized services for women who are victims of violence; developing guidelines for the media to promote more positive images of women; gathering research on the causes, consequences, and frequency of violence against women; and fostering "international cooperation for the exchange of ideas and experiences and the execution of programs aimed at protecting women." The articles in Chapter III thus create the pathbreaking international human rights norm of state responsibility in the prevention, punishment, and elimination of violence against women. Chapter IV identifies the mechanisms available in the inter-American system to protect women from violence, thus broaching the question of enforcement. The convention specifies a self-reporting requirement for states on the measures they have adopted to address the phenomenon of violence against women and any problems they have had in applying those measures. States are to include such information in a new section of their regular national reports to the CIM (Art. 10).

Chapter IV also specifies distinct roles for the Inter-American Court of Human Rights and the Inter-American Commission on Human Rights. Article 11 enables the court to give advisory opinions on the *interpretation* of the convention at the request of state signatories and the CIM; however, it is not given any authority to hear cases concerning states' violation of, or noncompliance with, the convention. Article 12 permits any person, group of persons, or nongovernmental entity to lodge petitions with the Inter-American Commission on Human Rights denouncing or complaining of violations of Article 7 (which addresses the duties of states to take steps to prevent, punish, and eradicate violence against women) according to the established procedures of the commission.

Chapter IV of the convention thus illustrates the willingness of American states to begin to allow some international scrutiny of their steps toward addressing the problem of violence against women through the CIM reporting mechanism and through the petition procedures of the Inter-American Commission of Human Rights. Yet there is no role for the Inter-American Court of Human Rights beyond interpreting the convention. This contrasts with the human rights mechanisms in the European Union, where the European Court of Human Rights is empowered to hear cases lodged by individuals against governments. It remains to be seen whether in practice the inter-American mechanisms meet the original Meeting of Consultation's goal of establishing "effective measures as a means of international denunciation of States for their shortcomings in this regard" (Organization of American States 1990, 18).

This review of the Convention on Violence against Women suggests that its importance lies in its definition of the nature and scope of violence against women and its identification of the moral, legal, and political duties of states to combat the problem. The convention clarifies and situates the issue of violence against women as a human rights issue within the international and regional human rights regimes. It begins to erode the distinction between the public and private spheres that has located violence against women as beyond the concern of the state. It creates important new norms in this area, most notably the norm of state responsibility to prevent and punish violence against women in both the public and private spheres, and identifies specific policy measures to be pursued. Moreover, its mechanisms to ensure compliance, while weaker than originally envisioned by the CIM, have nevertheless softened the boundaries between the local, national, and international. The convention opens new spaces within inter-American institutions for both the CIM and private individuals and NGOs to work towards holding states accountable for eradicating violence against women.

Conclusion

It is not yet clear exactly how the CIM can mobilize women's organizations at the national and grassroots levels to force states to comply with the terms of the Convention on Violence against Women. Because the CIM is a diplomatic organization and technically "above the fray," it must eschew political work of this sort. Moreover, its severely limited resources preclude its launching a massive public education effort or organizing an international issue network to mobilize political pressure on governments. Yet the CIM's work is acutely political, and its ability to bring together experts in this area from across the Americas in an organized and focused effort to develop an innovative convention shows that it is an important political force for women at the international level. The CIM is clearly concerned about, and interested in, connecting with women's groups at the national and grassroots levels, even if its ability to do so is limited.

Nevertheless, the CIM and its work remain obscure to most citizens and groups in the Americas. This is reflected in the research and press articles on violence against women consulted for this chapter. Among the scholarly articles focusing on human rights issue networks in Latin America (Sikkink 1993), women's human rights (Rao 1996), and the revitalization of the OAS (with a long section on human rights and democracy in the inter-American system) (Therien, Fortmann, and Gosselin 1996), the existence of the CIM and its work on the convention are totally ignored. Heise (1994, 3) only briefly mentions the convention's title in her otherwise authoritative World Bank study on violence against women, although even here the problem is cast as a health issue rather than a human rights or security issue. The convention does not fare much better in the popular press. Only a small notice in *Ms. Magazine* in January/February 1995 mentions the convention, with no analysis of its terms nor any discussion of the work of the CIM. Unless greater public awareness can be brought to the convention, the male-dominated states of the Americas will be free to continue to pay lip service to the problem of violence against women without being held fully accountable for its elimination. And unless women's groups and human rights NGOs across the Americas can form a coherent international issue network to complement the network of experts that negotiated the convention, the problem of violence against women will continue. This is not to ignore or underestimate the important work such national and grassroots groups are carrying out from below to press their governments for progress in this area. But the states of the Americas are now being pressured from both below and above to guarantee a woman's basic human right to live free from violence in all its manifestations.

Notes

An earlier version of this chapter was first published in *Aggressive Behavior* 24, no. 2, (1998): 135–46, copyright John Wiley & Sons, Inc. I wish to thank Caroline Murfitt-Eller, Mercedes Kremenetsky, and the rest of the staff at the CIM Secretariat for their hospitality and generous help in this research project.

1. The 1995 Human Development Report found that women held 30 percent of the professional positions in the United Nations, but they occupied only 11.3 percent of the senior management positions there. At the end of 1994, only four of twenty-seven executive heads of UN agencies were women.

2. In 1928, delegates from Uruguay, Paraguay, Ecuador, and Cuba signed the treaty. The Uruguayan delegate, Sofia Alvarez Vignoli de Demicheli, was the first woman ever to sign an inter-American treaty (Organization of American States 1992, 11–12).

3. The CIM is made up of three central organs: the Assembly of Delegates, the Executive Committee of the Assembly of Delegates, and a Permanent Secretariat headed by an Executive Secretary. The Executive Committee (ExCom) is elected by the assembly for two years and is composed of a president, vice president, and five member states' delegates. The ExCom meets every three months and carries out the formulation and implementation of the CIM's work.

5

Gender and Transnational Democracy: The Case of the European Union

Catherine Hoskyns

Regardless of whether they support aspects of its operations or oppose them, Europeans generally lack affective interest in the European Union (EU).[1] This was the somewhat surprising finding of Ulf Hedetoft, a Danish political scientist who between 1991 and 1993 conducted a series of in-depth interviews on cultural and political identity with a random selection of respondents in Denmark, Germany, and the United Kingdom. Respondents also lacked any feeling of participation in EU processes and politics. This was the case irrespective of which country they came from (Hedetoft 1994).

Hedetoft's findings demonstrate starkly the problem with democracy in the European Union. Early moves towards European integration were intended to bypass the national politics of the member states and engage with a technical elite capable of implementing a common market and creating a framework within which previously warring states could compete and cooperate (Featherstone 1994; Wallace and Smith 1995). A certain level of supranational structure was seen as necessary to deliver this. Popular participation and democratic institutions were not a priority, and the whole enterprise rested on what was termed "a vague but permissive public opinion" (Haas 1968, xii).

But by the 1990s, when EU governments decided to adopt a single currency and move towards economic and monetary union (EMU), people had become wary. The ratification of the Treaty on European Union (TEU, also called the Maastricht Treaty) proved difficult, with the Danes initially voting no, and the French voting a *"petit oui."* Policymakers as a result became concerned to reestablish the "permissive public opinion" of early years. But the resistance to the Maastricht Treaty had raised fundamental questions about the legitimacy of the EU and its policy process, and the debate about democracy took a sharper tone.

Symptomatic of the EU's "democratic deficit" is the difficulty experienced in developing a social policy. Attempts to "balance" economic integration with a stronger social dimension have either failed or produced ambiguous out-comes.[2] However, policies towards women constitute a notable exception. The women's policy of the European Union, starting with equal pay and then spreading out more broadly, has been one of the few well-developed areas of EU social policy. This development has taken place over thirty years and now includes Article 119 of the Treaty of Rome on equal pay, seven equality directives, at least twelve pieces of EU "soft" law (recommendations and resolutions), four action programs on equal opportunities, and over eighty equal treatment cases in the European Court of Justice (ECJ).

The aim of this chapter is to relate women's politics and the democracy debate in the EU and to suggest ways in which women's experiences of the EU and situations within it throw a different light on the points at issue. Such connections are not normally made. Although the European Commission from time to time presents the women's policy as one of its achievements, it does not in general make use of this experience in its proposals for the future. Yet the policy is instructive for efforts to democratize the EU because it evolved in a space where participation in EU policy processes was at least a possibility.

The chapter begins by looking at some of the issues in the EU democracy debate and goes on to examine what light women's experiences over more than thirty years of EU politics and policy can shed on these. Finally, I attempt a synthesis by looking in more detail, and in the context of these accounts, at the debates that took place within the Intergovernmental Conference (IGC), which reviewed EU procedures and practice and led up to the Amsterdam Treaty adopted in June 1997.

The Democracy Debate

The treaties that established the European Communities (EC) in the 1950s set up an advisory assembly of parliamentarians, and the intention may have been to develop more democratic structures at a later stage. However, EC institutions were molded in a tradition that favored "elite capture" over popular engagement. European planners effectively followed the constructs of dominant International Relations discourse: namely, that the international sphere is made up of states in interaction and that democracy is not an appropriate concept beyond the nation-state because ordinary people are not actors in that space and no "demos" exists. The logical consequence of such arguments was that this situation could alter only if Europe itself became a nation-state. The type of transnational politics that was facilitated as a result involved the creation of a dense array of technical and expert networks performing a variety of tasks and lobbying roles in and around the European Commission and other

EC institutions (Greenwood, Grote and Ronit 1993). These continued the priority given to elite contact and fell far short of creating "the substance of politics" at the European level.

The stagnation of economic integration in the seventies, following on the political unrest of 1968 and the 1973 oil crisis, raised concerns about the political base for the whole EC enterprise. In these circumstances, moves were made to initiate elections by direct suffrage to the European Parliament (finally held in 1979) in the hope that these might encourage more popular involvement (Wallace and Smith 1995). In the event, they did not: As turnout figures showed, people remained substantially uninterested. But this initiative started the trend, which has been followed ever since, of responding to arguments about lack of democracy by gradually increasing the powers of the European Parliament. Whereas the Council of Ministers long had primary power to decide on all EU policies, most are now adopted jointly by the Council and the Parliament through a process known as "co-decision."[3] This has had the effect of complicating the decision-making process while begging the question of whether an increase in the powers of the Parliament does in fact contribute to legitimacy and/or democracy.

The eighties intensified the contradictions. The move to increase economic integration still further by the adoption of the single-market program; the effectiveness and vision of the new European Commission president, Jacques Delors; and the "opening to the East" resulting from the collapse of communism all created unprecedented opportunities and risks for the European Community. These contradictory pressures culminated in the Maastricht Treaty on European Union which was signed in February 1992. This treaty embodied further changes to the status of the Parliament and in a symbolic gesture also created the category of "European citizen," though with little indication of what this might mean in practice.

At the same time, Delors, in an attempt to balance the economic moves, pushed to develop a stronger social dimension for the Union. But the 1989 Social Charter and the Social Chapter of the TEU, which were intended to develop the idea of "social solidarity," encountered difficulty due to increased financial restraints, the outright opposition of the British government, and, most important, the fact that trade unions and social movements were in no position to play a dynamic role at the European level. Partly to remedy this situation and to bring new constituencies into play, the Commission funded the establishment of a number of large umbrella organizations. The most important of these, from the point of view of democratic representation, were the European Anti-Poverty Network, the European Women's Lobby, and the Migrants Forum.

With the unprecedented publicity surrounding the date of 1992 for completing the single market, the consequences of removing internal immigration controls, and the decision (with virtually no consultation) to set a timetable for the merging of national currencies, the real shape and nature of the EU became suddenly more visible. Indeed, it became "visibly intrusive" and the gap between people being affected by something and their being able to participate to change it seemed huge (Hopkinson 1995). The result was to raise in a much more serious way the issue of democracy and its relevance to EU structures.

Up to this point, both practitioners and analysts had seen the EU as a voluntary association of already democratic states. Admission entailed a searching review of the practices of applicant states: the applications of Greece, Spain, and Portugal, for example, were frozen until authoritarian regimes had been overthrown. Once a state was admitted, however, it was considered inappropriate to query its democratic procedures using EU institutions, and internal conflicts—for example, the situation in Northern Ireland—were and are handled, if at all, with kid gloves. The European political system thus rested centrally on the belief that democracy functioned effectively (even if in different ways) at the nation-state level and that this ultimately provided legitimacy for the process. The need to make some concessions to the European Parliament, as already discussed, did not substantially alter this, although it did begin to establish an alternative center of power.

Post-Maastricht, the democracy debate has taken a new turn with a fresh awareness of the need to involve people more closely. In scholarship on the EU this has involved a move away from the state-centric discourse of International Relations. Thus, Joseph Weiler has pointed out that the EU system undoubtedly has "formal" legitimacy, since every stage of its construction was approved by member-state parliaments; however, "social" legitimacy would involve more trans-Europe community understandings and popular engagement in, and approval of, European processes (Weiler 1992). Jürgen Habermas questioned whether the democratic disparity in EU processes was "a passing imbalance that can be set right" or was in fact "highlighting a general trend that has for a long time also been gaining momentum within nation states" (Habermas 1992, 9). Also interesting has been the application of Arend Lijphart's ideas of "consociational democracy" to the EU. He developed his arguments in the sixties to explain how democratic systems worked in multicultural societies, such as Switzerland. In such systems, he suggested, consensus at the top among elites went along with the maintenance of considerable sectoral separation between communities. Applied to the EU, this paradigm helps to explain the nature of bargaining in the EU Council of Ministers and the reluctance to upset what has been called "a management coalition of nation states" with a track record of "decisional efficiency" (Chryssochou 1994).

What most of these attempts to reexamine the EU's political processes have in common is a perception that previous analyses of either the international system or the nation-states within it are unlikely to provide solutions to current dilemmas. Something new is needed that accommodates and seeks to relate both interdependence and the increasing fragmentation of social and political life.

The history of the EU women's policy and the engagement of the women's movement with EU processes provide materials for new conceptual under-standings of the EU and throw light on the possibilities for transnational democracy. I have discussed in detail the development of the women's policy elsewhere (Hoskyns 1996). Here I want to examine three other aspects: the combination of factors that caused this policy to develop, the scope of the pol-icy and how it has changed, and the kinds of politics, transnational and other-wise, that have emerged from it. All of these have a bearing on the democracy debate.

Women's Politics

Social policy continues to return as a European issue, particularly now that the operation of the single market and economic and monetary union are begin-ning to undermine the capacity of the individual states to deliver on key social issues. But the EU has so far avoided being a prime site for struggles over social policy and redistribution more generally, and nation-state governments have sought to retain primary control in this area. This can be explained on the one hand by the failure of social and political movements to organize effec-tively at the European level and on the other by the resistance of the EU polit-ical system to such involvements. However, to some extent at least, the EU women's policy has managed to buck this trend. How has this been possible?

Explanatory Factors

The development of the women's policy rested, I would argue, on a number of interlinked factors, which came together in the seventies. The first of these was the material need for women's labor, identified in the fifties and sixties as the best untapped pool to meet new demands (OECD 1975; 1979). Since the labor market was becoming European, there was at least a market rationale for facilitating this process at the European level and a need (perhaps) to transcend particularist national restraints.

This factor alone would not have been sufficient for the development of a women's policy without the parallel and unprecedented level of women's political activism across Europe in the seventies. Second-wave feminism was a phenomenon in almost all European countries and developed strategies that drew on women's alternative experiences and created public shock (Lovenduski 1986; Kaplan 1992). Although not primarily directed at institutional politics, certainly not at the European level, movement activities put the situation of women onto national agendas, and politicians carried at least an awareness of women's concerns into European negotiations. This enabled women within formal politics to be bolder and drew other women into a range of surrounding activities.

Importantly, campaigning for women's rights and feminist politics more generally, at both national and European levels, took place almost entirely outside the formal institutions of the labor movement, and labor leaders at times publicly opposed feminist politics. In the European process, this had the advantage, on the one hand, that it enabled policymakers to go ahead with measures for women without feeling that these were likely to disturb the "core balance" in industrial relations. On the other hand, it set women off on a separate track from labor movement policy more generally and has created long-lasting divisions that are now proving hard to mend.

The third factor in the creation of an EU women's policy was the presence of Article 119 on equal pay in the Treaty of Rome.[4] It put the issue of discrimination against women firmly within EC competence and made possible a structure of legal enforcement that grew stronger as the force of European law expanded. The importance of Article 119 in the development of the women's policy becomes clear when that development is compared to attempts to establish a similar policy on race discrimination, in the absence of such a legal handle.

These, then, were the main factors that caused the policy to develop in the seventies. As a result, an institutional infrastructure was created around it (a budget line in the Commission, a committee in the Parliament, expert networks, and research groups) that made it hard to dismantle. To the extent that the policy resulted from popular influence and organization and established some direct links between European institutions and specific groups and individuals, it had democratic potential. The realization of this potential, however, depended crucially upon whether the scope of the policy could be expanded beyond market requirements to meet women's real needs and whether some more permanent channels for influence and political engagement could be established.

The Scope of the Policy

In its initial stages, the women's policy was based centrally on the issue of equality in employment. This reflected both the needs of the market and the main areas of EC competence. At the same time, in the 1970s, feminists were concerned to break down the distinction between women's public and private roles and to show how issues to do with sexual politics, caring, and dependency shaped women's disadvantage and inequality across the board, and thus their position in the labor market. The principle of equality was also viewed by some feminists with suspicion, as, without a recognition of women's differences and a strong emphasis on positive action, its main effect seemed to be to push women to adopt and accept male characteristics and roles (MacKinnon 1987).

As the policy developed, these kinds of points were made in different ways and from different quarters. The policy remained centered on employment, but its scope broadened considerably, and issues such as parental leave, child care, and maternity rights came gradually onto the agenda. At the same time, the European Court in the eighties made some bold judgments that appeared to be pushing the concept of equality towards a recognition of women's differences—particularly with respect to part-time and pregnant workers.[5] More recently a new emphasis has been placed on women in decision-making to highlight the absence of women in politics and in other top policymaking roles.

Despite these small successes, both the court and European policymakers more generally appeared reluctant to use the women's policy to expand EC competence into issues that fell outside the market and employment. In a much cited ruling in 1984, the ECJ held that the equal treatment directive was "not designed to settle questions concerning the organization of the family, or to alter the division of responsibility between parents."[6] The court has also adopted a generally restrictive view of the application of the measures on equal treatment in social security, attempting here again to draw firm lines and enforce boundaries rather than (as it might have) use the references from the national courts to begin to establish the economic value of unpaid work or caring as an insurable risk. The class aspect of this has been demonstrated by Mel Cousins, who, after examining the ECJ's rulings in social security equal treatment cases in 1992 and 1993, pointed out that "women with childcare or other family responsibilities, who are living in poverty, who one might think most in need of equality of treatment, are in fact least likely to receive it under the directive" (Cousins 1994, 143).

Issues involving sexual politics (for example, violence against women, rape, sexual orientation, and abortion) have also been largely excluded from the policy, although a recommendation on sexual harassment was adopted in 1991 and the court has cautiously facilitated the right to abortion by ruling that it is a service to which normal EU rules about access and rights of establishment apply (Spalin 1992). In general, however, policymakers and the court have been reluctant to cross this boundary or allow the policy to "drift" (as they might see it) into areas that too directly affect or question male behavior (Elman 1996).[7]

The policy has also been restricted by the fact that equality for women has been a somewhat lonely principle at EU level. It has not until very recently been buttressed by other basic human rights principles, for example, on race equality, disability, or freedom of speech. As the policy has developed, the limitations of this have become clear, since the sex-equality measures are not easily applied in contexts of greater complexity and diversity. So the European Commission has always had difficulty in developing a policy for black and migrant women or poor women, since these group identities and conditions are barely recognized as a concern of the EU. This in turn reflects and reinforces the elite orientation of EU politics.

The EU women's policy has had great importance in establishing the principle of gender equality and in legitimizing gender politics at the EU level. However, as the above examples indicate, it is narrow in focus and only goes a small way to meeting the needs of the broad constituency of women. In particular, it has tended to maintain rather than break down the public-private divide that so disadvantages women, and it takes little account of the complex identities, reflecting class and race positions as well as gender, in which women now find themselves. The discourse used does not for the most part reflect feminist perspectives and analysis.

In these circumstances, it is not surprising that, despite the long history of the women's policy, many women still feel wary of the EU and unsure about what it stands for. However, policies of this kind are the result of debate and struggle. The level of engagement with the EU therefore depends not only on the issues but also on the interface between active groups and institutional politics, on the possibilities for transnational action and on the political opportunities available.

Networking and Transnational Politics

Transnational politics, to be effective or even exist, requires a focus and a material base. In respect of the EU's women's policy, these prerequisites were met through the framework of legislation and policy just discussed and the apparent need to address at the highest level the consequences of women's greater involvement in the labor market. In their pursuit of policies women have certain unique characteristics. While they are normally deeply rooted in local and national societies (though in a multitude of different ways), some at least are willing to look outside because, on the whole, existing national political systems have not met their needs. A potential has existed, therefore, for different kinds of women and women's organizations to bridge the gap between the national and EU levels of political activity.

Despite a lack of resources and structures, there has existed at the EU level what I have called elsewhere "a women's European policy network" (Hoskyns 1996, 17). This was at its strongest in the eighties and consisted of a number of different strands ranging from the executive level to the grass roots. It included the Advisory Committee on Equal Opportunities (consisting of representatives of the equality agencies in the different member states); the expert committees and study groups set up by the Equal Opportunities Unit in the European Commission to do research and generate policy proposals; the European Parliament's Committee on Women's Rights; the traditional women's organizations; and a variety of feminist groupings, for part of the time coordinated in a loose way through the European Network of Women.

The general network was informal rather than formal, and the different strands worked together only in an ad hoc manner and on particular issues. However, it had the capacity, rare in the context of the EU, to stretch down to the grass roots and up to the decision makers. During the eighties no formal coordination existed between traditional women's organizations and feminist groups, leaving them free to make contacts and take action. This showed that grassroots women were perfectly able to operate at the European level if given some resources and a friendly environment. Good use was made of the funding programs, and some imaginative projects were supported.

Gradually, however, a feeling arose that not enough was being done to aggregate the strength of women's voluntary organizations, and pressure grew also from the European Commission to create some composite body that it could consult on issues to do with women. As a result, in September 1990, after much anguished negotiation, the European Women's Lobby was formed. This was in theory an independent body, but it was funded for the most part through the Commission, from the EU budget.

The development of the lobby demonstrates the advantages and disadvantages of "peak organizations" of this kind (Hoskyns 1991). On the one hand, it has provided a focus, (usually) articulate spokeswomen, and good sources of information; on the other, it has experienced difficult problems with internal democracy, representation, and efficiency. The danger is that fluidity and diversity are traded for structure and coherence, with the result that some interests (and types of women) are prioritized and others marginalized. In effect, such organizations are being asked to do too much—before the necessary connections to the local, regional, and national have been constructed. The European Anti-Poverty Network and the Migrants Forum (also with many women involved) have faced similar problems. The danger here is that women may be co-opted into the existing forms of EU consociationalism, with a consequent reduction of their power to trigger more genuine forms of participatory democracy.

The "Return to the National"

Networking is all very well, but at what point does it turn into transnational politics, that is, politics that involves either sustained input into the political process by cross-national interests or a strong political system in which a variety of national interests bargain? One of the problems for social movements with the EU system is that it is by no means clear whom to lobby and where the focus for politics actually is. The Commission requires experts, sometimes gives out money and transmits and receives information; the Parliament appears to be acting politically but often is not; the Council of Ministers remains impenetrable, normally accessible only through national channels. There are many institutions without power, and meetings and projects that go nowhere. Such a system may be functional for those who know how to manage it, but it is dysfunctional for those with few resources and limited know-how.

As far as the women's policy is concerned, the opportunities for real transnational politics have proved to be very few. This is partly because it is often difficult to identify exactly what those processes are and gain access to them, and partly because it has proved hard to sustain a sufficient level of coordination and mobilization across the EU. What has worked much better for women has been either patient work inside the institutions or ad hoc spontaneous actions that demonstrate depth of feeling.[8]

It has also frequently been made clear, in the social field at least, that the European Commission itself is not anxious to encourage transnational politics of this kind. So the norm is for the Commission to supply materials, organize studies and workshops, and then when people become enthusiastic, to direct them back to the national level to lobby and bring pressure. This may be realistic in tactical terms, but it is an admission that there is no open political system that can accept a popular transnational input. Inevitably, this inhibits popular engagement at the European level and encourages "a return to the national."[9]

John Lambert's work would suggest that this is not the case with certain business and technical interests in the economic sphere, where transnational groups are normally built into the policy process and in some cases exert a stranglehold on what is decided (Lambert 1994). It may also be that environmental politics at the EU level is developing a different trajectory, given the more obviously international character of the issues and the groups involved. But Sidney Tarrow's detailed account of the 1994 "tuna war" illustrates the same phenomenon described for women's politics. In the course of the war, he writes, the lack of "political opportunities" in the EU system continually pushed activists back to nation-state mechanisms to pursue their claims. The result was to enhance and strengthen national confrontation rather than begin the construction of a transnational dialogue. He concludes that while organized business operates effectively in Brussels, other interests for the most part have their demands "heavily mediated" through the national route (Tarrow 1995).

It would seem, therefore, that the exclusion from transnational politics applies particularly to social, popular, and activist groups. And it is interesting that transnational political parties (which might be expected to give some voice to these kinds of interests) have not yet taken root within the framework of the European Parliament. This is presumably because party organizers do not as yet perceive sufficient openings and prospects of gain to make such a level of operation functional.[10] The Commission's favored structure for creating a European level of social policy is the "social dialogue" between employers and trade unions. For the first time, post-Maastricht, this dialogue is beginning to develop some energy. It may well be, however, that to create anything like a workable balance, social movements need to be built into the process as the "third partner."

To summarize so far: The EU was conceived by, and built for, elites, and this ethos still dominates. As far as women are concerned, the policies and procedures of the EU have brought some advantages in formulating rights in the area of employment and in creating a "gender framework" that facilitates links and contacts across the member states. The effects of these have, however, been limited by narrow interpretations of the EU scope. The strength of the women's network has enabled progress in the area of women's policy, but this network has also faced challenges with the formation of mainstream peak organizations. Furthermore, the EU's style of operations has proved difficult to deal with, as European institutions refer political and social demands back to the national level. And the EU's priorities, with their general disregard for class, race, or ethnic positions, exacerbate differences among women and make solidarity hard to maintain or create. These characteristics go a long way to explain Hedetoft's account of the "non-engagement" of EU citizens with EU processes, with which this chapter opened. The procedures of the EU thus present women with a double challenge: to protect themselves against the divisions and exclusions that EU politics can impose, and at the same time to inject some better practices into emerging EU governance.

The Intergovernmental Conference
from a Women-Centered Perspective

By way of expanding this last point, I want in the final section to take some of the issues discussed in the recent EU Intergovernmental Conference and see what a woman-centered perspective might suggest about them. This involves juxtaposing some very different assumptions, modes of presentation, and discourse. It encounters some of the difficulties Tickner identified in her comparison of feminist critiques of International Relations with more mainstream approaches (Tickner 1997).

The IGC, as its name suggests, was a process of negotiations among governments, very much on the consociational model. The purpose of the IGC was to review the procedures and practices of the EU, including the issue of legitimacy. The Parliament was given little access and the proceedings of the Conference itself were neither democratic nor transparent. The most "open" aspect of the IGC was the Reflection Group (RG), which was set up to draft a preliminary report. The RG conducted its own hearings, and all institutions of the EU submitted papers. These were then issued as public documents. All the members of the RG were men. One of the two "observers" from the European Parliament was a woman, Elisabeth Guigou from France.

I am taking the institutional (EU) points in this section largely from a schema developed by Grainne de Burca, which identifies three issues as being central to the legitimacy debate: citizenship, democracy, and transparency (de Burca 1996). My "women-centered perspectives" are taken from a disparate set of sources (by no means complete) that have the common characteristic that they seek to identify what may be special or different about how women perceive political issues or are involved in them. The fact that such texts are available, some of them relating directly to the EU, is a sign of the increasing involvement of women with international relations both as a discipline and as a practice.

Citizenship

The concept of European citizenship was introduced for the first time into the TEU in an attempt to build a popular identity for the Union. The formulation was extremely cautious, since the sole criterion was possessing citizenship of a member state (Article 8). The only substantial entitlements were the right to vote in local and European (but not national) elections, anywhere in the union. However, introducing the concept has been important since it dents the EU's preoccupation with people as paid workers and has opened up debate about what such a concept means and how it might be expanded.

The RG paid considerable attention to the idea of citizenship but came up with few concrete proposals. Clearly, there were fears among some members that developing European citizenship too far might pose a threat to national identity. The comments from the European Court of Justice put the emphasis on citizenship as status, in the sense that it entails formal legal rights given on a universal basis (i.e., to all of those who acquire citizenship).

Work by feminists produces some very different emphases. It sees citizenship as involving participation as much as status and takes into account needs as well as rights. Feminists are also far more conscious of the exclusions involved in citizenship: exclusions within, in the sense that some may be better able to enjoy rights and participate than others; and exclusions without, in the sense that citizenship is normally determined in the face of "others" who are noncitizens. There has been much debate also about whether citizenship as a concept should apply primarily in a political sense and to political communities, as well as over what its links are, or should be, to ethnicity and nation (Meehan 1993; Walby 1994; Lister 1997).

Democracy

The RG paid considerable attention to the issue of democracy, but again no clear definition emerged. The main debate continues to be that between the Parliament and the Council, well illustrated in the papers presented by the institutions to the RG. The Parliament argues essentially for an extension of the co-decision procedure and a simplification of the decision-making process overall; the Council, by contrast, continues to defend the existing arrangements and argues that the best guarantees of democracy are still the institutions and political ethos of the member states. The debate appears to be primarily about institutional relationships and processes, with little consideration of wider issues.

Looking at more women-centered material that deals with democracy, the focus once again is on participation, democracy being seen as the right to be heard and the right not to be excluded. Work by Cynthia Cockburn and Sue Cohen, which deals directly with experiences of EU politics, emphasizes these points. Cockburn, examining the workings of the EU social dialogue and the reasons for the general absence of women, develops the idea of "gender democracy" at the EU level. This combines an emphasis on participation and accountability with the notion of "fair representation" (Cockburn 1995). Cohen, discussing the operations of the European Anti-Poverty Network and EU action around poverty more generally, demonstrates through some very telling interviews how exclusions work even at this level and on this issue (Cohen 1995).

These accounts and others like them refute the "institutions only" approach to democracy. On this reading, extending the powers of the Parliament without any other changes might well exacerbate rather than heal the "distance" problem in European politics (Wallace and Smith 1995). What is needed is more attention to participation and political process and the creation of a genuinely public political space at the level of the EU.

Transparency

The need for greater transparency and openness in the EU's procedures is the area where there is probably most agreement that something needs to be done. The issue is contentious, with the new Scandinavian member states pressing for quite radical changes and two cases concerning disclosure of documents having been recently heard in the European Court.[11] However, the submissions from the institutions to the RG were quite bland, with the Council still emphasizing the need for confidentiality so that consociational bargains could continue to be made between member state governments.

Transparency and the supply of information can be said to be at the heart of democracy, and thus any pressure for increased participation is likely to go along this track also. This was the opinion of the Center for Research on European Women (CREW), a feminist organization that was set up in Brussels in the early eighties. CREW started a bulletin, *CREW Reports,* that reported regularly on events in Brussels from the point of view of women. The bulletin was extremely well informed, and its great achievement was to represent the EC as an exciting political arena. The element of gossip it contained did much to narrow the gap between the EC and its (female) public.

It may have been this effect that Danish Commissioner Ritt Bjerregaard was after when, in October 1995, she planned to publish *Kommissaerens Dagbog* (The commissioner's diary). After Commission President Jacques Santer rapped her over the knuckles for indiscretion, she agreed to withdraw the book. In a little-noticed comment, she explained that she felt the Commission needed a dialogue with the public and that she intended in her diary to demystify what goes on in Brussels "to get ordinary people to take an interest." In saying this, she seems to have had a better idea of what it would actually need "to get the public more involved with Brussels" than did her more conventional colleagues, mainly men (*Financial Times,* 25 October 1995).

These, then, are some examples of what it might mean to integrate perspectives drawn from women's writing and experiences more closely into the EU democracy debate. As can be seen, these perspectives put the emphasis far more strongly on participation and transparency than was the case in the closed, cautious, and institution-based deliberations of the IGC. However, it is interesting that the Amsterdam Treaty, finally adopted in June 1997 as a result of these deliberations, pays more attention than previous texts to human rights. For the first time, it includes a general antidiscrimination clause (Article 6a) that covers discrimination on grounds of "sex, racial or ethnic origin, religion or belief, disability, age or sexual orientation." The European Commission is currently using this article to propose EU-level legislation on race relations. The Amsterdam Treaty also enlarges the scope of the co-decision procedure and as a result once again extends the role of the European Parliament.

Missing from the text, however, is any real attempt to address the participation issue or the imbalance that exists between those who have access and influence within the EU and those who do not. In continuing to raise such issues, and in making clear that they have as much relevance at the international level as they do at the national, feminist theorists and activists make an effective critique both of International Relations as a discipline and of the practices of global governance. The EU, with its highly developed political framework and history of gender struggle, provides an instructive test bed for such interventions.

Notes

An early version of this chapter was given as a paper at the American Political Science Association Conference in San Francisco in September 1996.

1. In this chapter, I am using the term *European Union (EU)* in any context that involves either the present day or the whole span of EU development up to and including the present day. I have retained the term *European Community (EC)* for accounts of events that clearly took place before November 1993, when the name change came into effect.

2. These were the attempt to include a stronger social-policy element in the Treaty of Rome, the adoption of the ambitious Social Action Programme in the early seventies, and the Delors "social dimension" initiative of the mid-eighties.

3. The co-decision procedure, introduced in the Maastricht Treaty, divides the decision-making process more equally between the EU Council of Ministers and the European Parliament. In the event of disagreement, a complex conciliation procedure is initiated; if this fails, the measure falls. The Amsterdam Treaty expanded the scope of co-decision.

4. It is usually stated that Article 119 was included in the treaty for economic reasons and at the insistence of France. This is substantially true, but one needs to ask why did France insist and why did the other governments agree? The answers to these questions would seem to lie in the activism of women workers in France in the thirties, France's particular political situation after the war, and the extensive attention paid to equal pay by the International Labor Organization in the early fifties (for a fuller discussion, see Hoskyns 1996, chapter 3).

5. See esp. *Bilka,* ECJ Case 170/84, 1986 (part-time workers) and *Dekker*, ECJ Case C-177/88, 1990 (pregnant workers).

6. *Hofmann*, ECJ Case 79/83, 1984, para. 24.

7. There has recently been more concern at EU level with the issue of trafficking and violence against women and girls. Interestingly, this has been triggered not so much by pressures outwards from the women's policy but by panic in Belgium (where

the main EU institutions have their headquarters) over the uncovering of an international pedophile ring that was responsible for the killing and sexual slavery of young girls *(l'affaire Dutroux)*.

8. One such was the widespread pressure exerted to increase the number of women commissioners in the 1995 appointments to the European Commission. This was at least partially successful in that an unprecedented number, five out of twenty, were appointed.

9. The European Social Policy Forum held in March 1996 is a good example of this phenomenon. Sponsored by the Commission, it gathered together a large and representative collection of NGOs working across Europe in the social field. An excellent report by a prestigious committee of experts was presented to the forum, and debate was lively. However, there has been little coverage of this event, and there is no clear channel at European level through which its recommendations can progress. Organizations are left to continue campaigning, primarily at the national level.

10. The TEU, however, does specifically recommend the encouragement of transnational political parties, and this may give a new impetus (Article 138).

11. *Carvel,* ECJ Case T-194/94, 1995; *Dutch Government,* ECJ Case C-58/94, 1996.

6

Nongovernmental Organizations:
An Alternative Power Base for Women?

Irene Tinker

Women since time immemorial have organized themselves into groups to support their own activities and to assist others. In modern states, women's formal or informal organizations at national and local levels have offered charity, raised societal issues, engaged in networking, and generally provided the glue that holds society together; men have occupied most positions of power in state institutions. Today, women have expanded their organizing to the global stage and broadened the scope of their concerns to include population, environment, technology, energy, and human rights, to name a few. This process was encouraged and enhanced not only by the four United Nations World Conferences for Women (Mexico City 1975; Copenhagen 1980; Nairobi 1985; Beijing 1995) but also by other UN world conferences since the early 1970s.

The impact of embracing this global agenda has been two-fold. First, the agenda of women's organizations now not only includes "soft" issues of family and charity widely regarded as appropriate for women's concern, but it also encompasses advocacy positions that confront what has been a predominantly male discourse on each of these topics. Second, women have joined the myriad single-issue nongovernmental organizations (NGOs) and have taken with them their conviction that these issues are also women's issues. Today NGOs and women's organizations increasingly challenge the power and scope of traditional political institutions within the state and lobby international agencies to reinterpret development policies. As the civil society expands in most countries in response to this era of limited government, these new organizations are touted as the real arena for citizen participation and the foundation of present or future democracy. Are NGOs really the new panacea for contemporary government? Should women's organizations be considered NGOs, or do they form a distinct type of organization? Does women's involvement translate into greater political power, or does participation in NGOs once again marginalize women? Are women more likely to influence major decisions facing society through separate or integrated organizations?

What Is an NGO Anyhow?

The use of the term "nongovernmental organization" was adopted by the United Nations when it agreed to provide a mechanism for citizen-based organizations to participate in the Economic and Social Council (ECOSOC). Such organizations are private and nonprofit; they represent people acting of their own volition and describe themselves in their formal documents as self-governing (Weiss and Gordenker 1996a). As a residual category, the term covers a wide range of groups that are not commonly thought of today as nongovernmental organizations: trade union federations, business councils, international unions of scholars, lay religious councils, and professional associations. Women's organizations are also often distinguished from NGOs as the term is now used; this point will be further explored later in the chapter.

NGOs and the United Nations System

Nongovernmental organizations may file for consultative status with the UN, a designation that allows them access to meetings of the committees and commissions of ECOSOC. Members of NGOs may participate informally in these groups, roaming the chambers and halls to talk to delegates; they may also, by request, be given the floor in formal debate. Further, NGOs automatically receive all documents from these discussions and may request that their own documents be distributed. This interaction between UN staff and governmental delegates on the one hand and the NGOs on the other was so valuable that other agencies in the UN system identified their own lists of NGOs and granted them similar privileges.

As development issues began to dominate the UN agenda, new types of NGOs, concerned with issues such as agriculture, community development, population, environment, energy, technological transfer, and housing, sought consultative status.[1] Most international NGOs (INGOs) have affiliates or chapters at the national level in several countries. The objective of the INGOs is to monitor activities within the United Nations system of concern to their membership and to persuade the General Assembly to pass resolutions stating goals for national as well as international action. While such resolutions lack the force of law, they provide the national NGOs with a powerful tool that can be used to alter policies in their respective countries.

This policy role of INGOs was greatly enhanced as a result of the series of consciousness-raising world conferences that the UN convened, starting in 1972, on major development issues that had not been sufficiently addressed in the original UN Charter.[2] These world conferences are official meetings of the UN system; the delegates from governments, UN agencies, and official NGOs are charged with approving an official action document that has been discussed and debated in preparatory meetings in the preceding years.

Parallel to these official formal conferences, there have been open, unrestricted, often chaotic and contentious, NGO gatherings, called NGO forums. Loosely organized by the CONGO (Council of NGOs), these meetings typically feature seminars, panels, dances, films, and field trips, all meant to reflect the debates and disagreements among the wide diversity of interested people from around the world who are stakeholders in the issues under discussion. Some radicals considered even the NGO forums to be too close to the UN and its viewpoints and organized alternative NGO gatherings. During the UN Science and Technology for Development Conference in Vienna in 1979, the street theater groups set up an alternative to the "green" alternative to the NGO forum. Anyone, with or without affiliation to any group, could attend these NGO meetings, often without a registration fee.

In contrast, only "official" NGOs could attend UN conferences, although frequently NGOs working on the topic at hand could register for just the particular conference: fourteen hundred groups received recognition at the 1992 Earth Summit. Such accreditation allows NGOs to participate in the series of preparatory committees, or prepcoms, where the official document of an upcoming conference, often called a world plan of action, is discussed and refined, and where many of the most significant changes are made. NGOs not familiar with UN procedures often ignored these prepcoms and then became frustrated at the world conference when they realized the limitations placed on substantive changes at that time. At many conferences, about the middle of the first week when NGOs realized their impotence, some would organize a march on the official conference. At the 1980 women's conference in Copenhagen, activists actually invaded the chamber and halted debate. Usually, NGOs as well as many official delegates preferred the spirited discussions at the NGO forum to the measured minuet of official conference procedures.

Access to delegates is another matter. National and international officials are more available during the conference than in their protected home bureaucracies. NGOs lobby them about themes of the conference as well as on national policies. Often the delegates, official NGOs, and issue-oriented NGOs find common ground despite their earlier antagonisms. Commenting on the Earth Summit of 1992, Kakabadse and Burns write that "even NGOs that initially tried to work around their national delegations discovered that they would eventually have to find ways to work with them. The same holds for governments: Some that initially ignored NGOs ultimately found that they needed the substantive help of NGOs . . . or their political support back home" (1994).

Out of these world conferences have come global networks of activists from international and national NGOs. The Union of International Associations lists over fifteen thousand NGOs that operate in three or more countries and draw their finances from sources in more than one country (Gordenker and Weiss 1996). A measure of their effectiveness is the frequent efforts of some authoritarian governments to reduce or abolish the role of INGOs in the United Nations system in order to reduce the global reach of many powerful NGOs that are able to challenge national sovereignty on some issues. Another measure of their effectiveness is the growing attention given to these NGO networks by UN development agencies. From its inception in 1973, the United Nations Environment Programme (UNEP) sponsored the Environmental Liaison Committee to maintain a link with NGOs organizing at both the national and international levels. Following its creation in 1976, the United Nations Centre for Human Settlements, or Habitat, established the Habitat International Coalition, an umbrella group for NGOs and community-based organizations interested in shelter issues. The United Nations Fund for Population Activities (UNFPA) was until recently the major funder of the International Planned Parenthood Federation and many of its national affiliates. The United Nations Development Programme (UNDP) sponsored a new global organization in 1992 called SANE (Sustainable Agriculture Network). NGO relationships with the World Bank are discussed below.

The proliferation of NGOs active in the UN has led to demands by the organizations themselves for a greater say in the overall deliberations; some are even calling for an assembly of NGOs to parallel the General Assembly with its governmental representatives. Such a demand is based on the claim that NGOs reflect people better than do governments, a widespread but unproven assumption (Gruhn 1996; Tinker 1996; United Nations Development Programme 1993; ECOSOC 1994b). Yet a question persists: To whom are NGOs accountable? As elements of social movements, NGOs are rooted in a particular set of beliefs. At what juncture are they perceived as interest groups that may as often undermine the political process as support it?

The report by the Open-Ended Working Group on the Review of Arrangements for Consultations with Non-Governmental Organizations supports the desire of international NGOs to participate in global governance, using their expertise and practical experience in "the formulation of international legal instruments, polices and programmes, and [in] their implementation nationally and globally" (ECOSOC 1994a, 38). The working group stresses, however, that the vast growth in NGOs has occurred primarily at the national and local levels, an observation that led United Nations Secretary-General Boutros Boutros-Ghali to recommend that efforts be made "to build on and share experience and enhance multilateral agency/NGO/government operational collaboration at the country and grassroots level" (ECOSOC 1994c, iii). Support for NGOs is perhaps stronger than ever under the administration of the present UN Secretary-General, Kofi Annan. When 637 NGOs from sixty-one countries assembled in New York in September 1997 for the opening session of the first General Assembly under his leadership, he told them that UN/NGO partnership is "not an option, but a necessity" (Maran forthcoming).

NGOs and the World Bank

Collaboration between NGOs and governments is increasingly fostered by the World Bank as a condition for loans. Since early in the 1980s, the Bank has had an NGO committee that specialized at first on environment but has more recently enlarged its concerns. Finding consultation with NGOs extremely useful, by the end of 1980s the World Bank had begun to include NGO participation in 50 percent of its projects (Beckmann 1991). The committee has funded support staff and maintains a list of over eight thousand NGOs in its data base. Sunshine rules allow NGOs access to most internal documents of the World Bank, facilitating critique of proposed projects (Malena 1995). In an official Bank publication on NGOs, Samuel Paul acknowledges "the positive contributions of NGO interventions . . . to poverty reduction"; he notes the extremely limited knowledge available on this sector as of 1991 and calls for a "careful and dispassionate assessment of NGOs' distinctive competence and role in the development process" (Paul and Israel 1991, 1–2).

Debate continues within the NGO community about such close cooperation. Are the organizations working with the Bank being co-opted? The June 1991 issue of *Lok Niti,* the magazine published by the Asian NGO Coalition, ANGOC, is entitled "GO-NGO partnership: a marriage of convenience?" Its cover shows the groom, GO, and the bride, NGO, being married by the World Bank! Chandra De Fonseka asks, "What is the World Bank's interest in forming partnerships with NGOs? At the outset, altruism and similar philanthropic motivations can probably be rejected immediately. After all, the World Bank itself would wholeheartedly agree that as a bank, it does not operate in such rarified lines of business." He concludes that "poverty is bad for business" (1991, 4-5).

Paul Nelson, an NGO activist in Washington, D.C., reports on his observations over several years of NGO–World Bank interactions and suggests that the Bank promotes NGO connections to minimize criticism of its commitment to market solutions. Widespread complaints about disastrous social impacts of most structural adjustment policies convinced the Bank to attach policy conditions to loans to prevent all reductions of government spending from being taken from budgets for social programs. In his book, Nelson seeks the answers to two basic questions: "Are NGOs becoming tools of a development paradigm that most do not support? Or can NGOs shift the World Bank's practice and performance in areas of environmental impact, popular participation, and structural adjustment?" (1995, 4). He concludes that organizational rigidities minimize NGO influence and that NGOs' goals are "inevitably reshaped" by their relationship with the World Bank. NGOs, for their part, seek to influence programs and institute policy shifts without sufficient clout to implement them.

The Bank's program cycle has also been criticized within the institution. Noting that most NGOs are brought in to assist in implementation after the project has been designed, Carmen Malena (1995) supports consultation of NGOs "upstream," before the project is set. She argues that the current process does not allow NGOs to apply their distinctive attributes: their closeness to the community and knowledge of local circumstances and people. Involving NGOs early on would change the quality of NGO involvement.

NGOs' castigation of the World Bank and the International Monetary Fund reached a crescendo during the celebrations marking the fiftieth anniversary of the founding of the United Nations in San Francisco in 1945. A coalition of NGOs called Fifty Years Is Enough put forward demands for restructuring both institutions and rethinking their single-minded devotion to a single economic model (Danaher 1994). The role of these institutions in stabilizing the economies of East Asia in the financial crisis of 1997–1998 has propelled criticism from the NGO community into the U.S. Congress during debates about replenishing funds for the IMF. The value premises of the critics contrast with the narrow economic principles that continue to dominate the thinking within the World Bank. Will the humanitarian predilections exhibited by most NGOs alter the market-oriented paradigm so dominant today? Does this soft approach reflect traditional women's values, or are these values themselves becoming more central within the civil society? Does this mean enhanced power for women in NGOs?

Challenging the State

Not only are NGOs confronting multilateral agencies and the UN itself; the Open-Ended Working Group of ECOSOC is urging these intergovernmental organizations (IGOs) to work with INGOs *above* and *within* the state. The implication is that national NGOs, through international networks, have a mechanism to make an end run around the state and in the process contribute to undermining state sovereignty. As IGOs and bilateral agencies increasingly promote NGOs as the panacea for all the inequities and problems encountered when governments in the lower-income countries of Asia, Latin America, and Africa pursue rapid economic growth, they are offering an alternative decision-making structure within these states. Economic transition in many of these countries has been characterized by a withdrawal of the government from significant sectors of the society, thus fostering a civil society between government and market and providing space for NGO activities (Tinker 1996). Promoters argue that citizens, often constrained by oligarchical or authoritarian governments from participation in the formal institutions of power, can influence policies that directly affect their daily life and so help create a political culture and the social capital necessary to sustain democracy (Clark 1991, 1995; Diamond 1993; Renshaw 1994; Ritchey-Vance 1996).

Concerns about citizen activism and international interference have led many authoritarian governments, such as China and Vietnam, to prohibit the creation of indigenous NGOs and exclude international NGOs or limit their operation in their countries (Tinker forthcoming). Yet many tightly controlled governments find that they must trade greater openness to NGOs for international funding. Countries such as Indonesia try to contain NGOs by allowing them to function as service providers or advocate relatively safe issues, such as women's rights or environmental protection but not human rights, as long as their positions do not challenge the government (Walker 1996). When several environmental NGOs documented that a major source of the disastrous fires in Kalimantan in the fall of 1997 was linked to corporations controlled by people close to President Suharto, these critics were protected through their international networks, which ensured reporting in the global media.

In sum, the change in nongovernmental organizations from a focus on relief to a concern with sustainable development is a significant trend. More critical to global governance is the tendency of these increasingly articulate organizations to segue into advocacy and criticism of current international and national policies. While governments in many developing countries feel a loss of control, NGO networks and coalitions are propelled by great expectations for increased power and prestige.

Women in Nongovernmental Organizations

Historically, women have been more active than men in voluntary organizations, whether at the village level or with the International Red Cross. As the power of NGOs surges into the growing space of the civil society, do women themselves and women's issues in general benefit? After all, NGOs proclaim greater participation and broader democracy than other top-down institutional forms. If women and their concerns are in fact being integrated into NGO debates and programs, what is the role of women-only organizations? These questions are central when examining the functioning and efficacy of NGOs at all levels. Because this chapter focuses on global governance and power, I discuss first the origin and current roles of women-only organizations as they interact with the United Nations and other IGOs. Next I review methods women have chosen to influence debates on such societal issues as population and the environment. Finally I consider women's roles in mainstream NGOs.

Women's Organizations on the Global Stage

International women's organizations were founded over a hundred years ago to enhance women's attempts to influence governmental policies on social justice and temperance before they were granted suffrage; the first was set up by a Swiss woman in 1868. Leaders in many of these organizations served as delegates to the League of Nations, which did not have specific arrangements for NGO representation. Women from auxiliary wings of trade unions joined those from the women's organizations to set up in Geneva a Liaison Committee of Women's International Organizations, which monitored sessions of both the League and the International Labor Organization (ILO). These women, along with women from the Inter-American Commission of Women of the Pan American Union, were instrumental in adding language about women to the UN Charter in 1945 and securing the UN Commission on the Status of Women in 1947 (Galey 1995b). Many of these same women's organizations registered for consultative status at ECOSOC and continue to provide leadership in CONGO (Stephenson 1995).[3]

Organizationally, these first-wave women's organizations are formally structured with hierarchical officers and procedures that often reflect *Robert's Rules of Order.* Although these groups now have members from around the world, their leaders are drawn from the elite; their headquarters, and some would say orientation, are in the North. Most would consider women to have similar concerns everywhere for civil rights, education, and fair working conditions and so assume that there is one international women's movement.

Second-wave women's organizations have discarded tight structures in favor of more egalitarian forms and have preferred networks or coalitions to formal international organizations. These groups tend to be more active in outreach to the poor or disadvantaged (Basu 1995). Focused on issues in their own countries and skeptical of any generalized category of woman, these new-wave groups have worked together at UN World Conferences for Women and associated meetings, such as prepcoms, and have participated in invitational seminars and professional meetings. Given their preference for networks, they have not sought consultative status at ECOSOC; but many registered as NGOs for the women's conferences; the final list of organizations attending the Beijing NGO forum at Huairou numbered 1,761.[4]

Yet these newer women's organizations have had a profound influence on global governance. Two types of organizations predominated among those set up early in the 1970s: action-research centers, and groups working as agents to change the way women think or act. Both sought to alter the way donors conceived and implemented development programs and projects so that women's concerns and needs were included. Their activities were readily apparent, and both approaches were given recognition when the General Assembly agreed at its 1976 meeting to set up two new institutions for women as a result of resolutions at the International Women's Year Conference in Mexico in 1975 (United Nations Office of Public Information 1977). The UN Fund for Women, now renamed UNIFEM, was created to support grassroots women's groups. The International Research and Training Institute for the Advancement of Women, INSTRAW, was designed to conduct, collect, and disseminate research on women in development and to use this information to train government officials and NGOs to improve their projects.

Research Centers. The research groups were set up to assist in collecting data for the national reports on the status of women requested by the UN following the 1975 world conference. Founded by committed feminists, these groups sought new ways of creating knowledge that worked with poor women, not only to collect information, but also to collaborate with them in finding solutions to their problems instead of treating them as research objects (Tinker 1983, 1997). The report from DAWN (Development Alternatives with Women for a New Era), presented to the Nairobi conference by women scholars from the South, maintains that research organizations were the most effective of the new women's organizations in influencing policy and that they "aim to eliminate the distinction between the researcher and the researched, so that research becomes a process of mutual education" (Sen and Grown 1995, 92).[5]

Documenting women's invisible work in subsistence households, agriculture, and the informal sector was crucial if women's economic activities were to be acknowledged and supported by the development planners. The need for such data was immense, and funds were readily available from donor agencies, population organizations, and foundations. Free-standing research centers were not the only ones involved; university faculty formed women's studies centers whose research went beyond scholarly endeavors to action projects.[6] Agencies of the UN system such as UNESCO, ILO, and FAO commissioned studies; INSTRAW and UNIFEM supported research on basic needs such as water and technology. The secretariat for the 1980 UN Women's Conference funded research by women from the South to ensure a balanced interpretation of data.

Within the decade 1970-1980, the amount of research on women conducted throughout the world by women of all countries was indeed substantial. Internationally, the research findings influenced policies and programs of donor agencies and INGOs. Locally, these efforts spawned new organizations designed to work with poor women to ameliorate their problems; these groups were both integrated and women-only and focused on many issues new to more traditional women's concerns, such as community health, appropriate technology, household energy, and agriculture including crops and small ruminants. Women in these groups took their insights to the UN conferences on these topics, inserting language into official documents that ensured that women as well as men would benefit from new initiatives.

The excitement and legitimacy of the new research on women encouraged most international professional associations to hold panels on women and often to set up a women's caucus or committee to encourage women scholars to attend conventions. Frequent invitational conferences were held; the first conference on women in development was held in Mexico City in 1975, just before the UN's world conference. Participants were visible as delegates and presenters at both the official and the NGO meetings. The idea of creating Women's World Banking, an NGO that promotes credit for women, was formed during these discussions (Tinker and Bo Bramsen 1976). The action-research aspect led to the formation of the Association of Women in Development, which holds biennial conferences of scholars, activists, and practitioners from around the world.

The Copenhagen conference in 1980 was the site of the first meeting of the women's studies movement. The International Interdisciplinary Congress of Women was established to hold periodic meetings around the world on women's research and education. Typically decentralized, the Feminist Press publishes Women's Studies International, and the National Council for Research on Women maintains a roster of women's research centers around the world. The DAWN group of Third World scholars had begun meeting prior to the Nairobi conference and presented its report to the NGO forum; its leading scholars continue to influence development policy individually and through the organization.

Change Agents. The second type of women's organization that has had a global impact has concentrated on changing women's lives. Leaders of these groups often come from research organizations and academia. Emerging during the 1970s, they initially focused on the growing poverty among women, especially those heading households. Working as separate organizations or within NGOs, they organized poor women in rural and urban settings and assisted them in earning money, improving their housing and services, gaining access to health and family planning clinics, receiving agricultural extension information, and attending literacy classes; that is, they worked to include women in all aspects of development programs. Debate over the "success" of such programs continues among scholars and practitioners; activists know that the mere fact of organizing is empowering (Kabeer 1994; Tinker 1990).

Most women's organizations aim at more egalitarian decision making, though evidence suggests that this is difficult to accomplish; educated leaders often believe that they have the answers and manipulate, if they do not decree, certain decisions. Nevertheless, participation in groups outside the patriarchal family is mind-blowing for many women. Just hearing about new ideas, knowing that their problems are not theirs alone, and discussing alternative approaches to addressing their problems are provocative and stimulating. If at first most issues these groups took on related to poverty, relationships within the family and women's legal rights became more critical when households disintegrated. Domestic violence and rape became global topics openly discussed and addressed. Such issues span class and ethnicity and provide a foundation for a global women's movement encompassing many diverse institutions with their own issues. The global feminisms described by the authors in Basu (1995) attest to the many competing, and often conflicting, perspectives found among women's organizations.

In many ways, the network of research scholars provided the base for the contemporary international women's movement that embraces diverse feminisms. Grassroots groups at first tended to be fragmented over goals and ideology, but they have all emphasized participation and information, and their goal has been empowerment. As a result of all these activities, change is clearly happening at the local and state levels. What are the international implications of women's activism underscored by our greater understanding of women's roles and their economic and social contributions to society?

Women Influencing International Issues

International networks of women's organizations and coalitions have focused on identifying and inserting women's viewpoints into broader societal interests. Leaders of these groups often have their roots in women's organizations or research centers. Other groups were founded by women who previously worked within mainstream NGOs on issues such as population, environment, technology, energy, housing, and water and sanitation and who felt that their perspectives were ignored by the dominant male leadership. These groups have been influential in many recent international conferences.

For example, in January 1985, the Environmental Liaison Committee of NGOs, which advises the United Nations Environment Programme, held a meeting in Nairobi to consider how to include in its proceedings more voices of women and people of the South. Invitations had gone out to leaders of development and population organizations that had a better record of including women. During the first day, men from Europe and the United States dominated the debate, insisting that priority be given to global environmental issues such as acid rain and pesticides. Discouraged by the silence of contesting views, especially from women of the South, someone brought a procedural motion: speakers from North and South would have to alternate, as would male and female speakers. Before they could speak, the men of the North had to encourage, even beg, women of the South to talk. The tone and direction of the debate changed abruptly. Not only were issues of health and sanitation in squatter areas added to the agenda of UNEP, but also a women's caucus was established.

The Nairobi Women's Conference, which followed in June, featured a panel on women's stake in the environment. Presenters were members of Women in Development and Environment (WIDE), an organization that had been set up a few years before by the UNEP representative in Washington, D.C. Preceding the UN Conference on Environment and Development—the Earth Summit—in Rio de Janeiro in 1994, UNEP assembled over two hundred examples of successful environmental projects and brought the women who initiated them to a conference in Miami. A more political role for women at the Earth Summit was orchestrated by the recently established Women for Environment and Development (WEDO). This increasingly visible international coalition of women convened the World Women's Congress for a Healthy Planet in November 1991 to plan strategies for the Earth Summit and write a women's version of the official conference document, Agenda 21. Over fifteen hundred women from eighty-three countries attended. At the summit, WEDO held daily caucuses, just as the NGOs do for their members, to alert women about decisions taken and issues on the upcoming agenda. The visibility and sophistication of these efforts ensured that women's interests were included in the final document. Such briefings have become a permanent feature of subsequent UN conferences and prepcoms (Chen 1996).

In Rio, a division occurred among women's organizations over wording on family planning. In the following two years, leading up to the 1994 World Population Conference, women active in these overlapping issues met frequently to address the conflicting views. The International Women's Health Coalition coordinated the organization of meetings around the globe to draft and debate the Woman's Declaration on Population Policies. A final strategy meeting was held in January 1994 to rehearse individual and group responsibilities during the Cairo conference. The U.S. Network for Cairo '94 coordinated the activities of a broad spectrum of population, environment, and development organizations in support of the women's agenda. In Cairo, WEDO set up its daily caucus, briefing NGOs, official delegates, and the media (Chen 1996). The result was possibly the most feminist document to emerge from any UN conference. Principle 4 builds on previous UN conferences when it declares: "Advancing gender equality and equity, the empowerment of women, the elimination of all kinds of violence against women, and ensuring women's ability to control their own fertility, are cornerstones of population and development-related programmes." Other principles declare women's rights to health and education to be prerequisites for all population programs (Germain and Kyte 1995; see also Higer this volume).

Long-term preparation for the UN World Conference on Human Rights held in Vienna in 1993 also was instrumental in introducing the revolutionary concept that women's rights are human rights. In 1991 the Center for Women's Global Leadership at Rutgers University in the United States began planning for Vienna by convening women from twenty countries first to decide on goals for the conference and then to orchestrate a campaign to secure support for this new initiative that brought domestic violence into public view. In Vienna, WEDO held daily briefings for NGOs, while UNIFEM arranged daily meetings for delegates. A mock tribunal that heard women's own stories of human rights abuses provided dramatic documentation of the need to include women's rights in the final document (Chen 1996; Bunch and Reilly 1994; see also Joachim this volume).

The pace of UN meetings increased in 1995, when the World Summit for Social Development was scheduled for March in Copenhagen. WEDO joined with DAWN to coordinate daily caucus meetings and also arranged panels and dialogue sessions during PrepCom II. After the successes for women's issues at Rio, Vienna, and Cairo, women continued to stress unity in the face of attempts by religious and culturally traditional groups to roll back these advances. Although similar defensive strategies characterized much of the activity at the governmental conference in Beijing, the NGO forum in Huairou provided active NGOs with the opportunity to disseminate information about crucial issues to the twenty-five thousand to thirty thousand women attending (see also West this volume).

The women's groups that took the lead in coordinating lobbying at the four UN conferences were U.S.-based organizations with savvy leadership able to secure funding to enable women from around the world to participate in planning meetings as well as in the final conferences. All continue their activities; but while the International Women's Health Coalition and the Center for Global Leadership maintain a focus on health/population and on human rights, respectively, WEDO has expanded its membership abroad and broadened the scope of its policy papers to include issues of globalization and global governance. WEDO's primers on transnational corporations, the World Trade Organization, and the structure of the world and regional development banks were widely circulated in Beijing.

In 1996, perhaps the last of these major world conferences took place when Habitat II convened in Istanbul. Women's concerns came late to issues of shelter. The Habitat International Coalition was founded in 1976, but not until one of its few women members organized panels that promoted shelter issues for the 1985 Women's Conference in Nairobi did the topic gain recognition as a basic women's issue. A Women and Shelter group was formed and began publishing a newsletter that reported on both community programs and scholarly publications (Tinker 1993). This caucus held meetings and participated in prepcoms for the 1996 Habitat Conference in Istanbul; at the conference, it worked with NGOs to ensure that delegates considered women's rights to housing.

Since the beginning of the UN Decade for Women, leadership for women's issues has shifted from the older formal women's organizations to networks and coalitions of more diverse activist groups. Unlike earlier UN conferences, starting with the 1974 Population Conference, when changes in wording in the conference documents were the result of individual or ad hoc group efforts by NGO and government delegates, these new groups are diligent in their preparations for each topic and each conference. Not only are organized women more effective in changing policy statements, but also their national or local affiliates are able to lobby their own governments to follow the UN recommendations. The specialized groups, whether caucuses within mainstream NGOs or women-only NGOs, eloquently presented their perspectives at the most recent series of UN world conferences.

How much influence does all this lobbying activity have? If women's issues must first be inserted into single-interest or development policies, which in turn become the subject of negotiations at the agency or state level, do women's concerns simply fade away? At the 1995 NGO forum in Huairou, China, women working within the bureaucracies of bilateral agencies spoke at a plenary panel about problems in mainstreaming the women's development agenda. The speakers expressed great dismay and discouragement at their lack of progress toward including women and their issues at every stage of program design and implementation.[7]

One of these institutions was the World Bank, whose new president, James Wolfensohn, attended sessions at Beijing.[8] The Bank has been widely accused of fostering economic reform in countries undergoing structural adjustment in such a manner that social services are reduced and the social safety net for the poor is torn. Indeed, the reduction of government provision of these services is a major factor propelling the growth of existing service NGOs in those countries and the expansion of new NGOs into the provision of services. A group of women formed Women's Eyes on the Bank to monitor the implementation of the pledges made by Wolfensohn in Beijing. In addition, the World Bank set up the External Gender Consultative Group to work closely with policymakers. Leaders of women-only and mainstream NGOs have agreed to work within the Bank for reform in a symbiotic relationship with others involved in the Fifty Years Is Enough campaign.

Can external women's groups influence World Bank policies more than the long-existing but informal women's group within the Bank has been able to do? Women consultants have complained that policies concerning women are simply "tacked on" to program designs, if they are mentioned at all. The members of the External Gender Consultative Group want to start with a focus more on gender justice than on specifics of the project cycle (Alexander 1996). In some ways this is a more radical position than just proposing to restructure the Bank.

Women's Impact on Global Governance

Women today are charting several apparently contradictory paths to power and influence on the global stage. They are joining political parties and running with increasing success for elected office (Jaquette 1997), and once in office they are contesting everything from the rigidities of rules to the lack of women's restrooms to the juvenile verbal assaults in the British House of Commons. Women also hold many leadership positions within national and international NGOs that champion values that resonate with women's traditional concerns and provide a countervailing force to traditional state power. Although male dominance may still be present in organizational structures and decision-making processes in state institutions and NGOs, women's voices and leadership are increasingly evident.

An alternate route to wielding power is to appeal as women and mothers for a change in the values that underlie government policies and programs. Repelled by corrupt parties and patriarchal leadership, some women turn their backs on existing formal institutions and concentrate on forming organizations and networks of women outside the normal channels of power (Brasileiro and Judd 1996; Tripp 1996). In every country, women are taking charge of their lives; protesting domestic violence, sexual harassment, and male drunkenness; and demanding access to land and housing, microcredit and markets, employment and child care. The sum of these activities has pro-

duced the women's social movement that is fundamentally altering established institutions of society. The power of this social movement has
enhanced the role of women's organizations as they operate at the global
level. At the United Nations and its agencies, in discourse with the World
Bank, in negotiations at meetings of all types of NGOs, women have new
presence and authority.

Women-only communities or self-help groups benefit from the global
noise raised by the elite leadership within and outside mainstream institutions. But women leaders working within national legislatures benefit from
the rising public voices of women demanding a gentler and more equitable
world for women, their children, their families, and their communities.
NGOs, with their growing influence in an expanding civil society, are yet
another route for influence.

Is outside influence more likely to bring change in outmoded state institutions? Is the backlash against current trends toward gender equality a desperate
attempt to stop an inevitable shift in patriarchal relationships between women
and men? Is the lack of enthusiasm for women's issues among the younger
generations in the United States, for example, a reflection of women's
improved position? Around the world, male as well as female scholars and
activists believe that the women's movement has already irrevocably changed
society.

After a quarter of a century, the cumulation of women's activities globally
has challenged male control in the family by reducing women's economic
dependence on men. While women worry that such changes leave mothers
with the double roles of nurturer and provider while letting fathers off the hook
(Summerfield and Tinker 1997), many male scholars emphasize how these
changes alter the basic fabric of society. Amartya Sen reconsiders approaches
to the household with his discussion about women's improved bargaining
position within the household (1990); Ken Kusterer proclaims the imminent
demise of patriarchy (1990); Manuel Castells writes that "the transformation
of women's consciousness, and of societal values in most societies, in less than
three decades, is staggering, and it yields fundamental consequences for the
entire human experience, from political power to the structure of personality"
(1997, 136).

Translating the value shifts caused by the women's movement into new
political, social, and economic institutions is a monumental task. Women
need to pursue all available paths to power and influence, in women-only and
mainstream NGOs, in nonconventional community organizations, and in
political parties. The expanding civil society gives greater space to people's
organizations and so allows greater opportunities for women to mold their
own future.

Notes

1. The number of NGOs registered with ECOSOC in Categories I (global organizations with broad social and economic interests) and II (those with narrower issue or geographical concerns) has increased from 7 in 1948 to 42 in 1993 for the first category and from 32 to 376 during the same years for the second category, while other registered NGOs rose from 2 to 560, for a total of 978 NGOs in consultative status in 1993 (ECOSOC 1994b). The UN Web page on the Internet now lists 1,500 organizations in consultative status.

2. E.g., Environment, 1972, 1992; Population, 1974, 1984, 1994; Food, 1974; Women, 1975, 1980, 1985, 1995; Habitat, 1976, 1996; Water, 1978; Desertification, 1978; Agrarian Reform and Rural Development, 1979; Science and Technology for Development, 1979; New and Renewable Sources of Energy, 1981; and the World Summit on Social Development, 1995.

3. The International Alliance of Women and the International Council of Women have suffragist roots; they have run development projects in the South, but their major international activity focuses on UN affairs in Geneva and New York. The International Young Women's Christian Association, Zonta International, and Soroptimist International are charitable groups that provide grants to women's groups globally and promote their issues at the UN. International Federation of Business and Professional Women and International Association of University Women continue holding world conferences and have less presence at UN meetings.Some fifty women's organizations now have consultative status.

4. Information exchanges, although based initially in the North, were often international in reach. In 1975 the *Women's International Network [WIN] News* began publishing excerpts from UN documents and conference reports, as well as updates on issues of interest from women contributors. About the same time, two European women, one in Geneva and one in Rome, set up Isis as a clearinghouse and newsletter for information on women's health and violence issues. In London, Change produces reports and a magazine. The International Women's Tribune Center in New York City was set up to support the NGO community following the Mexico City conference.

5. Researchers are still struggling with the difficulty of carrying out feminist fieldwork that produces knowledge of use to those studied. For an excellent collection of opinions on this process, see Wolf 1996.

6. In Latin America under military dictatorships, university-sponsored projects were less vulnerable than those run by social change organizations. In Nepal before the restoration of democracy, for-profit consulting organizations provided a cover for action research and projects when activities of both NGOs and the university were constrained.

7. The panel was entitled "Institutional Mechanisms and Financial Arrangements" and was held on 5 September 1995.The chair was Rounaq Jahan, whose book reports her findings on mainstreaming efforts in two bilateral donors, Norway and Canada, and two multilateral agencies, the United Nations Development Programme and the World Bank (1995).

8. For background on women's offices in the World Bank, see Winslow 1995a.

Part II

Shaping Agendas: Feminist Strategies in Global Governance

7

The Women's International League for Peace and Freedom: Organizing Women for Peace in the War System

Mary K. Meyer

> All successful movements are organized. Nations organize for war; let women organize for peace.
>
> —Frances S. Hallowes, *Mothers of Men and Militarism*

A remarkable number of women's peace groups emerged around the world in the 1980s in response to the growing militarization and bitter wars of the decade. The women at the Greenham Common and Seneca peace camps, the Women for Peace in Sri Lanka, the Russian Commission of Soldiers' Mothers, the various Women in Black gatherings in the Middle East and beyond, and countless other grassroots peace groups brought women together to oppose the public violence within and between their societies. Such activism among women is not new. Recent feminist scholarship has demonstrated that "women through history, world-wide have protested against cruel treatment, indecent conditions, and subordination" (Eduards 1994, 182), and "millions of women," historically and across the globe, have had to think about and respond to "the underlying causes of war, militarism, and peace" (Enloe 1990b, 527), even if their specific local and temporal conditions have varied.

Yet the historical record suggests that most women's peace groups, and the peace movements to which they belonged, have had limited life spans, even if at one time they flourished. In her excellent history of women's peace groups in Britain since 1820, Jill Liddington (1989, 140) asserts that "a women's peace movement is always highly cyclical" because such movements are generationally linked to a particular war or militarization campaign. Another reason may be that women's peace groups have tended to avoid formal organizational structures to institutionalize themselves. Strong institutional structures are necessary to carry through the politics of peace movements; however, feminists have been suspicious of bureaucratic organizational structures that are hierarchical, undemocratic, and rigid. This raises serious problems for women's—or feminists'—challenge to the highly organized war system. Without enduring organizational structures that can sustain their challenge to militarism and war, women's peace groups can only be reactive to the war system rather than transformative of it.

Unlike most women's peace organizations, the Women's International League for Peace and Freedom (WILPF) has survived to challenge militarism and war for over eighty years. Indeed, WILPF is the oldest women's international peace organization in the world and one of the world's oldest non-governmental organizations (NGOs). What is it about this organization that has allowed it to span several generations and remain active for so long? WILPF's founders sought to institutionalize the international women's peace movement of the early twentieth century through an organizational structure that combines both mainstreaming and disengaging political strategies. This institutionalized organizational structure and its mainstreaming and disengaging strategies give WILPF its longevity and continued vitality in sustaining its challenge to the war system.

This chapter begins with a brief overview of WILPF's history, showing how its founders opened a space at the international level for women to challenge the war system and how they institutionalized their peace talk at the global level. The chapter then turns to an analysis of WILPF's organizational structure and its flexibility in combining mainstreaming and disengaging political strategies to keep those spaces open for women's continued peace activism. It concludes by considering whether WILPF provides a useful organizational model for contemporary global women's NGOs to consider in challenging other gendered global governance structures of the war system.

Historical Context

WILPF's history is rooted in the experiences of women's peace activism at the grassroots level in Europe and North America in the nineteenth and early twentieth centuries. Prior to winning suffrage, Victorian social values and the liberal state denied women much public space to carry out political work, forcing women peace activists to work on war and peace issues in the private space of the home. Yet numerous local women's peace groups appeared in the nineteenth century in Britain and the United States. In the 1850s some three thousand British women belonged to 150 Olive Leaf Circles, which met monthly to discuss peace ideas in Britain and abroad. These women wrote pacifist children's stories and parables, published a journal, sent "Olive Leaves" (short peace messages) to foreign newspapers, and corresponded with other Olive Leaf Circles forming abroad (Liddington 1989, 14–15). Thus, despite their confinement to the private sphere, they established links with women in similar groups in other towns and abroad.

Between the turn of the century and World War I, women peace activists in many countries were making a number of important transnational connections. A large number of women's leagues and associations focusing on disarmament and peace education were forming in Europe[1] and America alongside women's suffrage organizations. European feminists on the left developed analyses of militarism that linked women's suffrage to peace (Liddington 1989, 74–75). Women were soon traveling to other countries to meet with their counterparts and hold international meetings or congresses, thus creating personal, transnational connections among women organizing for peace and fomenting an internationalist sisterhood. The most famous such congress was the Women's International Peace Congress at The Hague in 1915, just eight months after the outbreak of World War I.

The Women's International Peace Congress was the brainchild of Dutch suffragist Aletta Jacobs who, with a generation of suffragists and peace activists from England, Germany, Holland, Austria, Hungary, Belgium, the United States, Canada, and elsewhere, called for an international congress of women to gather at the Hague in April 1915 to challenge the European war and discuss a permanent peace settlement. Social activist and writer Jane Addams (who in the same year had formed the Women's Peace Party in the United States) was invited to preside over the four days of the Congress, which attracted over twelve hundred women delegates from a dozen countries (Liddington 1989, 94–103).

The Hague congress set aside questions of responsibility for the European war and its rules of conduct, focusing instead on passing resolutions condemning the war and urging governments to cease fire, begin peace negotiations, and build a permanent peace based on principles of justice (Liddington 1989, 105). The resolutions also called for democratic control of foreign policy, women's enfranchisement, and "the organization of [a] Society of Nations" to include "a permanent International Court of Justice" and "a permanent International Conference . . . in which women should take part, to deal with . . . practical proposals for furthering International Cooperation" (quoted in Spivek 1995, 6). The Congress also created an International Committee of Women for Permanent Peace (ICWPP) based in Amsterdam that soon had twelve national sections. The British section took the name Women's International League, while the Women's Peace Party in the United States became a section in 1916 (Spivek 1995, 7).

After the Hague congress, two delegations, one of which was headed by both Addams and Jacobs, set out to present the congress resolutions to the heads of fourteen belligerent and neutral governments. The government of

Sweden offered to host a mediation conference if two belligerent states were agreeable, while President Woodrow Wilson received the resolutions as "by far the best formulation" put out by anybody to end the war (quoted in Liddington 1989, 104). But the war dragged on and a permanent settlement was delayed for over three more years, when President Wilson presented his Fourteen Points at Versailles (Liddington 1989, 103–6; Spivek 1995, 5).[2]

While the statesmen met at Versailles, the ICWPP organized a second international women's peace congress in Zurich in May 1919. Jane Addams again presided over the congress, which decided to send a delegation to Versailles to pressure the diplomats to change the onerous terms of the emerging treaty, lift the food blockade of Germany and Austria-Hungary, and include a Women's Charter in the peace agreement (Liddington 1989, 133–38; Spivek 1995, 8). The delegates at the Zurich congress also decided to institutionalize their peace movement further by adopting the name Women's International League for Peace and Freedom, or WILPF, and creating and basing its new international secretariat in Geneva. With a new headquarters and a small but "permanent" secretariat, WILPF both mirrored the model of the new League of Nations, which it promoted, and gave itself the means for its own continuation. Not content to remain an amorphous peace movement whose demise was probable given the end of World War I, WILPF's founders established an international women's organization and presence at the global level that sought to oppose war and imperialism and that promoted demilitarization (Vellacott 1993).

WILPF was an active supporter and defender of the League of Nations and played an important role in leading the disarmament movement of the 1920s. The League of Nations' demise after 1933 and the outbreak of World War II created a difficult international environment for WILPF, and debates within WILPF about how best to confront fascism and the war led to declining membership. But WILPF's leadership managed to keep the Geneva office operating thanks to the financial support of Jane Addams and the United States section of WILPF as well as the leadership of Gertrude Baer, a German feminist and lifelong WILPF activist. In 1945, WILPF participated in the United Nations Charter Conference in San Francisco. At WILPF's international congress in Luxembourg in 1946, a motion was considered to dissolve the organization, but its leadership decided to continue. In 1948 WILPF gained consultative status as an NGO in the UN's Economic and Social Council (ECOSOC). WILPF's early work on peace and disarmament issues received international recognition when its founder and first international president (1919–1931) Jane Addams received the Nobel Peace Prize in 1931; Emily Greene Balch, WILPF's first international secretary, received the Nobel Peace Prize in 1946 (Spivek 1995, 3, 8; Bussey and Tims 1980).

WILPF's early work was based on a number of theoretical influences that defined peace as something more than the temporary absence of war (negative peace). The generation of women activists that founded WILPF drew partly on earlier religious or maternalist arguments to justify their peace work (e.g., that women as mothers, life-givers, and nurturers have a duty to protect their sons from war's slaughter). Maternalist feminist arguments were particularly popular with German and Swedish activists (Liddington 1989, 93). Other first-wave feminist arguments posited women's suffrage and equal rights as essential to more democratic and peaceful foreign policies and hence a more peaceful world. A third ideological influence on WILPF's early work came from those women peace activists, particularly those on the left, who developed a materialist analysis of war (e.g., that war and militarism serve the interests of the armaments industry and the imperialist state).

A fourth important influence was the social reformist analysis developed by Jane Addams and others, who saw social ills such as poverty, social violence, and the oppression of women and others as the unacceptable costs of militarism (Liddington 1989, 6–8; Roseneil 1995, 4–7; Oldfield 1989; Vellacott 1993). Such women made connections between war and militarism and unacceptable social conditions at home and abroad. They envisioned a world of equality, social justice, prosperity, and progress if militarism and war could be eliminated. In doing so, they posited an image of "positive peace"[3] decades before peace studies scholars would invent the term. The materialist and social reformist analyses remained the most dominant ideological influences within WILPF for most of its history, contributing to the red-baiting of the organization during the Cold War.

Despite the red-baiting, WILPF continued to play an active and important role as an NGO within the United Nations framework in opposing the nuclear arms race and in pressing for disarmament as well as a variety of positive peace issues, including human rights, decolonization, and development. It advocated the Universal Declaration of Human Rights as well as the creation of UNICEF and the UN High Commissioner for Refugees (Spivek 1995, 11). WILPF's UN representatives have served on a number of UN commissions and special conferences, including the UN Commission on Human Rights (1959) and seven Conferences on Disarmament and Development (Spivek 1995, 11). WILPF also sends representatives to the United Nations Educational, Scientific and Cultural Organization (UNESCO), the International Labor Organization (ILO), the Food and Agricultural Organization (FAO), and other U.N. agencies. In 1976, its secretary-general, Edith Ballantyne, was elected president of the Conference of NGOs at the UN; its other representatives have served as officers on a number of NGO committees (Ballantyne 1989).

WILPF has not only presented a women's voice in United Nations peace, disarmament, and human rights forums, it has also reminded United Nations women's conferences that peace and disarmament are women's issues, too. As the oldest NGO to focus on women, WILPF played an active role in supporting the UN International Decade for Women (1975–1985) and the related UN women's conferences. In the 1975 Mexico City conference, which inaugurated the International Decade for Women, a small group of WILPF women struggled to include disarmament on the agenda and in the final conference document, but this was rebuffed by official government delegations as "politicizing" the Decade (Spivek 1995, 12; Foster 1989, 75–76). At the mid-Decade conference at Copenhagen (1980), WILPF was better able to get peace and disarmament issues on the broader program, thanks to the fact that Ballantyne was also serving as president of the Conference of Non-Governmental Organizations and therefore was chairwoman of the NGO forum at Copenhagen. Unlike the Mexico City conference, WILPF was a "visible force in Copenhagen" (Foster 1989, 79).

Again at the 1985 Nairobi conference, WILPF played a key role in seeing that peace issues would have an important place in the program. Ballantyne chaired the committee that organized the peace program of the conference, including the Peace Tent, which brought Soviet and American as well as Israeli and Palestinian women into dialogue. Thousands of women passed through the blue-and-white-striped Peace Tent, which was "ablaze with lively discussion day and night" (Foster 1989, 95). At the 1995 Beijing conference, WILPF was again largely responsible for organizing the Peace Tent, where women from Chechnya, the former Yugoslavia, Rwanda, and Burundi came together to share their experiences of war, make new connections, and speak about peace and cooperation. Once again, WILPF was the only NGO at the conference explicitly tying disarmament and demilitarization issues to other women's issues. WILPF called on governments to cut their military spending by 5 percent for the next five years and invest those funds in development. While governments did not want to discuss this idea in the official conference, the women and other NGOs at the parallel conference were much more open to it (Clement 1996). Nevertheless, the Platform for Action does pay attention to peace and disarmament issues and their impact on women (United Nations 1995a).[4]

WILPF's historical attention to the international level and its ability to institutionalize itself internationally as a nongovernmental organization are significant. By attending to the international level, where (male-dominated) states reproduce and participate in the war system, WILPF claimed and has occupied an important political space for women to keep peace and disarmament issues on the international agenda. This work within the United Nations and its consultative status in ECOSOC are important sources of WILPF's longevity as an organization and its legitimacy as an international actor.

It is difficult to assess how much of an impact WILPF has had. The world is still stockpiling weapons, wars still rage, and women still suffer as casualties and refugees of war while other women seek to join military organizations in their struggle for equal rights. But WILPF's representatives have been active and elected to leadership positions in the NGO community; they have supported and participated in seven UN conferences on disarmament; they have urged that women, the UN, and the NGO community remember to include disarmament and antimilitarism as central issues to the advancement of women. WILPF was also among the first to call and work for the Comprehensive Test Ban Treaty, which has recently received approval in the UN General Assembly. WILPF has a unique and focused voice that has had an impact on the UN agenda and made a difference at the international level. While WILPF is only one of hundreds of NGOs working within the UN system today, it was one of the first. Its internationalist commitment to the UN may seem quaint, naive, or too mainstream to some, yet WILPF's constant focus on disarmament and its direct challenges to governments to cut military spending in favor of economic and social justice demonstrate WILPF's commitment to changing the core values of the war system. WILPF has found important ways of helping to reshape international norms, even if international practice still falls far short.

WILPF: Structure and Strategies

Because it works within the UN system, WILPF can be categorized as a mainstreaming women's organization. Stienstra (1995, 144) defines groups that practice a politics of mainstreaming as those that "seek to reach the largest possible audience by working within or together with the existing social structures such as governments, educational institutions, and international organizations." As WILPF Secretary General Edith Ballantyne once said, "You have to work with the governments too because that's where the decisions are made" (quoted in Foster 1989, 85).

Nevertheless, WILPF's multitiered structure, the focus of its campaigns, the types of local actions it pursues, and the nature of its discourse also give WILPF the characteristics of a disengaging women's organization. Groups that practice a politics of disengagement critique the ways governments and other social structures address issues (Stienstra 1995, 144). Such groups develop alternative ideas and seek change by working outside of official structures through more radical actions (e.g., protests) and the networking of activities with other NGOs and grassroots groups at the international, national, and local levels.

WILPF is unique among women's peace organizations because its organizational structure allows for both mainstreaming and disengaging strategies. Mainstreaming has given WILPF an institutional base providing political space for "professional activists" in Geneva to make peace and disarmament issues "respectable" and keep them on international and governmental agendas. Disengaging strategies occur at the national and local levels, where activists can be more critical and creative, drawing on more radical influences from newer social movements and preventing WILPF from ossifying and becoming irrelevant. This flexibility built into WILPF's organizational structure is the key to WILPF's longevity and vitality.

International Level

WILPF has a hierarchical and multitiered structure that links its international office in Geneva with its national, regional, and local levels. It sees itself as "not a federation of national organizations, but an international community of women" of diverse backgrounds (Ballantyne 1986, 2). Its International Office in Geneva is currently headed by a secretary-general, an assistant, a number of interns, and the editor of its international magazine, *Pax et Libertas*. Its executive organ is the International Executive Committee, made up of representatives from each national section, who meet yearly. There are also a number of leading WILPF members who represent WILPF as volunteers in various United Nations agencies (e.g., at UNESCO, ILO, UNICEF, and FAO) in Geneva, New York, and Paris as well as in the NGO community. Once every three years, WILPF holds an international congress at which representatives from national sections meet to compare their work and discuss ideas for the next triennial international program (Gore and Jacobs 1989, 10). Recent congresses have been held in Baltimore, Maryland (1998), Helsinki, Finland (1995), La Paz, Bolivia (1992), Sydney, Australia (1989), and Utrecht, the Netherlands (1986). The International Executive Committee also meets in different cities around the world for its yearly meetings.

National and Local Levels

Beyond the international level, WILPF is organized into national sections that are in turn made up of local branches. In 1996, WILPF claimed some four hundred thousand members in forty-two countries worldwide. New national sections have formed recently in Africa, Latin America, and Asia, thus adding geographical and cultural diversity to the historically Western orientation of WILPF (Clement 1996). In the United States section, WILPF had over seven thousand members in 1996[5] organized into 110 local branches, the largest of which were found in Minneapolis, Cleveland, Santa Cruz, Cape Cod, Baltimore, and Detroit. Local branches may have as few as three members to over five hundred (Foster 1989, 3; Clement 1996). There are also at-large members who do not affiliate with any local branch.

WILPF's structure gives national sections the flexibility to address nationally relevant issues within the context of the triennial international program. For example, in 1988–1989, the Mauritius section campaigned to dismantle military bases on Diego Garcia; the New Zealand section promoted disarmament and the rights of the indigenous Maoris; the Japanese section promoted peace education, disarmament, and aid to Nicaragua; the Chilean section registered voters for the 1988 plebiscite to end Pinochet's dictatorship, denounced the arms trade between Chile and South Africa, and visited political prisoners weekly ("A World Full of Activists" 1989, 19–23). In the U.S. section in the 1980s and 1990s, WILPF organized creative national campaigns that challenged U.S. foreign and defense policies. U.S. WILPF's national campaigns included getting over half a million signatures for the Comprehensive Test Ban Treaty and a People's Peace Petition, organizing the Stop the Arms Race in Outer Space (STAR) campaign, making a Peace Quilt, sponsoring Peace Trains, creating and disseminating a Women's Budget challenging federal budget priorities, opposing war toys, signing the Women's Peace and Justice Treaty of the Americas, and (net)working with a variety of other groups against racism, apartheid, economic exploitation, environmental destruction, and violence against women. U.S. WILPF also endorsed a number of national boycotts, including those against Shell Oil, General Electric, Coors, and Chilean fruit imports during the Pinochet regime.

WILPF's literature keeps its membership informed of the activities of national sections from around the world as well as of other grassroots women's activism for peace and disarmament. During the 1980s, WILPF networked with the various new women's peace groups that appeared and supported the creative actions of groups like the Greenham Common Women's Peace Camp, the Ribbon around the Pentagon action, the Women for a Meaningful Summit protest, and others. The disengaging actions of these feminist peace groups soon began to influence many of the organizational structures and actions of local WILPF branches, at least in the United States. For example, in the mid 1980s, influenced by experimentation with other nonhierarchical organizational forms by women in other peace groups (e.g., Greenham Common), an article in the U.S. section's magazine, *Peace and Freedom,* noted the problem of feminist versus hierarchical leadership structures and gave examples of various models that local branches were using to create shared leadership and decision-making practices (Bowring-Trenn 1986, 14–15).

Local WILPF branches can be organized in a variety of ways, but all seek to find public spaces to work for peace. As with the national sections, the local branches have the flexibility to translate the international mission and address local issues of militarism, violence, and social justice in locally meaningful ways. In the United States, local branches typically hold meetings in public spaces, such as local libraries, community centers, church or town halls, and restaurants, although occasionally members' homes are used for meetings. Some local branches in the United States engage in more "respectable" or mainstream actions such as organizing letter writing campaigns to lawmakers; sponsoring discussions, speakers forums, and meetings with elected officials; and holding annual "Ways to Peace" essay-writing contests for school children. Others are engaged in more daring and creative disengaging actions. Among the more interesting examples, U.S. branches' activities at the local level in recent years have included:

- holding weekly peace vigils lasting for years at museums, post offices, and military contractors' plants
- creating a peace park at a county war memorial
- organizing an adopt-a-polluter pen pal correspondence with CEOs of polluting companies
- wearing "Schools Not Bombs" tee-shirts to a military base open house—and being thrown off the base
- helping to build a school in a Nicaraguan sister city
- painting shadows on sidewalks and holding paper lantern ceremonies on Hiroshima Day
- picketing war movies
- staging street theater
- preventing local police from being sent to train police forces in Central America
- creating the Clothesline Project (Cape Cod branch)
- sponsoring "I Don't Buy It" local radio commercials protesting federal budget priorities
- holding sit-ins in government offices
- running a "Swords into Plowshares" float in a local parade

- getting a nuclear-free-zone declaration on the local ballot
- organizing a Mother's Day protest at a Nevada nuclear test site
- having children place their colorful handprints atop a poster depicting bombs to blot them out
- networking and working with other local peace and justice groups on a variety of local projects

This range of campaigns and actions by the U.S. section and its branches in the 1980s and 1990s shows both mainstreaming and disengaging characteristics found in other women's or feminist organizations. It also shows that while WILPF's primary focus is antimilitarist, the organization also continues to devote a great deal of energy to other "positive peace" activities (antiracism, economic justice, etc.). These campaigns and actions may not receive the focused national media attention of more radical feminist peace actions like the Greenham Common or Seneca women's peace camps, but they do attract local media coverage and they demonstrate sustained and creative—and some-times humorous—local challenges to some of the core values of militarism rooted in the patriarchal state. These disengaging strategies also demonstrate WILPF's flexibility and openness to more radical grassroots feminist influ-ences that keep the organization alive and vital.

WILPF's Contemporary Discourse

WILPF's contemporary discourse also includes both mainstreaming and dis-engaging women's voices that resonate with its international membership. The organization's multitiered structure produces literature intended to mobilize members in relevant ways towards peace activism. Yet Foster (1989, 115) notes that WILPF has been reluctant to embrace the discourse and agenda of second- and third-wave feminism, particularly in its European and Third World sec-tions. Issues such as reproductive rights, sexual politics, and identity politics have not been at the forefront of WILPF's agenda, which may contribute to per-ceptions among some more radical feminist activists that WILPF is too conser-vative or mainstream in its approach. This is ironic, given WILPF's early con-nections between women's suffrage (first-wave feminism) and peace activism. Such perceptions overlook the fact that WILPF assumes that women are signif-icant political actors whose agency can and should be mobilized to challenge militarism and violence and to work on positive peace issues.

For example, a content analysis of the U.S. section's magazine *Peace and Freedom* from 1984 to 1996 reveals that the discourse used in the magazine's articles is decidedly antimilitarist, but the terms "patriarchy" and "feminism" were rarely used until after 1990. Yet for the entire period its articles are replete with empowering language stressing women's agency, solidarity, and empathy. A recurrent theme in most articles is "can-doism." From articles focusing on the work of a specific woman peace activist or a group of such women to more general articles about a peace issue with concluding tips on "What You Can Do," the message is almost always upbeat and empowering. Of course, the magazine's purpose is to inform and mobilize its members, but it does so in a way that can only be termed feminist.

It is also significant that the WILPF literature under consideration almost never resorts to essentialist arguments. Women are urged to organize peace actions not because they are "naturally" disposed to peace or to be life-givers but because they are political actors in a war system that hurts everybody, including women, and everything, including the earth. Occasionally one finds an article focusing on the issue of war toys or peace education for children in which a woman's role as mother is invoked, but maternalist arguments and language are avoided. This suggests that the maternalist arguments common a century ago are not relevant to WILPF's U.S. membership. Rather, the antimilitarist discourse most common in the WILPF literature under consideration is materialist in nature, reflecting old and New Left analyses of the links between militarism, capitalism, economic oppression, social inequality, and more recently environmental degradation. Yet even this materialist discourse is changing as a more explicitly feminist perspective has begun to inflect the language used by WILPF.

In 1992, outgoing Program Director Jerilyn Bowen urged U.S. WILPF to focus on larger "proactive programs that bring our priority issues together from a feminist perspective, programs designed to make the connections in a way no one else is doing" (Bowen 1992, 26). This view reflects not only a change within WILPF but also a changed international context, with the collapse of the Soviet Union and the end of the Cold War, the dismantling of Euromissiles, an uneasy peace in Central America, and talk of a "new world order." In responding to these changes, WILPF has continued to look for new ways to carry out its mission and engage its declining membership. WILPF's more recent attention to domestic violence and violence against women as part of its larger antimilitarist mission is a good example. Another is WILPF's 1992–1995 campaign to get citizen signatures in the United States and Latin America to its Women's Peace and Justice Treaty of the Americas, which sought to educate and link women across the Americas on such issues as women's economic exploitation, indigenous women's struggles, various forms of violence against women, and onerous international trade and debt structures.

These examples demonstrate that WILPF's discourse and the issues discussed in its literature are relevant to its changing membership and reflect the new peace issues (e.g., racism and violence against women and the environment) its members bring to WILPF's agenda. Together with its mainstreaming and disengaging political strategies, WILPF continues to tie the local to the global levels and mobilizes women in focused and dynamic ways. While the broader women's peace movement of the 1980s has lost its focus and energy and has largely disappeared, WILPF's formal organizational structure allows it to adapt to new times.

Organizing Women

Thanks to the recent work of feminist historians, we know that an important number of women's peace organizations have participated in peace movements in the modern era, from the Olive Leaf Circles in the mid 19th century to the No More War Movement after World War I; from Women Strike for Peace in the early 1960s to the women's antinuclear and antiwar movements in the 1980s. But few women's peace organizations and the movements they helped shape have been able to escape the cyclical or generational limits marked by a particular war or militarization campaign; instead, they end up fading into the past. While grassroots peace groups have been important in mobilizing and politicizing women who, thus empowered, have often moved on to other political work, they have not been able to sustain their direct challenge to the war system.

In the 1980s, the Greenham Common women were especially important in invigorating the peace movement and incorporating more radical feminist politics into their opposition to the war system. For over a decade the Greenham Common women successfully experimented with nonhierarchical models of organization and disengaging political strategies (see Roseneil 1995). Moreover, they invented powerful and sometimes humorous images that challenged—indeed, mocked—the militarist values of the war system. The placement of a determined feminist peace camp outside a U.S. Air Force base in England was a significant and daring step for a women's peace group. The Greenham women's more specific protests—like the Embrace the Base action, weaving webs of yarn through the fence surrounding the base, cutting the fence and running or singing and dancing inside the base, holding picnics atop missile silos, or painting peace slogans on aircraft, among other nonviolent actions—created powerful feminist peace symbols, even if many observers did not get the joke.[6] The Greenham peace camp enjoyed support from around the world and inspired women in many other countries, including WILPF members, to reconnect feminism and antimilitarism in new ways, to experiment with new forms of organization,[7] and to undertake similarly daring symbolic actions for peace.

Yet, because they eschewed a more formal organizational structure, the waves of Greenham Common women who visited or lived at the camp have now faded into memory, along with other women's peace groups of the 1980s. Like the Olive Leaf Circle women almost 150 years ago, such groups have succumbed to the cyclical or generational limitations of most peace movements. Despite their powerful and important contributions, such groups are inherently limited in time, place, and focus, while the patriarchal state and its war system continue to exist. Without more formal organizational structures that reach from the local to the international levels, such women's peace groups will only echo the binary logic of the war system. Without enduring organizational structures that can sustain their challenge to militarism and war through both mainstreaming and disengaging strategies, such peace groups can only react to the war system rather than transform it.

WILPF's experience demonstrates that women's peace politics can move beyond such limited or ad hoc forms of organization. WILPF is an important example of a women's international peace organization that combines the characteristics of mainstreaming and disengaging feminist organizations, both of which are necessary to have an effective political impact in the world. WILPF has not been immune to problems over the years, such as doctrinal debates (e.g., over the meaning of nonviolence), red-baiting, bureaucracy, limited diversity, multiple missions, declining and aging membership, and burnout, among others. Moreover, its fluctuating membership over the years has reflected the rise and demise of peace movements more generally. Nevertheless, it has outlived other peace organizations and movements while opening spaces for and connecting women's peace activism at the local, national, and international levels in flexible and effective ways.

The patriarchal state and its war system operate at the personal, local, national, and international levels. WILPF's example demonstrates that women's peace organizations can match these layers of political organization through a more formal structure that will last and be effective. Moreover, WILPF's experience shows that both mainstreaming and disengaging political strategies can be combined in one organizational model. WILPF's structure is not the only model, but it is an important one for other women's groups and movements to consider as they work to destabilize global patriarchy, improve women's status worldwide, and implement the positive peace objectives found in the Platform for Action of the Beijing conference. WILPF shows that to be all we can be, women must mobilize *and* organize for peace.

Notes

I wish to thank Ann Lyons, Director, and many others at the Women's Studies Centre at the National University of Ireland, Galway, for generously sharing their wonderful space, support, ideas, and encouragement during my sabbatical leave in spring 1997, which made revising and finishing this work possible.

1. In France alone, there were at least four pre–World War I era women's peace societies: L'Union Internationale des Femmes, La Ligue des Femmes pour le Désarmament, L'Alliance des Femmes pour la Paix, and La Société d'Education Pacifique. These became models for women's peace societies elsewhere.

2. One cannot help but wonder whether Wilson's idea for the League of Nations was entirely his own or whether it sprang from the Hague congress's proposals.

3. For a discussion of the terms "negative peace" and "positive peace" as used in the peace studies field, see Elias and Turpin 1994, 4.

4. See, e.g., in the Beijing conference's Platform for Action: Chapter IV, Section E, "Women and Armed Conflict," and Strategic Objective E.2., "Reduce excessive military expenditures and control the availability of armaments" (United Nations 1995a, 62 ff). See also Chapter VI, "Financial Arrangements," Section A, paragraph 349: "To facilitate the implementation of the Platform for Action, Governments should reduce, as appropriate, excessive military expenditures and investments for arms production and acquisition, consistent with national security requirements" (United Nations 1995a, 131).

5. This figure is down from an estimated thirty thousand members during the 1980s. The current membership campaign seeks to attract twenty thousand new members over five years, targeting college campuses as well as minority women to reinvigorate and diversify the organization with a new generation of women. To do so, WILPF has included program missions relevant to such women (e.g., fighting racism and more recently, domestic violence). The median age of the U.S. membership is currently in the late fifties (Clement 1996; Moore 1996).

6. Thomas R. Rochon (1988) totally missed the point in his discussion of the Greenham Common peace camp and related actions. He found such symbolic actions to be "too obscure for popular consumption" and "based on rather poor puns" (Rochon 1988, 111–20). Citing one survey from April 1983, he asserts that the camp did not win public approval, but he fails to analyze the gender breakdown of the respondents.

7. Other women's peace camps experimenting with nonhierarchical forms of organization (e.g., the Seneca Falls Women's Encampment) could not match Greenham's success (see Linton 1989).

8

International Women's Activism
and the 1994 Cairo Population Conference

Amy J. Higer

The international women's health movement (IWHM) emerged during the 1970s and 1980s. It began as a loose network of radical feminist activists based in the United States and grew into a global movement of women around the world sharing strategies, analyses, and information. The IWHM today is a complex configuration of formal organizations, informal networks, and individual activists.[1] It organized initially to challenge the safety of the birth control pill and other modern contraceptive methods. As the movement expanded, its agenda broadened to include issues of concern to women in Southern as well as Northern countries, including unethical marketing of Western products (e.g., infant formula), female genital mutilation, and coercive population control programs.

From its earliest days, women's health activists denounced what they viewed as the instrumental use of women in international population control policies (Hartmann 1987). Population control programs, they argued, paid too little attention to other aspects of health, even closely related ones such as sexually transmitted diseases and gynecological problems. Such programs also favored contraceptive methods that were likely to stress "effectiveness" over safety and to pose greater health risks for women (Dixon-Mueller 1993, 43). At the core of the critique was the contention that population policies justified risking the health and violating the rights of individual women for "the good of mankind" (Grant 1992, 72). Foreign-funded population programs were seen as especially problematic, in part because the programs' primary "targets," Third World women, had no voice in the policy process (Jaquette and Staudt 1988, 215). International population policies have played a major role in galvanizing women's health activism across international borders. By the end of the 1970s, resistance to population control policies had become one of the IWHM's solidifying issues and a major focus of its transnational networking.

122

Until recently, policymakers showed little awareness of, or interest in, the implications of population policies for women's lives. Planners and researchers were more concerned with the effects of population growth on economic development, environmental degradation, food supplies, and other macro-level phenomena. As a result, women's concerns remained peripheral to policy debates, both at the national and international levels.

This situation changed dramatically in the 1990s. Women's perspectives moved to the center of the policy debate and the IWHM became a visible player in international population policy. Nowhere was this change more evident than at the 1994 International Conference on Population and Development held in Cairo. The preeminence of women's issues was, by all accounts, the hallmark of the Cairo conference. Cairo's World Programme of Action formulated a new definition of population policy that emphasized the empowerment of women and downplayed the demographic rationale. It also articulated a broadened concept of family planning that placed such programs within a larger context of comprehensive reproductive health services (McIntosh and Finkle 1995, 223). The Cairo conference indeed has come to symbolize a women-centered approach to population policy. Many observers attributed this shift in emphasis to the influence of women's health activists (e.g., Cohen and Richards 1994, 233; Crane and Isaacs 1995; McIntosh and Finkle 1995, 235–39; and Sen 1994). Although the UN had held two international population conferences prior to Cairo (in Bucharest in 1974 and Mexico City in 1984), Cairo marked the first time that women's health activists made such a conference an explicit target.

In this chapter, I analyze the IWHM's internal political dynamics as it organized to shape the outcome of the 1994 Cairo conference. The following questions are addressed: Why did women's health activists select Cairo as a target of activism? What strategies and tactics did they employ to influence the conference? What kinds of debates and tensions emerged among activists during the conference process? What were the movement's goals and to what extent was it successful in achieving them? In a broader sense, this chapter asks: How does a transnational women's movement organize itself to effect change in a specific issue area? By examining the IWHM's internal evolution and dynamics, this analysis allows us to see not only the increased participation of feminist activists in UN conferences but also the movement's growing sophistication as a transnational lobbying force. The IWHM's strategies at Cairo call our attention to the things that feminists have learned over the years about UN population conferences and international organizing.

I argue that the Cairo conference illustrated both the strengths and the weaknesses of the IWHM as a transnational actor. In a positive sense, it challenged activists to advance a common agenda and strategy, develop internal processes of communication and dialogue, and build consensus and consensus mechanisms. In so doing, the movement achieved newfound power in international deliberations, stemming from its ability to disseminate new norms and language that shaped people's understandings. The IWHM's unity of purpose at Cairo, however, concealed deep philosophical and strategic divisions within the movement. These divisions became increasingly evident in the conference's aftermath. I argue that these fissures may impede the movement's political effectiveness in the future.

This chapter has four sections. First, I describe the IWHM's origins and its agenda for population policy in its early years. Second, I discuss the emergence in the 1980s of a pragmatic faction within the movement and its new policy-centered agenda. Third, I describe the movement's organizing strategies for Cairo. And fourth, I examine the ways in which participation in the Cairo process affected the internal politics of the IWHM. This final section also raises some questions about the movement's future prospects as an agent of change in the population field.

The International Women's Health Movement's Agenda in Population Policy

The Historical Context

The roots of present-day tensions among women's health activists with regard to population control policies can be seen in the early politics of the modern birth control movement. This movement began in the nineteenth century when women's rights advocates raised the demand for "voluntary motherhood" and soon split into radical and reformist factions (see Reed 1978; and Gordon 1983). The radicals sought to transform the socioeconomic order, while the reformers, led by Margaret Sanger, pursued narrower goals of disseminating prohibited birth control information and technology within the existing social structure. It was the reformist faction, under the banner of "family planning," that came to dominate the movement. In some analysts' view, by electing to pursue the short-term goal of establishing family planning clinics over long-term socioeconomic change, reformers thwarted the movement's radical potential for achieving reproductive rights and sexual equality (Fee and Wallace 1979, 205; and Sharpless 1995, 77). Thus, almost since its inception, the birth control movement was split between those who sought radical change in society and those who took a more pragmatic approach. I will suggest that a similar tension between "radical outsiders" and "pragmatic insiders" animates the current IWHM.

As is well known, in the early birth control movement the reformist faction decided to ally itself with the eugenics movement in order to broaden the appeal of birth control (Fee and Wallace 1979).[2] Reformers such as Sanger found political utility in racially motivated arguments for limiting birthrates among the poor. When eugenics ideology fell into disrepute in the wake of Nazi atrocities, both eugenics and birth control advocates found a welcome new ally in the burgeoning field of international population control, whose major proponents were American philanthropists and moneyed elites (Hodgson 1991, 6; Gordon 1983, 390). The institutional and ideological links between the birth control, eugenics, and population control movements left a legacy of distrust among many feminists (Davis 1990, 15). The racial aspects of population politics led to a furor over birth control in communities of color in the United States in the 1960s, culminating in charges by some African American leaders that family planning programs amounted to advocacy of black genocide (Joffe 1986, 23; Ross 1994). These protests against racist-tinged birth control policies presaged the women's health critique of global population control policies.

The history of the birth control movement is relevant for two reasons: first, it shows why feminists remain deeply skeptical of the motivations and objectives of those who advocate birth control on a mass scale; and second, it suggests that contemporary debates and tensions within the IWHM over the issue of population control have deep historical roots.

The Emergence of the International Women's Health Movement, 1970–1985

Although international population policies would seem to be a logical target for feminists, during the late 1960s and early 1970s the mainstream women's movement in the West did not organize against them (Jaquette and Staudt 1988, 214). Throughout this early period, most liberal feminists assumed that the goals of the women's movement and the global campaign to slow population growth were compatible. To them, having fewer children could do for Third World women what it had done for women in the industrialized world: improve women's health, extend female life expectancy, give women more time and energy to invest in children already born, and enable them to seek employment outside the home (220). In the beginning, the most formidable opposition to foreign assistance for population programs came from leftist critics in the Third World and from the burgeoning women's health movement in the West.

The women's health movement grew out of the surge of progressive movements in the late 1960s and 1970s. Women around the United States, mostly white and middle-class, formed small consciousness-raising groups to discuss formerly "taboo" subjects, such as sexuality, treatment by male gynecologists, and personal experiences with contraceptives and abortion (still illegal in most states) (Ruzek 1978). Catalyzing the movement's formation was the 1969 best-selling book by Barbara Seaman, *The Doctor's Case against the Pill,* one of the first publications to report on the dangers of oral contraceptives (Seaman 1969). The movement challenged what it perceived to be the foundations of Western medicine: profit-driven health care, controlled by providers in collaboration with pharmaceutical companies, and virtually unaccountable to consumers. It demanded more consumer knowledge, more alternatives to mainstream medical care, development of technologies that gave women more control, and the right of women to speak for themselves in health policy deliberations (Fee 1983, 26). The movement also called attention to race and class issues by emphasizing the ways in which women of color and poor women were treated unfairly by the health care industry.

The movement's rapid globalization in the 1970s was the result of several factors. First, a series of contraceptive method scandals alerted activists to the international dimensions of issues of contraceptive safety. U.S. feminists were outraged upon learning that Western-developed contraceptives, such as the Dalkon Shield IUD (a product that had been banned from Western markets), were being tested and marketed by international family planning and population organizations in dozens of countries around the world. Revelations about the "dumping" of unsafe contraceptives in the Third World "sent shock waves throughout the feminist community" (Jaquette and Staudt 1988, 221). Despite knowledge of the grave dangers these methods posed to women's health, little effort was made to inform women about them (Grant 1992, 151). Activists saw a need not only to share information about birth control technologies but also to collect and disseminate their own data, culled directly from women's experiences, rather than from studies commissioned by drug companies and the scientific community. As a result, global information-sharing networks proliferated (Isis International 1978).

A second impetus behind global expansion was mounting evidence of human rights abuses, including forced sterilization, in population control programs in Bangladesh, India, and Colombia. This evidence brought home to Northern feminists the coercive aspects of international population policies. That many Third World population control programs were funded by Western governments, with foreign aid often tied to the introduction of national population policies, only fueled feminist organizing and protest (Mass 1976).

Constituting a third galvanizing force were United Nations–sponsored events, including the two UN Development Decade (1960–1970; 1970–1980) and the UN Decade for Women (1975–1985). Both processes served to boost women's activism worldwide (and particularly in Southern countries) by facilitating linkages between women's health groups at the regional and local levels and by educating women about the workings of the UN process.

A final catalyst to global expansion was a series of international meetings that activists themselves have organized since 1977. These triennial International Women and Health Meetings were conceived as an alternative forum to UN women's conferences, where women could come together to focus on health problems ignored by governments, international agencies, and family planning programs (Isis International 1978). Initially dominated by Northern activists, the meetings grew more inclusive and diverse in the 1980s. The regularity of these meetings has helped facilitate and sustain women's health networking across borders.

The IWHM's early years were ones of internal consciousness-raising, mobilizing outside traditional policy channels, forging international linkages, and learning about the opportunities and constraints of pursuing change through institutional channels. The movement achieved some success in its campaign against international population control; by the early 1980s, the issue of contraceptive safety had become highly politicized, and the consciousness of perhaps millions of women about the potential dangers of contraceptives had been raised. The consciousness-raising activities of the early movement paved the way for subsequent activism, both by identifying the central issues for the movement and by conditioning the political environment for change (Spalter-Roth and Schreiber 1995, 112). The feminist critique of population control, for example, suggested to at least some population planners that policies that ignored women's priorities and concerns could undermine their own objective of slowing birthrates in developing countries (Hodgson and Watkins 1996).

In spite of these accomplishments, however, early activists did not have palpable effects on policy. This failure stemmed in part from the movement's use of outsider mobilization tactics and its refusal to work within a population policy framework. The IWHM participated only informally in the first two UN-sponsored international population conferences (1974 and 1984) and did not organize itself to influence the official proceedings. In the mid-1980s, however, this strategy began to change. Inside the movement, an internal faction of activists emerged to pursue a more accommodationist stance toward the population establishment. These "pragmatists" directed their energies at establishing a dialogue with population groups and began to assemble what would become the women's lobby for the Cairo conference.

The Emergence of IWHM Pragmatists, 1985–1992

The Political Context

Changes in the policy context in the 1980s had significant effects on the IWHM. Most of these changes stemmed from the right-wing assault on international family planning programs and abortion rights during twelve years of Republican rule in the United States. The Reagan administration's abrupt policy reversal on population, announced at the 1984 UN international population conference in Mexico City, symbolized this shift. Pushed by conservative domestic forces, the Reagan administration declared that it no longer considered population growth to be detrimental to economic development. Further, it argued, developing countries experiencing high population growth rates could reduce fertility by relinquishing government control of economies and adhering to free-market principles (United States of America 1984). The new policy also had an antiabortion clause that outlawed U.S. government funding of international family planning agencies that provided abortions, even if these services were not directly funded with American dollars. The following year, this "Mexico City policy" led to a cutoff in U.S. funds for the two largest international family planning organizations, the International Planned Parenthood Federation and the UN Population Fund.

The Mexico City policy changed the policy environment in several unintended ways. First, it shifted the distribution of power in the population field away from the United States. With power more widely dispersed across governments and multilateral institutions, the points of access for outside interest groups increased. Second, the policy helped to shatter the political consensus on population by challenging orthodox views. In so doing, it highlighted the validity of other critiques of population programs, including feminist ones (Hodgson and Watkins 1996). For those seeking to preserve international family planning programs, the policy also created an incentive to invoke alternative justifications for family planning assistance. One such justification was "improving" women's health. For example, the U.S. Agency for International Development, the most influential donor in the population field, began during this time to emphasize the contribution family planning programs could make to improving maternal and child health.

Third, the policy created a tactical incentive for cooperation between U.S. feminists and population planners. The two sides had a mutual interest in maintaining women's access to birth control services and found a common enemy in the Reagan administration. This incentive for cooperation facilitated the efforts of IWHM pragmatists who sought to move in this direction (see, e.g., WHO/HRP and IWHC 1991). Further, during this period feminists muted their criticisms of population control policies, fearing that such criticisms would play into the hands of those who sought to eliminate international family programs altogether (Cohen 1993, 65).

Also new in the political environment of the 1980s was the fact that many population planners themselves had began to question the effectiveness of prevailing approaches to slowing world population growth (Hodgson and Watkins 1996). In their view, birthrates, although in decline, were not falling fast enough. Feminist critiques of population programs in this way offered some promising new ideas for a field in search of new policy approaches and rationales.

For all of these reasons, many women's health activists saw the late 1980s as an opportune time to push population policy in a new direction. Working in collaboration with a network of feminists inside population agencies and private foundations, movement pragmatists began to articulate the intellectual foundations for a "women-centered" population policy oriented around women's reproductive health. This reproductive health approach would emphasize improving the quality of care in international family planning programs and promote a user's perspective on services (Germain 1987; Ford Foundation 1991). The approach would form the basis for the lobbying strategy that feminists would use throughout the Cairo process. The pragmatist effort was spearheaded by a New York–based group, the International Women's Health Coalition (IWHC). It is notable that IWHC's two leaders were women who had worked in the population field.

Meanwhile, a series of major UN international conferences in the early 1990s provided IWHM pragmatists with both a focus and a catalyst for action. These conferences addressed the environment (1992), human rights (1993), population (1994), social development (1995), and women (1995). They followed upon the 1985 UN Women's Conference in Nairobi, the largest-ever gathering of women worldwide up to that time. This cluster of conferences sparked an extraordinary mobilization of women's groups across borders, aided by an increased flow of resources into the movement by private foundations. In a tangible sense, the UN conferences gave women something to organize around, as well as an opportunity to learn the intricacies of the UN conference process. The 1992 environmental conference, UNCED, was a particularly valuable learning experience for feminists. UNCED marked the inauguration of a new feminist strategy to make major UN conferences a target of activism.

The Evolution of the Pragmatist Strategy

The period between the end of the UN Women's Decade in 1985 and UNCED in 1992 was one of intense activity for women's NGOs, particularly those engaged in international environmental politics. Feminist interest in this area stemmed in part from a long-standing concern with the environment. It also resulted from fears about the resurgence of neo-Malthusian arguments coming from some parts of the environmental lobby (Bretherton 1996, 100). A number of feminists formed new organizations specifically to address the role of gender in global environmental politics. Among these were the Committee on Women, Population and the Environment (CWPE), and the Women's Environment and Development Organization (WEDO). CWPE and WEDO represent two ends of the spectrum in terms of feminist approaches to international organizing.

CWPE, composed of feminists in the women's health and environmental movements, advocates a radical outsider position that recalls the IWHM's early years. Its agenda offers a useful synopsis of the feminist outsider stance on international population policy. CWPE calls for a reconfiguration of the international policy agenda to include global demilitarization, redistribution of wealth between and within nations, reduction of consumption rates in developed countries, and an end to structural adjustment programs. It rejects the argument that population growth is a primary cause of environmental degradation and stresses the interrelated causes of environmental problems (Committee on Women, Population and the Environment 1992). CWPE is primarily a consciousness-raising and networking group; it does not seek to engage directly in the policy process or to influence UN conferences. Because it has not oriented its own agenda and activities around UN conferences, CWPE, like other IWHM outsider groups, has been able to advocate an alternative policy framework that is not tied to existing institutional arrangements or priorities. For example, it rejects the institutional separation of family planning from primary health care, and environmental degradation from global consumption patterns.

Established around the same time, WEDO, unlike CWPE, was founded with the explicit purpose of putting women's issues on the UN agenda.[3] Although its own agenda does not differ significantly from CWPE's, WEDO's approach to international organizing does. It aims to expand women's access to the UN process by creating an international network of women's activists to pressure governments to adopt policies that advance women's interests. WEDO has been the primary sponsor of the Women's Caucus, an innovative lobbying strategy that has vastly increased the participation of nongovernmental organizations (NGOs) at recent UN conferences. By most accounts, WEDO has been extraordinarily successful; its organizing work has changed fundamentally the process through which NGO interests are represented in UN conferences. Its strategy of simultaneously mobilizing women outside official processes (e.g., by disseminating insider information to women's networks and by producing independent data on relevant issues) and coordinating lobbying efforts inside organizations has set the precedent for women's participation in UN conferences in the 1990s. Thus, whereas CWPE's outsider approach has enabled it to articulate an alternative policy framework to existing international institutions, WEDO's insider approach has allowed it to become a highly visible player at the policy table. WEDO made its debut during the UNCED process.

UNCED brought two new actors into the population debate: the Vatican and its allies, on the one hand, and the environmental movement, on the other. The arrival of both sets of actors would influence the IWHM's strategies in important ways. Antiabortion and fundamentalist forces, led by the Vatican, posed an obvious threat to women's reproductive rights and access to family planning. At the same time, however, a burgeoning alliance between population control and environment groups signified a potential resurgence of aggressive population control policies (Sen 1994). It became clear that feminists would need to articulate a distinctive position on population—that is, one that affirmed the right to family planning while at the same time criticizing the approaches and methods of existing population policies and programs (Sen 1995, 14).

It was during this period that movement pragmatists decided to endorse, at least implicitly, the demographic rationale as a foundation for family planning programs (McIntosh and Finkle 1995, 254 n. 23). By seeking to accommodate, rather than repudiate, population organizations, pragmatists looked to the sources of money and institutional resources for women's health. Thus activist Carmen Barroso could argue in 1990 that the existence of a demographic goal is immaterial, provided that program content is consonant with feminist objectives of freedom of choice and women's reproductive health (Finkle and McIntosh 1994, 25). Even more striking was activist Marge Berer's contention in a 1991 article that some cite as a turning point for the movement in terms of its population strategy. Berer argued that feminists must confront the joint realities that, just as an individual woman cannot sustain an unlimited number of pregnancies, the world cannot sustain an unlimited number of people (Berer 1991). Berer cautioned activists to either develop the concept of a "feminist population policy" or risk being isolated and ignored in the international debate. Not surprisingly, her article elicited sharp criticism from movement radicals.

In the end, UNCED exposed the emerging divisions within the IWHM over both strategies and priorities. Although feminists agreed on many goals (e.g., informed choice, access to safe contraceptives, the need to decriminalize abortion), they were deeply divided over the strategy of advancing women's rights through a population framework. For pragmatists, the Cairo conference offered a timely opportunity to further a key feminist goal: the right to control one's own sexuality and reproduction. For radicals, by contrast, the conference's population focus remained inherently problematic: given that governments would not consider dismantling population programs, the best they could hope for would be to soften some of these programs' most egregious abuses (Corral 1996, 17). The movement would expend considerable energy negotiating this internal tension as it prepared for Cairo.

The Cairo Conference, 1992–1994

The IWHM's Strategies for Cairo

Women's health activists were intensely engaged in virtually all aspects of the Cairo conference. Since the last UN population conference in Mexico City in 1984, feminists had become seasoned participants in UN intergovernmental conferences and had come to see them as a promising arena in which to expand their political access. Equally important, the IWHM also had benefited over the previous decade from an increased flow of resources from private liberal foundations seeking to counter the political ascendancy of the New Right (Barroso 1992). With this sudden influx of funds, transnational women's health networks could for the first time expend a sizable portion of their scarce resources on international organizing (Swenson 1994). It is notable, however, that while many women's health groups were beneficiaries, those that endorsed the pragmatist agenda received the lion's share of this new funding. Also new was that feminists now occupied positions of power in both population agencies and policy institutions. In short, for Cairo, the IWHM had greater financial resources and more points of access to the policy process than ever before.

Activists engaged in a wide range of activities to prepare for Cairo, from networking in their own countries to planning regional conferences to publishing books on women and population policy (e.g., Correa 1994; Dixon-Mueller 1993; Sen, Germain, and Chen, 1994). Two activities—the circulation of a "women's declaration" on population policy and the convening of an international conference—were especially important to the movement's organizing strategy. They also highlighted some of the tensions that were developing inside the movement.

In September 1992, a small group of women's activists met in London to evaluate UNCED's implications for feminist strategizing for Cairo (Correa et al.1994). The London group, led by IWHC, formed the Women's Alliance, made up initially of the nineteen activists in attendance. The alliance elected to pursue an insider strategy to influence the Cairo proceedings. Activists described the strategy in this way: "While there is substantial debate in the women's movement about population policies, and among Alliance members, the Alliance is specifically working within a framework of population policies in order to affect the outcome of [Cairo]. This is a deliberate strategy aimed to achieve concrete outcomes in the limited time frame set by ICPD" (Correa et al.1994). The Women's Alliance was formed at a propitious moment. Although the first preparatory meeting—or "prepcom"—for Cairo had already taken place, the bulk of the Draft Plan of Action had yet to be written. The alliance initiated two activities in preparing for Cairo. The first was a document called "Women's Voices '94: Women's Declaration on Population Policies," and the second was planning for an international women's health conference.

The "Women's Voices" declaration attracted significant attention in the population field in early 1993. Perhaps for this reason it became a point of controversy within the IWHM. Critics of the declaration objected to both the process by which it was written and its content. The alliance that drafted the declaration was dominated by movement pragmatists, many of whom were more closely identified with the policy world than with grassroots organizing. Some radicals suspected that the alliance's initial exclusivity reflected pragmatists' intention to distance themselves from radical views in order to gain credibility at the policy table.[4] "Women's Voices" in this sense became a symbol for radicals of the growing elitism of policy-focused groups. "Women's Voices" was even more controversial for implicitly accepting and, some charged, legitimizing, the population framework. It stated:

> We call for a fundamental revision in the design, structure and implementation of population policies to foster the empowerment and well-being of all women. . . . Population policies that are responsive to women's needs and rights must be grounded in . . . internationally accepted, but too often ignored, ethical principles. ("Women's Declaration on Population Policies," in Sen, Germain, and Chen 1994, 32)

Population groups endorsed the declaration, which provided ample evidence for radicals of how easily the movement could be co-opted by population interests if its strategy affirmed the population framework.

In retrospect, however, what is most interesting about "Women's Voices" is that it garnered the support of some radical groups. These groups felt that only by presenting a united front would feminists have their views taken into account at all by policymakers. They also believed that it was necessary to join the alliance so that their ideas would be included in the debate (WGNRR 1993). In essence, as one activist put it, "we cannot afford not to be involved" (Keysers 1994). Radicals' support for the Women's Alliance revealed the movement's changing perception of both its own potential power and the new

opportunities open to it in formal politics, specifically in UN global conferences. Still, movement radicals who endorsed the insider approach explicitly
lent their support only in the context of the Cairo conference. In other words,
while recognizing the advantages to be gained from presenting a united front
in negotiations, radicals remained ambivalent about pursuing change within
the existing policy framework.

The internal tensions generated by the Women's Alliance carried over to
other activities during this period. However, rather than further dividing the
movement, these events ultimately had a salutary effect in terms of strengthening the movement's unity of purpose and building cohesion for Cairo. Difficult issues were aired and debated, a dialogue was established among different factions inside the movement, and a minimal basis for a political
consensus was reached (Shallat 1993, 52–56). Although the issues were not
resolved, the agreement to present a united front in the Cairo process helped
keep disagreements within the confines of the movement, at least until the
conference was over.

The most important event in terms of negotiating internal tensions was the
Reproductive Health and Justice Conference, held in Rio de Janeiro in 1993.
The meeting's objective was to solidify a feminist agenda and to develop
strategies for participation in Cairo (IWHC and CEPIA 1994). Because the
Vatican had successfully exploited feminist disunity at UNCED, an additional,
implicit goal of the meeting was to unite women from North and South on
reproductive rights and health issues (Chen 1995). The conference organizers
limited the number of participants in order to achieve the meeting's instrumental goals. The challenge was to keep the numbers down while seeming to be as
inclusive and representative as possible. Given the controversy over the exclusivity of the London meeting, organizers seemed especially sensitive to ensuring diversity of participants and giving women from Southern countries an
ample voice. By most accounts, this effort was successful, and "the strongest
voices came from women of color and women from Southern countries, with
Northern women assuming a lower profile." Indeed, a major topic of discussion was process and accountability mechanisms within the movement (Yanco
and Canepa 1994).

During the five-day conference, activists drafted a twenty-one-point statement. This document was considerably broader in scope than "Women's Voices." In addition to encapsulating points of commonality among participants, it
also acknowledged points of difference. The drafting process involved all 218
women, working in four languages, in what was described by two participants
as "a most extraordinary editorial exercise," remarkable for its democratic participation and for building solidarity among diversity (Yanco and Canepa
1994). The statement began with an indictment of "inequitable development

models and strategies" for being "the underlying cause of growing poverty and marginalization of women, environmental degradation, growing numbers of migrants and refugees, and the rise of fundamentalism everywhere." It continued with an attack on existing arrangements in the international political economy, singling out structural adjustment programs in particular as a primary cause of a number of chronic social ills (Rio Statement 1994). Differences of opinion were noted on such issues as whether population policies could be made more democratic, women-centered, and integrated with health and development priorities, and whether all population policies were inherently harmful to women. Overall, the Rio Statement was regarded as more representative of the IWHM's political agenda than "Women's Voices." For this reason, the conference helped produce cohesion in the movement. This sense of solidarity was especially valuable for feminist lobbying efforts at the final prepcom for Cairo in April 1994.

The vehicle that feminists used to shape the proceedings at all three Cairo prepcoms was the Women's Caucus, organized by WEDO. The Women's Caucus functioned as the organizational hub for feminist activism at the NGO forum and was the largest NGO activist group at Cairo (McIntosh and Finkle 1995, 239). Because it was conceived to provide a channel through which activists could participate in, and influence, the intergovernmental meeting, the Women's Caucus embodied the pragmatist approach to international organizing, with both WEDO and IWHC playing influential roles. At the same time, what was most innovative about the Caucus was not simply that it helped activists gain access to the conference process but also that it worked to change the rules by which the process had, in the past, restricted NGO access. In other words, the Caucus not only learned the rules of the game but also learned which of those rules needed to be changed in order to increase the participation of women's NGOs.

The Caucus's main goal throughout the Cairo process was to lobby government delegations and persuade them to include language in the Draft Plan of Action that reflected feminist concerns. Every official delegate received a copy of the Women's Caucus Draft Revisions and Priorities to which delegates could refer in their negotiations. The Caucus used this tactic effectively to shape the formulation of the annotated outline for the final document (WEDO 1994). Like lawyers using precedent to argue their case, Caucus strategists drew upon language of past UN documents, including those from human rights and women's conferences, and made explicit that existing human rights apply to population policies and programs. As the Caucus itself put it, "it [was] not designed to either increase or decrease the scope of currently recognized rights" (Women's Caucus 1994). WEDO founder Bella Abzug described the Caucus as "a constant voice, a constant presence. Since many countries are lazy or ill-informed, they were happy to get our analysis." Before the activist Women's Caucus, NGOs that had UN consultative status were limited to presenting position papers and lobbying individuals. "A nice process," said Abzug, "but it didn't have much impact." Since UNCED, the Women's Caucus has become, in Abzug's words, a "semi-institution" at the UN, now supplied with photocopiers and faxes (Abzug 1995).

Women's health activists, working through and alongside the Women's Caucus, employed a number of other tactics to influence the Cairo process. They shared information with other advocacy networks; worked within their respective countries to influence the drafting of national position papers; produced useful data that might serve as the basis for a policy shift; and pursued an aggressive media strategy, issuing press releases and placing advertisements in major newspapers. IWHC and WEDO were particularly adroit at using the media to disseminate their message. According to Gita Sen (1994), it was "no accident" that news stories about Cairo often focused on the role of women in shaping the conference agenda.

The final crucial component of the Caucus's strategy was to keep the focus on reproductive health and rights and leave broader economic and social issues for other UN conferences. By setting aside other priorities, including those articulated by activists at the Rio conference, pragmatists hoped to maintain credibility as negotiators and maximize their chances for shaping the international agenda on reproductive rights.

At every step of the way, IWHM pragmatists dominated feminist organizing. They distanced themselves from radical views that they judged to have little chance of winning approval, worked intensively with sympathetic population insiders to find language that might be acceptable to both sides, and secured a significant number of places on national delegations. Most important, they endorsed the idea that population growth rates should be lowered and that their differences with population groups were over means and not ends.

Pragmatists benefited from a number of new developments in the surrounding policy context. It is significant, however, that many of these changes also resulted from pressure from women's groups. Perhaps most important was the unprecedented role that NGOs played at Cairo. As noted, prior to Cairo, only NGOs accredited by the UN Economic and Social Council (ECOSOC) could participate in the process.However, criticism of ECOSOC accreditation, largely from NGOs themselves, helped change the rules. The effect was to expand greatly the number of NGOs that could influence the process. Although there is wide variation among NGOs in terms of political interests, agendas, and political and economic power, it is significant that the vast majority of NGO representatives in Cairo were women. Seven of eleven members of the NGO steering committee were women, including prominent feminists from Southern countries (Correa et al.1994).

Also new was the increased number of NGO representatives on official delegations. This was due, at least in part, to feminist pressure. The Women's Caucus advocated redress of the situation in which "the overwhelming majority of NGO observers were women and the overwhelming majority of government delegates were men" (Correa et al.1994). As Gita Sen noted, the presence of women NGO representatives on government delegations was critical. "What was working at Cairo, and not recognized by governments at first, was that women inside and outside delegations, and women working across countries that traditionally do not speak to each other, were talking to each other." Highly secretive information was passed along in this way to the Women's Caucus. The Caucus, in turn, could strategize faster and produce well-thought-out, clear revisions to the draft. According to Sen, this increased women's credibility among official delegates, who were "astounded at what women knew." Since most delegates were not population experts, they were grateful for the immediate analyses and the language on matters being negotiated (Sen 1994).

Finally, pragmatist efforts were also aided by a change of U.S. policy following the election of Bill Clinton. Clinton's reversal of the Mexico City policy and his support for abortion rights helped create a more favorable climate for feminist activism. The Clinton administration also endorsed a platform that promoted a broader approach to population and development, an emphasis on women's empowerment, and a need to ensure access to high-quality family planning and reproductive health care (United States Mission 1993). All of these goals dovetailed with the feminist agenda. Moreover, the United States actively solicited the input of the NGO community, particularly women's groups. More than half the U.S. delegation's members were women's advocates, including several prominent women's health advocates (Sinding 1994). For all of these reasons, U.S.-based pragmatists saw new opportunities in the Clinton administration and effectively exploited this new access to policy elites in order to influence the emerging U.S. position on Cairo.

In sum, at Cairo, the IWHM was more organized, politically knowledgeable, and skillful than at any previous UN population conference. It also had more access, points of leverage, and representation with regard to the official conference. In the end, feminists had reason to be pleased with Cairo's outcome. The Plan of Action paid central attention to women's rights and reproductive health, and nearly every delegation head mentioned the role of women, women's empowerment, women's education, and women's rights as central to the purpose at hand (Bernstein 1994). For the first time at a major international

meeting, governments openly and extensively discussed formerly taboo subjects such as abortion, female circumcision, violence against women, and sexual health and rights. By the conference's end, delegates had reached a broad
consensus on the premise that economic development and population decline is
most effectively fostered by promoting women's rights (see, e.g., United
Nations 1994, principle 4). Implicit in this consensus was the pragmatist argument that once women become more empowered through education and the
ability to exercise their reproductive rights, they will opt to have fewer children
and population growth will slow. For these reasons, the Cairo conference must
be seen as a watershed event in the IWHM's decades-long effort to influence
population control policies.

For Cairo, the IWHM was able to strike a successful and workable balance
between goals within its capabilities, goals that sustained the unity of the
group (at least provisionally), and goals that were theoretically desirable (Willetts 1982, 141). A successful formula, however, is not necessarily an uncon-
tested one. Feminist cohesion masked considerable conflict over internal
process and external goals.

Cairo's Effects on the IWHM

As the conference drew to a close, the *Trinidad Guardian* reported on 12 September 1994 that some activists, frustrated with the narrow focus of the debate,
staged protests to denounce what they saw as the "blatant absence" of development in the discussions on the Draft Programme of Action. With banners
bearing slogans such as "Keep your aid, cancel our debt" and "Two cars per
family in the North, one child per family in the South," a sizable number of
women's activists, particularly from the South, demanded to know what happened to the "D" in ICPD. From their perspective, the most significant omission was the failure to address the detrimental effects of structural adjustment
programs and other internationally imposed debt-servicing schemes. Many
also opposed the way in which the issue of women's health was carved up into
discrete bureaucratic categories. To feminist dissenters, it made little sense to
isolate women's reproductive health from other health issues and from the
enabling environment for adequate health care.

Radicals and pragmatists therefore held different views on the meaning of
Cairo. This discrepancy is well illustrated in the following assessments by two
participants. On 14 September 1994, the *Los Angeles Times* quoted activist
Joan Dunlop as saying that the Cairo plan was "very close to everything we
hoped it would be; it's like 98 percent," while the Women's Global Network on
Reproductive Rights newsletter of July-September declared: "We find the

[Plan of Action] to be nothing but an insult to women, men and children of the South who will receive an ever-growing dose of population assistance, while issues of life and death will have to await the Social Development Summit of 1995 in Copenhagen." The question of who the "we" represents in these statements lies at the core of the problem.

The Cairo process served to amplify the voice of pragmatists while marginalizing the views of those who rejected the pragmatist agenda. One reason for this was structural. Over 90 percent of the language in the Cairo document was agreed upon before the conference even began. NGO access to the prepcoms was therefore critical. The NGO activists that attended three prepcoms, however, tended to be self-selected; they had sufficient resources, foreign sponsors, and/or sufficient knowledge of the UN conference process to know the strategic importance of these meetings. The result was that activists who attended the prepcoms and who were responsible for shaping the Women's Caucus's agenda tended to be a more elite group than both those who attended the conference itself and those representing the grass roots of the movement. Thus the IWHM at Cairo was characterized by far more diversity than it was at the Cairo prepcoms.[5] This suggests that, although the Women's Caucus is a promising innovation for feminist organizing at the UN, it has not overcome perennial difficulties for social movements over questions of representation— who speaks for whom in the policy debate, and whose voices are left out? When movement pragmatists chose to expend their energies and resources on international lobbying, and when they succeeded in winning a seat at the policy table, they confronted the vexing question of how to share power with those who remained on the outside.

On this score, they may have paid insufficient attention to the concerns of outside voices. The fact that pragmatists opted to focus their energies on gaining a foothold in the policy world and tailored the women's health agenda to satisfy institutional and policy needs may reflect a politically astute strategy in the face of considerable opposition. However, by not pushing on debt relief issues, despite the fact that economic issues and alternative models of development comprised the entire first seven points of the twenty-one-point Rio Declaration, they risked having alienated the very movement they claimed to represent. As a result, the post-Cairo period is likely to be one of increasing fragmentation and stratification of the movement.

The issue of movement cohesion is an important one. As John Kingdon has noted, cohesion is another resource that gives a group some advantage in affecting the agenda. If a group is plagued by internal dissension, its effectiveness is seriously impaired (Kingdon 1984, 52–53). Because their connection to formal politics is already tenuous, transnational movements rely even more heavily than other interest groups on resources such as cohesion in order to wield political influence. By paying insufficient attention to questions of how to share power with those who remained on the outside, pragmatist organizing tactics at Cairo, though successful in the short term, may have served over the long term to sharpen the distinctions between insiders and outsiders.

Conclusion

This chapter has examined the international women's health movement's efforts to shape population policies at the international level. By sketching the movement's origins and evolution and examining its role at the 1994 population conference in Cairo, it showed how the movement's activities and strategies have changed over the past two decades from outside mobilization tactics to inside lobbying. This change reflects a shift in the balance of power in the movement from "radical outsiders" to "pragmatic insiders."

The Cairo conference was the first time the IWHM organized on behalf of its own interests to influence the outcome of a UN population conference. Pragmatist insiders saw in Cairo an opportunity to advance a core goal: to redirect the existing flow of population resources in ways that would bring more benefits to more women. Radical outsiders remained skeptical about this accommodationist stance. At Cairo, the movement was able to close ranks and mobilize behind the common goal of shaping the conference's outcome. The movement's participation in the process, however, exacerbated internal tensions over both strategies and long-term goals.

By taking a historical approach and focusing on the internal dynamics of this movement, we gain insight into the nature of feminist organizing in international institutions. Two insights in particular are worth noting. First, at the level of international policymaking, UN conferences have become an important arena of feminist activism. Whereas women's health activists participated only informally in UN population conferences prior to Cairo, they made the 1994 conference a key target. Because conferences provide more points of access than other international institutions, women's health activists increasingly have expended their scarce resources on learning how to operate effectively in this arena. By employing a sophisticated and innovative set of tactics, feminists have used UN conferences to achieve some potentially meaningful reforms.

Participation in existing institutional arenas, however, has some pitfalls. A second insight gleaned from this analysis is that movements that elect to operate within a given institutional context must tailor their own agenda to suit institutional frameworks and needs. By choosing to work within the population policy framework to advance a women's health agenda, IWHM pragmatists had to repackage the movement's core ideas to fit the needs of policymakers. By so doing, they alienated many radicals, who saw their voice diminished and their priorities marginalized. The unity of purpose that activists achieved at Cairo gave way to fragmentation in the conference's aftermath. The movement's ability to wield influence in international institutions in the future is likely to depend upon its ability to negotiate internal tensions around issues of representation and democratic process. This task is even more crucial for the type of organizing that will be necessary to ensure that the recommendations of Cairo are translated into changed policies and practices on the ground.

Notes

1. Activists themselves frequently cite the following networks as comprising the movement: the Women's Global Network for Reproductive Rights (WGNRR), based in Amsterdam; Isis International, based in Manila and Santiago; Isis International Cross-Cultural Exchange, based in Kampala, Uganda; the Boston Women's Health Book Collective, based in Somerville, Massachusetts; the National Black Women's Health Project, based in Washington, D.C.; the International Women's Health Coalition, based in New York City; Development Alternatives for Women in a New Era (DAWN), based in Rio de Janeiro; Women Living under Muslim Laws; the Latin American and Caribbean Women's Health Network, based in Santiago; WAND, based in Barbados; Catholics for a Free Choice, based in Washington, D.C.; and FINRRAGE (Feminist International Network for Resistance to Reproductive and Genetic Engineering), based in Dhaka, Bangladesh.

2. The eugenics movement propagated an ideology in which economic and social inequalities were conceptualized and interpreted as fundamentally biological phenomena. Thus, the poor were rendered biologically unfit for anything but their impoverished condition.

3. WEDO was founded by former congresswoman Bella Abzug in connection with the Women USA Fund Inc., a nonprofit, educational organization in New York City, and the Women's Foreign Policy Council.

4. This comment is based on information provided to the author on the condition that the source not be revealed.

5. This observation about the composition of the Women's Caucus relies upon interviews with Caucus members.

9

Shaping the Human Rights Agenda:
The Case of Violence against Women

Jutta Joachim

The date was 20 December 1993. The weather in New York City was windy and cold. On this typical winter day a very atypical event was under way. The 180 states in the UN General Assembly adopted by unanimous consent the Declaration on the Elimination of Violence against Women. The declaration condemns gender-based violence in both the private and public spheres and obliges UN member states, at least on paper, to work towards its elimination. While it thus promises benefits for women, the fact that it was passed poses a puzzle for scholars of international organization, since only a decade ago gender violence was considered an exclusively domestic and cultural issue. How and why did the issue of gender violence against women become part of the UN's agenda? Why was the issue added only in the 1990s, even though women have been the victims of male violence for centuries?

International women's organizations were responsible for moving the issue of violence against women out of the private and into the public realm, and, specifically, onto the UN's agenda. Efforts to place the issue on UN agendas date back to the 1970s and were spearheaded by a small group of international women's organizations and supported by a large international constituency. Among the most important organizations in this effort were the Center for Women's Global Leadership, the International Women's Tribune Center, the International Women's Rights Action Watch, and the International Women's Network. These otherwise very different organizations were drawn together by their belief that gender violence is unjust and violates women's fundamental rights and freedoms; their conviction that it is caused by structural inequalities between women and men; and their goal of increasing the pressure on states to take measures against gender violence by making the problem more visible internationally.

By tracing the activities of international women's organizations within the

UN between 1970 and the present, I seek to illuminate the ways in which these groups, generally assumed to be weak, were able to shape the agendas of states. I show that in the case of gender violence, international women's organizations derived their influence primarily from the dynamic interaction of two factors: the political opportunity structure in which international women's organizations were embedded and the institutional and ideational resources that these organizations mobilized through time. While the former opened a window for international women's organizations to place the issue of gender violence on the UN's agenda, the latter empowered them to take advantage of it. I tell the heroic story of how these organizations introduced, diffused, and legitimized the issue of gender violence within the UN, which obstacles and opportunities they encountered, and what resources they mobilized to overcome the former and seize the latter.

Introducing the Issue within the UN:
The UN Decade for Women, 1975–1985

The first opportunities for international women's organizations to place the issue of violence against women on the UN agenda were provided by the three World Conferences on Women that the UN organized in connection with the UN Decade for Women between 1975 and 1985 (Mexico City 1975, Copenhagen 1980, and Nairobi 1985). These conferences gave international women's organizations a forum for drawing attention to their issue. First, these conferences had been specifically organized to identify new and pressing issues concerning women. Second, a large number of UN member states were represented, and the conferences received a lot of media attention. Finally, they were accompanied by nongovernmental organization (NGO) forums that took place around the same time and in the same location as the governmental conferences and that provided a space for NGOs from around the world to network, exchange information, develop a common position, and lobby governments as they frequently turned to forum participants for ideas and information (Fraser 1987, 9–13). However, several obstacles initially prevented international women's organizations from seizing these opportunities and placing the issue of gender violence on the agendas of the first two conferences.[1] While some of these obstacles were structural, such as the makeup of political alignments and the absence of influential allies, others were imposed by a lack of resources, the most important of which were a consensual international constituency and substantive as well as procedural expertise.

Mexico City, 1975, and Copenhagen, 1980

To understand the exclusion of gender violence from the agendas of the Mexico City and Copenhagen conferences, one needs to look at the broader institutional context at the time these conferences took place. The existence of three competing blocs among UN member states in the 1970s and the early 1980s (West/North, East, and South) hampered international women's organizations in their efforts to place gender violence on the governmental agendas in Mexico City and Copenhagen. To begin with, each of the three blocs dominated the conference agendas with what they considered important women's issues, namely, equality, development, and peace. Women's equality, particularly in terms of their legal rights, was being pushed by the West; women in development, calling for more resources and greater access to development programs, was added by the South; and, maintaining the position that women had already achieved equality under socialism, the East sought greater participation by women in the promotion of peace and disarmament (Allan, Galey, and Persinger 1995, 29-44).

In addition, the tensions and rivalries between these blocs were responsible for the politicization of the Mexico City and Copenhagen conferences. In particular, the conferences became a battleground for the ongoing North-South conflict. The South took advantage of its majority position and used the platform for action to promote the new international economic order, condemn and sanction apartheid, and denounce Zionism as a form of racism.[2] Northern governments, in turn, expressed their disagreement with these positions by abstaining and, in the case of the United States, Canada, Australia, and Israel, voting against the platform (Jaquette 1995, 45).

Moreover, the political alignments at the time deprived women's organizations of influential allies. The women who served on national delegations and could have been advocates for women's concerns became, willingly or unwillingly, the voices of their governments and the bloc to which they belonged (Stienstra 1994, 127). The support that international women's organizations received from UN member states such as the United States, Canada, and Australia also mattered little and might have even worked to their disadvantage, since, as a result of their decline within the UN, the position of Western-bloc countries was not a favored one (Jaquette 1995, 46). This is reflected in the resolutions introduced by these governments on the subject of domestic violence, which had no support from governments of the other two blocs (United Nations 1980, 67, 222). Finally, international media coverage turned out to be of little help, since television, radio, and the press chose to focus on the political spectacle rather than on women's concerns.

If bloc politics hampered international women's organizations agenda-setting efforts, why were they unable to avoid this problem? One contributing factor was the divisions among the women who attended the parallel NGO forums, which made it difficult for these organizations to mobilize a constituency for their issues. These divisions had several sources. First, the women attending the NGO forums were as much affected by, and caught up in, the East-West/North-South conflicts as their governmental counterparts. This was particularly apparent in the fierce debates that ensued among women over one type of gender violence: female genital mutilation. While several Northern women's organizations condemned the operation as "a barbaric practice imposed on women by male-dominated primitive societies" (Toubia 1995, 232), several Southern women's organizations defended it as a cultural practice and took the criticism of Northern women's groups as yet another expression of "Western imperialism" (McIntosh et al. 1981, 780). Second, women were divided by their different understandings of feminism (Jaquette 1995, 48; Stienstra 1994, 128), which reflected their different cultural backgrounds and experiences and led them to advocate different strategies for increasing the visibility of the gender violence issue. Liberal feminists, for example, viewed the UN, and more specifically the women's conferences, as an appropriate vehicle for accomplishing this goal. In contrast, radical feminists rejected this venue and instead organized the International Tribunal on Crimes against Women in Brussels in 1976. Their reasons for doing so are reflected in a statement by one of the tribunal participants. In her opinion,

> the International Women's Year would, in all probability achieve little beyond window dressing, and that, more seriously, it might succeed in leading women to believe that these patriarchal governments and the male-dominated UN itself have [their] best interest at heart. This could all too easily result in a co-optation of women's energy, a blunting of our anger at our true situations, . . . and a co-optation of the women's liberation movement, or sections thereof. However, rather than putting [their] energy into criticism of [the International Women's Year], they [the organizers] wanted to engage in counteractions that would be both radical and constructive. (Russell and Van de Ven 1976, 218–19)

The tribunal provided an alternative forum where women could discuss their issues and concerns free from governmental interference. More than two thousand women from approximately forty countries participated and heard testimonies about "all man-made oppression" that ranged from forced motherhood to economic crimes to traffic in women.

However, the divisions among women were not the only reason international women's organizations failed to place violence against women on the conference agendas. Their lack of both procedural and substantive experience also played a role. For many of these organizations the UN Women's Conferences were their first encounter with the UN. Few of them knew how the agenda-setting process worked, how they could gain access to governments, how to present their information, or how to lobby (Bunch 1995).

With respect to substantive expertise, women's organizations had little more than anecdotal evidence, stemming from their own experiences or those of their friends, that gender-based violence was a problem for women throughout the world. One reason for the paucity of information was the taboo that surrounded discussion of the issue in many countries and the still-prevailing perception that gender violence was not a problem (Schuler 1992). However, the lack of information was also reflective of a more general condition—the fact that statistics about women's status were generally unavailable. This prompted governments to include a strong section on research and data collection in the platforms of action (United Nations 1975, 32–33; United Nations 1980, 45).

Nairobi, 1985

The Mexico City and Copenhagen conferences had not resulted in the inclusion of the gender violence issue in the platforms of action and were viewed by some as political fiascoes that had done more harm than good to the international women's movement (Jaquette 1995, 45). However, through these conferences international women's organizations were able to mobilize a consensual constituency and gain more knowledge about the UN, which enabled them to place the issue front and center on the agenda of the Nairobi conference. Violence against women in all its manifestations was included in the *Forward-Looking Strategies,* the final conference document, as a priority issue for the coming decade (United Nations 1985, 70).

Inspired by the discussions and interactions at the first two conferences, women throughout the world began to organize around the issue of gender violence. In Brazil they established women-only police stations (Eluf 1992); in Peru they started a program designed to encourage community whistle-blowing against batterers (Miles 1996); in India they waged campaigns against dowry deaths and police rape (Kalkar 1992); from Trinidad to Toronto they established rape-crisis centers and transition houses; and in the Philippines they organized to prevent sex tourism (Skrobanek 1992). In addition, national, regional, and international networks began to emerge, facilitating cooperation and communication between different women's groups. Two such networks that were particularly active at the international level were the Women's International Network (WIN) and the International Women's Information and Communication Service (Isis). WIN, established in 1975, collects and publishes information on violence against women, specifically female genital mutilation; Isis, founded at the Tribunal on Crimes against Women in 1976, facilitates collaboration between Northern and Southern women's organizations by maintaining headquarters in both Chile and Italy and functioning as a clearinghouse and documentation center on violence against women. Further, in response to the conferences in Mexico City and Copenhagen, women organized more international meetings on the issue of gender violence. For example, they held an international meeting on female genital mutilation in Dakar, Senegal, in 1982 (Schuler 1992) and gathered for a Global Feminist Workshop to Organize against Traffic in Women in Rotterdam, the Netherlands, in the spring of 1983 (Barry, Bunch, and Castely 1984). Through these different types of activities women began to develop a shared understanding about gender violence, its different manifestations, and possible strategies to increase its visibility. This shared understanding was particularly apparent at the NGO forum in Nairobi, where more than thirty of some one hundred workshops were devoted to gender violence and where violence against women was identified as one of several priority issues in the NGO forum consensus document (Bunch 1995).

Through their participation in the first two conferences and through lobbying workshops that the forum organizers conducted at these conferences, women also became more experienced in dealing with UN member states and bloc politics. This was reflected not only in the various resolutions concerning gender violence, which in contrast to previous conferences were supported by governments from almost every region (United Nations 1985, 254), but also in the employment of linkage politics. Women tried to gain governmental attention by framing gender violence as an obstacle to peace (Patton 1995, 73).

The impact of the resources mobilized by international women's organizations, however, cannot be understood fully without also considering the broader institutional context in which international women's organizations were active. Even though neither the Cold War nor the North-South conflict had dissipated, the women's conference in Nairobi was less politicized than the previous two conferences. One explanation for this was that both North and South had a keen interest in making the conference a success, though for different reasons. The South's motivation was the locale of the conference. Hosting a successful UN conference in its own hemisphere was a matter of international prestige. The North, and particularly the United States, could not afford another diplomatic defeat. One way the United States sought to bring about a less politicized and, for the West, acceptable final document was through a change in decision-making rules. Rather than having decisions made by general agreement and two-thirds majority of those present and voting, which had originally been planned and which would have been easier to accomplish, U.S. delegate Maureen Reagan managed, after extensive diplomatic maneuvering, to gain approval for the much more tedious, but more meaningful, process of agreement by consensus (Patton 1995, 61–76).

Other contributing factors to a less politicized conference were the astuteness and the negotiating skill exhibited by the individual women who chaired the different negotiation committees at the governmental conference. To keep the conference focused on women's issues and to facilitate consensus, these women relied heavily on UN negotiation procedures, and invoked the prerogatives that came with their offices.[3] One of these women was Margaret Kenyatta of Kenya, the president of the conference. During the final plenary session, when the proposed inclusion of the phrase "Zionism is racism" in the Forward-*Looking Strategies* threatened once again to deadlock the negotiations, Kenyatta called a recess to resolve the dispute through substitute language, deleting "Zionism" and inserting "all other forms of racism and racial discrimination." When the plenary session resumed hours later, Kenyatta announced the substitute and then used her gavel to end discussion, signifying the consensus approval of the paragraph just before the Iranian delegation sought a vote on the substitute (Patton 1995, 70).

The Nairobi conference and the inclusion of gender violence on its agenda constituted an important turning point for international women's organizations. This success enhanced the visibility of gender violence and as a result facilitated the spread of the issue to other agendas within the UN. However it also imposed certain constraints on international women's organizations. First, the *Forward-Looking Strategies* were nonbinding, meaning that the implementation of the recommendations would be subject to the will of individual governments. Second, through its inclusion on the agenda of the Nairobi conference, the issue of gender violence became recognized as a "woman's concern," which limited the agendas on which it would be included.

Diffusion of the Issue, 1985–1990

Following the Nairobi conference, international women's organizations succeeded in placing the issue of gender violence on the agenda of the Commission on the Status of Women (CSW). This was an important achievement for three reasons. First, because the CSW had been established in 1947 with the explicit mandate to promote women's rights, it was recognized within the rest of the UN as the expert on women's concerns. Second, it could provide access to other UN organs, specifically the UN Economic and Social Council (ECOSOC), of which it was a subsidiary body and to which it made recommendations on urgent problems in the field of women's rights. Finally, the inclusion of the issue on the CSW's agenda was an important achievement considering the obstacles that international women's organizations faced at the outset. One of these obstacles was their lack of access to the CSW's agenda. Since most of these organizations had only been established during the 1970s, they had not yet been granted the consultative status that would have given them the prerogative to attend CSW meetings and to make oral or written statements. Another obstacle was the perceived private nature of gender violence, on the one hand, and, on the other, CSW's public mandate restricting the commission's promotion of women's rights to political, social, civil, and cultural fields (Galey 1984, 464–65). International women's organizations were able to overcome both of these obstacles with the help of influential allies within the CSW who were willing to function as conduits for these organizations' expertise. However, the support from these allies came at a price: limiting the scope of gender violence to that occurring only in the family.

Among the allies were several older women's organizations that had been established at the turn of the century. The most active within the CSW were the International Alliance of Women (IAW) and the International Council of Women (ICW). These two organizations had several important resources that the younger organizations lacked: They had consultative status; they were experienced in dealing with the CSW, since they had been attending its meetings since its establishment; and, as a result of the first two factors, they were recognized by governmental delegations as legitimate participants (Stienstra 1994, 96–132). Throughout the 1980s these organizations urged governments within the CSW to take up the issue of violence against women in the family.

International women's organizations also found supporters in individual CSW member states. The delegates from Canada and the United States gave the most outspoken support. In almost every meeting of the CSW between 1985 and 1990, they introduced resolutions on behalf of international women's organizations, drawing attention to violence against women in the family. Their leadership was not surprising. As a result of the activism of women's groups, violence against women had been on these countries' domestic agendas since the late 1970s and early 1980s.

Finally, the Division for the Advancement of Women (DAW), the secretariat of the CSW, played an important role. DAW was almost a natural ally, since it maintained close contact with women's organizations in general and relied on their information for the preparation of reports and documents (Stienstra 1994, 133). DAW commonly elicited such information by holding meetings of expert groups, including the 1986 meeting "Violence within the Family with Special Emphasis on Women." The meeting brought together more than twenty international nongovernmental experts, many of whom had affiliations with women's organizations (United Nations Branch for the Advancement of

Women 1986). The background papers prepared by the experts for the meeting for the first time provided comprehensive statistics and analyses about gender violence in the family. They showed (1) that the problem was not confined to one country or cultural system but rather was global in nature; (2) that gender violence in the family manifested itself not only in physical or sexual violence but also in mental, emotional, and financial violence and violence related to customs such as dowry; and (3) that remedies needed to include immediate help for women who were victims of violence in the family as well as structural reforms (United Nations Branch for the Advancement of Women 1986, 16–17). DAW prepared a report on violence against women in the family based on the expert group meeting and presented it to the CSW at its thirty-second session in the spring of 1988. In response the meeting adopted a resolution entitled "Efforts to Eradicate Violence against Women within the Family and Society." In the resolution, which was adopted by consensus, CSW member states recognized that violence against women in the family "exists in *various forms* in *everyday life* in *all kinds of societies*" (emphasis added) and recommended to ECOSOC that concerted and continuous efforts were required for its eradication (CSW 1988, 27).

While the CSW's recognition of the problem of family violence gave credibility to the issue of gender violence in general, there was still no reason for international women's organizations to rest. First, other forms of gender violence needed addressing (e.g., rape, traffic in women, sexual harassment in the workplace). Second, the recommendations made by the CSW to ECOSOC did not bind UN member states in any way. Finally, CSW's recognition of the issue reinforced the perception that gender violence was only a women's concern.

Legitimizing the Issue of Gender Violence: The 1990s

It was not until early 1993 that the General Assembly adopted the Declaration on the Elimination of Violence against Women, giving the issue additional legitimacy within the UN. The decision came as a surprise to many, especially since the General Assembly's agenda was generally restricted to economic and security issues and, in comparison with the UN Women's Conferences and the CSW, was even less accessible to international women's organizations. Three events—the end of the Cold War, the 1991 expert group meeting on the Elimination of All Forms of Violence, and the 1993 UN World Conference on Human Rights—gave international women's organizations the opportunity to place the issue of gender violence on the General Assembly's agenda. Moreover, international women's organizations were able to seize the opportunity because by the 1990s they had mobilized an international constituency and gained sufficient procedural and substantive expertise.

The End of the Cold War

While the Cold War had only a few years earlier hampered the agenda-setting efforts of international women's organizations, its thaw now provided opportunities for these groups. In particular, it freed up agenda space. In the absence of the East-West conflict, issues that UN policymakers had once considered important began to appear meaningless. Looking for new issues to fill the vacuum, UN policymakers decided to hold a series of specialized conferences in the early 1990s, starting with the UN Conference on Environment and Development in Rio de Janeiro in 1992, followed by the World Human Rights Conference in Vienna in 1993 and the International Conference on Population and Development in Cairo in 1994. Some of these specialized conferences provided forums for international women's organizations to increase the visibility of gender violence. Moreover, the end of the Cold War led to a redefinition of "security." In contrast to a focus on the military strength and defense capabilities of states, the rights and well-being of people were now receiving greater emphasis. This shift in emphasis was reflected both the UN's increased attention to issues such as AIDS, human rights, and refugees and its increased willingness to intervene in the civil wars of countries such as Somalia, Rwanda, and the former Yugoslavia to protect the lives of vulnerable groups. Further, the cessation of superpower hostility set in motion an institutional realignment during which the three ideological blocs that had dominated UN politics until the late 1980s were replaced by three economic ones—the European Union, the Group of 77, and the JUSCANZ (Japan, the United States, Canada, Australia, and New Zealand). These three new blocs provided new possibilities for communication and cooperation within the agenda-setting process (Gordenker and Weiss 1996, 24).

Finally, through the end of the Cold War, the UN became more accessible to NGOs. During the early 1990s, the UN began to relax its standards of accreditation for NGOs. Consultative status was no longer granted only to international NGOs but also to regional and grassroots NGOs (Willetts 1996). In addition, the UN expanded the prerogatives of NGOs with consultative status (Rowlands 1992, 215–17). Previously relegated to the visitor balconies and the corridors, these NGOs were now allowed onto the negotiation floors. The effects of these decisions were felt for the first time at the environmental conference in Rio de Janeiro in 1992, where more than fourteen hundred NGOs were accredited. This was the largest number ever for any UN conference and allowed NGOs to play a significant role in shaping the intergovernmental agenda (Donini 1996, 84). International women's organizations seized the opportunities provided by the end of the Cold War and put the issue of gender violence on the agenda of the General Assembly.

The Expert Group Meeting on Violence against Women in All Its Forms, Vienna, 1991

In the fall of 1991, CSW convened another expert group meeting to discuss a range of measures to eradicate violence against women, including the elaboration and strengthening of the general recommendations of the Committee on the Elimination of Discrimination against Women (CEDAW), the monitoring body of the Convention on the Elimination of All Forms of Violence against Women; the appointment of a special thematic rapporteur on violence against women; the Declaration on Violence against Women; an optional protocol to the Convention on the Elimination of All Forms of Discrimination against Women under which states would submit to the judgment of CEDAW, and even a convention on gender violence. However, only the first three measures received serious attention during the meeting, as they were found less time-consuming to develop and implement. The optional protocol and the convention were viewed as long-term measures that would be implemented if the recommendations, the declaration, and the rapporteur proved ineffective (CSW 1992a). Here I will focus only on the Declaration on the Elimination of Violence against Women, since it was drafted during the expert group meeting and became the main vehicle for moving violence against women onto the agenda of the General Assembly.

The declaration that the experts drafted over the course of their four-day meeting was quite radical by UN standards. It defined violence as "any act, omission, controlling behavior or threat, in *any sphere,* that results in or is likely to result in physical, sexual or psychological injury for women" (emphasis added). Further, it condemned violence not only in the family but also in the general community, as well as violence perpetrated or condoned by the state, on the grounds that women are entitled to the equal enjoyment and protection of all human rights and fundamental freedoms—political, economic, social, cultural, and civil. Finally, it declared the eradication of violence against women the responsibility of both states and the international community (CSW 1992a, 12).

The draft declaration was presented to the CSW at its thirty-sixth session in Vienna in 1992. Although most of the CSW members welcomed and supported it, many felt that the definition of violence against women required further elaboration and revision. They therefore decided to convene an intersessional working group that would continue the work on the draft declaration. The working group provided an opportunity for international women's organizations to lobby the thirty participating governments to support the declaration, since the organizations had been invited as observers and advisers. But the working group process also presented a challenge, since the entire declaration had been put into brackets, indicating disagreements over its content (CSW 1992b). International women's organizations were able to seize the opportunity and confront the challenge because they had, as one interviewee put it, "done their homework" (Sullivan 1995). In particular, organizations such as the Women in the Law Program of the International Human Rights Law Group, whose director was a lawyer, made statements; prepared background papers providing explanations, analysis, and evidence that such a declaration was indeed needed; and developed alternative language, all of which helped governments reach a consensus. At the end of the meeting all of the brackets had been removed, and much of the original text of the draft declaration had been preserved and in some cases even strengthened. The revised draft declaration was reintroduced at the thirty-seventh session of the CSW, where it was approved by consensus and recommended for adoption to the General Assembly, which in turn adopted it by unanimous consent and without changes on 20 December 1993 (CSW 1993, 9–15).

The World Conference on Human Rights, Vienna, 1993: Women's Rights as Human Rights

The swift adoption of the Declaration on the Elimination of Violence against Women within both the CSW and the General Assembly cannot be understood without consideration of the inclusion of violence against women on the agenda of the UN World Conference on Human Rights in Vienna in the summer of 1993. Both the declaration and the Programme of Action adopted at the end of this conference identified gender violence and all forms of sexual harassment and exploitation, including those resulting from cultural prejudice and international trafficking, as incompatible with the dignity and worth of the human person and called for their elimination (United Nations 1993). International women's organizations won the inclusion of such language despite several obstacles. One major roadblock was the prevailing discourse within the UN Commission on Human Rights (UNCHR) in Geneva, the organizer of the Vienna conference, according to which violence against women could not be considered a human rights issue for three reasons: (1) it occurs primarily in the private home of the family, in which international governmental organizations have no right to interfere without a specific mandate; (2) it is perpetrated by private individuals rather than the state, and (3) it does not occur in gross patterns (Bunch 1990, 488). International women's organizations were able to overcome the obstacles imposed by this discourse as a result of the work of the Center for Women's Global Leadership, a women's and human rights organization in New Brunswick, New Jersey, that functioned as an organizational entrepreneur and facilitated the mobilization of a powerful "rights frame."

Shortly after the UN Commission on Human Rights had announced the decision to hold the conference, the Center for Women's Global Leadership conducted three leadership institutes. These institutes brought together twenty women from different regions of the world who had emerged as leaders in their communities or countries in the struggle against gender violence. Many of them had participated in the expert group meeting in 1991. These institutes sought to provide a forum for the development of strategies to ensure the inclusion of gender violence on the Vienna conference agenda. After two weeks of intense discussions, seminars, and workshops, institute participants decided to launch a three-year global campaign leading up to the conference; during this time the Center would coordinate internationally enacted framing activities that would symbolically link gender violence and human rights (Bunch 1995).

Among the most spectacular activities were the Sixteen Days of Activism against Gender Based Violence. The Sixteen Days linked 25 November, the International Day against Violence against Women, with 10 December, International Human Rights Day.[4] Women mobilized around the world to draw attention to violence against women within their countries. For example, in San Jose, Costa Rica, representatives of fifty women's groups met to develop a policy paper addressing violence against women that could be used by policymaking agencies throughout the country; in London thousands of women from all over Britain united at Trafalgar Square to mark 25 November and to demand an "end to the double standard which condones male violence"; and in South Korea women's organizations held demonstrations and a memorial service for the victims of gender violence (Center for Women's Global Leadership 1992). With the help of the International Women's Tribune Center, a global fax–and–e-mail network headquartered in New York City, the Center circulated a global petition. The petition called on participants of the Vienna conference to "comprehensively address women's human rights at every level of its proceedings" and to recognize "gender violence as a universal phenomenon which takes many forms across culture, race and class, . . . as a violation of human rights requiring immediate action." While initially translated into only six languages, the petition ultimately circulated in twenty-four and was sponsored by over a thousand groups that gathered almost half a million signatures from 124 countries by the time the conference was convened in 1993

(Center for Women's Global Leadership 1993).

An article by Charlotte Bunch, the director of the Center for Women's Global Leadership, was published in the prestigious *Human Rights Quarterly* in 1990 and gave further meaning and impetus to these activities. "Women's Rights as Human Rights" provided the theoretical underpinnings of the emerging rights frame. In particular, it offered an explanation for the separation of human rights and women's rights, attributing it to the narrow, Western definition of human rights, which favors civil and political rights over economic and social rights. The article stated that "much of the abuse against women is part of a larger socio-economic web that entraps women, making them vulnerable to abuses which cannot be delineated as exclusively political or solely caused by states" (Bunch 1990, 488). Moreover, the article provided a threefold rationale for the consideration of women's rights generally, and violence against women specifically, by human rights organizations. First, statistics demonstrate that gender violence kills women daily. Second, the arbitrary definitions of what constitutes the "private" are subject to interpretation and are often used to justify female subordination at home. Third, violence against women is profoundly political, "result[ing] from structural relationships of power, domination, and privilege between men and women in society" (Bunch 1990, 491). The title of Bunch's article, "Women's Rights as Human Rights," became the slogan of the three-year campaign leading up to the Vienna conference and was printed on buttons, T-shirts, and posters (Carillo 1995).

Because the rights frame resonated so strongly with many women throughout the world, it helped mobilize an international constituency that empowered the Center and other international women's organizations concerned with violence against women to influence the agendas of the meetings held in preparation for the Vienna conference. At almost all of the regional conferences, women's groups prepared consensus documents and successfully lobbied for the inclusion of gender violence in the regional platforms of action. Their achievements, in turn, provided women's groups attending the international preparatory meetings with a mandate and a lobbying tool to hold governments accountable to their commitments at the regional level (Bunch and Reilly 1994, 5–6).

Thus, at the conference in Vienna in June 1993 the Center for Women's Global Leadership could skillfully employ the human rights frame and the international constituency to ensure the inclusion of gender violence on the conference agendas. At the most visible location at the NGO forum held prior to the official conference, the Center established a Women's Rights Place, which provided opportunities for exchange, networking, and strategizing. In addition, it orchestrated a global tribunal, modeled after the Nuremberg trials, during which more than thirty women from every region of the world testified about the violence they or their friends had suffered and for which a jury of five internationally renowned judges prepared a statement. Further, the Center organized a women's caucus that met every morning before the official conference and provided a space for women to discuss the developments at the governmental conference and possible lobbying strategies. Finally, the Center hired a women's media consortium to publicize women's activities at the conference through press conferences, media kits, and press releases. At the governmental conference, the Center formed a representative group of six women, many of whom had participated in both the leadership institutes and the expert group meeting in 1991. They reported to governmental delegates about the tribunal, asked delegates for a minute of silence for all the women around the world who had died or been badly injured by domestic violence, and delivered to the conference floor the half-million signatures gathered through the global petition. These symbolic activities were paralleled by the tireless lobbying activities of representatives of women's organizations, who provided governmental delegates with analysis and alternative language at every possible moment in every possible place (Bunch and Reilly 1994; Carillo 1995).

While the resources mobilized by international women's organizations were impressive and reflected these organizations' growing experience in dealing with the UN, they do not explain why the rights frame captured the attention of international policymakers, making them question their beliefs about the relationship between human rights and women's rights. Several changes within the international environment helped the rights frame gain acceptance. The mass rapes of women during the civil war in the former Yugoslavia made policymakers aware of the political nature of gender violence (women were raped by soldiers and not by private individuals), its pervasiveness (more than two thousand women were raped), and its cross-cultural nature (women on both sides of the conflict were raped). The impact of these rapes on policymakers is reflected in the resolutions adopted by the CSW (CSW 1992b, 5), the UNCHR (United Nations Commission on Human Rights 1993), and even the General Assembly (United Nations General Assembly 1993b) condemning the systematic rape and abuse of women in areas of armed conflict in the former Yugoslavia.

In addition, the activities of influential allies inside and outside the UN contributed to the frame's resonance. Responding to pressure by women's organizations, several traditional human rights organizations such as Amnesty International and Human Rights Action Watch adopted a new focus on women's rights in the early 1990s. Although these groups investigated only gender violence that was perpetrated or condoned by the state, their missions to countries as diverse as Pakistan, Brazil, Kuwait, and Haiti provided further proof of the political and global nature of the issue and enhanced its credibility, since these organizations had a reputation for presenting reliable and well-researched information (Bunch 1995).

As to the allies inside the UN, the Development Fund for Women (UNIFEM) had a major role to play. Throughout the 1980s, UNIFEM showed little interest in the issue of gender violence. Appeals by Southern women's organizations to UNIFEM to incorporate the issue in its program activities were rejected by the agency's board of directors with the argument that violence against women was not a development concern (Carillo 1995). UNIFEM's board of directors changed its position in response to a paper written in the early 1990s by Roxanna Carillo, then staff member of the Center for Women's Global Leadership, entitled "Violence against Women: An Obstacle to Development." Drawing on the UN's own definition of development—the creation of an environment that enables people to enjoy long, healthy, and creative lives—and with the help of international statistics, Carillo was able to link the rights frame to the development frame and cast violence against women as a development issue. In particular, she was able to show that gender violence interferes with women's personal development, as it limits their ability to pursue options in almost every area of life, including the home, schools, workplaces, and most public spaces. Moreover, owing to its severe health and psychological impact, it prevents women from contributing effectively to a country's economic development. Finally, gender violence leaves women unable to assist in development projects, as their participation and empowerment is frequently seen by their husbands as a threat and penalized with abuse (Carillo 1991). Shortly after the publication of the paper, UNIFEM offered Carillo a position, which she accepted and used to establish a women's rights program within the agency. The program became a major ally of international women's organizations within the UN. It sponsored the global campaign leading up to the Vienna conference and financed women's travel to it from the South. UNIFEM also now functioned as a channel of communication between governments and women's organizations. For example, at the official conference, UNIFEM organized a parallel women's caucus, which brought together representatives of women's NGOs, governmental delegates, and representatives of UN agencies and provided a space for lobbying and exploring possible means for collaboration (Bunch and Reilly 1994, 102–3).

Finally, the absence of an agenda for the Vienna conference helps explain why international policymakers responded to the rights frame. Even though this was the first human rights conference in twenty-five years, governments and human rights organizations could not agree on its agenda and as a result did not have an agreed-upon text until the last international preparatory meeting in Geneva in the spring of 1993 (Bunch and Reilly 1994, 6–7). Disagreement centered on a split between governments and NGOs from the North and those from the South as to which rights should have priority, socioeconomic rights or civil and political rights, and which should be considered universal. The lack of consensus provided a window for international women's organizations that had an agenda (getting gender violence on the agenda of the human rights conference), an issue that cut across traditional categories of rights, and an international constituency.

Conclusion

What implications does the Declaration on the Elimination of Violence against Women have for women around the world? Skeptics would probably say very few. Even though the declaration was adopted by consensus and is couched in forceful language, it is still up to the individual UN member states to follow through on its implementation. In light of shrinking budgets, the rise of fundamentalist movements, and the stress suffered by many governments in transition, such as the former communist countries, the elimination of violence against women is likely to be put on the back burner. But while these are certainly legitimate issues, those who are skeptical about the effect of the declaration ignore some of the positive steps that governments have already taken. For example, in the early 1990s the Japanese government delivered a public apology to the tens of thousand of women forced by its military as sex slaves in a vast network of government-run brothels during World War II. India has shifted the burden of proof in the case of custodial rape so that the state now has the responsibility to show that the alleged rape did not take place. And Canada now grants asylum to female immigrants if they have reason to fear gender-based violence upon their return to their home countries. More important, skeptics ignore the resources that women have won through the agenda-setting process that will make it more difficult for governments to ignore the declaration, including (1) an international constituency, (2) the recognition of women's rights as human rights, and (3) the appointment of a special rapporteur on violence against women.

While a constituency around the issue of violence against women began to emerge in the early 1970s with women's organizations from Western Europe and North America, by the late 1980s it had broadened to include women's organizations from Africa, Asia, Latin America, the Caribbean, and the Middle East. Held together by international networks and a collective consciousness that gender violence is unacceptable, this international constituency can push forward the implementation of the Declaration. The organizations that belong to the constituency not only offer help to victims through shelters, counseling, training, and education but also enable women to pressure governments at every possible level—community, national, regional, and international—to live up to their international commitments.

The recognition of women's rights as human rights gives force to the Declaration by making states accountable. With the integration of women's issues into the human rights mechanism, it is no longer possible to argue that gender violence is "beyond" the responsibility of states. With this shift in emphasis, states now have an obligation to offer protection to victims of gender violence independent of whether it occurred in the private realm of the family or in the streets; to investigate allegations of violence; and to punish the perpetrators, whether they are private persons or public officials.

Finally, the appointment of Radhika Coomaraswamy as special rapporteur for violence against women by the UNCHR has important implications for the efforts to stem gender violence. Coomaraswamy is likely to contribute to a greater understanding and awareness of gender violence, since part of her mandate is to collect information about the causes and types of violence against women. She is also in a position to shame states engaging in or condoning gender violence by exercising the right to investigate situations or allegations forwarded to her by concerned parties.

These resources are certainly not sufficient to bring about the implementation of the Declaration on the Elimination of Violence against Women and cannot compensate for the lack of funding or the lack of will on the part of UN member states. Nevertheless, they do hold the potential for moving us a bit closer to the Declaration's goal.

Notes

1. Violence was not mentioned at all in the Platform of Action adopted at the Mexico City conference and was mentioned only briefly in connection with health in the platform adopted in Copenhagen. There, paragraph 140f calls on UN member states "to improve the physical and mental health of all members of society through . . . the development of policies and programs aimed at the elimination of all forms of violence against women and children and the protection of women of all ages from the physical and mental abuse resulting from domestic violence, sexual assault, sexual exploitation, and any other form of abuse" (United Nations 1980, 31).

2. Since the adoption of a proposed wording or paragraph required only a two-thirds majority of those present and voting, many of these issues found their way into the Platforms of Action of Mexico City and Copenhagen.

3. Among them were procedures, such as the establishment of contact or open-

160 *Jutta Joachim*

ended working groups, that are frequently used at specialized conferences to develop compromise language.

4. The first feminist *encuentro* for Latin America and the Caribbean, held in Bogota, Colombia, declared the first International Day against Violence against Women in 1981 to commemorate the brutal murder of the Mirabel sisters by the Trujillo dictatorship in the Dominican Republic on 25 November 1960. The date 10 December marks the anniversary of the proclamation of the Universal Declaration of Human Rights in 1948.

10

Realizing Women's Human Rights: Nongovernmental Organizations and the United Nations Treaty Bodies

Alice M. Miller

The human rights of women and the girl-child are an inalienable, integral and indivisible part of universal human rights. The full and equal participation of women in political, civil, economic, social and cultural life . . . and the eradication of all forms of discrimination on grounds of sex are priority objectives of the international community (United Nations 1993, para. 18).

If the goal of full realization of human rights for all is to be achieved, international human rights instruments must be applied in such a way as to take more clearly into consideration the systematic and systemic nature of discrimination against women that gender analysis has clearly indicated (United Nations 1995a, para. 222).

Non-governmental organizations, women's organizations and feminist groups have played a catalytic role in the promotion of the human rights of women through grass-roots activities, networking and advocacy and need encouragement, support and access to information . . . in order to carry out these activities (United Nations 1995a, para. 228).

These quotations set out three strategic elements of women's human rights work at the United Nations. The first quotation, from the 1993 Vienna World Conference on Human Rights, embraces the goal of much of international women's human rights activism of the last ten years: global recognition of the universality of women's human rights. The second statement, from the Beijing Fourth World Conference on Women, names a practical reality: until human rights treaties themselves are gendered, the legal basis of much of women's rights activism will remain inconsistent and ad hoc. The third statement recognizes the critical role that nongovernmental organizations (NGOs) play in realizing these promises. Yet, although Beijing highlighted the importance of national NGOs and women's groups, these groups face great difficulties in becoming actors at the international level where critical changes in the elaboration and application of the legal basis for women's human rights claims must occur. Taken together, these statements indicate an important area of work for women's human rights activists at the United Nations.

Women's human rights NGOs have played a key role in the recent recognition of women's human rights as "a priority concern of the international community." First, they successfully drew international attention to the marginalization of women's human rights in the international system of rights protection (Bunch and Frost 1998; Cook 1994; Amnesty International 1995; Human Rights Watch 1995). They also successfully campaigned for increased gender analysis and new standards to strengthen protections for women. These campaigns resulted in such advances as the adoption of the UN Declaration on the Elimination of Violence against Women (United Nations General Assembly 1993a; Joachim this volume), the inclusion of sexual violence in the statutes of the two ad hoc war crimes tribunals (Statute 1991, 1994), and the recognition of women's essential roles as agents and beneficiaries of development as well as the need to promote and protect women's human rights as the basis of family planning and sustainable development policies.

Women's NGOs have made many of these advances in ad hoc venues created by the UN, such as through the recent cycle of world conferences beginning with the UN Conference on Environment and Development in Rio de Janeiro (1992), the World Conference on Human Rights in Vienna (1993), the International Conference on Population and Development in Cairo (1994), the World Summit on Social Development in Copenhagen (1995), and culminating in the Fourth World Conference on Women in Beijing (1995). However, as we end this cycle (with a proposed World Conference on Racism scheduled for 2000), NGOs, including women's NGOs, look to solidify these political advances on the ground, both in law and practice.

This chapter focuses on one aspect of the process of "making rights real" — the use of the UN's treaty monitoring system by women's NGOs. Such a focus sharpens our understanding of the obstacles and potentials faced by women's NGOs working with the formal tools of the UN. It reveals important practical and conceptual concerns for NGOs and suggests steps for building the necessary political commitments and normative framework for increased women's rights protections.

The chapter begins by noting the positional differences between established international human rights NGOs and the more recent women's human rights NGOs working at the international and national levels with regard to the UN human rights treaty system. A brief overview of the structure of the UN human rights treaty system follows, with attention to the structure and functions of

UN treaty bodies as well as the historical marginalization of women's rights and the lack of a gender perspective in human rights obligations. The chapter then considers the role of women's NGOs in helping to integrate gender into the human rights system and explores their potential for using UN treaty bodies to improve human rights protections for women. Finally, an examination of different types of treaty work by national and international women's NGOs reveals how a fully functioning treaty system in the UN can and should include the international participation of women's NGOs as a goal. I use examples drawn from training and technical assistance activities of the Women's Rights Advocacy Program of the International Human Rights Law Group based in Washington, D.C.[1] These examples are presented from the perspective of an international NGO working at the international and national levels with national NGOs. It must be stressed that this perspective cannot substitute for the national NGOs' voices themselves.

As noted by a representative of Amnesty International, "although international NGOs have had a number of opportunities to develop their roles [in the UN], the role of national NGOs remains rather unexplored" (Clapham 1997). The global participation of national women's NGOs should be explored for the intrinsic values of self-representation and empowerment. Ironically, women's groups are emerging to claim a place in the traditional world of human rights protection at a time when the entire system is facing calls for reevaluation and revision. The international work of women's NGOs has the potential to transform the workings of international institutions. Our challenge is to be a central and constructive part of that process to ensure the full integration of gender in human rights protection and enjoyment.

Differences in Human Rights NGOs' Positions vis-à-vis the UN System

NGOs comprise a wide range of not-for-profit groups that are constituted as independent, nonpartisan entities, usually with an identified mission or mandate. NGOs are neither monolithic nor identical in mandate, methodology, or perspectives at the national, regional, or international level (see also Tinker this volume). NGOs working in the area of international human rights serve many different functions: they undertake scrutiny and criticism, demand transparency and government accountability, present documentation and information, publicize results, and provide outreach to other NGOs to increase awareness and form networks.

At the international level, NGOs with a demonstrated structure as independent entities and a charter consistent with UN goals can participate in special capacities in the formal activities of such international governmental organizations (IGOs) as the United Nations, the Council of Europe, the Organization of African Unity, and the Organization of American States. To become accredited observers at the UN, NGOs formally apply to gain "consultative status," which allows them to walk the halls of the UN, enter the sessions of UN political and nonpolitical bodies, and, under certain circumstances, to speak. An important change occurred in 1996, when the Economic and Social Council (ECOSOC) voted to open this process to national and regional as well as international NGOs (ECOSOC 1996). This reform allows local women's NGOs to speak for themselves and increase the diversity of voices at the UN.[2]

In recent years, many new NGOs have emerged from the local and national levels to work at the international level, such as women's NGOs and groups working for the human rights of lesbians, gay men, or persons with disabilities. Many of these new NGOs have different needs and expectations from the UN than do the more established international NGOs. They also perceive the established international human rights NGOs to be standing near the center of power in the UN system. This positional difference has resulted in tensions between international NGOs and the emerging national groups — especially women's groups, which have been concerned that international NGOs have not paid sufficient attention to women's human rights (Bunch 1990; Amnesty International 1998; Sullivan 1995b). These tensions manifest themselves in at least three ways.

First, many established human rights NGOs have suffered from the same myopia as the UN in overlooking women's human rights by prioritizing civil and political rights over the interrelated and indivisible continuum of all human rights—civil, cultural, economic, political, and social (Bunch 1990; Charlesworth, Chinkin, and Wright 1991; Amnesty International 1998). In both international NGO and UN work, these priorities have obscured women's lives. Discrimination and gender roles often remove women to "private" spaces and out of the forums in which they could claim violations of such traditional civil and political rights as voting, association, protest, expression, or freedom from torture by government agents. Thus, part of the recent struggle of women's rights NGOs has included the campaign to place the issue of women's rights on the agenda of major international human rights NGOs such as Human Rights Watch, the International Commission of Jurists, and Amnesty International.

Second, other international women's rights NGOs, such as Women, Law and Development International (WLDI) and the International Women's Rights Action Watch (IWRAW) have labored to move out of the marginalized area of "women's work" and into the mainstream of UN human rights work. However, this presents an additional challenge to regional women's rights organizations. Southern-based NGOs such as Women in Law and Development Africa (WILDAF), Asia Pacific Women Law and Development (APWLD), and numerous Latin American networks that arose after the 1985 Nairobi World Conference on Women are still campaigning to get their "women's human rights" message heard by the mainstream human rights organizations on their continents. Moreover, they struggle against the dominant voices of Northern-based women's NGOs, which have greater resources, ease of movement, communication capabilities, and access to key information within IGOs.

Third, human rights NGOs differ about what should be their relationship to governments and IGOs, whether they should be characterized as governmental "partners," treaty expert "partners," oppositional monitors, or critics. Interestingly, the language of partnership occurred more frequently among women's groups at the Beijing Fourth World Conference on Women than among traditional human rights groups at the Vienna Conference on Human Rights. These references to partnership may stem from the focus of some women's groups on private, nonstate-actor violence against women, which requires calls to governments for investigation and prosecution. It may also derive from the fact that the women's machinery in national governments is disempowered and marginalized, leading women's groups that are often allied with such machinery to call for its strengthening. However, this question should not be dealt with superficially or simplistically, as many women's groups have radical feminist analyses that are critical of the patriarchal nature and coercive power of the state.

Despite these tensions, however, NGOs have contributed to developing the terms of gender analysis and pressuring intergovernmental bodies within the UN to live up to their rhetoric on women's rights. As illustrated in other chapters in this volume, the recent UN world conferences allowed NGOs at all levels, even those not accredited to the UN, to participate as advocates in powerfully organized ways, leading to the creation of international lobbies on women's human rights in such areas as health, especially sexual and reproductive rights; development; and violence against women in the home, the community, and armed conflict. These organized advocacy efforts led to the political commitments in Rio, Cairo, Copenhagen, Vienna, and Beijing to mainstream or integrate women's human rights. These political commitments are theoretically being transformed into more monitorable commitments through various UN bodies. However, without an informed and lively constituency of NGOs from all regions to monitor the "mainstreaming of a gender perspective into all the policies and programmes of the UN system," their words may remain tokenistic and unenforced (ECOSOC 1997).

The UN's Human Rights Treaties and the Treaty Bodies

Human rights work can mean everything from the political demand of women's rights groups for equality at a street demonstration in Goma, Zaire/Congo, to a legal brief in the Supreme Court of India challenging discriminatory inheritance laws by invoking a human rights treaty, to the San Francisco, United States, Board of Supervisors' vote to incorporate formally into local law the UN Convention on the Elimination of All Forms of Discrimination against Women. These actions have in common the reference to human rights standards formally accepted by many nations through international human rights treaties, conventions, or covenants. Over the last fifty years, the United Nations has developed an array of standards and machinery to promote and protect human rights. All of this work is based on the UN Charter, which makes the promotion and protection of human rights and fundamental freedoms one of the foundational bases of the UN.

The 1948 Universal Declaration of Human Rights, the first set of formal human rights standards adopted by the UN General Assembly, was further elaborated through a series of human rights treaties to make its promises enforceable. The six core human rights treaties are the International Covenant on Civil and Political Rights, the International Covenant on Economic, Social, and Cultural Rights (often called the UN Bill of Rights), the Convention on the Elimination of All Forms of Racial Discrimination, the Convention on the Elimination of All Forms of Discrimination against Women, the Convention against Torture, and the Convention on the Rights of the Child. These treaties form the backbone of the enforceable human rights claims; they represent a common language for governmental promises to respect, ensure, and fulfill human rights for all persons without discrimination.[3]

Each of these treaties was drafted by governments—with input and lobbying by NGOs—in various UN bodies and then formally adopted as a human rights treaty by vote of the UN General Assembly. Once adopted, a treaty is "opened for signature," and each government takes the steps required under its domestic legislative and legal system to ratify the treaty, thus becoming legally bound by its terms. Each treaty contains the substantive articles outlining the rights it protects and the basic steps (e.g., law review and reform, review of practice and policy) that the ratifying nation (or state party) must take. Each treaty also sets out the state party's fundamental obligation to report regularly and publicly to the relevant UN treaty body on the steps that the government has taken to revise laws or practices to meet the obligations of the treaty. Additionally, three of the treaties (the International Covenant on Civil and Political

Rights, the Convention on the Elimination of All Forms of Racial Discrimination, and the Convention against Torture) allow individuals to lodge complaints with the UN treaty bodies.

The UN has a number of Charter-based human rights bodies charged with formulating and monitoring human rights standards, such as the Commission on Human Rights and the Commission on the Status of Women, whose members are representatives of governments, as well as subbodies (e.g., the Sub-Commission for the Protection of Minorities and Prevention of Discrimination) made up of experts appointed to act independently of governments. A branch of the UN Secretariat is also charged with human rights support work, while the UN's specialized agencies, funds, and programs (e.g., UNICEF and the UN High Commissioner for Refugees) have major responsibilities for protecting human rights.

In addition to these mechanisms, there are a number of treaty-based mechanisms, in most cases created by each treaty to monitor and evaluate the implementation of its obligations. These treaty bodies are committees of independent experts that meet regularly at the UN in New York or Geneva. These committees receive reports from governments and give evaluations in public meetings with representatives of those governments on how the government is doing in implementing the obligations of the treaty. The treaty bodies summarize their main concerns, including positive and negative findings as well as guidance, in final remarks called "concluding comments." In addition, all the treaty bodies may issue "general comments" or "general recommendations" that interpret and elaborate on the nature and scope of the treaty obligations they monitor.

All of the treaty bodies have recognized that they need alternative sources of information to carry out their mission. Many have established formal rules of procedure for interactions with UN agencies and NGOs to collect information and suggestions for priority concerns. However, the international NGOs have been the predominant suppliers of information to these bodies; very few women's-rights-focused groups have submitted information to treaty bodies other than the committee that monitors the Convention on the Elimination of All Forms of Discrimination against Women (CEDAW).

This is the formal world of the UN that many activist women's NGOs are trying to enter. NGOs are increasingly turning their attention to the application of human rights treaties to women's lives, in part through the monitoring role of the treaty bodies. While there are powerful reasons to become active in the non-treaty-based bodies at the UN, such as the Commission on Human Rights or the Commission on the Status of Women, this chapter focuses on the treaty bodies.

Integrating Gender: NGO Contributions
to Human Rights Protections for Women

While some steps toward integrating gender have occurred within the UN treaty system, very few institutionalized advances have taken place. This lack of progress can be fairly attributed not only to residual prejudices but also to an even more fundamental problem: there is very little concrete understanding of exactly what a gender analysis is with regard to any one right or to rights as a whole. While the treaty experts themselves must increasingly play a critical role in developing the framework for gender analysis, the paucity of UN resources for training on these topics suggests that the experts' main lessons will come from the NGOs.

NGOs can play a critically important role by demonstrating what gender-specific reporting means. Indeed, perhaps their most useful contributions are well-documented, fact-based submissions to the treaty bodies combined with carefully shaped analyses of the nature of the legal obligations to respect, ensure, and fulfill women's human rights. They can demonstrate "the form which a violation takes; the circumstances in which it occurs; the consequences of the violation for the victim; and the availability and accessibility of remedies" (Sullivan 1998).

Understanding the nature of governmental obligations around protecting and promoting the rights of women and girls requires a number of different steps. It includes a gendered understanding of "classic" human rights concerns such as the right not to be arbitrarily deprived of life. This right, which is usually applied to state killings or the death penalty, could be elaborated as a question of state responsibility for maternal mortality if the state blocks or fails to facilitate adequate access to contraception, abortion, nutritional information, and so on. Gender analysis would also expand the understanding of the right to be free from torture. It would require a greater understanding of the forms of torture, including sexual, mental, and physical, directed at men and women as well as the specific forms directed primarily or exclusively at women. It would examine government complicity or acquiescence in acts of torture committed by nonstate actors and the underlying nature of discrimination against women. It would examine the gendered nature of the harms suffered by men and women with an eye to constructing more complete and effective methods of prevention as well as compensation and redress.[4] Finally, gender analysis would link the classic civil rights concepts of torture and bodily integrity with the social and cultural rights concepts of mental and physical health.

In addition to these commonly addressed fundamental rights, the entire range of civil, cultural, economic, political, and social rights as enjoyed by women must be better understood in their most concrete, fact-based terms.

Such issues as women's rights to participate in the public life of their country—touching on issues of citizenship, political participation, culture, and development—should be better articulated. This requires increased documentation coupled with nuanced questioning of steps taken by the government to remove gender-based obstacles to women's enjoyment of such rights.

Developing more fully the analytical and factual bases for holding the state internationally accountable for abuses by nonstate actors, including abuses by corporate as well as individual entities, is a critical aspect of the work of the UN treaty bodies. Many local NGOs—especially but not exclusively women's NGOs—focus extensively on this issue. Major abuses of, and obstacles to, women's enjoyment of fundamental rights arise in the private sphere—through home-based violence, unequal rights within marriage contracts, restricted access to property, or lack of choice in the sexual and reproductive spheres.[5] NGOs are deeply concerned with the state's failures to take action, particularly on key legislation to criminalize acts of violence against women. Other violations occurring through inaction could be the systemwide failure to train police to investigate or prosecute allegations of domestic violence or a failure to prosecute domestic abuse as aggressively as other crimes of violence.

The potential role of the treaty bodies in this area is vital because they can provide the legal framework for the overall development of the critical standard of "due diligence," by which a state can be held accountable for acts committed by others under its jurisdiction or control. This standard, included in the UN Declaration on Violence against Women, further builds from the obligation "to ensure" the enjoyment of rights contained within the treaties.[6] All these steps are essential to apply the content of human rights guarantees concretely to women.

International NGOs have played key roles in recent initiatives on gender integration within the treaty system. Their vigorous advocacy at the 1994 annual meeting of the chairpersons of the human rights treaty bodies resulted in the bodies' agreement to amend their guidelines and require that states parties report on the status of women with respect to the rights articulated in each treaty. The Human Rights Committee became the first to do so. International NGOs also participated in an expert group meeting on gender integration in Geneva in July 1995 as well as a 1996 roundtable of the human rights treaty bodies, "Human Rights Approaches to Women's Health with a Focus on Reproductive and Sexual Health Rights."

Although only a few national women's NGOs were present at these meetings, the expert group meeting recognized that gender integration requires the treaty bodies to make procedural and substantive changes (United Nations 1995f). Among its recommendations concerning the sources of the treaty bodies' information and other working methods, the expert group recognized the critically important role that local women's NGOs must play in documenting and facilitating the flow of gendered information to the UN. It also recommended more "aggressive steps to disseminate [information on the human rights work of the UN, which] could include media outreach, when appropriate to the mandate of the activity, using such means as radio, popular newspapers, etc." (United Nations 1995f, recommendation 6).[7] Thus, the efforts of international NGOs at these meetings resulted in part in emphasizing local and national NGOs' role in enforcing human rights protections.

NGOs and the United Nations: Multiple Spheres of Action

Local Advocacy Based on Treaty Obligations

Many women's NGOs have no interest in engaging with the UN at its headquarters in New York or Geneva. They wish to use the human rights treaties ratified by their governments as tools for local accountability. Local activists, who are often engaged in direct services to women, have turned to the international system in part because the language of women's human rights is seen as empowering. The promises made by governments in ratifying human rights treaties can be the basis for effective public education on women's rights, for advocacy on the obligations to change discriminatory laws, or for direct litigation to find laws or practices invalid. Typically, local activists want to find out whether their government is bound by certain treaties, what facts they need to document violations of various treaty articles, and the strategic uses of those analyses in campaigning for law or policy reform, such as changing police practices or health clinic services.

Currently, some international NGOs, such as the International Human Rights Law Group, are collaborating with local groups to develop programs for technical assistance to accomplish these goals. Workshops and other programs can provide local activists with the opportunity to elaborate new and valid ways of applying treaty guarantees. For example, participants in a 1996 Bangkok workshop hosted by the Global Alliance against Traffic in Women demonstrated gendered violations by India of Article 9 (arbitrary detention) of the International Covenant on Civil and Political Rights. NGOs noted the situation of women arrested in brothel raids and held indefinitely in detention in India because authorities would only release the women into the custody of male relatives. These relatives from either Bangladesh or Pakistan would not rescue such "dishonored" women.

Thus, through documentation, human rights analysis, and advocacy, activists seek to use treaty obligations as tools to hold their governments accountable at the national level. As yet, however, they are still unsure about sending their information on to New York or Geneva. They lack knowledge about when to do so and how to ensure that the review of their information is fed back to them for their own use. If they get a timely response from the UN treaty body, they can publicize how their government was questioned on discriminatory practices; but there is currently no information structure to accomplish this.

Local women's NGOs face severe obstacles to the effective use of the specific aspects of the treaty system. In particular, the scope of the reservations to the Convention on the Elimination of All Forms of Discrimination against Women is an obstacle to raising questions about certain abuses, such as religion- or custom-based inequalities within the family (CEDAW 1997). Interestingly, many governments have ratified non-women-specific treaties with guarantees of equality within the family and nondiscrimination between men and women, reinforcing the need for women's rights activists to know the whole treaty system, not only the CEDAW treaty, to claim rights strategically. Yet many women's groups are trained only on CEDAW as the primary treaty setting out definitions of discrimination against women.

Activists often combine exaggerated expectations of the treaty system with great skepticism about law and the state-centered nature of the system. They have few illusions, however, about the low level of state compliance with obligations, although they generally express great interest in the "public shaming" capacity of treaty review. While these local women's NGOs may never appear in New York or Geneva, their work should be supported for its power to amplify the concrete effects of the human rights system.

International-Level Advocacy

The Committee on the Elimination of Discrimination against Women (also known by the acronym CEDAW), the body responsible for monitoring implementation of the CEDAW treaty, has historically been separate from the other treaty bodies in the UN structure. It has received the least financial support for its operations and the least time for meetings. Many, including a number of international NGOs, have noted that CEDAW lagged behind the Geneva-based treaty bodies in developing formal and informal links with NGOs, both as sources of independent information and as constituents to strengthen the promotion of women's human rights at national and international levels.[8] Specific steps have been taken to strengthen CEDAW, partly because its work to articulate the nature of discrimination can then inform the work on women's rights within the other treaty bodies and partly because of the intrinsic benefits of having a strong focal point for women in the UN system.

In 1996, UNIFEM and a Malaysia-based NGO called International

Women's Rights Action Watch–Asia Pacific began an innovative project to further the work of CEDAW by focusing on the potential role of women's NGOs. Other collaborating international NGOs, such as the Law Group and ILANUD (Instituto Latinoamericano de Naciones Unidas para la Prevención del Delito y Tratamiento del Delincuento/UN Latin American Institute for the Prevention of Crime and Treatment of Offenders), soon joined them.[9] The project has worked with activists from countries scheduled to submit their official treaty report to CEDAW.[10] Key elements of the project are (1) identifying a sponsoring organization based in the South; (2) allocating pre-reporting grants of money to identified women's NGOs in those countries to enable them to form coalitions with other groups and collect information on women's rights relevant under the Convention; (3) providing guidance and support when the NGO is preparing an alternative report or "shadow report";[11] (4) holding a special, intensive multiday training session at CEDAW offices in New York with trainers from all five regions to provide background, substantive understanding of the Convention, and advocacy skills; (5) organizing a weeklong (or longer) mentored stay in New York to watch CEDAW in action, make informal contacts, and observe the dialogue with governments and the development of concluding comments; and (6) receiving from UNIFEM follow-up information, such as CEDAW's concluding comments and other results of the session. Each of these components is critical; however, an NGO's work before and after action at CEDAW in New York is the real test of the usefulness of the project.

CEDAW is revising its practices, particularly with regard to receiving information from NGOs, and has improved the reporting process (see CEDAW 1997). However, although the process is technically public, the NGOs involved in the project all had great difficulty in obtaining their own governments' report to CEDAW prior to leaving their countries for New York. Also, the lack of translation into local languages is a barrier to using the governments' report and CEDAW's responses for education and outreach at home.

The case of Morocco's report at CEDAW's 1997 session demonstrates some of the potentials of this kind of treaty work. A newly formed coalition of Moroccan NGOs produced a detailed alternative report. Its shadow report prioritized critical issues and carefully critiqued the government's claims that Islam justified discrimination. The report gave extensive, concrete recommendations for action by the government (Association Démocratique des Femmes du Maroc 1996).[12] CEDAW members appeared to use this shadow report as they questioned the government closely. The Moroccan NGO representative herself was extraordinarily keen to understand and use the political space opened up by the session to approach her government, with which she had never had any direct contact. Representatives of the government contacted her directly for a follow-up meeting. She felt strongly that this approach validated her work as well as the work of the NGO coalition and would strengthen the coalition members' ability to approach the government on their return home.

Despite its positive potential, the UNIFEM training project also illustrates that the increasing number of venues for national-international NGO exchange is not without controversy. As noted above, criticisms of the positional and representational differences between international and national NGOs in the UN treaty bodies have surfaced, resulting in calls for greater accountability of international NGOs to national NGOs. National NGOs have raised concerns that international NGOs are co-opting their voices and information while controlling access to the treaty bodies. If left unaddressed, these concerns could lead to damaging schisms in NGO work. Moreover, national NGOs that choose to act internationally may face distrust or hostility from within the national NGO community for their loss of grassroots "validity."[13] International and national NGOs each have roles to play. But the participation of national groups bolsters specific values such as increased empowerment and advocacy capacity. Increased local capacity advances the goal of holding governments accountable to their own people and, in turn, can usefully amplify the impact of the treaty committee's work at the national level.

Obviously, this potential is dependent on a great many other factors, including the relative openness with which the NGO can operate domestically as well as internationally and in conjunction with international NGOs. An assessment of risks and benefits of local NGO action in the national environment should set the background for negotiating an appropriate division of labor between the "umbrella," or supportive, international NGO and the national NGO. For example, local NGOs that fear retaliation if they are connected with the release of certain information may choose to send it to an international NGO for submission to the treaty body. At the same time, local NGOs increasingly seek recognition as credible suppliers of information and may wish to be credited for other information or to submit reports in partnership with international NGOs.

Conclusion

At least three principles can be extracted from this summary evaluation. First, the responsibility for protection of women's human rights belongs to all treaty bodies and can be found in all treaties, not only in the UN Convention on the Elimination of All Forms of Discrimination against Women. Second, gender integration should be a priority in the role definition of both national and international NGOs, whether their mandates explicitly focus on women or not. Third, both national and international NGOs play critical and potentially complementary roles in the UN and internationally.

While the treaty bodies (except CEDAW) are increasingly trying to "ask the woman question," gendered questions on specific rights are still inconsistent and sporadic, and questions directed at incidents of reported violations of the human rights of women are often conceptually incomplete. The treaty bodies have not yet fully addressed questions about women's human rights in their specific recommendations and concluding comments, which have great potential use by NGOs in their domestic advocacy. The treaty bodies must increase their understanding of the obstacles women face. At the very least, any discussion of the professionalization of the treaty bodies must recognize that knowledge of women's human rights should be a key qualification for experts, male and female.

Concrete understanding of the substantive issues of women's rights will be advanced by the increased and effective participation of national women's groups. All the human rights treaty bodies would benefit from greater national NGO information and advocacy. Participation and advocacy would also contribute to important new conceptions of state responsibility, particularly the development of notions of international accountability of states for abuses committed by nonstate actors. Moreover, increased NGO participation would enhance domestic NGOs' capacity to amplify the impact of the treaty bodies' recommendations and criticisms by organizing educational campaigns on international standards and publicizing treaty bodies' concluding comments at the national level. Strengthening the capacity of treaty bodies to respond to national NGOs, especially women's NGOs, could thus yield a kind of constructive synergy.

The arguments for participation of women's NGOs need to be weighed against the negative factors, which include diversion of time and scarce resources into an overwhelmed, often politically compromised international system with weak direct enforcement power. These are real concerns. At minimum, there is a great need for improved transparency, both in the workings of the UN system and the actions of governments. Scheduling meetings in-country and facilitating the travel of experts, among other steps, would greatly benefit national NGOs. The question of resources dedicated to NGOs must also be addressed if the language of partnership in whatever guise is going to be used. Commitments to widen the pool of NGOs with the capacity to operate in international forums—as critical constituents or even potentially as experts in the future—must be made at all levels.

The experience of women's NGOs at world conferences and summits in Rio, Vienna, Cairo, Copenhagen, and Beijing also bears reiterating. Activists brought their demands to the international level so that the claim to the universality of women's human rights would be addressed concretely at local, national, and international levels. The source of legitimacy for enforcing this claim to universality lies to a great extent in the normative power of UN treaties as well as in participatory values. Yet, we cannot lose sight of the fact that women's groups, recently arrived to claim "international human rights," cannot move automatically into the implementing spheres of agencies and other UN entities. They face great dangers that they will find their not-yet-solidified rights mixed in with other considerations at the programmatic level, as most agencies do not have rights protection as the basis of their activities.

In sum, there is a fertile but tricky field to negotiate for national NGOs, especially women's NGOs, to participate fully in the UN treaty system. On the one hand, there is a great interest among local and national women's groups in using the treaty system for human rights protection. Much of this interest emerges from the explosive growth of human rights as the language of empowerment for women in all regions; the dramatic priority given rhetorically to women's human rights through the world conferences has stoked this interest. On the other hand, this interest is tempered by justified skepticism, and in some cases active distrust, about both international structures and traditional law-based or legal-style activity. There is limited information within women's groups about the actual nature of the work of the treaty bodies and the content of the human rights treaties. This is compounded by the domestic gaps between women's groups, which are often based on development models, and the traditional rights groups, which are often focused on law and the prioritization of civil and political rights. Recognizing that this discussion is set within the larger debate about the relationship between rights and development and the future of the nation-state, the task is to open up the space to let the NGOs define their roles for themselves.

Notes

I would like to thank Sheila Dauer, Amnesty International USA's Program on Women's Rights, Susana Fried, Center for Women's Global Leadership, and Ilana Landsberg-Lewis, UNIFEM, for their insightful comments on earlier drafts of this chapter.

1. The Women's Rights Advocacy Program (WRAP) of the International Human Rights Law Group was established in the fall of 1992 to build the capacity of local and national women's groups to use human rights language, methods, and mechanisms as tools in their work. By collaborating at national and international levels with women's groups, WRAP contributes to the progressive strengthening and development of standards to hold governments accountable for violations of women's civil, cultural, economic, political, or social rights.

2. Choosing to apply for consultative status is not without problems and trade-offs. ECOSOC can refuse to accept an NGO on the basis of political or ideological opposition of member governments; the cost and time required to apply are considerable and may result in a diversion of scarce resources. See Wiseberg 1996 for a

description of the strengths and limitations of the new process.

3. The concepts of "respect, ensure, and fulfill" are central to understanding the promises of governments. First, governments or their agents must not themselves violate rights; second, they must ensure that rights are not abused by nongovernmental agents; finally, they must create the conditions in which persons can enjoy their rights. See, generally, Henkin 1981; Alston 1991.

4. For a comprehensive application to reproductive self-determination for women of the full range rights articulated in the various articles of human rights treaties, see Rebecca J. Cook (1995).

5. The work of the special rapporteur on violence against women has begun to synthesize a great deal of the fact-based and analytical research on violence against women, its causes, and its consequences. Her first report addressed violence against women in the family (UN Doc. E/CN.4/1996/53 and Add.2) and her second report examined violence against women in the community (UN Doc. E/CN.4/1997/47).

6. See discussions on the crucial question of state accountability for private actor abuses of women's human rights by Celina Romany (1994); Rebecca J. Cook (1994a); and Donna Sullivan (1995b).

7. These meetings also prioritized the development and application of a framework for state accountability for violations of women's human rights (see United Nations 1995f, paras. 38–55).

8. For the weaknesses of the CEDAW in this regard, see Clapham 1997, 18–20; Byrnes 1989; Jacobson 1991; and Wright 1993.

9. ILANUD is a UN-related organization based in Costa Rica and directed by Alda Facio.

10. The countries involved in this project were Bangladesh, Canada, Morocco, the Philippines, Turkey, and Zaire (now Republic of Congo).

11. Guidance for creating "shadow reports" is contained in a short paper prepared by the Women's Rights Advocacy Program of the International Human Rights Law Group, which sets out the reasons for producing shadow reports (e.g., providing alternative information to the treaty bodies; building coalitions; creating benchmarks for domestic education and activism using standards agreed upon by the government). Copies of the *Draft Guidelines* can be obtained from the Law Group at ihrlg@aol.com or by phoning (+ 1-202-232-8500). The IWRAW/Commonwealth *Manual on Reporting under the Women's Convention* also provides comprehensive information for reporting, supplementing the UN's Manual on Human Rights Reporting (United Nations 1997).

12. UNIFEM is currently asking the participants for permission to put the shadow reports on line so that other NGOs can see various models of NGO reports.

13. Similarly, many activists involved in the World Conference for Women in Beijing commented on the clear tensions between national and international NGOs and among national NGOs that opt to participate in international forums. The NGOs that focused on government activities in the formal conference were quite distanced—literally and politically—from the NGOs that focused on the events of the NGO forum. In some countries, the splits between national NGOs that chose to work in the formal governmental sector and those that focused on the NGO forum are still being felt.

11

The United Nations Women's Conferences and Feminist Politics

Lois A. West

The last quarter of the twentieth century will be remembered for rapid progress in improving the status of women worldwide and the corresponding international spread of feminism. Women who have worked with the United Nations have provided much of the impetus for the internationalization of feminism. Much progress has been made: Girls and women are better educated; improved communication networks have helped raise women's consciousness of discrimination; public barriers to women's political participation are breaking down; and women are becoming more prosperous; women's health is improving; women are fighting to eradicate violence and to end their victimization. Social change for women is happening rapidly and globally, but there is still no society where women enjoy the same opportunities as men. Women remain the "second sex," defined as "the Other" in relation to men. Discrimination hits women the hardest in terms of time and money (Buvinic 1997), and globally, across all societies, women have less income and less free time than men. A significant reason for the continuing inequalities is that women are forced to operate within "masculinized" organizations and structures.

This chapter describes women's activism in relation to the four United Nations women's conferences in 1975 (Mexico City), 1980 (Copenhagen), 1985 (Nairobi), and 1995 (Beijing). It reviews the politics surrounding UN women's conferences to examine the ways in which feminist activism has affected international politics on women. I argue that women's presence at UN conferences has redefined global agendas. Through international nongovernmental organizations (NGOs), computer networking, and other new communications technologies, feminists have been able to insert women-oriented concerns and agendas into international discourse and practice.

But feminists have also, for the last several decades of the twentieth century, organized to re-create political processes from a woman's standpoint and to define power in new ways, not as political zero-sum games (see Dominelli and

Gollins 1997). The NGO forums that have accompanied United Nations women's conferences have constituted a kind of counterpolitics that has provided alternative structures for networking and organizing. As social movement events, they have focused the organized and noninstitutionalized efforts of excluded groups to change national and international political processes. Such events are important for mobilizing movement participants and for revitalizing the global movement. As a form of counterpolitics, they have contributed to social change but also spawned resistance and backlash politics by male-dominated forces of tradition that are seeking to reestablish hegemonic masculinities (Connell 1995).

This chapter is not simply an academic exercise. I attended three of the four UN women's conferences and the parallel NGO forums not only as a feminist activist but also as a writer and recorded my experiences in feminist publications (see, e.g., West 1980). I was able to attend two of the conferences with my world-traveled mother, whose religious interests and peace activism were a nice counterweight to my American feminism. We found each event wonderful in its own way. Yet there were real differences between the intergovernmental conferences and the NGO forums: while feminist practices defined the forums, the masculine organizational forms of governments and the United Nations circumscribed the official conferences. Women's political activism, spontaneity, and cutting-edge concerns defined the NGO forums and continuously challenged the hierarchical political structures and forces of masculinized tradition fostered by the intergovernmental conferences. At the same time, women (and women's concerns) were increasingly making their way into the formal structures of the UN conferences, even moving beyond the women's conferences into other UN conferences in the 1990s, as more elite women (who did not necessarily have an entirely elitist agenda) came to represent their governments. This dialectic between feminist activism at the NGO forums and the politics of intergovernmental conferences is the focus of this chapter.

The United Nations Women's Decade Conferences, 1975–1985

Women were actively, albeit quietly, organizing in the international arena prior to the establishment of the League of Nations in 1920. Among the first women's international nongovernmental organizations (INGOs) were the Women's International League for Peace and Freedom (WILPF), organized in 1915 (Galey 1995a, Meyer this volume), and the International Alliance of Women, which in 1926 echoed WILPF in linking equality, development, and peace as international issues for women. These issues became the later themes for the UN Decade for Women (Fraser 1995, 81). Women's INGOs promoted the establishment of the United Nations in 1945 (Stienstra 1994), but it was not until the creation of the UN Commission on the Status of Women (CSW) in 1947 that women were first formally organized as a separate, diplomatic force in the UN arena. The CSW initially worked on issues of legal equality for women and then in the 1960s concentrated on economic and social development (Galey 1994, 113; Galey 1995b).

International Women's Year, Mexico City 1975

The CSW's quiet work to develop an international women's agenda during its first three decades was linked to the larger United Nations agenda through the UN International Women's Year (IWY) and the first UN women's conference in Mexico City in 1975 (Allan, Galey, and Persinger 1995). In the Mexico City World Plan of Action, governments agreed for the first time on a global public policy to end discrimination against women internationally and to support equality for women with men (Mair 1986). This was also the first time that women constituted a majority of representatives at a UN conference—73 percent of government representatives and 85 percent of government heads in attendance were women, although there were more wives of leaders than women heads of state, who at that time only numbered three (Allan, Galey, and Persinger 1995, 33).

Despite the strong presence of women, the elite nature of the governmental meeting was painfully obvious. Significantly, representatives from INGOs and NGOs, individuals, and the media who had gathered to observe the conference convened an alternative meeting called the Tribune. Allan, Galey, and Persinger (1995, 39) argued that the Tribune was an attempt to organize the "potentially thousands of observers who flock[ed] to the site." Sapiro (1994, 481) argued that it was a reaction to the perception "that some women delegates were being used to foster their governments' own aims." In either case, the Tribune solidified into a social movement organization, the International Women's Tribune Center, which became a permanent international center for research, documentation, and communication on the plan of action and subsequent conferences (Allan, Galey, and Persinger, 1995, 41). It helped create feminist alternatives to the traditional patterns of male-dominated networking available up to that point.

Thus, the early efforts of elite women working within the UN structure motivated the creation of oppositional processes on behalf of larger constituencies of women who felt excluded from elite politics. The Tribune marked the beginning of NGO parallel conferences where the real concerns of women did not get lost in the elite structures of UN conferences. But compared to subsequent conferences, the worldwide media barely noticed the Mexico City conference, with its 133 government representatives, or the Tribune, with its 6,000 attendees.

The most notable development following the first UN women's conference was the adoption by the United Nations General Assembly of the Convention on the Elimination of All Forms of Discrimination against Women (CEDAW) on 19 December 1979 (Winslow 1995b, 179). While the UN conferences negotiated nonbinding plans of action, the Convention is a binding treaty obliging governments to end discrimination against women. The CSW, which developed the Convention, gave women the free space to adopt what was essentially a feminist document without ever using the term "feminist" (Fraser 1995, 78). CEDAW is significant because it gives individual women a legal instrument to fight discrimination. The actual formal signing-on to CEDAW first took place at the opening ceremonies of the 1980 Mid-Decade Conference in Copenhagen (Fraser 1987, 126).

The Mid-Decade Review: Copenhagen 1980

UN policymakers who had orchestrated the 1975 International Women's Year quickly realized that a year was not enough time to address the agenda laid out in Mexico City. Thus, the IWY became the UN Decade for Women. A mid-decade review was planned for Copenhagen in 1980 and a conference marking the end of the decade was scheduled for 1985. The meeting of interested observers in Copenhagen was no longer called the Tribune but the NGO Forum; eight thousand women attended. At the official conference, 145 governments were represented (Seagar 1997, 13).

The Copenhagen conference and forum were considered the "most conflictive" of all the conferences of the women's decade (Jaquette 1995, 45). The official conference agenda became submerged under specific nationalist causes—Zionism was equated with racism and the Palestinian cause was celebrated, resolutions condemned governments for authoritarianism and apartheid, and the developing countries of the South condemned the developed North for political and economic neocolonialism. At the NGO Forum, Iranian women revolutionaries held a news conference celebrating the outcome of their revolution as they called for a return to the veil as a symbol of anticolonialism, and Ukrainian women demonstrated for a free Ukraine. Conference President Lise Ostergaard remarked, "I get a strong feeling here that the UN conference is being politicised, by dealing with . . . special situations of women in crisis" (Hall 1980). Were these signs of feminism dominated by masculinized nationalism, or could one argue that women were expressing some kind of incipient feminist nationalism (see West 1997)? The movement split between those who

PHOTO BY LOIS A. WEST.

Fig. 11.1. Women demonstrate at NGO Forum, Copenhagen, 1980.

felt that women were being used by male-dominated political and revolutionary movements to further masculine agendas and women in those movements
who, like the PLO's Leila Khaled, felt that they could not separate their national struggles from their feminist ones and should not be asked to do so (Interview: Leila Khaled 1980).

The End of the Decade: Nairobi, 1985

By the end of the UN women's decade, feminist issues that had been invisible ten years before had become mainstreamed. At the third women's conference in Nairobi, Kenya, attendance at the parallel forum almost doubled to
15,000 participants. African representatives included at least 3,000 Kenyan

women, many from rural areas (Cagatay et al. 1986). The official conference included 1,546 women delegates, 81 percent of the 1,899 representatives of the 157 governments (Patton 1995, 65). The official conference demonstrated progress in addressing a broad range of issues, including a condemnation of all forms of violence against women and calls to end degrading media images of women and reeducate abusive men. Despite this significant consensus, the official conference "ignored, eliminated, or expressed reservations on some issues such sexual preference/same sex relationships, equal pay for work of equal value, the right of married women to own property" (Patton 1995, 73).

At the NGO Forum women's economic status emerged as one of the central themes. As in Copenhagen, where Danish women gave tours of women's organizations, Kenyan women's groups organized tours for foreigners to their organizations to provide us exposure to their daily lives, which were taken up with securing the most basic of human needs—getting adequate drinking water, food, housing and employment.[1] At the Forum, African women activists described which development policies worked and which did not and demonstrated in very practical ways how their grassroots organizing could mitigate the effects of failed, exclusionary development policies. A network of Third World women (Development Alternatives with Women for a New Era, or DAWN) had been organizing since the previous conference to develop alternative economic analyses and proposals (Cagatay, Grown, and Santiago 1986), and these efforts coalesced into a series of critique workshops (Mair 1986, 590). These critiques did not make their way into the official document except to highlight the problems of women and poverty.

In the area of women's human rights, North African women doctors described their work on eliminating clitoridectomies and female genital mutilation. Concerned to move beyond policy into activism, feminists held weeklong workshops at the Forum (attended by five hundred people) on how to implement CEDAW. Out of these workshops grew the International Women's Rights Action Network, a global network to publicize and encourage the implementation of CEDAW (Fraser 1995, 90). Feminist organizing led to the mainstreaming of women's issues and to the notion, spawned by the concepts set forth in CEDAW, that women's rights are human rights (see Fraser 1995; Joachim this volume).

The 1995 Beijing Conference

The Context

The 1995 Fourth UN Conference on Women in Beijing represented a symbiosis of efforts by elite women working in the United Nations and international arenas and grassroots women working at the local levels that internationalized feminist movements to an unprecedented degree. It also saw an organized, antifeminist backlash of conservative, traditional, religious movements and states. Three important developments shaped the politics of this conference: (1) the recognition in reports by the United Nations that women's global status was not improving significantly; (2) the introduction into diverse UN conferences of a women's agenda, effectively mainstreaming what had been "women's issues"; and (3) the proliferation of feminist NGOs and the rise of new communications technologies (e-mail, the World Wide Web), leading to the globalization of women's networks.

In 1987, the United Nations devised a System-Wide Plan for Women and Development (1990-1995), which instigated a program to develop statistics and indicators on women's status, improve public information and networks on women's issues, and improve the quality of information and policy analysis. The International Research and Training Institute for the Advancement of Women (INSTRAW) became an important part of the process (Pietilä and Vickers 1994). These efforts made data available on women's status internationally that made possible better analysis of regional and global trends (see United Nations 1991a, b; 1995c, e; United Nations Department of Public Information 1995, 1996; United Nations Development Programme 1995; for reviews, see Chamberlain 1996; Guan 1996). Particularly important was the development of new measures—the gender-related development index (GDI) and the gender empowerment measure (GEM) (United Nations Development Programme 1995). The GDI provides a way to assess how countries compare to one another on quality of life indicators. The GEM measures women's power in terms of their share of national income and their labor force participation.

A second significant trend beginning in the early 1990s was that feminists began to mainstream women's issues into the traditionally male-dominated agendas of the non-women's UN conferences (both the NGO forums and the official conferences). At the UN Conference on Environment and Development in Rio de Janeiro in 1992 (known as the Earth Summit), women succeeded in inserting into the Plan of Action a chapter concerning women's issues as they relate to environment and development (Charlesworth 1996, 540). According to Freeman, "by far the largest group at the NGO Forum, and the most effective during the whole preparatory process, were the women . . . organized . . . dedicated, and they had the benefit of extraordinary leadership in the person of Bella Abzug, co-chair of . . . the Women's Environment and Development Organization (WEDO). . . . She was able to shift the focus of the Earth Summit and every other UN conference toward what she always called the 'gender perspective'" (1996, 14).

At the 1993 World Conference on Human Rights in Vienna, "the women's groups, urged on by UNIFEM, impressed many participants with their campaign to gain acceptance of the principle that 'women's rights are human rights.'" (Freeman 1996, 14). A section "The Equal Status and Human Rights of Women" was included in the Vienna Plan of Action and emphasized the need to eradicate violence against women in both public and private life (Charlesworth 1996, 540; Joachim this volume). At the 1994 Conference on Population and Development in Cairo, chapter 4 of the Program of Action focused on empowering women as a means of improving women's health (Charlesworth 1996), and consensus was reached that "educating and empowering women [is] the most effective way to reduce population growth rates and promote sustainable development" ("Conferences Summarized" 1996, 17; see also Higer this volume).

The third significant factor affecting international politics on women in the 1990s was the high degree of feminist organizing. Since the 1970s, feminist organizations were proliferating almost everywhere, spurred in many instances by the UN women's decade (Basu 1995; Margolis 1993; for a guide to movements see Shreir 1988). Even if they did not call themselves feminists, women were organizing to improve the lot of females in their societies. Women marched in the late 1970s against dowry burnings in India, organized all-women's political parties in Iceland in 1975 (on the heels of Mexico City) and in the Philippines for the 1986 elections following the ouster of Ferdinand Marcos. By the mid-1990s, the Inter-Parliamentary Union in Europe was organizing meetings to help women parliamentarians improve their electoral chances. Women's studies proliferated and internationalized (see Women's Studies: A World View 1996) as did grassroots organizations that organized into GROOTS—Grassroots Organizations Operating Together in Sisterhood (Basu 1995; Azad 1996).

In such auspicious circumstances, the Fourth World Conference on Women (FWCW) and the parallel NGO Forum were an overwhelming success in terms of numbers and representation. Over thirty thousand women attended the NGO forum (five times the attendance in Mexico and double that in Nairobi) in the Beijing suburb of Huairou, and 189 governments were represented at the formal downtown Beijing conference (Seagar 1997, 13), with a majority of delegates being women (although states still sent male-headed delegations). At the Forum, every class status from peasant to worker to movie star, and every race, ethnicity, religion, nationality, and sexual preference seemed to be represented, and for the first time a large number of young people, babies, and men attended (Ahmed 1996).

The Chinese government had initially been very enthusiastic about hosting the women's conference after failing to be chosen to host the international Olympic games. This openness helped to empower the Chinese women's movement; Wang Zheng notes that "the word feminism not only began to appear fre-

©JIMMY MARGULIES. REPRINTED BY PERMISSION.

Fig. 11.2. Hillary Clinton goes to Beijing.

quently in official women's journals and newspapers but also became a positive word. . . . Many women participants saw the FWCW and the NGO Forum as the greatest opportunity of the century for them to break China's intellectual isolation and to push the boundaries of women's activism in China" (Wang Zheng 1996, 195). Attendance at regional preparatory conferences throughout China and at international meetings empowered many Chinese women and was their first exposure to international feminism (Hsiung and Wong 1997).

However, in the aftermath of the 1989 Tiananmen Square massacre and in anticipation of large numbers of potential critics and demonstrators, Chinese government officials in early 1995 developed cold feet about hosting the conference and reacted by making the NGO Forum difficult for women to attend. They tried to limit and control the Forum by moving the site from Beijing to a difficult-to-reach suburb at the last minute, making visas difficult to obtain, and mishandling logistics to the point of disorganization.

An international honor to China had now become an international threat to China's political stability or, rather, to state control of power, in the eyes of the nation's top leaders. The decision to isolate the NGO Forum expressed not only the leaders' determination not to let this event disturb China's political status quo but also the state's suspicion and hostility toward women's spontaneous activities. (Wang Zheng 1996, 196)

Fig. 11.3. Welcome to the Beijing Women's Conference.

The response of the Chinese women's movement was to go underground with its feminism. Chinese women said, "Just keep a low profile and wait for the paranoia to pass" (Wang Zheng 1996, 197). Those on the outside attempting to get into the system played by the government rules. Tibetan feminists who wanted to attend the conference came through Western countries, hiding their Tibetan identities. This was the first women's conference to confront the power of a male-dominated security state so directly.

The repressive security apparatus evident at the Forum consisted not only of hundreds of plainclothes male security officers (there were females, but they were significant for their low numbers) but also of security operatives within workshops—an unprecedented event for a women's conference. I had organized or been involved in workshops at two previous NGO forums. At the Beijing forum, I ran two thematically unrelated workshops that were curiously assigned to the same room, with the same (and only) man, a male science professor from a local Beijing university, attending both. I thought he might have been there as a security monitor for the television equipment—but why a professor? One Chinese source said, "The government had placed an English-speaking spy in every tent and meeting room to take detailed notes on every workshop—the content of the presenters' speeches, the questions asked, who asked them, and the answers—and if anything inappropriate happened, this spy was to call the police immediately" (Lee 1996; see also *New York Times*, 3 September 1995).

Politics at Beijing: Backlash and Outcomes

While attendance at the Beijing conference and the NGO forum exceeded anything seen previously, feminists for the first time at a UN women's conference faced an organized opposition. The proliferation of feminist groups and the success at mainstreaming a women's agenda into non-women's conferences had mobilized a backlash from conservative male-dominated religious institutions, states, and movements that solidified in Beijing. In the United States, Richard G. Wilkins, a Brigham Young University constitutional law professor, argued that "UN conferences have become captives of a well-organized left-wing lobby" (1996, 288); and "for the past twenty years, the best-organized, best-funded (often with government subsidies), and most-vocal NGOs have been feminist organizations controlled by the Women's Caucus, headed by former Cong. Bella Abzug . . . The power of this group (vaunted by Abzug herself) is formidable" (289). Recounting his experience at the 1996 UN conference on shelter in Istanbul (Habitat II), Wilkins was "astounded at the breadth of the Women's Caucus' total domination of the official NGO presentations before the UN body charged with drafting the Habitat Agenda" (294). He warned that the Beijing platform of action was "a particularly far-reaching document" that was "incorporated directly into U.S. policy—without formal adoption of that document (or its stated objectives) by Congress" (298). Wilkins's statements fall within a long anti–United Nations tradition among the right wing in the United States, and also demonstrate a distinct backlash against the women's conferences and feminist agendas (see Faludi 1991).

On an international level, the countermovement was disorganized but came together on the Beijing plan of action and attacked what it considered "radical feminist" ideas. In the United States, right-wing commentators like Cal Thomas decried the conference for its antifamily agenda and control by radical feminists. The Christian Broadcasting Network had various news commentators lambaste the conference on the same grounds, and conservative Republicans in Congress sought to withhold U.S. support for federal officials' attendance at the conference. The Rockford Institute Center on the

Family in America, a right-wing think tank, produced a newsletter, which it circulated at the official conference, criticizing "the Nordic Factor" as a Scandinavian plot designed as a conscious campaign against nature;[2] the deliberate elimination of the private; the dismissal of marriage; disdain for men; the affirmation of "reproductive rights"; and "schizophrenia over women and the economy," in that the plan of action advocated for working women as well as homemakers (Carlson 1995). During the conference, Abzug was singled out for nasty criticism by Republicans Bob Dole and former president George Bush; Bush thought she was cochairing the conference (Morgan 1996, 82)!

This backlash was not solely a Western countermovement. The Grand Imam Sheikh of Al-Azhar circulated a "statement pertaining to the Fourth International Conference" that said:

> The Beijing Conference is only one stage in a connected series aiming at innovating new ways of life. Contravening religious values and destroying well-established customs and traditions without considering that these values, restrictions, and traditions have protected many nations from collapsing into the dungeon of sexual promiscuity, the disorders of psychological troubles or slipping into the quagmire of moral decay and disintegration [sic]. (Al-Azhar 1995, 3)

At the UN conferences prior to Beijing, the Vatican, Roman Catholic–dominated countries, and fundamentalist Muslim governments had raised objections, especially about reproductive rights and issues of sexuality. In Beijing, these same forces contested parts of the official Platform for Action during the five regional preparatory conferences. This resistance took the form of bracketing the parts of the Platform the countermovement found objectionable, thus reserving them for discussion at the conference rather than agreeing on language ahead of time. This resulted in "almost 40 percent of the text enclosed in what came to be called the Holy Brackets" (Morgan 1996, 80). A great deal of wrangling went on about the use of the term "gender," which was bracketed because the sheikh, for one, thought the term had the "intent to squash and abolish the difference between male and female by reducing the human being into a depraved creature, to be neither male nor female" (Morgan 1996, 4). Interestingly, Mary Ann Glendon, a Harvard law professor who headed the Vatican delegation, was instrumental in helping to unbracket gender.

In spite of this organized resistance, governments approved some significant phrases: the Platform for Action refers to the family "in its various forms"; it mainstreams the idea that "women's rights are human rights"; and it recognizes that the human rights of women include "their right to have control over and decide freely and responsibly on matters relating to their sexuality, including sexual and reproductive health, free of coercion, discrimination, and violence" (Platform for Action 1996, 191). It reaffirms that rape as a strategy of warfare is a war crime that can be prosecuted as such. It urges governments to measure women's unpaid work. It calls for an enforcement protocol for CEDAW. For the first time, the Platform considered the needs of girls—from eradicating violence against girls to securing their primary school education and eliminating discrimination in schools. Countries agreed to develop strategies to alleviate poverty, especially absolute poverty in all its forms; to end female genital mutilation, prenatal sex selection, and violence against women; to alleviate the effects of armed conflict on females; to empower women to participate in decision making; and to provide the institutional mechanisms for the advancement of women. The Platform said that the media should end gender stereotyping, and women should be included in policymaking about the environment (International Women's Tribune Center 1996).

Right-wing critics alleged that the Platform focused too much on sex and not enough on the family. The Vatican criticized its "exaggerated individualism." The Associated Press reported on 21 September 1995 that Sudan promised to ignore it where it conflicted with Islamic fundamentalism. The *Long Beach Press Telegram* on 12 September 1995 quoted a conservative Canadian women's group as saying that the Platform "imposes Western feminist cultural values worldwide and as such is a racist document." Where the Platform upheld the rights of information and privacy for young women with regard to family planning issues, conservatives pitted parental rights against the rights of female teenagers. The NGO Coalition for Women and the Family circulated documents at the official conference arguing that "Sovereignty Begins at Home. The rights of parents are natural and pre-exist the state."

Platform supporters criticized the plan for not linking women's human rights to economic rights and for not dealing with the effects on women of economic globalization, especially with governments cutting social services and welfare programs. Barbara Hopkins took issue with the sometimes inappropriate language of the Platform: "The language of war is used to describe policies to improve women's health and policies aimed at eliminating domestic violence" (1996, 535). Despite these limitations, the Beijing Platform of Action represents a mainstreamed international feminism that subsumes feminist goals under an umbrella of human rights.

Impacts

One way to measure conference outcomes is by developing specific indicators: Was there a program of action developed and initiated? Did it get put into place? Did it get funded? How was it funded and by whom? Did it have a positive impact or any impact at all? The provision of quantitative data on the status of women was one positive outcome of the UN conferences, but it carried many ambiguities as well. The United Nations apparatus as well as national governments produced regional and global status reports prior to each conference. In addition, NGOs analyzed specific issues (women in poverty, the environment and women). But individual government reports tend to put a glossy spin on anything and everything their countries do for women. This was also true for country progress reports after Beijing.

In the United States, the President's Interagency Council on Women published an upbeat follow-up report. But language such as "despite serious budgetary constraints" and "redirecting existing funding to meet these objectives" (President's Interagency Council on Women 1996, 27) highlighted problems with government implementation in an age of declining federal funding sources; programs seemed more symbolic than programmatically real. Moving oversight of the Council to the first woman secretary of state, Madeleine Albright, signaled the Clinton administration's commitment to keep the Beijing objectives alive (President's Interagency Council on Women 1997). Albright's attendance at the Beijing conference and her continuing support of the UN objectives for women were important markers, if only symbolic ones, of U.S. support for the international policy objectives on women, but as of this writing they do not appear to mark any real advances in the sharing of resources.

The Chinese government published a report on the situation of women prior to the Beijing conference (People's Republic of China 1994) for English-speaking foreigners. Following the conference, Hsiung and Wong (1997) argued that for ordinary Chinese women, rather than just the Communist Party elite, the conference had a positive impact. But this impact got lost because of the way Chinese women were framed in international feminist discourses and in the official party line. Where the party focused on how much progress Chinese women had made since the 1949 revolution, feminists used different statistics to construct a negative analysis of the situation of women in China and the communist state. Hsiung and Wong argue that this put Chinese women between two rigid ideological frameworks that did not acknowledge the significant impact the conference had on developing a Chinese feminist movement and a distinctive brand of Chinese women's nationalism. Between the discourses of Western feminists and the Chinese state, Chinese women became objectified and posed as mindless objects. Yet Chinese women were able to benefit from involvement in preparations for the conference that extended women's networks, created sizable staffs, increased resources for women's issues, and helped elite women connect with ordinary women's issues.

In 1996, the Women's Environmental and Development Organization published a country-by-country analysis of follow-ups to Beijing. The report argued that there was a need to close the gap between rhetoric and reality. Of the twenty-six countries WEDO reviewed a year after the conference, "few ... report[ed] any new resources allocated to implement the Platform" (WEDO 1996b, 6). The report argued that positive outcomes included governments reporting back and popularizing the Beijing Platform, implementation of aspects of the Platform through ad hoc governmental commissions, innovative actions by women in political positions of power, and involvement of women's NGOs in collective campaigns. "Perhaps the most significant milestone is the apparent acceptance of mainstreaming—that gender perspectives are essential to all programs and issues" at the United Nations (WEDO 1996b, 8).

These impacts seem meager. However, Staggenborg argues that organizational and social movement analysts must rethink the criteria for evaluating success: "Groups that are unsuccessful in terms of organizational maintenance and policy outcomes may be effective as the centers of movement communities and as the originators of cultural changes. Although the successes of many feminist organizations tend to be hidden, they are likely to have an impact on subsequent rounds of collective action" (1995, 353). Further, the feminist movement has achieved cultural change, and the markers of such change include the creation of alternative institutions and pools of activists, models of collective action, and ideologies to attract supporters.

The United Nations women's conferences were significant markers of such cultural change. At the level of discourse and symbols, they marked the progress women were making vis-à-vis men—the breakdown of barriers between the public and private, the unprecedented independence of women, the degree to which women are coming to understand or be conscious of their social conditions. But the NGO forums also enacted alternative forms of power, a feminist politics. They brought to life a participatory democracy that generated immeasurable discussion, combined with consumerism for and by women, cultural education and exposures, hoopla, fun, and festivities. They resembled women's world fairs that mixed serious political and economic concerns with street demonstrations, socializing, ad hoc women's markets, and shopping. Spontaneity, disorganization, networking, consensus, and coalition building all coalesced to define these movement events as counterpolitical spaces.

At Beijing, telecommunications and advanced technologies facilitated such politics, enabling new networks, expanding participation, and providing a means to argue points of view. In preparation for the conference, women used e-mail to communicate about logistical problems and to organize women, panels, and their own travel arrangements. Several Web networks were set up just to disseminate information on the conference and allow prospective participants to communicate. At the NGO forum, Apple Computer, Hewlett Packard, and the Women's Networking Support Program of the Association for Progressive Communications staffed a formidable computer center that generated 1,700 free e-mail accounts and 100,000 visits to the international World Wide Web, and included the use of e-mail, electronic conferencing, databases, Internet navigation tools, access to conference documents, and user support (Technology Links Forum 1995). Networking went on before, during, and after the conference. People communicated and organized around issues raised through these networks, allowing a kind of virtual participation for those unable to attend—you could be there on the Web without being there in person. Political causes were played out over the networks. For example, prostitutes' rights advocates were upset with the content of the Platform as well as the debate on prostitution, and sought to organize women at the conference to help rewrite the Platform.

The openness of the forum continually challenged the hierarchical political structures and forces of masculinized tradition fostered by the governmental conferences. Official UN conferences are frequently constrained by a politics of consensus that leads governments inevitably to omit matters considered by a minority as remotely controversial. The NGO forums had no such constraints; controversial topics could get raised in an atmosphere of openness, making the forums more intellectually cutting edge. Previously contentious ideas and beliefs of feminism often found their way later into the official conference discourse, and language once used only by radical feminists entered the so-called policy mainstream. I can remember being criticized at earlier conferences for decrying women's "oppression" and invoking "liberation" and "power" instead of using less-threatening words, like "discrimination" and "equality," but Benazir Bhutto's speech at the Beijing conference embraced all five of these concepts (Morgan 1996, 79).

But the hoopla of the forums was not without critics. To Jill Nicholls, the nonhierarchical "creative, imaginative and fun" structures of the 1980 forum looked like a fragmented movement: "The trouble with a loose friendly structure is that it can keep us where the Big Boys want us—in a shambles on the fringes" (1980, 16). Yet according to Jane Jaquette, "Many would argue that the Forum [in Copenhagen] was a more significant international meeting than the official conference" because it further internationalized the feminist movement (1995, 56). Like its Tribune predecessor, it provided feminist alternatives or laid out issues not yet addressed by the official conference.

The last twenty years have produced great cultural changes in the status of women, including the consciousness-raising of women and men. These changes have involved ideological shifts as well as specific policy and organizational outcomes, processes that occurred within the context of the United Nations women's conferences and in other arenas. It is important to emphasize that, while there are no quantitative measures of the impact of the conferences on the development of local and regional women's movements, there were women from all walks of life at all the conferences. Our contributions may not have made it into the forum's daily newspapers, and we most surely were not accounted for by name, but women from all regions of the world were in attendance. Our numbers grew over a twenty-year time span with a dynamism and force that cannot be discounted because of a lack of empirical measures. At the Beijing conference, the sheer number of women from a majority of countries in attendance crossed every imaginable stratum of class, race, age, ethnicity, religion, sexuality, and nationality. The numbers demonstrated that women organized and international feminism thrived. These women were crucially responsible for helping develop an unprecedented international consensus of women's rights.

Notes

1. In the 1980s, "exposure tours" became a mainstay for movement-based organizations seeking foreign support, understanding, and an international audience. To give just one example, some of the most effective tours were run by human rights, labor, and church-based organizations in the Philippines, where foreign human rights groups could document abuses for the foreign press.

2. The Nordic Council of Ministers had regionally organized Denmark, Finland, Iceland, Norway, and Sweden around a Nordic Model for Gender Equality that, not surprisingly, got the highest marks for the GDI and GEM, with Sweden getting the highest GDI value (United Nations Development Programme 1995, 2). The ministers defined the Nordic model as "based on the assumption that women and men must have the same rights, obligations and opportunities in all essential areas of life. This broad concept of equality imposes—in turn—demands on the fundamental structure of society. . . . The goal—an egalitarian society" (Nordic Council of Ministers 1994, 21). The model supported states setting quotas for women's representation on appointed boards, committees, and councils. Finland required a minimum of 40 percent women on government committees (Nordic Council of Ministers 1995, 43). Norway set up a public committee to prepare a job evaluation system to institute comparable-worth and pay equity standards for the entire labor market (1995, 35).

PART III

CONTESTING LANGUAGE: GENDERED RULES IN GLOBAL GOVERNANCE

12

What Is a Worker? Gender, Global Restructuring, and the ILO Convention on Homework

Elisabeth Prügl

What does it mean to be a worker? In the summer of 1996, the International Labor Conference, the policymaking body of the International Labor Organization (ILO), significantly expanded the meaning of "worker" by adopting a convention (international treaty) on homework that sets international labor standards for people who work at home for pay. The convention was the outcome of years of organizing and lobbying on the part of the Self-Employed Women's Association (SEWA) of India and a coalition of homeworker advocacy groups from Asia, Europe, and Africa. It constituted a remarkable step in the context of a restructured global economy in which firms increasingly favor a flexible workforce that effectively lacks protection under labor laws. Because home-based workers are disproportionately female, the debates about the convention provide an ideal case study of the way in which economic regimes of accumulation and modes of regulation build on and create a gender order, constructing notions of femininity and masculinity together with the category worker.

Home-based work has preoccupied debates in international forums at least since the turn of the nineteenth century. At that time, activists and reformers created shared interpretations of industrial homeworkers as exploited dupes who served the needs of capitalists by helping them circumvent new labor laws. They deplored not only the working conditions of homeworkers but also the unhygienic environment of homes and the dangers of contagion this posed for consumers.

The early debate on home-based work coincided with the emergence of a Fordist "regime of accumulation." According to writers in the so-called regulation school, a regime of accumulation fixes the relationship between production and reproduction in particular historical time periods. Under Fordism mass production along a strict division of labor combined with mass consumption to secure steady rates of profit. A "mode of regulation" accompanies every regime of accumulation; it encompasses the social and political rules that ensure that the behavior of workers and consumers conforms with the regime of accumulation. Under Fordism, laws guaranteeing job security and social security ensured worker compliance as well as sufficient worker income to stoke demand and economic growth (Lipietz 1987; Boyer 1990; Harvey 1989).

Modes of regulation entail messages about gender, about proper definitions of womanhood and manhood, that distribute privilege among economic actors. The gendered regulatory edifice of Fordism tended to domesticate women, to define them as housewives and outside the working class. As "domesticated workers" home-based workers constituted an ambiguous entity and an urgent cause for reformers intent on ordering society to ameliorate exploitation and poverty. On the one hand, the puny wages of homeworkers and their deplorable working conditions provided moral arguments for minimum wage legislation, often de facto and sometimes (e.g., in the United States) de jure restricted to women defined as "not-real workers." On the other hand, the fact that homeworkers provided employers a venue to circumvent emerging factory laws sustained arguments in favor of banning homework, framed as supplemental work of housewives that threatened the work of the male breadwinners.

A dismantling of Fordism and the creation of a new regime of accumulation provided the context for the debate on homework in the 1990s. This restructuring entails a change in modes of regulation, including an adjustment of the rules that define labor relations. In this chapter, I introduce the debate around the ILO convention on homework in order (a) to document that constructions of womanhood and manhood are part of a mode of regulation; (b) to show that gender and class positions and locations in the international division of labor foster divergent notions of gender that not only fix power relations between women and men but also create and support inequalities of class and inequalities between people in economic centers and peripheries; and (c) to highlight some characteristics of current arguments about labor regulation circumscribing the possibilities of new modes of regulation under conditions of globalization.

Restructuring and Homework

In the late twentieth century, Fordism appears to be on its way out, as customized small-batch production has tended to replace mass production in many sectors of manufacturing. Many workers have lost job security, governments increasingly seek to foster private initiative by suspending Fordist regulations, and international rules stabilizing the Fordist regime of accumulation have crumbled (Harvey 1989, 174–79). Fordism flourished after the Second World War but reached a crisis in the early 1970s. Declining productivity, profits, and growth, low rates of investment, surplus capacities, mass unemployment, decreasing real wages, and accelerated inflation all indicated a crisis. Many corporations responded by relocating production to countries in the periphery to take advantage of low-cost labor. Assembly workers and industrial homeworkers employed in footloose manufacturing industries in the core lost their jobs to a largely female factory workforce in free-trade zones in Asia, Latin America, and North Africa in the 1970s (Fröbel, Kreye, and Heinrichs 1980, 61 and appendix, table 2; Nash and Fernandez-Kelly 1983). As the need to respond quickly to changes in demand joined imperatives for increased earnings and cost savings, companies sought to meet global competition not only by cutting direct labor costs but also by becoming more flexible. They increasingly subcontracted labor-intensive production and service work to small firms and employed "contingent workers," including home-based workers, who could be easily hired and fired. In this way they did not have to pay wages when they had no orders, and the wages they did pay contingent workers were usually lower than those paid to full-time factory workers. Furthermore, resorting to subcontracting and contingent workers allowed firms to circumvent unions and the high costs of negotiated wages and employment guarantees. New information technologies facilitated flexibilization, and global competition encouraged the spread of the new "just-in-time" strategies (Storper and Scott 1989, 15; Mitter 1986; 1991; 1994; Pineda-Ofreneo 1990; Ward 1990).

A "globalization of states" has accompanied this globalization of production. States no longer serve as buffers for the impacts of unfettered market forces but increasingly adjust the domestic regulatory structure to the demands of global capital (Cox 1996a). The prescriptions of neoclassical, liberal economics have guided the economic policies of governments in North America and Europe, replacing Keynesian demand management. According to neoclassical liberalism the industrial and social policies of the postwar era constitute "structural rigidities" that impair the free play of market forces and impede efforts to overcome the economic crisis. The solution is to eliminate these rigidities by deregulating both product and labor markets, that is, by dismantling the Fordist mode of regulating the economy: The technocrats' supply-side interventions replace Keynesian demand management and corporatist forms of interest intermediation.

Industrializing neomercantilist states in Latin America, Asia, and Africa often postponed the impacts of the crisis by borrowing heavily in private financial markets only to face difficulties repaying their debts (Cox 1987, 274–79). In the 1980s, the World Bank and the International Monetary Fund (IMF) adopted neoclassical prescriptions for indebted countries intent on regaining economic growth. Structural adjustment and stabilization programs were antithetical to Keynesian demand management, often discouraged bargaining between workers and employers, and prescribed cuts in welfare programs. In order to attract foreign capital, governments in the South deregulated their economies and dismantled existing labor protection. Some pursued active policies to encourage subcontracting, on the one hand enticing local companies that produced for domestic markets to draw on rural-based small firms and home-based workers, on the other hand fostering arrangements under which home-based workers produced for an international market (Mitter 1990, 33; Samarasinghe 1993, 38-39; Perera 1995, 103).

Globalization has had ambiguous consequences for women. In the North, some women workers in manufacturing lost jobs as companies searched for low-wage labor; others found jobs as "flexible workers," often laboring in sweatshop conditions. In the South, many suffered the effects of structural adjustment, often having to work double and triple shifts and extending their daily schedules as they could no longer afford to buy processed foods and as governments slashed social spending, leaving the care of the sick, elderly, and children to the unpaid work of women. Here as well, women found jobs in world factories and subcontracting chains but under often deplorable conditions. In the North and the South, home-based workers became ideal workers in a restructured global economy, providing flexibility and costing little. In industrialized countries the decline in the number of home-based workers slowed and sometimes even reversed during the 1980s. Homework increased in Germany, the United Kingdom, France, Italy, Greece, the Netherlands, Spain, Switzerland, the United States, and Canada (Hakim 1984, 9, 11; Federal Republic of Germany 1985, 133; 1988, 70; Bequele 1988, 37–38; Council of Europe 1989, 16; Portes and Sassen-Koob 1987, 46; Rose and Grant 1983, 78). Case studies from Latin America and Asia similarly indicated an increase in the phenomenon. In Latin America and Africa, the economic crisis of the 1980s and monetary stabilization policies forced even more women into unregulated employment (International Labour Organisation 1991, 78; Safa and Antrobus 1992, 61; Benería 1992, 92; Tripp 1992; Daines and Seddon 1993; Nash 1993b, 129).

Social movements, including reinvigorated labor movements as well as women's movements, are resisting the effects of globalization and, in a process reminiscent of the resistance to the effects of the self-regulating market in the nineteenth century, are struggling to find new modes of regulation that supersede globalization (Cox 1996e, 155–56). These modes of regulation will differ from Fordism, entailing changed notions of gender and workers as some women (and men) with family responsibilities have welcomed work arrangements that allow them more easily to combine family work and wage work (Jurik 1998; Boris and Prügl 1996). Not surprisingly, debates about post-Fordist modes of regulation, like the debates about state intervention and the creation of welfare states in the early part of the twentieth century, strongly contest rules of gender. These contestations are especially fierce because they take place at a time when a global women's movement is well institutionalized and plays an active role in debates about globalization.

The ILO and Homework

When the victors of World War I created the ILO through the Treaty of Versailles in 1919, they did so because of commitments they had made to labor unions during the war to ensure their collaboration in the war effort. The Bolshevik revolution and the fear that it might spread to other countries bolstered these commitments. Labor unions and socialists agreed that social welfare could be advanced through international action, and their leaders actively participated in the negotiations to create the ILO. The organization constituted the regulatory counterpart of welfare states at the international level. It was to work towards the regulation of working hours and wages, the establishment of social security protection, and the assurance of the free operation of trade unions (Haas 1964, 140–42).

The ILO is unique among international organizations because of its tripartite structure, which gives a vote to nongovernmental organizations. Governments, unions, and employer organizations all participate in the annual assembly of the International Labor Conference, the International Labor Office (the ILO's secretariat in Geneva) routinely consults all groups on various matters, and it offers technical support to all. Under U.S. hegemony, tripartism in the ILO took a corporatist form in which a vision of harmonious worker-management relations substituted for a view of class relations as inherently conflictual (Cox 1996c). Yet conflict between the "social partners" has increased in the struggle for post-Fordist modes of labor regulation as employers seek to undermine labor regulation, questioning the very purpose for which the ILO was founded and putting unions permanently on the defensive.

Corporatist forms of interest mediation, including the ILO's tripartism, have excluded a significant number of workers who lack job security and never came to share the fruits of industrial growth. Many were women. Because these workers (including home-based workers) constitute a significant part of the post-Fordist workforce, they are now on the agenda of the ILO. The ILO convention on homework is the first to deal with contingent workers. Not surprisingly, debates leading up to the convention were highly contentious and notions of gender played a prevalent role.

Since the 1950s, when newly industrializing countries requested help from the ILO in modernizing their economies and creating employment, research and technical assistance programs have become a significant part of ILO activity. Technical assistance and standard-setting feed into each other and are mutually supportive. The idea for the ILO convention on homework grew out of the activities of the ILO's Programme on Rural Women. During the 1980s, the Programme sponsored a series of studies in which the home-based work of rural women (including crafts production) was identified as an exploitative practice resembling the industrial subcontracting that had preoccupied global debates in the early part of the century. Much of the evidence came from India, where subcontracting arrangements frequently tied women to traders and employers in the garment and textile industries, food processing, and livestock rearing (Singh and Kelles-Viitanen 1987). In the Narsapur district, women formed the backbone of the lace industry, crocheting at home lace that their husbands and middlemen marketed. Much of the lace was exported, and the women earned puny wages. Census enumerators did not count lacemakers as workers; the general perception was that they were nonworking housewives (Mies 1982). In Allahabad, women rolled cigarettes for contractors, making significant contributions to household income and shattering the image that secluded women did not work (Bhatty 1981). A study of rural women in Turkey found carpet weavers working in quasi-independent production and as subcontractors. Even though they were the main weavers, their work was not counted in national economic statistics, and typically their male relatives controlled the income (Berik 1987).

Academic studies proliferated, complementing the findings of ILO-sponsored research (Longhurst 1982; Alonso 1983; Benería and Roldán 1987; Roberts 1989; Weiss 1992; Nash 1993a; Boris and Prügl 1996). This research informed ILO projects for home-based workers in the late 1980s and into the 1990s. The organization collaborated with the Self-Employed Women's Association to conduct legal camps and workers' education classes for home-based *bidi* (cigarette) rollers in India to teach them about their legal position, minimum wage laws, and entitlements to welfare benefits (Rose 1992, 124). It launched a project to promote the welfare of home-based workers in rural Indonesia, Thailand, and the Philippines by creating organizations of home-based workers that would fight for legal rights as well as empower these workers economically (Lazo 1996). In the Philippines the project fostered the formation of a national umbrella group and local organizations of home-based workers. In Thailand, it succeeded in creating an economic support network gaining home-based workers easier access to market outlets, credit, raw materials, and technology (Lazo and Yoodee 1993). In Indonesia, government interference limited activities to a local action project geared towards improving the health of home-based workers in one village (Yayasan Pengembangan Pedesaan 1993).

As evidence accumulated in the 1980s of the deplorable working conditions of home-based workers, staff in the Programme for Rural Women began to float the idea of an international labor standard. An interdepartmental task force, formed in 1984, considered the feasibility and advisability of creating such a labor standard and suggested that further study was necessary. As a result, departments allocated funds to collect, synthesize, and distribute information on legislation in different countries; to produce monographs on homework in six countries; and to convene regional tripartite seminars in Asia and Latin America and a meeting of experts in Geneva. Homework now surfaced in debates at the International Labor Conference, and the ILO's Governing Body decided to put the issue on the official agenda of the 1995 International Labor Conference as a possible item for standard-setting. Two years of debate resulted in the adoption of the ILO convention on homework and a parallel recommendation outlining specific desirable government actions.

Feminists in the ILO did not accomplish this feat by themselves. Of substantial importance was the lobbying, networking, and advocacy of SEWA. SEWA's homeworker protection bill was stalled in the Indian parliament, and SEWA saw an international standard as a way to induce the Indian government to act. While feminist allies moved the issue in the ILO, SEWA lobbied international union federations, gaining the support of the International Union of Food and Allied Workers (IUF) and, importantly, the International Confederation of Free Trade Unions (ICFTU), which the ILO considers the most representative international federation of trade unions. SEWA also fostered links with nongovernmental homeworker advocacy groups in Europe, Southeast Asia, and South Africa that led to the formation of an international network, HomeNet International, with headquarters in Britain. HomeNet members sought support from their own governments and unions for an ILO convention and gave international visibility to the issue by participating in feminist conferences and writing in feminist publications.

In a sense, the purpose of HomeNet and its members was to change the definition of what it meant to be a worker. While the women's movement had undermined the notion that women were nonworking housewives, it was quite a different matter to decide how to incorporate them into modes of labor regulation that presumed a clear spatial separation of home and work and helped maintain a highly unjust gender order. When home-based workers entered into conversations about labor, they destabilized basic elements of the Fordist regulatory structure and the gender order it supported. The way in which different parties defined "worker" in the debate about the homework convention sheds light on emerging gender constructions.

Post-Fordist Identities

The most significant accomplishment of the ILO convention on homework is that it requires governments to "promote, as far as possible, equality of treatment between homeworkers and other wage earners" (International Labour Organisation 1996b). The convention defines homeworkers as employees who should gain access to basic labor rights and protections and be guaranteed the same wages as those who work outside the home. Few countries have laws about homework, and employers frequently treat homeworkers as self-employed and therefore not covered by labor law or collective bargaining agreements. Gaining an international standard that defined homeworkers as no different from other wage workers thus constituted a significant victory for homeworker advocates and their labor allies. It signaled a fundamental reversal of early-twentieth-century constructions of homeworkers as outside the working class and of home-based women workers as not-real-workers.

V. Spike Peterson has argued that it is difficult to include women in categories that were built on the basis of male experience: "Either females cannot be added (they are marginalized), or they must become 'like men' (they are masculinized) or *they are included, and the meaning of the category is transformed to include femaleness*" (1996, 17, emphasis in original). What, then, does it mean that homeworkers have been defined as equal to other wage workers in the convention? Are homeworkers simply added to the category worker? Do they fit that category? Or are they transforming it?

A legal definition gains meaning only through social practices. Therefore, to answer the question about the meaning of the category worker in the ILO convention on homework, it is necessary to look at contexts. Indeed, constructions and reconstructions of women and worker identities have been ongoing in local contexts throughout the processes of restructuring since the 1970s. The debate on homework shows the divergent constructions of one set of social actors, that is, those who participate in global debates, and who in this way participate in establishing a global mode of post-Fordist regulation and an associated gender order. Their different class positions and their positions in the hierarchies of core and periphery influence the arguments they put forward.

As feminists asserted themselves within the labor movement, many unions put aside their traditional hostility towards homeworkers and were prepared to expand the definition of a worker. At the 1996 International Labor Conference, voices portraying homeworkers as outside the working class, "competing with organized labour, organized work places, and avoiding payment of just taxes to the State" were not contradicted, but they were not very loud either (International Labour Organisation 1995a, 34).[1] International union confederations, including the International Textile Garment and Leather Workers Federation (ITGLWF), the IUF, and the ICFTU, had changed their policies at the end of the 1980s from a preference for banning homework to calling for regulation and expressing their solidarity with home-based workers. At the 1996 International Labor Conference unions allowed homeworker advocates full access to their deliberations and were eager to receive the input of advocates. They suggested that Ela Bhatt, General Secretary of SEWA, be allowed to address the conference and deplored employers' opposition to this.

But unions held tight to the language of Fordism and, to some extent, the gender rules that supported it. They shifted the boundaries between home and work but closely guarded the dichotomy itself and the rules it informed. In the language of labor leaders, homeworkers were still, above all, "invisible, marginalized and isolated" with "few or no skills," many being immigrants or members of ethnic minorities (International Labour Organisation 1995a, 30 and 41). In Peterson's terms, unions included homeworkers in the category workers by marginalizing them. They considered homeworkers submissive victims of unscrupulous employers who denied them minimum wages and legal benefits. Homework had advantages primarily for employers because it allowed them to evade labor laws. Homeworkers did not choose this form of employment but were left with no alternative because of a lack of child care, illegal immigration status, or racism and sexism in society. Thus, in the words of the union member from the Netherlands, "if you offered women a choice, they would choose factory work" over homework (ILO Meeting of Experts 1990).

Homeworker advocates, in contrast, challenged the conception of homeworkers as victims, passive, dispersed, and difficult to organize. The difference became clear during the 1995 International Labor Conference when conflict arose over a photo exhibit that HomeNet had organized and displayed at the entrance to the meeting room of the Committee on Homework. Australian union representatives criticized the exhibit as "too pretty" because it showed British homeworkers in tidy homes, Indian homeworkers in colorful saris working together in front of their houses, and Philippine homeworkers collaborating on decorative craft items. The Australians added their own images of homeworkers: black-and-white photos showing tired immigrants stooped over sewing machines in dilapidated houses. HomeNet representatives defended their pictures, insisting that it was necessary to get away from the image of homeworkers as victimized dupes who had no power to change their own situation.

Advocates conceded that homeworkers were exploited but insisted that they could take fate into their own hands, that they had the power to act. Renana Jhabvala, a leader of SEWA, characterized home-based workers as follows:

Vulnerability makes it very difficult for her to organise. But the extreme pressures have in some ways made such a woman strong. She is able to survive under such crushing conditions only because of her deep faith, her courage, her love for her family and her indomitable will. She is weak, but her weakness is due to the pressures of society. She is weak as a social being in her relations to others, as a political being and in her social status. However, as a person she is strong, for her very social weakness requires that she be strong internally. In order to survive in a desperate struggle as the weakest in society she must develop internal resources of courage and strength. It is these strengths she draws on in the rare cases when she tries to fight back, to organise. (Jhabvala 1994, 117–18)

And with some help she did organize, resisting isolation, low wages, and exploitation.

In taking the needs and experiences of home-based workers as definitive, advocates transformed the category worker. First, they challenged Fordist gender rules that defined workers in opposition to housewives and that constructed homeworkers as not-real-workers and their incomes as supplemental. In line with the themes of the Women-in-Development (WID) movement, advocates argued that homeworkers made a crucial contribution to family survival. Their work was as important as that of male income earners, and was often more important Because homeworkers were workers and breadwinners, they should not be merely a marginal addition to the category worker but should be recognized as historical agents. As Ela Bhatt of SEWA insisted, homeworkers were "not demanding charity but their rightful place in the labour movement" (International Labour Organisation 1995b, 59).

Second, homeworker advocates challenged the definition of workers as dependent employees. Drawing on Gandhi's vision of a rural society based on cooperatives and village industries, SEWA leaders saw self-employment not just as a scheme of employers to deprive workers of their benefits but as an ideal to be achieved. In their view, the self-employed were not capitalists depending on their own labor, a construction currently prevalent in the West (Linder 1992). Instead, the self-employed resembled dependent workers: They were weak and needed legal protection. SEWA rejected the separation between employees and the self-employed as artificial and inappropriate, and it organized all informal workers regardless of employment status. SEWA's members included home-based producers and casual workers as well as petty vendors. Some were in subcontracting arrangements, some catered to final consumers, and some took jobs from large clients as available. All worked under extremely adverse conditions and in situations with little negotiating power. At the 1990 Meeting of Experts, Ela Bhatt argued that the definition of a worker should include "whoever contributes to the economy of the country or the household" (ILO Meeting of Experts 1990). The Fordist category "worker," styled as a dependent employee laboring under the supervision of an employer, could not encompass the needs of SEWA members: their desire for flexibility, their preference for working at home, and their need to integrate productive and reproductive activities.

Bringing both the self-employed and employees under the umbrella of labor regulation is precisely what employers and governments informed by neoclassical liberal principles wanted to avoid. They agreed with homeworker advocates on the difficulty of keeping employees and the self-employed apart but, unlike them, used this as a reason for opposing all new labor regulations. For these employers and governments, home-based women workers became stand-ins for the flexible labor force of the future. They surmised that homework, freed from bureaucratic regulation, constituted a fount of wealth and progress in the post-Fordist economy. Rather than an evil, the U.S. employers' delegate intoned at the International Labour Conference, homework was "an opportunity to spur economic growth, create jobs, eliminate poverty, increase productivity and provide real options to the traditional workplace" (International Labour Organisation 1995a, 43). Regulation, by contrast, would be "counterproductive to meeting the preferences of workers, job-creation, a rising standard of living for workers, business growth and competitiveness" (International Labour Organisation 1996a, 17–18). Indeed, in the words of the employers' vice chairman of the conference's Committee on Homework, the convention "had little to do with home work as a vehicle for job creation and the alleviation of poverty and had everything . . . to do with creating machinery and bureaucracy to hold back progress" (International Labour Organisation 1995a, 23). Therefore any attempt to regulate homework needed to be resisted by all means.

Employers did not want to merge homeworkers and workers but sought to relegate the category worker (defined as employee) to the scrap heap of history. They complained that the ILO debate engaged, in the words of the delegate from the United Kingdom, "language from the 1920s," an "old paradigm," to regulate the flexible producers of the new economy (International Labour Organisation 1995a, 26). Employers identified four types of homework: pre-industrial, industrial, telework, and mobile professionals. The concern of employers from the North was mostly to preserve the advantages of telework that involved the use of new communications technologies when working at home. Telework, they insisted, had many advantages: reduced expenses for clothing and meals, reduced travel time, and increased productivity. Because telework was "dynamic and constantly changing," it was "premature and inappropriate" to regulate it (International Labour Organisation 1996a, 4).

Where advocates sought to integrate into the definition of worker women's needs arising from the requirements of reproductive labor, employers tried to disembody and degender homeworkers and create them as operatives in a new world of producers detached from the constraints of place. Their "new paradigm" envisioned professional home-based workers connected to the rest of the world through advanced technologies. The employer delegate from Canada presented himself as an example. "I am a homeworker," he declared. "My office is at home, and at home I am hooked up with all the high-tech equipment that enables me to function effectively. . . . I happen to have a cottage 15 miles by boat out on an island in the middle of Lake Huron. That place will be my workplace for most of the summer, naturally with all the technical equipment I need." He sneered at the suggestion that his type of homeworker would need an international convention: "Will the inspector come and visit me at this workplace by taxi boat at great expense to the taxpayer? Will the inspector determine that occupational health and safety rules require that my employer get rid of the bears and rattlesnakes? I am also a long way from a doctor and hospitals. Do I contravene the first-aid regulations?" (International Labour Organisation 1995b, 224–25).

With the stigma of the weak and exploited female removed, homeworkers became the stars in the futuristic plot of a technology-based flexible economy that transformed the spatial configuration of private and public, masculine and feminine, that defined spheres of work under Fordism. In this plot, the home became the home office, and cottage industry became management from the lodge in the country. Technology had made the Fordist spatial separations of home and workplace irrelevant, enabling a merger of the feminine "private sphere" with the "private sector" of the economy. Ruled by neoclassical liberal economic principles, this combined sphere housed a reconstructed worker: a manager-entrepreneur whose world of work was in cyberspace.

In sum, the effort to include home-based workers, mostly women, in the international labor code brought to light divergent understandings of what it means to be a post-Fordist worker. Unions subsumed home-based workers under the Fordist worker category as employees but attached negative values to these workers, effectively defining them as marginal. In contrast, both homeworker advocates and employers from the North transformed the category itself. Starting from the needs of home-based workers, homeworker advocates destabilized the opposition between home and work, which is fundamental to definitions of employment status, and merged employees and the self-employed. Northern employers also challenged the boundaries of worker status with the intent of dismantling labor protection. All strategies involved definitions of gender. While unions held on to a masculinist definition of worker and implicitly devalued feminine types of work, employers degendered home-based workers in order to project them as androgynous workers of a future in which the spatial boundaries between public and private, masculine and feminine are suspended. In contrast, homeworker advocates constructed home-based workers as part of the core of a new labor movement that takes account of women's experiences and transforms the regulatory structure of work.

Conclusion

Whether post-Fordism really constitutes a new mode of regulation or whether it is Fordism in a new disguise, the facts of the matter are that governments and companies have weakened social protections for workers, that unions in the North have lost considerable power, and that there is foment among workers in many parts of the world. International organizations and global movements have served as forums to debate new ways of regulating a globalized economy. The debate on homework makes clear that modes of regulation do not impose themselves—indeed, there is no one logical form to complement a particular regime of accumulation. Modes of regulation are the result of a political encounter between different discourses, frames, or interpretations arising from the gender and class locations of various actors.

In the case of the ILO convention on homework, unions and homeworker advocates won the understanding that homeworkers should legally be defined as employees. Yet, what it means to be an employee is far from obvious. As this chapter has shown, notions of proper womanhood and manhood influence definitions of the category worker. Because gender props up inequalities beyond those involving women and men, feminist struggle affects all areas of society. More than simply "adding women," feminist struggle entails a transformation of fundamental categories.

Note

1. There are still a number of national unions that favor a total ban on homework (International Labour Organisation 1990, 27).

13

Women in the Neoliberal "Frame"

Anne Sisson Runyan

Although debates have begun on what feminists should make of global governance, there is less focus on what global governance is making of feminism. In particular, how is global governance, in its current stunted form of economic-regime building, "framing" women in ways that can undermine feminist struggles?

In her scathing critique of the Fourth World Conference on Women held in Beijing in 1995, postcolonial feminist and cultural critic Gayatri Spivak argues that "the financialization of the globe must be represented as the North embracing the South. Women are being used for the representation of this unity—another name for the profound transnational disunity necessary for globalization" (Spivak 1996, 2). Spivak contends that the "United Nations is based on the unacknowledged assumption that 'the rest of the world' is unable to govern itself," and, therefore, it puts on lavish shows of "global national unity" to replace the role of the state that is being marginalized in the face of global capital. She characterizes the Beijing conference as an example of "Woman" as "global theatre, staged to show participation between the North and the South, the latter constituted by Northern discursive mechanisms—a Platform for Action and certain power lines between the UN, the donor consortium, governments, and elite Non-Governmental Organizations (NGOs)" (2). According to Spivak, "what is left out" of this performance piece "is the poorest women of the South as self-conscious critical agents, who might be able to speak through those very nongovernmental organizations of the South that are not favoured by these object-constitution policies" (2).

At the heart of these "object-constitution policies" is a pervasive faith in free market capitalism since the "triumph of the West." This faith is informed by neoliberal economics and embraces the following agenda:

"Liberate" business from oppressive government controls; cut taxes on corporations and capital gains in order to free money for business ventures; cut government spending of social welfare to make up for lost tax revenues; privatize as much public assistance as possible, including health care, prisons, communications, transportation, and education; and open up trade to benefit home multinationals. (WIDE, NAC-Canada, Alt-WID, CRIAW 1994, 2)

This is essentially the agenda pursued through structural adjustment programs (SAPs) imposed by the International Monetary Fund on debt-ridden countries of the South since the onset of the debt crisis in the early 1980s. It is now also being applied in the countries in the former Soviet bloc and in the West itself, from where neoliberalism has been emanating and gaining momentum with the rise of neoconservative political leaders on both sides of the Atlantic, also since the early 1980s.

In the view of University of Delhi law professor Upendra Baxi, the almost worldwide imposition of this neoliberal agenda is being enabled by the seemingly more benign and progressive discourse of global governance. In her analysis of the 1995 report of the Commission on Global Governance, which came out under the warm and fuzzy title *Our Global Neighborhood,* Baxi praises the report for its courageous attention to such things as "global civil ethics," "people's right to security," "demilitarizing international society," "standards for corporate behavior" to protect labor and the environment, and recommendations for democratizing the UN system through innovative structures and mechanisms such as an "assembly of people" and a "forum of civil society" to complement and advise the General Assembly, a "Trusteeship Council for the global commons," a "new economic security council"; and for the creation of positions to put "women at the center" of UN decision making. However, she is deeply troubled by a number of inadequacies and problematic assumptions and prescriptions in the report.

Baxi is primarily concerned that the report attempts to resolve the tension between the rise of global capital and the rise of social movements for human rights, equality, social welfare, democratization, and environmental protection by denying that there is much tension at all. In its treatment and celebration of "the emergence of a vigorous international civil society," the report lumps together nongovernmental organizations, which typically represent progressive social movements, with civil society organizations (CSOs), which typically represent private sector interests (Baxi 1996, 534). The effect of this is to privilege the voice of global capital in "people's assemblies" and "civil society fora" designed to parallel the UN. As Baxi explains:

It will no longer be the NGOs that would enjoy the limited (if not limiting) privilege of being associated with the United Nations, despite the fantastic growth of their presence and power. Just when they come of age and begin to make their collective presence felt, the report's conception of 'global governance' prescribes that their privileged space be shared by CSOs. Making space for the 'citizens movement' may even lead to bizarre developments; for example, the US National Rifle Association finding a space in the UN forum of civil society. Regardless of such possibilities, it is clear that the forum will need to have a fair share of 'private sector organizations' from commerce, industry, and 'corporate alliances,' whose spheres of influence would be even further reinforced and legitimated by such accreditation. (536)

Furthermore, the report of the Commission on Global Governance is silent on such things as how transnational corporations would be held accountable for human rights violations and how civil society organizations and corporate actors compromise women's bodily security and rights through pharmaceutical testing, sex industry trafficking, and assaults on reproductive freedoms. The report ends up being essentially a primer on "how the United Nations, the states, and NGOs can be good neighbors to transnational capital and technology" (537).

Thus, the neoliberal frame, even when cloaked in "people-friendly" global governance, is about creating what Baxi calls "market-friendly NGOs" that can cooperate with, and be co-opted by, but do not oppose CSOs, states, and international organizations that support a neoliberal agenda. This gives weight to Spivak's fears of "a proliferation of feminist apparatchiks who identify conference organizing with activism" (Spivak 1996, 4) and thus fail to resist the ways in which women are being "framed" by the neoliberal agenda.

"Framing" Women

A notable example of how the neoliberal agenda seeks to limit and subsume strategies for women's advancement is the "Draft Regional Platform for Action: Women in a Changing World—Call for Action from an ECE Perspective" (4 October 1994), which was prepared for the High-Level Regional Preparatory Meeting for the Fourth World Conference on Women held in Vienna on 17–21 October 1994 (see ECOSOC 1994a). The ECE (Economic Commission for Europe) region had only recently made its debut as an Economic and Social Council (ECOSOC) world region. Comprising fifty-four countries through the amalgamation of North America (United States and Canada), Western Europe (including Turkey), the countries of the former Soviet bloc (referred to in the ECE Draft Platform as "24 economies in transition"), and

Israel, this region represents a new construction of the "West" (by bringing together the Eurocentric world through a newly shared neoliberal ideology). It also represents a more unified "North" (the fusion of the so-called developed world—with the exception of the Japan–Australia/New Zealand—Asian NIC triangle)[1]—and constitutes the single wealthiest region. Of course, such categories mask huge differences and significant inequalities among the states in this conglomeration (e.g., the countries of the former East are heavily dependent on, and peripheral to, the "core" of the West) as well as within the states of this "region" (there is much "South" in this "North" where growing pockets of the poor live). Despite this unwieldiness, the ECE region carried the banner of the neoliberal agenda.

This was first evidenced by the member states of the ECE region taking on as their major concerns with respect to women's advancement the themes of the economy and political participation. These themes were among twelve put forward by the Commission on the Status of Women as a framework for the Beijing Platform of Action and as subjects for the ECE, Asia-Pacific, Latin America and the Caribbean, Africa, and Arab regional meetings. The other ten themes were poverty, education, health, violence against women, armed conflicts, human rights, the media, the environment, the girl child, and mechanisms to promote the advancement of women. By privileging the economy and political participation, the ECE region's governments signaled that they would determine the discourse and strategies around women in the global economy and define the parameters for women's political participation. Furthermore, by marginalizing other themes, the ECE region's governments (and particularly those of the core states) could set the agenda for women's economic and political participation without having to deal with the kinds of issues, such as human rights and the environment, that are treated as "externalities" by neoliberal economics. Thus, the ECE region was able to set the economic and political agenda according to the frame of neoliberalism.

A perusal of the ECE draft platform provides further evidence of the framing of women's economic and political advancement according to the neoliberal agenda. Indeed, the "Regional Framework" of the draft platform explicitly spells out that agenda (see ECOSOC 1994a, 5–9). Speaking to the effects on women in the ECE region of "'a global process of restructuring of economic, social, and cultural relationships'" (para. 3, p. 5), the draft platform states that the

"feminization" of the labour force contributed to economic growth and brought many women a measure of economic and social independence. Globalization, privatization, technological change and the development of new activities in dynamic sectors, such as service industries, provided opportunities for fostering this contribution. (para. 4, pp. 5–6)

This is followed by an admission that there have been some downsides to this process for women, particularly in the countries of Eastern and Central Europe and the Commonwealth of Independent States (CIS), which are described euphemistically as undergoing "'transformation stress'" (para. 5, p. 5). However, the platform then concludes that the problem is not globalization but rather that "the opportunities opened by new technologies, more flexible production system and the development of services are not being sufficiently tapped" (para. 8, p. 6). In other words, the ills that have befallen women in the process of globalization (which are portrayed as unintended consequences) can be alleviated by an intensification of it.

Moreover, later in the "Regional Framework" section, it is argued not only that women "have been the major beneficiaries" of the "globalization of the economy" and the "boom in the service sector" as a result of "computer-based technologies" but also that the strategy for women's future economic development that will contribute the most to the growth of economies overall is to stimulate women's "entrepreneurship" (paras. 19 and 19 bis, p. 9). Women are to become the new "enterprise zones" to fuel globalization further.

This directive is particularly reflected in the submission of the International Trade Centre UNCTAD/GATT for the Vienna meeting, which focused almost exclusively on women entrepreneurs as "a resource base" for the expansion of trade in "economies in transition" (United Nations International Trade Centre UNCTAD/GATT 1994, 3). Observing that "women entrepreneurs are mainly active in the informal sector" because they lack access to "credit, property investment, capital, training or information," the submission recommends that women's "entrepreneurial base represents a potential whose productivity can be *selectively channelled* into the formal sector, in particular the external trade sector, if provided with an enabling environment" (3; emphasis mine). An enabling environment, according to the submission, is one that includes "price liberalization and market reform, enterprise reform, trade liberalization and the creation of a legal and constitutional framework of a market economy" achieved by a "partnership between the State and the private sector" (3).

The assumption that only market mechanisms, properly released from the state, will unlock the entrepreneurial potential of women (a very problematic conception in itself, burdening women with job creation for which the state and large-scale enterprises are abandoning responsibility) wholly neglects the fact that, as at least the ECE draft platform acknowledges, "the labour market in the region has not yet been organized in such a way that people can fulfill their obligations to the family" (para. 9 bis, p. 7). There is no mention in the International Trade Centre UNCTAD/GATT submission of what would constitute an "enabling environment" for women entrepreneurs with respect to a reorganization of responsibilities within the "private" realm of reproduction, nor is there any admission that an intensification of market forces that requires women to become entrepreneurs may undermine social reproduction. Relatedly, although the "Regional Framework" section of the draft platform concedes that women's formal political participation has declined (para. 9, pp. 6–7), particularly in the national legislatures of the "economies in transition," the draft platform maintains implicit faith that market economies (equated with liberal democracies) can produce equality in decision making.

Countering the Neoliberal Agenda

This neoliberal framing was a major target of the Vienna NGO Forum, which took place just before the ECE intergovernmental meeting (13–15 October 1994). The NGO Forum was organized into daylong concurrent workshops on the general themes proposed by the UN Commission on the Status of Women that were to feed into an alternative document to the ECE draft platform. The"Vienna NGO Forum 94 Call to Action" was subsequently read into the official record of the ECE meeting. It was no small task to reduce the collective work of fourteen hundred women with multiple agendas into a twelve-page document (the size limit mandated by the ECE meeting), but it is significant that almost one-third (indeed, the first third) of the call to action was devoted to measures to counter globalization forces. These measures came out of the deliberations of the "Globalization of the Economy and Economic Justice for Women" workshop at the NGO Forum organized by a coalition of WIDE (Network Women in Development Europe in Brussels), Alt-WID (Alternative Women in Development in Washington, D.C.), NAC (National Action Committee on the Status of Women in Toronto, Canada), and CRIAW (Canadian Research Institute for the Advancement of Women in Halifax, Canada). The North American contingent of this coalition had been active in the campaign against the North American Free Trade Agreement; and the European organization of WIDE and the U.S.-based Alt-WID, both long concerned with women and development issues in the South, had been turning their attention to the effects of structural adjustment policies on women in the North through neoliberal global restructuring (see Kerr 1994).

This coalition produced an alternative framework paper entitled "Wealth of Nations—Poverty of Women" to guide the discussions for the daylong workshop on globalization at the Vienna NGO Forum. Countering the optimistic rhetoric associated with globalization found in the ECE region draft platform, the alternative paper documented that women have been, not the beneficiaries, but significant victims of this process not only in the South but also in the

North, and especially in the former East. Working women in the ECE region, from the poor and working classes through the middle class, have been disadvantaged "in terms of wages and benefits, occupational segregation, working conditions, lack of job mobility, and the increasing incidence of contingent work" with little relief in terms of "tax breaks or child care" policies (3). Women in manufacturing have lost their jobs in large numbers, and subcontracted industrial homework is on the rise, taking advantage of the labor of particularly vulnerable immigrant and minority women. The vast majority of women in the region are employed in the so-called service sector, which is increasingly characterized by "part-time, temporary and seasonal employment patterns and . . . technological innovations which reduce the number of workers needed to perform a task" (4). Rural and urban women alike are having to step up reproductive work in the face of declining incomes, unemployment, and the erosion of social services, while bearing the brunt of "declining health and education, growing increases in substance abuse, in domestic violence, . . . homelessness and . . . migration" (5).

Not only are minority, immigrant, migrant, and refugee women among the poorest and most exploited labor, but also they face increased racist attacks and more draconian immigration policies across the region as the loss of jobs as a result of restructuring produces "scapegoating" (7). The number of female-headed households is growing, as are their poverty rates, already the highest in Western Europe and North America (7). Women in Central and Eastern Europe are facing unprecedented unemployment rates, fueled in part by the loss of state-funded "maternity health care, maternity leave and child care," which makes women unattractive employees to privatized industries that want to avoid having to provide such benefits (6). Finally, women generally are "scapegoated for not fulfilling their responsibilities when the family and social fabric begins to unravel" (8) under the weight of restructuring, leading to an intensification of pro-patriarchal family policies directed toward removing women from the workforce and/or justifying a reduction in state-provided social services and benefits.

The alternative framework paper concludes that the globalization of the world's economies is "having similar effects on women and people on the margins of all countries," calling "us to an alternative North/South debate" directed to forming "a solidarity that is mutual, as women in all regions of the world struggle against the same economic forces," although their deleterious effects play out somewhat differently in different locations (9). To that end, the paper calls for recommendations relevant not only to women's situations in the ECE region but also to "the key role the ECE countries play in relationship to other countries and regions in the world" and its effects on women's conditions elsewhere (9).

The recommendations from the workshop that found their way into the "Vienna NGO Forum 94 Call to Action" document focus heavily on increasing the transparency and accountability of North/West-dominated international financial institutions (IFIs), transnational corporations (TNCs), and commercial advertising, which are held especially responsible for purveying neoliberal ideology and practices. The recommendations also call upon all ECE governments to become more responsive to their own citizens as opposed to TNCs and their IFIs; to provide for "sustainable development and peace" by forgiving Southern debts, reducing militarization, and redirecting peace dividends; to ensure a gender perspective in all economic development decision making that empowers women within and outside the ECE region; to redefine the value of paid and unpaid work, ensuring the provision of services, benefits, and antidiscriminatory policies in all sectors of the economy; and to end direct and structural violence committed against "women of colour, including indigenous, migrant, immigrant, and refugee women" (see Vienna NGO Forum 1994).

These calls for action and the alternative framework upon which they are based were later reviewed and revised in Beijing. There the organizers of the ECE region NGO Forum workshop on globalization held a joint workshop with the DAWN (Development Alternatives with Women for a New Era) group, a coalition of women from the South formed in the closing year (1985) of the UN Decade for Women, to initiate a "new North/South debate" and a new basis for solidarity that would resist the stultifying Northern "embrace" of the South that Spivak sees. The beginnings of this dialogue took place at the NGO Forum '95 for the World Summit for Social Development in Copenhagen, 3-12 March 1995, in a roundtable entitled "Women Reclaim the Market" sponsored by the Women's Global Alliance for Development Alternatives, a joint project of DAWN, Alt-WID, NAC, CRIAW, and others.

Reclaiming Women's Agendas

The so-called Social Summit was convened explicitly to address the social consequences of globalization, which the Draft Declaration and Draft Programme of Action of the Summit (see United Nations 1995d) described in the following manner:

> Globalization, which is a consequence of increased human mobility, enhanced communications, greatly increased trade and capital flows and technological developments, opens new opportunities for sustained economic growth and development of the world economy, particularly developing countries. Globalization also permits countries to share experiences, to learn from one another's

achievements and difficulties and a cross-fertilization of ideals, cultural values and aspirations. (United Nations 1995d, 3–4)

The underside of this rather rosy picture (which tellingly de-emphasizes economic processes in favor of highlighting social and cultural benefits) was presented in this fashion:

At the same time, the rapid processes of change and adjustment have been accompanied by intensified poverty, unemployment and social disintegration. Threats to human well-being, such as environmental risks, have also been globalized. Furthermore, the global transformations of the world economy are profoundly changing the parameters of social development in all countries. The challenge is how to manage these processes and threats to enhance their benefits and mitigate their negative effects on people. (United Nations 1995d, 4)

Thus, the task is framed as a problem of managing the seemingly autonomous forces of globalization that are represented as a fait accompli. The admission that state intervention may be required to offset the underside of globalization signals a slight departure from neoliberalism, but throughout the document there remains a commitment to the promotion of free markets and free trade with a "need to intervene in markets" only "to the extent necessary" (9). Indeed, Baxi refers to the summit as being essentially about the promotion of "trade-related human rights" (Baxi 1996, 537), a concept similar to what ecofeminist Vandana Shiva calls "trade-related feminism" in which "the empowerment of women" is reduced to a "means towards economic success," thereby making "the freedom of trade and not the freedom of women" the central issue (Shiva 1995, 37).

Given that state intervention is likely to be limited despite some of the lofty rhetoric of the Draft Declaration and Draft Programme of Action for the Social Summit and with the knowledge that "it is misleading to simply pose the state against the market, for the state can likewise contribute to the 'social, economic, and ideological processes that subordinate women'" (Rowbotham and Mitter 1994, 220), the participants in the "Women Reclaim the Market" roundtable at the NGO Forum for the Social Summit stressed the need to break the neoliberal monopoly over the meanings and operations of the "market" (see Women's Global Alliance for Development Alternatives 1995). They argued that there are many "markets"—or places of exchange that respond to supply and demand mechanisms to meet human needs—in which women, and especially poor women, are the major actors. Roundtable participants called for a reevaluation of what kinds of markets to promote. The task is not just to manage "the market" but rather to reduce the power of global markets, supermarkets, sex markets, and arms markets that undermine women's economic, political, and social advancement.

These resistances suggest a still far from co-opted or cooperative feminist NGO system; however, there was acknowledgment at the Beijing NGO Forum during the "Regional Perspectives" plenary session on 1 September 1995 that women had very little representation in a "de facto 'global government'" already "in existence that is beholden to no constituency save its own interests" (David 1995, 3). This manifested itself in myriad ways in Beijing, ranging from the eleventh-hour isolation of the NGO Forum from the IGO meeting, when the Forum was banished to the Huairou site fifty miles distant from the UN conference in Beijing, to the unprecedented contentiousness over the Platform for Action, wherein "two pages of text alone had generated thirty-one pages of amendments" and the word "gender" was bracketed throughout (Baden and Goetz 1997, 11). But perhaps the most telling example of "global theatre" designed to frame women and tame NGOs was the case of the "Forum bag" that was provided by the U.S. garment company, Esprit.

As reported in the 5 September 1995 issue of *Forum '95: The Independent Daily of the NGO Forum on Women,* a leaflet charging that Esprit used sweatshop labor was distributed at the plenary session on strategies for dealing with the globalization of the economy. The anti-Esprit campaign called for Forum participants to send the Esprit labels from their conference bags to the company with letters demanding that it ensure that all subcontracted labor had decent wages and working conditions (see Hurtado 1995, 5). On 6 September the Forum daily paper reported that "Irene Santiago, Executive Director of the NGO Forum, has strongly refuted the allegations against Esprit, the US company that provided 38,000 carrier bags for women attending the Forum" ("Campaign Refuted" 1995, 16). The article quotes Santiago and an Esprit spokeswoman at the Forum who maintained that Esprit was socially responsible because it had begun asking its subcontractors to sign guarantees that they were not using exploited labor and because it was sponsoring store displays and radio shows on the Forum. The Esprit representative went so far as to say, "We would certainly invite people to send the company the tags, if they want—maybe with a thank you note—and ask about our policies" ("Campaign Refuted" 1995, 16).

This tension between NGOs and CSOs, which the Report of the Commission on Global Governance denies, was settled in favor of a CSO through the good offices of the UN. As Baxi observes, the Commission sees CSOs and NGOs as the "primary vehicles of 'participation' in governance"; however, "their participation has to, indeed, 'graduate into manageable modes'" (Baxi 1996, 542). This NGO attempt at confrontation constituted what the Commission would call "an unmanageable 'mode' of participation" (542), which was met with a managed and management response. The moral of the story is that feminists must continue to resist the neoliberal frame or fall prey, as Spivak warns, to providing "an alibi for exploitation" (Spivak 1996, 4).

Notes

Major portions of this chapter were first published under the title, "Women and the Neoliberal Agenda of the North" in *Women in Development: Trade Aspects of Women in the Development Process,* edited by Eva Haxton and Claes Olsson (Uppsala, Sweden: United Nations Youth and Student Association of Sweden, 1995), 104–17. The author wishes to thank the editors of that compendium for giving their permission to allow that piece to be reprinted, in revised form, in this volume.

1. Asian NICs are the newly industrializing countries of Asia, such as Hong Kong, Singapore, South Korea, Thailand, and Taiwan.

14

An Ecofeminist Critique of the International Economic Structure

Stephanie Hallock Johnson

Patriarchal power manifests itself in the daily operations of the international economic system. Both women and the natural environment fall prey to domination on a global level through the production and consumption patterns created and maintained by the international market. The ramifications of the international economic system for the natural environment are most readily apparent in underdeveloped regions and, by extension, in the lives of the rural people who depend on the natural world for their survival. Since the daily tasks of providing for basic needs usually fall to the women in these communities, women are the most acutely aware of the results of environmental destruction. The actions these women have taken to reclaim the natural environment as their home have created the groundswell that has grown into an international ecofeminist movement.

Radical French feminist Françoise d'Eaubonne coined the term "ecofeminism" in 1974. D'Eaubonne combined ecology and feminism in her rather heavyhanded critique of traditional European feminist movements, which she felt excluded not only many groups of women but also several fundamental issues. A Marxist by training, she also harshly criticized the capitalist system for its oppression of both nature and women and focused on the role of overpopulation in destroying the natural environment.

A group of North American women picked up the threads of d'Eaubonne's connections between the feminist and ecology movements. Both movements expanded rapidly in the 1970s. Awareness of the ramifications of environmental degradation grew in response to the publication of numerous texts written by ecologists. At the same time, the feminist movement lost its radical label as economic conditions forced women into the workforce where they encountered lower wages than men, glass ceilings, "mommy tracks," sexual harassment, and general discrimination based on gender. Serious threats to the environment, and more particularly women's reproductive systems and children's health, sparked the beginnings of an ecofeminist movement in the United States. The partial meltdown at the Three Mile Island nuclear energy plant in Harrisburg, Pennsylvania, in March 1979 forcefully demonstrated the linkages between the protection of women, the protection of nature, and the dangers of modern science.

At the same time, a number of grassroots, women-oriented movements sprang up in underdeveloped regions of the world. The natural environment upon which women in underdeveloped regions directly depend for survival is being destroyed by inappropriate production methods, leaving women without alternatives for food and fuel. The most often cited example of grassroots ecofeminist action in underdeveloped regions is the Chipko (tree-hugging) movement in India. Stripping and subsequent erosion from cash-cropping threatened the traditional ecological use of the forests for food, fuel, fertilizer, water, and medicine. Because ancient Indian cultures worshiped tree goddesses and viewed forests as sacred, tree-hugging had been an important spiritual rite. The women of India revived this rite from 1972 to 1978 to save their forests from rampant destruction in the name of economic "growth." In Kenya, the Women's Greenbelt Movement emerged when the National Council of Women began planting trees on World Environment Day in 1977 to reestablish community woodlands that had been destroyed for lumber production. The founder of the movement, Wangari Maathai, established the program with the cooperation of the Ministry of the Environment and Natural Resources to promote "environmental rehabilitation, conservation, and . . . sustainable development" (Maathai 1988, 5). These and other local movements (many of which never make the news) have proven that it is possible to serve the needs of human society without destroying the viability of the earth to sustain human life.

Throughout the 1980s, a body of ecofeminist literature built a solid foundation in the works of Ynestra King, Carolyn Merchant, Starhawk, and Andrée Collard; however, it suffered sharp divisions from within in terms of its fundamental concepts.[1] Originally, texts focused solely on the condemnation of the patriarchal system that seized control of primitive partnership cultures and firmly entrenched itself through the spread of male-God-dominated religions, capitalism, and the scientific discoveries of the Age of Enlightenment. Ecofeminists claimed that these so-called advancements in human civilization led to the worldwide subordination of all things "Other" than white, Western males, including women, nonwhite humans, nonhuman life, and the natural environment.

Despite the many differences between ecofeminists, Karen J. Warren (1994; 1996) has identified a central core of assumptions in ecofeminist perspectives. First, there are intrinsic connections between the domination of nature and the domination of women (and other oppressed humans), and the only way to rectify the injustices inflicted by such domination is to unite the feminist and ecology movements. Second, a system of patriarchy exists in human society that leads to the domination of Other, and its roots are firmly planted in history. Third, the domination of all things Other expresses itself conceptually in human thought in the form of dualisms, in which polar opposites are placed at binary odds with one another. One pole is socially constructed with masculine qualities deemed to possess a higher value than the socially constructed feminine qualities that belong to the other pole. Fourth, the meaning of the term "power" has been twisted to justify and legitimize the domination of all things Other; but the true definition of power is the ability to accomplish something, not the ability to dominate. These assumptions can serve as a guide to critiquing capitalist principles and practices that constitute a central part of current structures of global governance.

The Ecofeminist Critique of Capitalist Principles and Practices

Both the scientific revolution and the development of global capitalism gave rise to a most significant series of events for human relations with the natural environment. The theories that legitimated such events still shape contemporary global structures governing these relations. The invisibility of both women and nature in contemporary economic theory and practice is rooted in the writings of the fathers of Western scientific and economic thought stretching back to the sixteenth century.

Celebrated as the Father of Modern Science, Francis Bacon contributed significantly to the revolution in human thought that sanctioned destructive behavior towards the natural environment. The new worldview that Bacon propounded was based on the concept of nature as a machine rather than a living entity. As such, nature should be "bound into service," made to perform as a "slave," "constrained," and "forced out of her natural state and squeezed and molded" (Merchant 1992, 46). It is no accident that the language Bacon used was fraught with sexual connotations and hostility towards the feminine: His ideal state for human society is founded upon patriarchy and hierarchy.

Bacon's worldview laid the groundwork for the modern experimental method. He demanded the constraint of nature (in the laboratory), dissection by hand and mind, and the discovery "by the hand of man" of "hidden secrets" (hard facts) (Merchant 1980, 171). Bacon's primary work, *New Atlantis,* inspired the works of scientists like John Drury, Samuel Hartlib, Joseph Glanvill, Robert Boyle, and René Descartes. Together, these men shifted human thinking from the animistic, organic assumptions of primitive societies to a view of nature as a mechanical framework that should be manipulated by humans to meet the needs of human society most efficiently.

This shift in human thinking led to what Carolyn Merchant has identified as "the death of nature."[2] It was based on concepts of machinery and production, hierarchical social order, and Bacon's formulation of positivistic scientific methodology. The view of nature as a collection of inert particles to be shaped by external forces (i.e., human action) legitimized the manipulation of nature to meet human needs and desires. The use of force, the definition of power as *power over* rather than *power to,* and a hierarchical system of domination all became prominent features of human society.

The scientific revolution of the seventeenth century was a direct result of the expanding needs of an emergent international capitalist system. Rapid production and the expanding market economy required the gathering of raw materials, often in colonial territories. The mechanically fueled production process (as opposed to the use of human and animal power, water, wood, and wind) required coal, iron, copper, silver, gold, tin, and mercury, the acquisition of which required extensive mining and refining processes.

> Over the course of the sixteenth century, mining operations quadrupled as the trading of metals expanded, taking immense toll as forests were cut for charcoal and the cleared lands turned into sheep pastures for the textile industry. Shipbuilding, essential to capitalist trade and national supremacy, along with glass and soap-making, also contributed to the denudation of the ancient forest cover. The new activities directly altered the earth. Not only were its forests cut down, but swamps were drained, and mine shafts were sunk. (Merchant 1992, 45)

The rise of modern science thus led to the domination and destruction of the natural environment, including nonhuman life, and facilitated the development of industrial capitalism.[3] It also involved the denigration of women.

Industrial capitalism developed a decidedly patriarchal persona, one that forever changed the role of women in society. In societies based on subsistence agriculture, women provided the means for the survival of the family. Women's daily work of growing and preparing food and birthing and rearing children was respected as an essential contribution to human society. With the development of capitalism, however, labor became valued monetarily. Since profit is derived from surplus value and women's subsistence work did not create a surplus value, women's work could not create profit and was accorded no economic value. In this view, women's work did not contribute to capitalism because it did not generate capital. Furthermore, as capitalism privatized and monetized the ownership of land, it reduced women's ability to ensure family subsistence. Capitalist ventures induced men to leave home as wage laborers;

women's unpaid labor could no longer ensure the viability of the family land-holdings, and the land was soon expropriated or bought by capitalists. If the wife could find employment outside the home, her earnings were considerably less than a man's because she was defined first and foremost as a mother, and her income as merely supplemental. When a woman left the home to work, the health and nutrition of her family suffered. The capitalist labor force, therefore, was not seen as a suitable realm for women.

With the spread of capitalism, women lost control of trades at which they had formerly excelled. Whereas they once provided the necessary goods for the survival of human society, women were banished from agriculture, spinning and weaving, baking, butchering, fishmongering, and brewing. In another dramatic shift, with the development of scientific medicine, women lost their status as experts not only in caring for children but also in birthing them. Until the seventeenth century, midwifery was the exclusive domain of women. With the advent of "scientific" medicine and especially the medical diploma, midwives were banished from the birthing process. Natural remedies passed from mother to daughter for generations became signs of witchcraft, which was punishable by death. Since, for the most part, only men could attend medical school, women were effectively removed from caring for their families' health. Modern science even went so far as to repudiate the importance of women in the reproduction process. William Harvey (who discovered the circulation of blood in 1628) studied reproduction and generation in hens and extrapolated his findings to humans. Basing his investigations on the work of Aristotle, Harvey "discovered" that

> Among animals where the sexes are distinct, matters are so arranged that since the female alone is inadequate to engender an embryo and to nourish and protect the young, a male is associated with her by nature, as the superior and more worthy progenitor, as the consort of her labor and the means of supplying her deficiencies. (Merchant 1980, 158)

As modern science developed to meet the needs of the expanding capitalist production and consumption system, it consistently marginalized both women and the natural world from the "rational" world. Likewise, as capitalism developed and expanded, economic thought sought to discover and rationalize economic rules, which further marginalized women and nature. According to Adam Smith, the Father of Modern Economics, human self-interest is the "invisible hand" that guides the free market to an efficient allocation of resources. Smith assumed that when the needs of each individual are met, the welfare of society will be maximized. However, he defined the needs of the individual solely in monetary terms, which could be easily measured in the free market by the new science of economics. The egoistic pursuit of financial gain was thus disconnected from other human values and morality. The result has been a human society concerned primarily with the accumulation of money, often at the cost of personal needs. This has not led to social welfare. Instead, it has increased tension in society as human value is determined by monetary value. The division between the "haves" and the "have-nots" is constantly growing.

In today's international economy, economic value is reflected in the gross national product (GNP), the primary statistic used to measure a country's wealth (and therefore worth). Liberal capitalist economic thought dictates that increasing the GNP leads to greater prosperity for all humans in all countries. However, the mere fact that a dollar is spent or earned does not mean that the standard of living has somehow improved. Money is often spent "to deplete scarce resources, pollute the environment, and dispose of wastes. . . . In the GNP, [these] are masked as income, and everyone is presumed to be better-off because of it" (Stead and Stead 1992, 82). Pricing natural resources according to their market value leads to the annihilation of limited and nonrenewable resources. The result is massive deforestation, soil erosion, polluted aquifers, and species extinction in countries that lack the knowledge and capabilities to produce and trade technological goods. Quality-of-life factors and the social costs of producing and consuming are not factored into the GNP statistical picture. In most underdeveloped regions, social costs, including those resulting from the destruction of the environment, are disproportionately borne by women. "The diversion of resources to the market economy generates ecological instability and creates new forms of poverty for women" because they must walk further for fuel wood, food products, and clean water (Shiva 1990, 197).

Related to the supreme value that money is accorded in liberal economic thought is the idea that "more is better." Ecofeminists and ecologists, in contrast, believe that "there is a sufficient level of economic consumption beyond which human welfare and ecological balance are significantly eroded" (Stead and Stead 1992, 87). By focusing on the pursuit of money, liberal economics ignores other human goals, such as purpose, happiness, emotional fulfillment, and intellectual and spiritual enlightenment. Furthermore, liberal economics cannot recognize that the way to achieve these goals is often through simplicity and reduced consumption of limited resources and energy.

In liberal economic thought and practice, the needs of current generations supersede the needs of future ones. Economists rationalize this approach in a variety of ways. They argue that there is no sense in saving things when we do not really know what future humans will want or need, or that new technologies will be developed to replace anything that may be lacking. Others believe that the human race will become extinct anyway (because of exogenous factors), so we might as well use what we have been given in the time we are here. The net effect is the destruction of nonrenewable resources and radical altering of the environment, which will limit the survival options of future generations. Modern economics may readily accept intergenerational damage to the natural environment; but as ethical humans, we should not.

Closest to ecofeminists' hearts is the need for a massive restructuring of the way that labor is valued in the international economy. What is traditionally considered "women's work" in virtually all human societies is the very labor that keeps humans alive. Yet, remarkably, the economic value accorded to this labor is zero when it is performed by the wife/mother and much too low when performed by hired help. Bearing children and raising them, keeping a home clean and warm, caring for the sick and the elderly, and gathering food and preparing meals are all activities crucial to the survival of the species, and these activities need to be assigned economic value. Assigning economic and social value to women's work is a vital step towards more equitable gender relations in human society. In a society preoccupied with financial gain, revaluing women's work monetarily accords it the respect it deserves. It may also degender such work and entice men to participate equally in reproductive activity.

The Ecofeminist Alternative

Ecofeminism constitutes a radical political program with a vision for a different type of economics. While ecofeminist principles are often interpreted as advocating a denial of modern society and a return to traditional ways of living, ecofeminists do not wish to stop time. They simply want to ensure that progress is tempered by an ethic of care for nature. Development programs should be infused with ecofeminist principles to create a sustainable level of progress that respects the needs of nature as well as the true needs of humans.

Maria Mies and Vandana Shiva have developed a new vision of an "ecologically sound, non-exploitative, just, non-patriarchal, self-sustaining society" (Mies 1993, 297), which they call the subsistence perspective, or the survival perspective. It is grounded in a sharp criticism of industrial society (which they also refer to as the market economy or capitalist patriarchy). The economic model of capitalism is based on the "colonization of women, nature, and other peoples," which renders it "neither sustainable nor generalizable worldwide" (Mies 1993, 298). Yet it is exactly the model that informs virtually all mainstream development projects. The "new vision" that Mies and Shiva suggest is based on grassroots movements, such as the Chipko movement.

One of the most basic principles of the subsistence perspective is that economic activity exists to meet the needs of people rather than to create disposable commodities and profit in the form of capital. The subsistence perspective requires that we return to a sense of community survival, where humans can be self-sufficient, particularly in food and other basic needs. Recapturing a sense of community will ensure that natural resources will not be depleted beyond their ability to regenerate. Community-oriented economic activities are based on a new relationship to nature. They take nature as a living entity in and of itself, as well as a support system for all that is interconnected with it (including humans). Humans should not dominate nature; rather, they should learn to live in respect and reciprocity with nature. Community-oriented economics also fosters new relationships among people. Living in harmony and respect is extended to nature and all human beings. This requires that we replace the urge to value everything monetarily with a sense of emotional, spiritual, and aesthetic value. A subsistence perspective values community, reliability, stability, trustworthiness, and interconnection.

A subsistence perspective is based on and promotes participatory or grassroots democracy—not only with regard to political decisions but also with regard to all economic, social, and technological decisions. A sense of community demands that we rely on one another and make decisions accordingly, rather than shove our responsibilities off on elected officials.

Because a subsistence perspective recognizes that the different dominance systems and problems are linked and cannot be solved in isolation, we must re-establish problem-solving techniques that address issues in an interconnected fashion. Thus social problems (patriarchal relations, inequality, alienation, poverty) must be solved together with ecological problems. Ecofeminism is predicated on this notion of the interconnectedness of all life on earth. This demands new approaches to science, technology, and knowledge. A grassroots-, women-, and people-based science will reintroduce humans to older survival wisdom and traditions, as well as use modern knowledge in such a way that people maintain control over their technology and survival base. Current conceptions and manifestations of science and technology maintain men's domination over nature, women, and other people. The goal of an ecofeminist "technology" is social justice.

A subsistence perspective also requires new attitudes to work that construct it as both burden and pleasure. The main aim is happiness and a fulfilled life, which requires that work be balanced with other pursuits that pervade everyday life. This also requires a reintegration of spirit and matter, so that we must not be forced to choose one or the other but, rather, can enjoy a life filled with both. Likewise, we must keep in mind that nature is provided for our use but not for our ownership. Water, air, soil, and other natural resources are commons that have been entrusted to our care and require a community responsibility for their preservation and regeneration.

The interconnections postulated by ecofeminism require that both men and women take responsibility for creating this new society. It is not up to women alone to repair the damages caused by human society; men must share in this task as well, including subsistence work such as household tasks, child-rearing, and caring for the elderly and sick. As the dichotomies of human society are washed away and an economy based on self-reliance, mutuality, and self-provisioning emerges, the need for destruction in the name of nationalism, ideology, or economic gain will disappear. A subsistence perspective will be the most significant contribution to the demilitarization of men and society. Only a society based on a subsistence perspective will be able to live in peace with nature, other humans, and future generations. A society based on these ecofeminist principles creates harmony because it does not base its concept of a good life on the exploitation and domination of nature and other people.

Notes

1. Because ecofeminism draws from so many disciplines, I recommend the following introductory texts: Diamond and Orenstein (1990); Caldecott and Leland (1983); and King (1990).

2. Carolyn Merchant's 1980 text, *The Death of Nature,* represents one of the first attempts to link the women's movement and the ecology movement. Published just after the Three Mile Island partial nuclear meltdown and just before the first official ecofeminist conference (in Amherst, Massachusetts, in 1980), Merchant's book does not employ the term *ecofeminism.* Merchant does, however, provide a remarkably complete history of the oppressions of women and the natural environment, highlighting the inextricable linkages between the two.

3. Carolyn Merchant (1992, 41–60; 1980) provides excellent discussions of the linked development of capitalism and science.

15

Trafficking in Women: Alternate Migration or Modern Slave Trade?

Emek M. Uçarer

> Grazyna is divorced and has two children. When she lost her job, she had
> financial problems. Then she met a man, who told her about a possibility to
> work in a restaurant in Germany. He promised her a very good salary. Grazyna
> agreed. In Germany, she was told that she had to work as a prostitute. After she
> refused, she was raped. Then she was taken to the Netherlands and was forced
> to work as a prostitute in a window. She was beaten and blackmailed, her pass-
> port was withheld and she was raped.
>
> —Leaflet distributed in 1995 to potential Eastern European victims
> by the Dutch Foundation against Trafficking in Women

Trafficking in women and girls has become a booming transnational business.
It occurs at the nexus of a complex set of factors that exploit its victims. While
many factors compel women to seek employment outside their countries of
origin, vulnerable women are often caught up in exploitative and abusive trafficking networks. Trafficking in women raises serious questions about
women's human rights. The deceitful way in which women are trafficked suggests that this phenomenon is a contemporary and unique form of slavery.

So far, efforts to address trafficking in women have largely remained within
the jurisdiction of sovereign states. Recipient countries generally treat trafficking
in women as a migration issue. They respond to the problem in an ad hoc manner, concentrating their efforts on legislating barriers to trafficking at the borders,
including attempts to tighten border controls, scrutinize visa policies, and deport
individuals—primarily the trafficked women—who have been caught in the act.
But efforts to combat the problem in this way are removed from current reality.
Tougher immigration rules are ineffective against crafty traffickers, and they pay
insufficient attention to the social causes and consequences of trafficking.

There are compelling arguments to regard trafficking as a human rights
issue rather than as a migration issue. This alternative line of reasoning

focuses on the sexual exploitation and abuse suffered by trafficked women. It seeks to criminalize the behavior of the traffickers rather than the trafficked and to provide some redress for the abuse that trafficked women suffer. Yet this approach focuses on the consequences of trafficking (i.e., the violation of women's human rights) rather than its causes. Moreover, while human rights concerns have influenced debates about trafficking in women at the global level (e.g., at the League of Nations and the United Nations), success has been limited in developing effective international rules that can stem this growing phenomenon. Recently, there have been efforts in the European Union to combine the migration and human rights approaches in combating trafficking. Such an integrated approach promises to deal more effectively with this transnational criminal activity that abuses vulnerable women and girls.

This chapter seeks to define trafficking in women, identify its causes and consequences, and outline recent national and international responses to this phenomenon. It highlights the two frameworks that have surrounded the phenomenon—one emphasizing trafficking as a migration problem, the other accentuating its human rights dimension—and seeks to demonstrate what types of policies these two approaches inform. It argues that neither approach by itself is sufficient to address the problem and suggests that the European Union's leadership in developing a more holistic approach addresses the dual victimization of trafficked women, both as migrants and as human beings.

Trafficking in Women as a Migration Issue

The theoretical literature in the migration field frames contemporary migration as occurring at the nexus of pull factors, push factors, and other intervening variables (Martin 1997). *Demand-pull* factors make certain countries, such as Western industrial societies, attractive to individuals who have decided to seek their fortunes outside their ordinary place of residence. Among these factors are the level of development and prosperity in the target country, the leniency of immigration legislation, geographic access, the prospect of employment, and sometimes official invitations. *Supply-push* factors have to do with the circumstances in the country of origin, such as unfavorable economic, social, or political conditions. While historically migration occurred at the equilibrium of the push and pull factors, a unique aspect of contemporary migration is that it is driven largely by the push factors in an era when receiving countries attempt to control immigration by offsetting, if not eliminating, the pull factors.

In addition to this pull-push, supply-demand calculus, there are other intervening variables, in this case the trafficking networks that arrange to smuggle the trafficked individuals into the countries of destination (Martin 1994). All three components are at work in trafficking in women (International Organization for Migration 1996a, b, c, d).

According to the definition recently formulated by the International Organization for Migration (IOM), trafficking occurs when an international border crossing involves a facilitator who may provide information, fraudulent or stolen travel and identity documents, legal and illegal transportation, lodging at transit points, guided crossing of borders, and reception and employment in the country of destination. In addition, money or some other form of payment changes hands. Finally, entry and/or prolonged stay in the country of destination is often—but not always—illegal (International Organization for Migration 1996c, 2).

Defining trafficking along these lines squarely frames it as a migration issue, implying that the trafficked individual is neither necessarily exploited in the country of destination nor trafficked and kept against her will. Significantly, the definition omits any reference to gender. Yet, trafficked women differ from other trafficked migrants in ways that raise serious human rights concerns and must be understood within a wider phenomenon, namely, the trade of human beings. While other types of trafficked migrants, such as illegal male laborers, admittedly face harsh circumstances upon their arrival, it is generally accepted that exploitation, coercion, or deception is far more likely to be the norm in the case of trafficked women, often with consequences that constitute a direct threat to their well-being. While there are exceptions, the predominant portion of trafficked individuals are women and young girls who are often sexually exploited. This lack of reference to gender reflects the IOM's effort to define trafficking in the broadest terms possible in order to find some consensus. Nonetheless, this type of language obfuscates the power differential in favor of both the traffickers and the men who demand a steady supply of women and girls.

A working definition of trafficking in women must take into account the illicit nature of transporting women for economic gain, implicating the traffickers, who often get away with what they have done. These activities include "facilitating the illegal movement of migrant women to other countries, with or without their consent or knowledge; deceiving migrant women about the purpose of the migration, legal or illegal; physically or sexually abusing migrant women for the purpose of trafficking them; (and) selling women into, or trading women for the purpose of, employment, marriage, prostitution or other forms of profit-making abuse" (International Organization for Migration 1996c, 2). The current IOM definition of trafficking includes none of these activities and thereby frames the issue in terms that are disempowering for women, especially for those who have already been trafficked.

Emergent Trends

Treating trafficking as a migration issue, the IOM has focused on studying paths of trafficking, push and pull factors, and the mechanics of trafficking. While the existing research is rudimentary at best, certain trends can be recognized. These studies find that trafficking in women is on the rise and that it is largely a North-South phenomenon. The initial flows are predominantly from the poorer to the wealthier countries. As an IOM report bluntly puts it, "women from rich countries are not trafficked to poor countries." Trafficked women come mainly from Africa, Latin America, Southeast Asia, and Central and Eastern Europe. Subsequent movements often occur between bordering industrialized countries, as women are trafficked to other areas as their visas expire or as they are deported.

Certain groups of women are trafficked predominantly to certain countries. Women from the Dominican Republic are generally trafficked to Spain, Italy, Austria, and the Netherlands, whereas those from Thailand are trafficked predominantly to the Netherlands and Germany. Moreover, there seem to be established patterns that link specific regions in the sending countries to specific recipient countries, suggesting that chain trafficking might be taking place as a result of increased experience in trafficking.

Push Factors: The Profile of Trafficked Women

Some countries, such as the Dominican Republic, Thailand, Brazil, and the Philippines, have disproportionate numbers of women working overseas in prostitution; current estimates put the number at over 50,000 women (International Organization for Migration 1996b, 1). The majority of trafficked women come from impoverished urban areas. If they come from rural areas, they are often involved in chain trafficking from the same village to the same country in Europe. They are generally between twenty-four and twenty-eight years of age, and by far the majority are divorcees or single mothers who bear the sole responsibility of looking after their children. These women are generally poorly educated, often not having gone beyond primary school, and come from poor or troubled family backgrounds (International Organization for Migration 1996b, 1–2; see also 1996c). Interviews conducted by IOM researchers with these women indicate that the main motives for leaving are poor economic prospects in countries where the minimum salaries hover under $100 per month. Another important motivator is unemployment. The main goal of trafficked women is to provide their families with the financial means to raise their children or to provide for long-term financial security.

An important intervening variable that facilitates trafficking of women is the existence of an established market for sex tourism in the country of origin. An existing market not only allows potential traffickers to hone their skills in preying upon unsuspecting women but also permits them to "export" existing prostitutes or channel them into more lucrative markets. Indeed, exporting prostitutes can be a very profitable business both for the traffickers and for the owners of the establishments that "buy" trafficked women. As reported in the *Wall Street Journal* on 1 March 1996, in Poland, a trafficker receives approximately $700 for each Polish woman delivered to a brothel; in Berlin, a foreign woman working in a brothel earns $350 per day and is allowed to keep approximately $13. Finally, in addition to economic factors, the sending countries are often geographically close to destination countries, generally have lax emigration controls, and have local trafficking networks that are often ignored because of widespread corruption.

Pull Factors: The Profile of Destination Countries

Several factors contribute to the targeting of certain developed countries as suitable destinations for trafficking. Particularly in the European Union, some destination countries have well-defined ties with the source countries through their colonial history and linguistic and cultural ties. The recent increase in trafficking from Eastern Europe to bordering EU member countries suggests that geographic proximity and the ease with which borders can be crossed clandestinely provide favorable circumstances for trafficking. Some of these destination countries already have relatively high clandestine immigrant populations from the source countries that act as network groups to promote chain immigration and trafficking.

Additionally, the lack of prohibitive sanctions against trafficking creates further incentive for traffickers. While the *New York Times* reported the execution of four traffickers in China on 7 January 1992, the prosecution record in Europe has generally been poor. This can be attributed to the domestic laws of the states involved, which may not regard prostitution and exploiting prostitution as criminal offenses. Even where the law allows for the punishment of the trafficker, lack of evidence against the trafficker—partly because the trafficked women are unwilling to testify against them for safety reasons and partly because they are usually deported before they can bring a case against the traffickers—prevents the judicial system from taking appropriate action.[1] This hole in the judicial system works to the advantage of traffickers, significantly reducing their risks and creating a situation of impunity. Perhaps as important, however, is the fact that there is a growing demand in these destination countries for foreign and "exotic" prostitutes that turns trafficking into a very lucrative business (International Organization for Migration 1996c, 8).

The Mechanics of Trafficking: Profiles of Traffickers

The International Organization for Migration (1996c, 10–11; 1995, 3–4) outlines three types of traffickers. Occasional traffickers operate on a relatively small scale in border regions. Typically, they can smuggle individuals or groups across poorly guarded borders in their own vehicles and drop them off at predetermined sites across the border. The financial gain from these types of activities is not the main source of the traffickers' income but rather a supplement. Thanks to its intermittent and small-scale character, this type of trafficking does not require sophisticated organization that would breach a wide variety of laws. Somewhat more sophisticated are the small-scale trafficking rings, which are substantially better organized. These organizations use the same routes to traffic individuals routinely from particular source to particular destination countries. Finally, the most sophisticated are the international trafficking networks engaged in various kinds of criminal activity ranging from producing fraudulent, stolen, falsified, or other mala fide documents to undertaking risky smuggling operations involving transit countries. Displaying a high degree of adaptability to changing circumstances, these organizations have the flexibility to change routes, methods, and transit countries as needed in response to efforts to tighten controls in the transit or destination countries.

While trafficking almost always conjures up images of sneaking across the border in the trunk of a car, not all border crossings are initially illegal. Research shows that women are often brought into a destination country legally after having obtained certain types of visas that are issued to artists, dancers, au pairs, language students, or entertainers; they then overstay their legal welcome. The traffickers are responsible for applying for and obtaining these visas, thus abusing the immigration regulations of the recipient country.

In sum, the migration approach views trafficking within the economic framework of supply and demand. The evidence provided by IOM's studies strongly highlights the root causes of trafficking, namely, the economic conditions that push desperate, poor, and often unsuspecting women into a pattern of exploitation by traffickers. And while these studies acknowledge the macroeconomic pull factors in destination countries, they tend to ignore the gendered nature of demand for trafficked women and girls in those countries. Media attention to the issue usually reflects concerns about the inability of the state to defend its borders against "shady" migrants, leading policymakers to respond by devising various border control mechanisms. Such policies are not concerned with the plight of the trafficked women, nor do they get at the root causes of the phenomenon to eradicate the abuse. Instead, they are reactive instruments that always lag one step behind the ingenuity of traffickers.

Trafficking in Women as a Human Rights Issue

Framing trafficking in women as a human rights issue predates the designation of trafficking as a migration phenomenon. International efforts earlier in this century sought to develop international rules to prohibit trafficking and raise awareness about its human rights dimension. International organizations have been instrumental in creating multilateral momentum, providing forums within which to debate the issues, and keeping the debate on the international agenda.

The human rights framework on trafficking emphasizes the sexual exploitation and abuse of women—questions the migration approach avoids. Some have argued that for trafficking to violate the human rights of the trafficked, a distinction has to be made between voluntary and involuntary prostitution in individual cases. Women who willingly consent to being trafficked—knowingly putting themselves at risk of being prostituted—have little or no right to recourse, in this view. But this raises difficult questions regarding what constitutes voluntary and involuntary prostitution. Even human rights and women's rights nongovernmental organizations (NGOs) are divided on the issue. The majority of NGOs would subscribe to the notion that trafficking is a form of violence against the human dignity of women, a position espoused by the Coalition against Trafficking in Women. Many feminist NGOs argue that there is no such thing as voluntary prostitution (Raymond 1995). Others portray prostitution as a profession, the practice of which cannot be prohibited without encroaching on the human rights of "sex workers." The International Committee for Prostitutes asserts that women ought to have a right to prostitute themselves and that preventing them from doing so in the name of protection is a breach of their human rights.

The lack of consensus on key concepts in this debate—prostitution, voluntariness, abuse, coercion, trafficking—has complicated contemporary efforts to develop an effective human rights framework to address trafficking in women. Another problem with the human rights approach is that, unlike the migration framework, it seeks to rectify primarily the consequences of trafficking and tends not to address its root causes. A third problem is the divergence of national legal approaches in dealing with prostitution. Divergent legal and moral traditions have limited international efforts to develop broad-based and effective international rules to suppress the trafficking of women.

There are essentially three legal approaches to prostitution. Each follows a different moral tradition, and each accordingly prescribes different consequences for aberrant behavior. *Prohibitionism,* practiced largely in the United States, China, and some other Asian countries, outlaws prostitution and punishes the individuals engaged in it as well as their clients. *Regulationism,* introduced by the Napoleonic Code and practiced in the majority of the European countries, provides for the control of prostitution to contain the health consequences (such as the spread of venereal diseases and most recently of AIDS). This approach allows for exploiting the prostitution of individuals legally regarded as adults. In turn, the public authorities monitor brothels, and prostitutes are registered and must undergo regular health checks. Finally, *abolitionism* recognizes prostitution to be incompatible with human dignity but declares it a private matter. It seeks to abolish the regulatory practices, which are seen as discriminatory measures against prostitutes whose human rights should be respected (Hirsch 1996).

These different approaches, which divide the world into blocs of countries that follow different rules, have important implications for the trafficked women. The legal recourse that can be sought or the methods of prosecution available against the perpetrators of trafficking depend greatly on which one of these approaches informs the response mechanisms of a recipient society. They also have significant consequences for international rulemaking. Part of the difficulty in garnering international support for global guidelines under the aegis of international organizations can be attributed to these divergent traditions.

International Rulemaking on Trafficking in Women

At the beginning of the twentieth century, international law recognized trafficking for the purpose of sexual exploitation as an international criminal activity that harmed the human dignity of its victim. International agreements sought to establish common policies to combat the prostitution of underage individuals and the sexual exploitation of women of full age under duress. Significantly, these early international legal efforts sought to address what was termed the "white slave traffic," and it appears that there was consensus that this was a gender-specific phenomenon. In other words, they recognized (white) women and young girls as the primary targets of cross-border pimping. The subsequent development of international rulemaking on trafficking under the League of Nations and the United Nations followed a curious path that progressively included additional groups of individuals and resulted in the deracializing and degendering of the issue (see table 15.1).

The first instrument to deal with trafficking was signed on 18 May 1904. As spelled out in its title, the International Agreement for the Suppression of the White Slave Traffic concerned itself with the fate of white victims only. The Paris Convention for the Suppression of the White Slave Traffic followed in 1910. Although gender was not specified in their titles, both instruments sought to establish a common policy against the prostitution of women and

Table 15.1
International Instruments Relating to Trafficking in Women

Date	Instrument/Occasion	Content/Relevance
18 May 1904	International Agreement for the Suppression of the White Slave Traffic	First international arrangement adopted for the suppression of white slave traffic.
4 May 1910	International Convention for the Suppression of White Slave Traffic (Paris Convention)	Art. 2: "any person who, to gratify the passions of others, has by fraud or by the use of violence, threats, abuse of authority, or any other means of constraint, hired, abducted or enticed a woman or girl of full age for immoral purposes . . . shall also be punished."
30 Sept. 1921	International Convention for the Suppression of Traffic in Women and Children	Deletes "white" from the term "white slave traffic" and extends the definition to other races and includes minors and children
11 Oct. 1933	International Convention for the Suppression of the Traffic in Women of Full Age (Geneva Convention)	Art. 1: "whoever, in order to gratify the passions of another person, has procured, enticed or led away, even with her consent, a woman or girl of full age . . . shall be punished." Applies to all women of full age, not just white women.
2 Dec. 1949 21 March 1951	UN Convention for the Suppression of the Traffic in Persons and the Exploitation of the Prostitution of Others (with Final Protocol)	Art. 17: "adopt or maintain such measures . . . to check the traffic in persons of either sex for the purpose of prostitution."
10 Dec. 1979	UN Convention on the Elimination of All Forms of Discrimination against Women	Art. 6 calls on all UN member states to take all appropriate measures to suppress all forms of trafficking in women and exploitation of prostitution. Has been ratified by 130 member states.
1992	Recommendation No. 19 of the Committee on the Elimination of All Forms of Discrimination against Women	Elaborates on the factors contributing to trafficking, including poverty, unemployment, and armed conflict.
June 1993	UN Conference on Human Rights, Declaration and Program of Action	Particularly Chaps. II and III deal with trafficking.
Sept. 1995	UN Conference on Women, The Platform of Action	Chap. D, para. 123 calls for the implementation of the 1949 Convention. Strategic Objective D, para. 131 calls for criminal and civil measures against traffickers.

underage girls who were abused and/or constrained. Thus, even before the League of Nations came into existence, the signatories to the Paris Convention agreed to criminalize the forced traffic and prostitution of white women and girls.

The 1921 International Convention for the Suppression of the Traffic in Women and Children lifted the race category and extended the definition of trafficking to include minors and children, but not men, as victims. The 1933 Geneva Convention expanded on the Paris Convention by declaring the trafficking of women of full age, even with their consent, a criminal activity. Superseding the Paris Convention, the 1949 New York Convention deemed all individuals involved in the trafficking of persons and their exploitation through prostitution to be liable to criminal punishment, regardless of whether such trafficking occurred with the consent of the trafficked individual or under duress. Its preamble states that "prostitution and the accompanying evil of traffic in *persons* for the purpose of prostitution are incompatible with the dignity and worth of *the human person* and endanger the welfare of the individual, the family and the community" (United Nations, Treaty Series 1951, vol. 96, no. 1342, 270; emphasis added). Thus, up to and including the 1933 convention, the treaty texts continued to make explicit reference to women as the objects of trafficking. By contrast, since the 1949 convention, there has been a steady move away from gender-specific language.

The 1949 New York Convention was the last legal attempt under the aegis of the UN to formulate binding international rules. However, implementation of this instrument has been fraught with monitoring and enforcement problems, as it was ratified by less than half of the UN member states. Divergent legal traditions made the contents of the convention unacceptable to some countries. The absence of a common position among European states when the convention was signed illustrates this divergence of practice. Greece, the Netherlands, and Luxembourg voted in favor of the convention; France and the United Kingdom voted against; Belgium, Denmark, and Sweden abstained. States cited a variety of reasons, ranging from constitutional incompatibility to outright unacceptability of the underlying assumptions of the instrument, to justify their abstentions or refusals to sign and ratify the instrument. Major sending countries such as Thailand and the Dominican Republic likewise refrained from becoming parties to an international legal instrument that could incriminate their citizens.

The United Nations and Agenda Setting

With only weak international laws in place to deal with a growing problem, the issue of trafficking in women has reappeared on the UN agenda, particularly as a result of the UN Decade for Women. The 1979 United Nations Convention on the Elimination of All Forms of Discrimination against Women calls on states to suppress all forms of trafficking in women and the exploitation of prostitution (Art. 6) (United Nations, Treaty Series 1981, vol. 1249, no. 20378, 14). By the 1990s, the issue was included in a broadening discussion of women's human rights. The 1995 Fourth World Conference on Women (Beijing conference) sought to raise awareness, facilitate goal-oriented thinking, and generate discussion on trafficking, casting it in terms of another form of violence against women. The Beijing Platform for Action identified the "effective suppression of trafficking in women and girls for the sex trade" as a "matter of pressing international concern" (United Nations 1995a, para. 122). Strategic objective D.3 of the platform deals with eliminating trafficking in women and assisting victims of violence due to prostitution and trafficking. It calls for the ratification and implementation of the 1949 New York Convention. It urges addressing the root causes of trafficking by stepping up concerted action against traffickers by the relevant law enforcement authorities. It also urges the allocation of resources for the rehabilitation of victims and the development of educational programs to prevent trafficking (paras. 130–31).

Following the Beijing conference, the UN Commission on the Status of Women (CSW) pressed the issue within the Economic and Social Council (ECOSOC). The CSW was instrumental in preparing the draft resolutions on mainstreaming the human rights of women (CSW 1996a) and violence against migrant workers (CSW 1996c). Both resolutions focus on the need for multilateral cooperation to combat trafficking, and invite UN member states to develop new, legally binding instruments. The CSW also drafted a resolution that was more specifically directed towards trafficking in women. Submitted to ECOSOC by Fiji, Ghana, Nigeria, the Philippines, and Thailand (the first time source countries played such a role), this resolution called for the implementation of the Platform of Action of the Beijing conference, invited governments to "consider the development of standard minimum rules for the humanitarian treatment of trafficked persons consistent with internationally recognized human rights standards," encouraged UN specialized agencies, governments, and NGOs to gather and share information on trafficking, called upon governments to take appropriate preventive or prohibitive action against trafficking, and pledged to keep the issue on its future agenda (CSW 1996b).

These recent efforts have clearly placed the issue of trafficking in women on the UN's agenda within the context of mainstreaming women's rights as human rights. While these efforts are helping to raise and shape the debate, real progress (in the form of hard law) at the global level to eliminate trafficking in women continues to be elusive.

The European Union and Trafficking in Women

Some have argued that rather than addressing trafficking in women at the global level, efforts ought to be concentrated at the regional level, where it is arguably easier to forge consensus. Europe is one region where governments and intergovernmental organizations are slowly developing a more comprehensive agenda relating to trafficking. Significantly, recent efforts have been made within the European Union to synthesize the migration and human rights approaches to develop an integrated and effective response.

Trafficking in women as a political issue has gained salience in Europe since the fall of the Berlin Wall. While before 1989 most of the foreign prostitutes—partly trafficked—were recruited in Asia, South America, and Africa, the current trend shows an important increase in those who are trafficked from Central and Eastern European Countries (CEECs). Not all EU member states have been equally targeted by traffickers. Continental Europe appears to be more affected by trafficking than the northern and the northwestern periphery (e.g., Sweden, the United Kingdom, and Ireland). While the actual numbers are disputed owing to problems with data collection, it is estimated that approximately 200,000 Eastern European women work in Germany. In Austria, while there were only 50 cases of trafficking discovered in 1990, the numbers jumped to 316 cases involving 752 women in 1994, most of them from the CEECs (International Organization for Migration 1996a, 8). The Dutch Foundation against Trafficking in Women, a women's rights NGO, reported in 1995 that 69 percent of the foreign prostitutes who were trafficked to the Netherlands were from Eastern Europe, predominantly from Russia, Ukraine, Poland, and Hungary. It is estimated that for each trafficked woman whose case reaches the authorities, three others remain unreported. In fact, the existence of individuals who are accused of trafficking 200 women points to the magnitude of the problem that goes undetected (International Organization for Migration 1996c).

The recognition that effective policies need to be devised at the regional level is leading to collective efforts to respond to trafficking. Within the EU, cooperation on trafficking in women falls within the purview of the newly established "Third Pillar,"[2] which can approach the problem from the perspective of legal cooperation and migration policies alike, thus potentially allowing for a healthy dialogue between the two approaches. Most of the work on trafficking in the European Union is done by the European Parliament and the European Commission through a process that allows consultation with other intergovernmental organizations such as the Council of Europe. Although NGOs are not yet very successful in influencing the official debate, their voices are increasingly being heard by the public, European bureaucrats, and policymakers, while EU institutions are becoming more comfortable with engaging NGOs to implement projects.

European Parliament. Among the European institutions spearheading debate on trafficking in women is the European Parliament (EP). On 14 December 1995, an Italian member of the European Parliament, Maria Paola Colombo Svevo, submitted a report to the EP's Committee on Civil Liberties and Internal Affairs on Trafficking in Human Beings that formed the basis of the EP's resolution on the same subject (European Union Parliament 1995). On 18 January 1996, this resolution was unanimously adopted by the EP. The Colombo Svevo Resolution urges member states to "identify trafficking as a violation of human rights and a serious crime" (European Union Parliament 1995, para. 15). It calls on EU member states to create a legal framework that would penalize trafficking as well as protect victims and introduce preventive measures targeting countries of origin. The resolution calls on member countries to develop a common, multitrack policy of dissuasion to combat trafficking that would rest on a combination of "prevention, deterrence, prosecution and rehabilitation," possibly the best combination of measures. (European Union Parliament 1995, para. 7). The resolution also calls on the EU "to take action at an international level to draft a new UN convention to supersede the obsolete and ineffective" 1949 convention and to exert its leverage at the UN to appoint a special rapporteur for the traffic in human beings to the UN's Commission on Human Rights (para. 31). This resolution forms the basis of current programs developed by the European Commission.

European Commission. Combating trafficking in women ranks high on the agenda of Anita Gradin, the Swedish commissioner who was confirmed for a five-year period in 1995. Gradin was quick to involve the Commission in the regional efforts to combat trafficking. Following up on the Colombo Svevo Resolution, Gradin tasked the Commission with organizing a conference on trafficking in women. This conference took place in Vienna on 10–11 June 1996.

The Vienna conference (organized and funded in part by IOM) brought together experts from source and destination countries, representatives of EU institutions, other European international organizations such as the Council of Europe, and, to a lesser extent, NGOs. Engaging the experts in group sessions that examined trafficking from multiple perspectives, including migration policy, judicial cooperation, law enforcement, police cooperation, and social policy, the conference made numerous recommendations for a multitrack policy that would criminalize trafficking, prosecute traffickers, and assist vulnerable women and victims of trafficking. These recommendations also emphasized judicial and police cooperation at both national and international levels (European Union Commission 1996b).

Since the Vienna conference, the European Commission has taken steps to develop Europe-wide programs to stop trafficking in women. In its 1996 Communication on Trafficking in Women for the Purpose of Sexual Exploitation, the Commission laid the groundwork for a pilot program on the sexual trafficking of persons (appropriately referred to as the STOP program), which was designed as an incentive and exchange program for persons responsible for combating trafficking. The STOP program seeks to improve existing data collection, research, exchange of information between authorities, and training. Some 6.5 million ECU (European Currency Units) have been allocated to fund the program over a five-year period (European Union Commission 1996a, 7–8). In 1997, the European Commission launched the Daphne Initiative, which provides funding for NGOs targeting violence against children, youth, and women. In line with the human rights framework, the Commission now appears to regard trafficking as a type of violence against women and thus has demonstrated its commitment to stem trafficking and develop measures to protect trafficked women.

The Commission has also sought to improve cooperation and coordination between sending and recipient countries in such areas as information campaigns, training of national civil servants to help them detect and respond to trafficking, and judicial cooperation to assess and strengthen national legislation as well as European and international laws relating to trafficking. Since the Vienna conference, Belgium has launched an initiative to adopt an EU instrument to combat trafficking in persons.[3]

While still at an early stage, the EU's efforts to address trafficking are promising. They combine the concerns of the human rights framework about the exploitation, violence, and abuse suffered by those who are trafficked with the attention of the migration framework to the causal factors of trafficking. These efforts are also based on an informed debate on trafficking and have established cooperative programs linking EU institutions, governments, and NGOs.

Conclusion

Trafficking in women is a growing phenomenon that has largely eluded national and international efforts to eradicate it. Unfortunately, as Jonas Widgren observes, "there will be more victims in the decades to come" (Widgren 1996, 1). The migration framework that seeks to understand this phenomenon points to factors that compel individuals to leave their usual place of residence and cross international borders, the expansion of criminal networks that specialize in trafficking, the relative ease with which borders can be penetrated, and, to a lesser extent, the emergence of regional markets for trafficking. The human rights

244 Emek M. Uçarer

framework points to the lack of an appropriate and adequate legal structure that criminalizes the traffickers rather than the trafficked, protects the human rights of the trafficked, and provides support to victims of trafficking. Policy approaches that use only one of these frameworks will not be effective.

Historically, the diversity of national legal approaches to prostitution (which are themselves highly gendered and deserve further analysis) has limited international legal efforts to eradicate trafficking. More recently, renewed attention to trafficking as a gendered phenomenon that violates women's human rights has led to calls for global action. However, a debate persists over which women's rights are at stake and how they can best be protected. As the United Nations and the European Union begin to take up these questions, it is clear that stronger cooperative efforts by governments, intergovernmental organizations, and nongovernmental organizations are needed to stop this transnational criminal activity that abuses vulnerable women and girls. A human rights–cum–migration approach may ultimately bring about a more informed dialogue and more effective policies at the national, regional, and global levels.

Notes

1. The sanctions against alien smuggling;aiding and abetting smuggling; harboring smuggling; creating fraudulent documents; and transporting undocumented individuals vary greatly across countries. Alien smuggling carries with it a penalty of between one year (the Netherlands) and ten years (United States), with two years being the most common (Denmark, Finland, Italy, Norway, Sweden). A similar range applies to aiding and abetting smuggling and harboring smugglers. The penalty for document fraud varies between six months (Switzerland, United Kingdom) to fifteen years (United States). A variety of fines are applicable to carriers and employers of undocumented aliens. For a comparative analysis of the fines and penalties that relate to trafficking in persons, see Czech Republic (1996, 10).

2. The 1992 Treaty on European Union (Maastricht Treaty) restructured the European Community and renamed it the European Union (EU). The post-Maastricht architecture of the EU consists of three pillars: The first pillar is the original Treaty of Rome as amended by Maastricht and centers on economic integration (the common/single market); the second pillar centers on common security and foreign policy; the third pillar centers on the competence area of justice and home affairs, including judicial cooperation and cooperation on migration issues.

3. Belgium is the only EU member state that has explicit legislation for combating trafficking in human beings and child pornography. Partly as a result of this Belgian initiative, and partly because the Commission would like to consider trafficking within a broader framework, current EU efforts do not specifically target trafficking in women but rather refer to the broader category of trafficking in human beings.

16

Gender Construction and the Protection Mandate of the UNHCR: Responses from Guatemalan Women

Erin K. Baines

"Protection," according to the United Nations High Commissioner for Refugees (UNHCR), "is at the heart of the responsibility that the international community bears toward refugees" (UNHCR 1991a, 7). Outside their country of origin, refugees lack the protection that their own governments should provide and thus are vulnerable to human rights abuses. As one of the largest and fastest-growing international organizations dealing with refugees, the UNHCR strives to take all necessary steps to protect the rights of refugees and to find permanent solutions to their problems.

Until the 1980s, refugee women were assumed to have the same protection needs as refugee men, and the UNHCR claimed to apply its policies equally to both. Yet feminist investigations revealed that UNHCR policies and practices had different outcomes for refugee men and women (Forbes Martin 1992). In 1985, the UNHCR recognized for the first time that "refugee women and girls have special protection needs that reflect their gender" (UNHCR 1991b, 7). Over the following decade, a series of policies and guidelines sought to extend UNHCR protection to refugee women and meet their specific protection needs. What were the assumptions of the UNHCR's policies regarding gender roles and responsibilities in politics, economics, and the family, and how have they changed? Do the new UNHCR policies on refugee women significantly challenge or transform previous constructions of gender? What impact have policy changes had on refugee women, and how have refugee women responded?

According to Sandra Whitworth, an analysis of international organizations that is sensitive to gender involves exploring "the ways in which knowledge about sexual difference is sustained, reproduced, and manipulated. . . . It means uncovering the ideas about sexual difference which inform different international activities, and discovering the impact which these ideas have on . . . practices" (Whitworth 1994, 4). Gender is conceived of here as a social construct that differentiates appropriate modes of behavior for men and women—including notions of what is masculine and feminine—in ways that become embedded in a variety of social institutions such as the family, workplace, church, state, and international organizations and institutions (xii). Thus, the actions and policies of international organizations are but one part of a complex process that perpetuates, or reproduces, gender relations. Therefore, we should be interested in "the extent to which international practices themselves contribute to the particular understanding which we hold of gender in any given time or place" (4).

At the same time, feminist approaches to international organizations and global governance should be wary of the tendency to overgeneralize the experiences of women in relation to global forces. Global gender relations may limit or provide opportunities to women and men, but they do not determine outcomes. Indeed, global gender relations are constantly in flux; they may be contested and transformed by the "practices and struggles of actors engaged in relationships with each other and the institutions in which they are involved" (Whitworth 1994, 65). A major challenge facing feminist scholars is to understand the connections between the local and the global, to contemplate how agents, individually and collectively, may challenge global constructions of gender.

This chapter argues that the 1951 UN Convention Relating to the Status of Refugees reproduces public/private distinctions prevalent in liberal political theory, obscuring the link between gender-related forms of persecution and the need for international protection. As a result, female asylum seekers fleeing gender-related persecution often are not recognized, and the protection needs of refugee women in assistance programs in refugee camps often are not met. This chapter considers how the UNHCR recently has attempted to integrate refugee women into its protection mandate and asks whether these initiatives challenge traditional constructions of gender. To address this question, the chapter analyzes the relationship between Guatemalan refugee women in Mexican camps and UNHCR initiatives on gender. It highlights the interplay of the local and the global in the constitution and reconstitution of gender.

Gender Construction and the UNHCR's Protection Mandate

Women and their dependent children constitute between 75 and 80 percent of the world's twenty-three million refugees (Forbes Martin 1991). In times of political and economic turmoil, women are among the first to suffer repression, in part owing to "laws and social mores which dictate gender-specific behaviour and treatment" (Kelly 1993, 626). For instance, the number of beatings women suffer increases when men are laid off from work or cannot find employment. Left to head their families when husbands are soldiers in a war, women are often targets of violent attacks by opposition forces. Fleeing their country, women are sexually attacked by border guards, pirates, or guerrilla forces (UNHCR 1995b).

Sexual violence is often a cause of flight for refugee women. In times of war, rape has been used as a strategy of genocide and humiliation. The mass rape of Bosnian women by Serbian men during the war in the former Yugoslavia was a strategy that sought to exile Bosnians from their land (Stiglmayer 1992). The Guatemalan army used rape to humiliate indigenous communities in highland villages, often before murdering members of the community. Rape has also been used as a cruel means of ethnic cleansing. This was the case in Ecuador, where multinational agribusiness companies hired mercenaries who raped more than 50 percent of Yuracruz women in order to assimilate indigenous Yuracruz people (Copelon 1995, 200). Additionally, women have been abducted by soldiers in wartime and sold into prostitution (UNHCR 1995c).

Despite their frequency, gender-related violations are not specifically recognized by international refugee law as a form of persecution or as grounds for claiming refugee status. Gender-related forms of persecution include "situations where a woman is persecuted as a woman, that is to say where the form of persecution is uniquely or primarily inflicted on women" (Macklin 1997).[1] Forced abortion, sterilization, impregnation, and female genital mutilation are all forms of gender-related persecution in this sense. "It also includes situations where a woman is persecuted . . . because of her attitudes about women" (Macklin 1997). For example, the expression of feminist views in a state hostile to feminism may lead to persecution.

The 1951 UN Convention Relating to the Status of Refugees defines a refugee as a person who "owing to well-founded fear of persecution for reasons of race, religion, nationality, membership in a particular social group or political opinion, is outside the country of his nationality and is unable or, owing to such fear, is unwilling to avail himself of the protection of that country" (UNHCR 1951, 2). According to Doreen Indra, the 1951 convention is silent on the "ways in which gender may play a major role in how refugees are created, and how distinct the refugee experience can be for men and women" (1987, 3). Indra explains that the grounds for refugee status offered in the Convention reflect the experiences of men within the public sphere, neglecting or obscuring altogether the private-sphere experiences of women. As a result, the Convention reproduces the idea that oppression suffered in the private sphere is somehow neither political nor connected to the public sphere. This in turn severs the connection between gender-related forms of persecution that women suffer and state responsibility. Referring to the Refugee Convention, Indra points out the irony of this false separation:

> It is remarkable that sex and gender oppression are not even mentioned, whereas oppression arising from parallel forms of invidious status distinction such as race or religious conviction are central. Thus an individual risking death at the hands of the majority group institutions for maintaining a minority religion (say, Bahá'í in Iran) fits the definition, whereas a woman (again, say in Iran) facing death by the same institutions for stepping out of her 'appropriate role' or for deviating from misogynous sexual mores does not. (1987, 3)

Emphasis on civil and political violations in the 1951 Convention obscures the grounds for gender-related persecution. This problem is compounded by the fact that international human rights laws and norms, informed by the separation of public and private spheres in liberal theory, fail to recognize gender-related violence as a human rights issue. As a result, "survivors of sexual violence perpetrated by the military or paramilitary forces or in prison camps by officials may find it difficult to establish that their victimization was linked to their religion, race, political opinion, nationality or membership of a particular social group and may find that their victimization is perceived of as a random and individual act" (Connors 1997, 120–21).

In 1985, the UNHCR made some progress toward the recognition of gender-related persecution, urging states to recognize women who suffer inhumane treatment "due to their having transgressed the social mores of the society in which they live" as a "particular social group" under existing Convention grounds (UNHCR 1995a). Unfortunately, this conclusion is not binding on states. Furthermore, its wording presents the idea that women bring harsh treatment upon themselves. In reality, sexual and physical violence against women occurs regardless of their actions; in many cases it occurs simply because they are women (Macklin 1997). As Davar observes, linking a woman's actions to the violence she suffers is similar to making rape victims responsible for their rape (Davar 1993, 3). Despite this shortcoming, the recommendation has spurred efforts in several Western countries, including Canada, the United States, and Australia, to include gender-related persecution under the "particular social group" category. However, to date, no case has considered gender or sex alone as sufficient reason for claiming refugee status, even under the more flexible category "particular social group" (Connors 1997, 126).

Efforts to reformulate or reinterpret the Convention definition may help some refugee women escape persecution. But most never make it to the borders of Western countries to apply for asylum in the first place. The majority of the world's refugees arrive in so-called developing countries and lack the necessary resources to move on to a third country of asylum. If a woman is poor, uneducated, and solely responsible for the care of her children, her mobility is even more restricted than that of her male counterpart. Moreover, changing the definition of a refugee, while essential to the development of an international norm on gender-related violence, does not address the immediate protection needs of refugee women who may spend many years in camps. Unfortunately, life in refugee camps often increases women's vulnerability to sexual violence (UNHCR 1995b). Emergency and long-term assistance programs that do not consider the needs of refugee women reinforce unequal power relations between men and women, contributing to women's subordination to men and even vulnerability to abuse (Bonnerjea 1985, 13).

Refugee women are the invisible majority in assistance programs, marginalized at nearly every step in decision-making and distribution processes (Camus-Jacques 1992; Forbes Martin 1992). For example, the distribution of goods and services within camps is usually conducted in consultation with male leaders. This method often results in malnutrition, poor health, and increased workloads for refugee women who are not consulted (Bonnerjea 1985, 13; Camus-Jacques 1992, 148). This is particularly true for female heads of households who may be left out of distribution processes altogether. Furthermore, training and educational programs tend to be targeted at men. As a result, girl refugees are often unable to obtain an education and refugee women the skills to get a job.

The exclusion or marginalization of refugee women can be explained in part in terms of assumptions relating to gender roles embedded in assistance processes. These processes reflect the public/private split prevalent in liberal political theory. They encode the assumption that refugee men are the sole income earners of family units and that they are active in the public sphere while refugee women are engaged in reproductive work in the private sphere. Thus the economic stability and well-being of a community are thought to have been met if the needs of men are met. Assistance workers presume that this understanding resonates with the cultures of refugee groups. As Sima Wali argues, "rendered voiceless and powerless, refugee and displaced women are expected to defer their needs to the political and religious dictates of the male hierarchy. Unfortunately, Western and international assistance agencies often perpetuate this condition by granting food, relief assistance, and protection to male refugees. Often, they justify such action by claiming it [is] 'culturally appropriate'" (Wali 1995, 337).

The invisibility of refugee women in UNHCR assistance practices masks and marginalizes the experiences and priorities of refugee women in camps. For example, health care programs in refugee camps often fail to recognize the specificity of women's needs or to reflect sensitivity to cultural norms. In overcrowded camps, the health of all refugees is precarious, but women especially have problems getting care. Owing to traditional gender relations and cultural medicinal practices, many female refugees are unlikely to seek the services of Western heath care providers, who are mostly male. Gynecological problems and complications related to pregnancies in particular go untreated for these reasons. Another example is camp design. Poorly lit areas, mixed-sex housing, and services provided in remote areas can lead to sexual violence (UNHCR 1995a). The alarming increase in violence against women within refugee camps has forced the UNHCR to confront the fact that protection and assistance are intimately linked (UNHCR 1993).

A crucial step in the protection of refugees in camps is providing adequate documentation. Without documentation, the refugee cannot enjoy the social services or employment opportunities of her or his country of asylum, nor be protected under the principle of *non-refoulement.*[2] Historically, legal documentation of refugee status has been granted to male heads of household (UNHCR 1991a, 38). This has resulted in great stress for married women who, dependent on their husbands' documents, are unable to decide independently if they wish to resettle, integrate, or return to their country of origin. This reality is further complicated for women who have separated from their husbands either by choice or in forced circumstances after leaving their home country. Without their own documentation, refugee women separated from their husbands are denied the freedom to decide their own future, and in some cases they are forced to repatriate against their will. In addition, the practice of documenting only male heads of household has resulted in female heads of household not receiving documents. In these cases, the UNHCR is clearly not upholding the principle of non-refoulement nor protecting the interests of refugee women.

In 1990, the high commissioner, with the support of major donor countries and global refugee women's groups and networks, appointed a senior coordinator for refugee women, Canadian Ann Howarth Wiles. The coordinator's office is responsible for integrating issues related to refugee women into all UNHCR programs. This includes assessing the "effectiveness of existing protection and assistance measures in preventing physical violence, rape, exploitation and discrimination against refugee women, and propos[ing] solutions as appropriate" (Overholt 1996, 2). Howarth Wiles wanted to ensure that the issue of refugee women was not treated as a special program and thus marginalized within the UNHCR; she therefore focused on initiatives that would benefit refugee men and women equally. This led to a "people-oriented approach" to camp design and programming. For example, the policy on refugee women stressed that a "programme which integrates refugee women will have taken into consideration factors influenced by the male/female roles in a society and include these in the planned activity with a view to benefiting the whole target population not marginalizing a portion of it" (UNHCR 1991b, 6). It emphasized the importance of identifying the gendered division of labor in refugee camps: projects must go beyond including women as daughters, wives, and mothers to understand how they also are income earners for their families, providers of fuel and water, and producers of food.

In 1991, the coordinator's office released the Guidelines on the Protection of Refugee Women. The guidelines highlight the frequency with which refugee women encounter gender-related violence during flight and in exile. They suggest fairly straightforward measures for preventing sexual violence, including designing camps to promote physical security; ensuring access to food and other distributed items; urging local authorities to investigate, prosecute, and punish perpetrators of, sexual violence; and instituting public information and education campaigns to inform refugee women of their rights. The guidelines provide practical advice for responding to incidents of violence, including protecting the victim from further abuse, reporting and documenting cases of abuse, and providing medical assistance. Impressed with the importance of implementing both the policy on refugee women and the guidelines, the Sub-Committee on the Whole of International Protection ordered that they be distributed and implemented throughout UNHCR field offices.

What has been the significance of introducing a gender perspective into UNHCR protection policies? Do the new policies represent changed constructions of gender? What difference do they make to refugee women? Most feminist analyses of global governance focus on gender construction at the international level (Whitworth 1994). Such analyses often lead to the overgeneralization of women's experiences, neglecting diversity as well as sources of resistance and change. They underestimate the interplay of the global and the local in the construction of gender relations. The remainder of the chapter strives to determine the extent to which the introduction of gender policies and guidelines by the senior coordinator for refugee women challenges traditional constructions of gender by extending protection to refugee women. The experiences of Guatemalan refugee women provide insight into the way UNHCR policies open important political spaces and offer new opportunities to refugee women. They illustrate gender construction at the intersections of the local and the global.

Responses from Guatemalan Refugee Women

In the 1970s, indigenous Mayan peasants in search of a better life settled in the northern highlands of Guatemala. They formed profitable cooperatives, and villages began to flourish, despite an inhospitable climate. However, in the 1980s the civil war in Guatemala grew more intense, and the new villages came under increasing threat. The Guatemalan army, convinced that the highland villagers were supporting the guerrilla movement, began a campaign of terror in the region. Scorched-earth tactics, forced conscription, kidnapping, disappearances, torture, and rape forced highland peasants to flee from their newfound homes. At the peak of the repression, between 1980 and 1985, fifty thousand to seventy-five thousand Mayan peasants were murdered and four hundred highland villages were completely destroyed. In total, over two hundred thousand peasants were forced to flee deep into the jungles and into bordering Mexican states. A further one million Guatemalans were displaced within the country as a result of the war (Salvado 1988, 1).

Most of the refugees settled in the Mexican state of Chiapas, but, at the insistence of the Mexican government, some went to camps in Campeche and Quintana Roo. The refugees organized the Permanent Commissions of the Representatives of the Refugees (CCPP) to lobby various governments and international agencies, initially with regard to living conditions in the camps. The CCPP quickly became involved in negotiations with the Guatemalan government for a safe return of refugees, and an accord was signed on 8 October 1992. Under the terms of the accord, over thirty thousand refugees returned to Guatemala by 1997 (Kznaric 1997, 62). Although divisions have occurred within the CCPP and new refugee organizations have formed, the organization continues to play an important role in most returned communities, working toward economic and political stability.

The UNHCR became involved in organizing the camps in Mexico in the early stages of the refugee movement and later fully supported the return process. The UNHCR regards the Guatemalan repatriation process as a success and as a good model for other countries to follow. Regional cooperation and refugee participation are referred to as decisive factors in the returnees' successful readjustment. In particular, the UNHCR has pointed to the organization of Guatemalan refugee women as a vital force in the return process and in the construction of the returned communities (Garcia 1995; Lozano 1996, 5).[3]

In the 1990s, refugee women's organizations formed to support a peaceful resettlement and to help build new communities. The Mamá Maquín is the largest of these organizations, with close to eight thousand members (Garcia and Garcia 1995). Other organizations include the Ixmucané Organization of Guatemalan Women, the Union of Guatemalan Refugee Women, and Madre Tierra, which was formed in 1993. The majority of the women in these organizations are from one of the twenty-one indigenous groups in Guatemala. They have organized returns, conducted cultural and educational workshops, and developed income-producing initiatives. Refugee women involved in the organizations have moved beyond the economic and cultural reconstruction of their communities, however. Through their actions they are also negotiating and redefining gender roles.

Sandra Garcia identifies at least four factors that facilitated the organization of Guatemalan refugee women and an awareness of gender in the camps (Garcia 1995). First, the International Conference on Central American Refugees (CIERFCA) promoted and provided a framework for the cooperation of NGOs, refugee groups, and the Guatemalan state in the return process. Second, a Central American NGO specializing in women's issues, CIAM (Centro de Investigación y Acción de la Mujer/Women's Center for Research and Action), began working with the refugees in Mexico, raising awareness and providing support. CIAM and the Mamá Maquín were important partners in building a knowledge base about the situation and the priorities of Guatemalan refugee women living in Mexico. Third, following its policy to collect more information on refugee women in general, the UNHCR in Mexico conducted an evaluation and presented its findings at a regional conference on the topic, the Regional Forum of Refugee and Repatriated Women (FoReFem). These findings were then incorporated into the CIERFCA approach. FoReFem, which was held in February 1992, provided an important networking medium for participants. Here, displaced and refugee women could articulate their demands to governments and the international community in a forum designed specifically for and by them. Fourth, Guatemalan women organized themselves in a way that connected them to each other in solidarity, ensuring that they would not be left out of decision-making processes and securing a forum to articulate their demands. For example, a number of refugee women's organizations formed the Committee for the Support of Refugee Women, which included members of local NGOs and the UNHCR. Through this committee, groups such as the Mamá Maquín were able to articulate to the UNHCR as well as other agencies what refugee women wanted, thus becoming a part of decision-making processes.

The UNHCR began working with refugee women's groups in early 1991, after conducting a survey in some 60 of 120 camps in conjunction with the Mamá Maquín and CIAM. The survey underscored a number of obstacles that refugee women faced, including the fact that refugees represented four major ethnic groups (Chuj, Kanjobal, Mam, and Jacalteca) as well as ladinos (mestizos) and other minority ethnic groups. Each indigenous group has a different language, and most refugee women were monolingual. What is more, refugee women had a high illiteracy rate, up to 90 percent (Lozano 1996, 2). This meant that facilitating communication among refugee women was difficult. One of the first programs organized by the Mamá Maquín and supported by the UNHCR was to offer literacy classes in Spanish.

Results of the survey raised awareness of the gender-specific protection needs of refugee women, highlighting the problem of domestic and sexual violence in the refugee camps. Domestic violence is prevalent in Guatemala and continues to be one of the greatest inhibitors of women's rights and freedoms. Laws against gender violence are inadequate (de Cerraza 1997), and the attitude is that women are to blame. As one woman put it: "If you go to your family, then your family says 'well, don't do anything that can provoke the violence.' It's up to you—if you want the violence, then it's up to you" (Best 1993, 8). Close to 85 percent of refugee women in the camps stated that they believed that they must obey their husbands, and 32 percent felt that men had the right to beat them (Mamá Maquín and CIAM 1995). Sexual violence as a tactic of military intimidation was widespread during the civil war. During the late summer months of 1994, the military reportedly raped more than eight hundred women in Chimaltenango alone (Smith-Ayala 1991). Forced abortions and sterilizations of highland indigenous women were common state practices during the war, since, according to common attitudes, highland women's "wombs produce[d] guerrillas" (Mamá Maquín and CIAM 1994, 14). State strategies, then, were both sexist and racist.

In the survey, refugee women expressed the desire to learn more about their rights as women. In response, the UNHCR—taking direction from the guidelines—supported a campaign against domestic violence and sponsored a number of workshops informing women about their constitutional rights and about human rights, including those codified in the UN Convention on the Elimination of All Forms of Discrimination against Women (CEDAW). The Mamá Maquín, together with CIAM, conducted most of these workshops. A woman-run radio station in Chiapas also transmitted information on the subject and broadcast special programs on violence against women. According to the Mamá Maquín, only through women's "self-discovery of gender subordination, discriminatory and sexist attitudes, and defense of our rights in a collective and organized fashion [can we have] . . . an impact on cultural modes of subordination" (Mamá Maquín and CIAM 1994, 98).

Responding to requests for legal assistance and protection, the UNHCR established a Legal Protection Committee in Mexico in 1992. Owing to an increased awareness of their rights, large numbers of refugee women came to seek legal protection from this committee. According to Terry Morel of the UNHCR, the number of reported cases of gender-related violence increased from zero to 40 percent of all human rights cases between 1992 and 1994 (Morel 1998). The Mamá Maquín considered these public denunciations as a symbol of the advances Guatemalan refugee women had made in terms of being aware of and demanding their rights. In the meantime, the UNHCR strives to prevent gender-related violence from occurring in the first place and provides legal, medical, and psychological assistance when it does occur.

The UNHCR in Mexico recognized that a key to refugee women's empowerment and sustainable change was their own organization, so the UNHCR sought to strengthen the autonomy of groups such as the Mamá Maquín by supporting their initiatives in the areas of literacy, health care, legal rights, leadership development, preparing for return, and ensuring women's right to vote in the returnee communities (Morel 1998). Refugee women, in turn, have recognized the importance of the UNHCR's support: "We value the role that the UNHCR has played in the growth of the Mamá Maquín. The UNHCR has protected us and helped us in our search for assistance in training and for international recognition of our rights. The UNHCR has also provided projects that have helped women meet their needs" (Garcia and Garcia 1996, 264). Some members of Mamá Maquín said that the experience of exile had changed their lives, opened up new ways of looking at life, and even empowered them: "In our country, as women, our work was that of the kitchen and having children. [Living] in Mexico has been an education, like a school for us" (Women's Commission for Refugee Women and Children 1992, see also Mamá Maquín and CIAM 1994). The highly politicized nature of camp life and the support of international agencies opened a space to Guatemalan refugee women that other Guatemalan women did not have. As a result, many refugee women said that "we are now organized and we are learning. We have a voice and we, as women, also can speak" (Women's Commission for Refugee Women and Children 1992).

Field-workers in the UNHCR also learned from refugee women. At first, they excluded Guatemalan refugee women from programs with the UNHCR and the Mexican government because "no one had thought of inviting them to the meetings and it was much easier to communicate with the men" (Morel 1998; see also Garcia 1996). The introduction of the senior coordinator's guidelines and the accomplishments of Guatemalan refugee women's organizations shifted this attitude significantly. In a recent review of the strategies and outcomes of refugee women's initiatives on health, literacy, work, and human rights in Chiapas, the UNHCR concluded that "the promotion of women's organizations and development projects with women to meet their immediate and strategic needs are essential to realize more sustainable and profound changes" (Lozano 1996; translation mine). The review goes on to acknowledge that women's participation in refugee camps must involve more than the creation of separate organizations, "to include women in the participation of structures traditionally dominated by men, together with consciousness raising and the introduction of real changes in the exercise of community leadership" (Lozano 1996, 5, translation mine). In contrast to its assumptions in the past (Garcia 1995), the UNHCR in Mexico has begun to learn that refugee women want to participate in assistance and protection programs and are fully capable of doing so (Morel 1998).

The UNHCR policy on refugee women and guidelines on protection provided an important framework for staff in Mexico in 1991 when they began working with refugee women (Morel 1998). The guidelines also legitimized the initiatives of field staff, who are sometimes accused of tampering with culture when they work towards empowering refugee women. Yet as one staff member countered: "It is important to recognize that our projects are constantly empowering men: training, resources, recognition, status, etc. This is good, but when we do not do the same for women we are increasing the gap between the two and hence, women's dependence and subordination" (UNHCR in the Americas 1997, 7). While there was resistance among implementing partners at first, work by interested field staff in the UNHCR has led to a general recognition that gender-related protection issues are essential to the whole refugee population (Lozano 1996).[4] Initially, the UNHCR worked exclusively to support the initiatives of refugee women's organizations. Today, the organization seeks to integrate gender in all aspects of its programming. Women's organizations, Lozano notes, have greatly improved women's self-esteem and personal empowerment in refugee camps, and gender-sensitive UNHCR programming reinforces this empowerment.

Of course, the transformation of gender roles in any community is complex. In Mexican camps and returned communities in Guatemala, refugee women encountered tremendous resistance from men, often in the form of domestic violence. Some Guatemalan men felt that their masculinity was threatened when women, particularly their wives, challenged traditional boundaries relating to their role: "If our wife goes out, if we help her in the house, later other *compañeros* come and criticize us. They say, 'you look like an old woman. That's woman's work'" (CONGCOOP 1994–1995, 6).

Kathleen Sullivan (1996) found that some refugee women were discovering ways to negotiate workloads and responsibilities with men in their communities. In the border camp of El Porvenir, midwives organized and networked with international agencies not only to receive official training and recognition of their skills but also to build a place of their own, La Casa de la Mujer. The midwives originally encountered resistance from the men in their communities but, through a process of compromise and negotiation, were able to solicit the help of the men in the actual construction of the building. In the process, Sullivan argues, everyone involved learned more about gender relations (1996, 278). La Casa has come to represent a place where women can meet to discuss issues of importance to them and, what is more, has established their participation in public affairs (Sullivan 1996, 277).

While some of the women of El Porvenir have found peaceful solutions to address tensions between men and women, women in other communities have encountered gross violations of their human rights. In the Ixcán region of northern Guatemala, the Mamá Maquín are very active, participating in decision making, operating small cooperatives, and providing meeting spaces in offices or cooperative buildings. Although the political climate in the Ixcán is complex and tensions are high between various sectors, male leaders in some communities have expressed deep resentment toward the members of Mamá Maquín in particular. Members of the CCPP and local *juntas directivas* (decision-making bodies in the communities) have sought to discredit Mamá Maquín members by labeling them subversives aiding the revolutionary movement. In a meeting in April 1997, members of various communities carried a banner stating that the "Mamá Maquín was the base of the guerrillas" (Violence in Ixcán Grande 1997, n.p.). In the community of Pueblo Nuevo, tensions rose to a climax when men in the community, including members of the junta directiva, burned the office of the Mamá Maquín and then placed a large cross on the ashes to symbolize the death of the organization. María Guadelupe García Hernández, a Mamá Maquín representative, said she suspected that the sexist attitudes of men in the communities were in part responsible for this, as women who participated in community affairs were viewed as trespassing into men's territory (Violence in Ixcán Grande 1997). However, in his analysis of the tensions in the Ixcán region, Roman Kznaric suggests that these tensions were a result of the political mobilization of refugees in Mexico in combination with a competition for scare resources in returned communities. International organizations gave refugees a new language of rights: "Contact with the UNHCR and other NGOs gave refugees access to a transnational political 'space.' The refugees' effective appropriation of such universalistic discourses as human rights in their organized struggles to return suggests that these organizations have acted as agents of change" (Kznaric 1997; Pritchard 1996, 104). Kznaric points out that women in the Mamá Maquín adopted a discourse of women's rights that helped to legitimize a right to direct their own development. Male members of the community selectively adopted the same human rights discourse, claiming the rights of refugees to be free from military threat while denying the Mamá Maquín the right to organize freely. These tensions remind us that transforming gender relations is a constant battle. According to Terry Morel, who had long supported the inclusion of refugee women in UNHCR programming in Mexico: "With gender work . . . every time you take an action and you think you have solved the issue you have to take 20 more actions to follow up. . . . It's a Pandora's box and I think the challenge is not to give up, but to be more creative and have much greater clarity and understanding of gender power relations when planning responses" (Morel 1998). Morel goes on to point out that while the strengthening of women's self-esteem and organization are key to gender change, so too is strengthening women's negotiating skills with men. Reflecting upon the tensions and incidents of violence in Ixcán, the UNHCR began to work on notions of masculinity, offering some initial workshops to discuss the issue (Sayavedra 1997, 20–21; UNHCR in the Americas 1997, 1).

The experiences of Guatemalan refugee women demonstrate the potential impact of global policies on local actors. The UNHCR's attempts to integrate the protection needs of refugee women into legal definitions and camp programs opened important political spaces for Guatemalan refugee women to organize and begin to work towards their objectives. However, it was ultimately the actions of Guatemalan refugee women themselves that made changes in their communities possible. While the UNHCR may have opened spaces that are otherwise unavailable to refugee women, it was Guatemalan women who filled those spaces. As the Mamá Maquín argued in reference to consciousness raising:

> Each culture has a model of subordination that constantly undergoes changes. This dynamic of change is determined by internal and external forces outside the women's control (for example, refuge, aid, and poverty). Work with women from a gender perspective necessarily includes an integral analysis of gender, class, and ethnic inequalities which allows women to better understand and influence these changes in their favor. The legitimization of these changes implies that women must be their author. (Mamá Maquín and CIAM 1994, 97)

In turn, global organizations must begin to listen to, and learn from, women acting in local contexts. In the case of the UNHCR, Guatemalan refugee women demonstrated that they were willing and able to participate in assistance programs. What is more, refugee women in Mexican camps showed the UNHCR that they were "very clear on their rights as women and their right to protection" (Morel 1998). If protection is at the heart of UNHCR responsibility to refugees, then an understanding of the gender relations within refugee camps is vital to carrying out that task.

The experiences of refugee women's organizations in Guatemala demonstrate the need to contextualize the issue of gender construction and change in global governance. Gender relations exist within and across different levels of social organization: the family, the community, the state, and international organizations. The separation of the public and private spheres in the UNHCR's protection mandate perpetuates the assumption that gender-related persecution and violence are not international or political issues. This assumption reinforces patterns of violence and subordination at the state and local level. On the other hand, the UNHCR's efforts to integrate a gender perspective into its programs have opened a strategic space for Guatemalan refugee women to renegotiate gender relations. Intersecting constructions of gender are not static but are constantly renegotiated by a variety of actors within given historical contexts; they sometimes conflict and at other times complement one another. The experiences of Guatemalan refugee women demonstrate this point well, as gender relations continue to be negotiated and challenged within both refugee communities and the UNHCR.

Notes

I would like to thank the Social Sciences and Humanities Research Council of Canada and the Killam Foundation at Dalhousie University for providing the support I needed to complete this chapter. I would also like to thank the following people for their thoughtful comments and suggestions on earlier drafts: Kelly Frame, Mary K. Meyer, and Elisabeth Prügl. Thanks to Terry Morel for her help in providing information on the UNHCR in Mexico.

1. In feminist refugee studies, forms of persecution inflicted on a woman's body are referred to as *gender-specific*. Forms of persecution inflicted on a woman because she is a woman are referred to as *gender-based*. *Gender-related persecution* is a term that captures both forms and reasons for persecution specific to women.

2. The principle of *non-refoulement* in international refugee law safeguards the refugee from forcible return to her or his country of origin.

3. Terry Morel of UNHCR in Mexico cautions that the work on gender in Mexico should not be considered *the* successful answer. She explains that the UNHCR sometimes overlooked important things and that constant improvements and corrections are being introduced. However, she does believe that "there are many lessons to be learned in what has been a genuine attempt to support the refugee women and to recognize the importance and validity of their participation and their role in refugee life."

4. Morel notes that some implementing partners, such as COMAR (Comisión Mexicana de Ayuda a los Refugiados), were faster to embrace some initiatives on gender than others; in particular, gender and health issues were fairly quickly addressed, while education and employment projects are slower to develop.

17

Of Roots, Leaves, and Trees: Gender, Social Movements, and Global Governance

Deborah Stienstra

When I write, I am privileged to look out at a fifty-year-old Manitoba maple tree. Its unique ecosystem with squirrels, birds, grubs, bees, leaves, roots, and trunk reminds me of the groundedness necessary for theory, or the ways in which we need to locate or root theory in specific historical times and places. In this chapter, I reflect on how social movements, and especially women's movements, are shaping, and are shaped by, global governance and international organizations. As I have thought about gender, social movements, and global governance, the tree has become even more than a touchstone; its tiny communities, which are so reliant on each other for survival, have become a metaphor for my thinking on this topic. To understand global governance in the late 1990s, we need to explore the work of social movements. To explain social movement activity, we need to consider gender and other power relations. To understand why global governance has been shaped the way it has, we need to explore gender relations. The interconnections between gender, global governance, and social movements form as unique and complex an "ecosystem" as does my tree.

As the editors suggest in the introduction to this volume, the study of global governance has acquired some space in International Relations, as scholars try to account for the interconnections between state decision making at the domestic and international levels and the increasing importance of nonstate actors. While some scholars have attempted to add nongovernmental organizations (NGOs) to a liberal pluralist framework, that framework is unsatisfactory for trying to understand the more encompassing relationships between states, intergovernmental organizations and social movements.[1] A more useful approach is to explore how specific states and the institutions of the interstate system, like the United Nations and the International Monetary Fund, use and are shaped by global civil society.

"Global civil society" is not a neutral term. Some limit their definition of it to nonstate actors like NGOs. In this chapter I use "global civil society" to refer to the institutions that make up society outside of the state, including the media, educational institutions, churches, unions, families, NGOs, social movements, and transnational corporations. These institutions are in a dynamic relationship with states and intergovernmental organizations. Several key questions guide this work: How are social movements part of global civil society? In what way(s) does global civil society engage with international organizations and global governance? How does gender affect both social movements and global governance? How can and do social movements have an impact on global governance? The ecosystem of these three sets of forces— gender, social movements, and global governance—comes to life in the metaphor of my tree.

The chapters in this book contribute to and challenge our understanding of these relationships. They all argue that we need to look beyond the specific interactions between women and states or interstate organizations. Most argue implicitly or explicitly that the inclusion of gender and/or women in global governance could only have taken place with the support and encouragement of women's movements in local and global settings. Some suggest that this takes place as a result of the personal connections of some women in elite positions with particular women's movements. Others suggest that women's activism in relation to international conferences and organizations has created the opportunities for action or shaped the agendas under discussion. Still others argue that women's movements need to understand and challenge broader forces at work in global governance. In this chapter we will consider both the theoretical literature and questions around global civil society and social movements, as well as some specific ways in which norms are evident in and shape social movement activity.

Global Civil Society

All too often in International Relations, scholars adopt a focus on the state, whether on the actions of an individual state or its bureaucratic or political decision makers reified as an actor in international affairs. Little attention has been given to those parts of society that interact with and shape, or are shaped by, the state or the interstate system. Society is often described in opposition to the state, something that provides a context but fails to have any significant role in the world of politics. Some years ago, Robert W. Cox suggested that "neorealist theory in the United States has returned to the state/civil society relationship, though it has treated civil society as a constraint upon the state and a limitation imposed by particular interests upon *raison d'état*, which is conceived of, and defined as, independent of civil society" (Cox 1996c, 96). While many realists have incorporated a very limited analysis of NGOs in their studies of international regimes, they fail to explore the more dynamic relationships between state and society.

While global civil society has been addressed by an increasing number of scholars, the most promising work has been written by critical theorists such as Cox and Stephen Gill. This approach is in contrast with the use of global civil society by liberal pluralists such as Ronnie Lipschutz (1992) and Paul Ghils (1992). Liberal writers suggest that global civil society can be seen as analytically separate from the state, as an arena where there is autonomy from the state and especially where international NGOs seek to pressure the state and make it more responsible (Macdonald 1994, 274–75). This resembles liberal analyses of pluralist domestic societies where "interest" groups are seen to place constraints on governments. Critical theorists reject the separation of civil society from the state, arguing that the state needs and uses civil society to ensure that consensual hegemony is maintained. Using the work of Antonio Gramsci, Cox (1996b) argues that states maintain a hegemonic presence in the world by the creation of consent based on shared principles and institutions, like the United Nations or the World Trade Organization, which maintain these principles. As Gramsci and Cox both point out, the state in this instance is not, nor can it be, considered simply the decision maker or administrator who holds on to the levers of government within a given geographical territory. Instead, "the State is the entire complex of practical and theoretical activities with which the ruling class not only justifies and maintains its dominance, but manages to win the active consent of those over whom it rules" (Gramsci 1971, 244). In order to do this, the state relies on the institutions that make up civil society to reinforce, or respond to, the underlying principles of consent.

Gramsci's argument is based on his assumption that the primary and foundational social relations at work in capitalist societies are class relations. Cox extends this to world orders, suggesting that class relations are the most important for understanding power in world politics. As a result, most critical theory work has focused on the relationships between the global "class" of capitalists, their transnational corporations, banks, states, and workers. In contrast, feminists and others have suggested that power intersects with a series of social relations based on class, gender, race/ethnicity, and sexual orientation (Stienstra 1994, 28). These reinforcing relations of power arise from historical patterns of inequality or domination. No one is necessarily more important than another, but the relative strength and importance of each is found in a particular historical context. In this chapter, I rely on the broader understanding of social relations, arguing that these relations of power form a basis from which to understand and explore international relations.

The component parts of civil society differ across space and time. In the latter half of the twentieth century, social movements are becoming an increasingly important part of global civil society. The peace, environmental, women's, gay and lesbian, fundamentalist Christian, and Islamic movements continue to have a presence in global politics, especially as seen in the United Nations conferences held between 1992 and 1996. These movements are at once easily identifiable and amorphous. We know, for example, that Greenpeace is part of the environmental movement, but we are not always clear about who is part of the women's movement. Also, we slip between describing nonstate activity in terms of social movements and NGOs.

Social Movements

I distinguish between social movements and nongovernmental organizations as two different levels of institutions within civil society, with different levels of member consciousness, participation, and organization (Stienstra 1994, 27–29). This is in contrast to others like Irene Tinker (this volume) who argue that NGOs are the most useful unit of analysis. Social movements are defined as groups with a self-consciousness or awareness of being a group and with some level of organization, although not all members necessarily participate in those organizations. Social movements arise in response to structural, technological, or other changes in society or world order. Some of these changes may reflect changes in social relations. Some social movements may work to remove the inequality of particular power relations, while others may seek to reinforce those inequalities. Social movements are also not monolithic; they reflect dominant power relations, especially those defined by gender, race, sexual orientation, and class.

Social movement theory suggests that social movements arise in order to "do politics differently" by providing greater opportunity for citizen participation and by re-creating what we understand to be political spaces (Melucci 1988, Tarrow 1994). This may entail challenging the existing power system by confronting the state violently or nonviolently, or by organizing boycotts of corporations that engage in practices the movement deems unsuitable. Social movements may seek to ensure greater participation for their members or increased accountability in existing power structures. Movements may also seek to raise the profile of an issue or change the discourse or ways of speaking about the issue at hand. For example, the environmental movement has successfully made "greening" a part of corporate and government discourse. Finally, social movements may also create alternative spaces where it is possible to do things differently. For example, the women's movements in Europe and much of North America have established shelters for battered women. These are not only refuges for victims but also places where many attempt with varying degrees of success to use feminist processes of decision making.

Social movements may include the full range of NGOs described by Tinker and Alice M. Miller (this volume). Although social movements are not limited to organizations, they do need organizations to mobilize resources over a sustained period of time. Organizations provide structure and leadership to social movement activity and are able to mobilize resources and place demands on the state and other institutions. But we need to ask why and how leaders become leaders and how they maintain their roles, especially in terms of power relations. For example, in the women's movement, we can see that leadership has often been provided by women's NGOs based in the North. This has shaped the movement in a particular way, often excluding the participation of women from the South. Usually NGOs that have been in existence for many years and have access to a significant volunteer base and monetary resources have greater access to the United Nations. This shapes who can and does provide leadership within a movement. Higer (this volume) highlights the consequences of similar tensions in leadership in her discussion of the international women's health movement.

Gender, race/ethnicity, class, and colonization also shape the internal relations within movements. For example, in the women's movement during the preparations for the Beijing conference, there was considerable dispute between two groups, the Women's Environment and Development Organization (WEDO) and the organizers of the NGO Forum. Both felt that they should manage the presence of women's NGOs at the Fourth World Conference on Women because of their leadership role within the women's movement. Their conflict reflected the tension between a primarily New York–based group that had considerable experience in lobbying at United Nations conferences (WEDO) and the Forum, which claimed to be more regionally based and representative and thus able to speak more credibly for the women's movement. Existing power relationships often determine leadership within social movements. The women's movement's leadership reflects these power relations, and women's groups based in the North or whose members are primarily white, middle-class, well-educated women have usually held a leading role within the movement.

By considering the different aspects of nonstate activity at the level of social forces, social movements, and organizations, we can also consider more readily the ways in which all of these engage with states in the forums of international organizations and in global governance more generally. Liberal pluralists would lead us to believe that we should look especially to the intersection between NGOs and states. If NGOs are effective, they will be able to change state actions to fit their own agendas, and we should be able to find evidence of this from the written record. This is also often the perspective of the elite NGOs that have much access to the United Nations. They measure success by how many words or phrases of their own they were able to have inserted into international agreements. In the women's movement, the work of WEDO stands out as a prime example of this (WEDO n.d.). Miller (this volume) argues that NGOs have been especially effective in getting words in place in the human rights arena but that their goals need to shift to monitoring and ensuring compliance with the legal standards. Both of these aspects of NGO activity are necessary and valuable, but considering them as the primary arena for engagement between states and social movements fails to deal with the dynamic relationship that exists between the two sets of forces.

Norms, Social Movements, and Gender

Critical theory suggests that we may find more interactions between civil society and the interstate system than we care to admit because the state and civil society are mutually reliant. At the core of global governance are commonly held norms and principles that have been created as a result of the interconnections between states and global civil society. What are these norms and principles, and how are they evident within structures and practices of global governance? I use "norms" and "standards" interchangeably to refer to the set of assumptions, beliefs, and intersubjective meanings that govern and form the basis of social practices. These are often difficult to pin down but are reflected in the language of interstate agreements, the agendas of international conferences and their resulting documents, the priorities of international organizations, and the areas where no work is done and silence is maintained. The standards are developed by states with the participation and support of global civil society in all its manifestations. They are reflections of dominant power relations at work at the particular time and place in which they were developed, and they are maintained through international institutions.

Different types of norms can be distinguished on the basis of their scope. For example, there are more comprehensive norms that encompass the span of a world order and more focused norms that deal with a particular issue or situation. The comprehensive norms often provide a framework within which the more specific norms are developed. For example, if we look at the specific norms related to disability found in the United Nations, we see how comprehensive norms of the liberalization of the global economy have circumscribed and shaped the specific norms (Stienstra and Kellerman 1998). Some norms may work at both levels, the comprehensive and the specific. For example, assumptions of gender shape the structures and practices at a world-order level, but there are also specific norms such as the Convention on the Elimination of All Forms of Discrimination against Women (CEDAW), which is more focused and specific. Other norms are evident primarily at the specific level. Meyer (this volume) discusses how specific norms related to violence against women were negotiated within the Inter-American Commission on Women. D'Amico (this volume) illustrates how the specific norm of including women in the Secretariat of the United Nations, especially at senior positions, has shifted over the history of that organization.

We can identify the norms by considering the definition of who is a legitimate actor in a given setting, what is said and left unsaid, who is present, and who is absent. We may see that different actors and practices are at work in comprehensive and particular norms. For example, when we consider how the more specific norms around women are established within the context of the United Nations, we see that despite the attempts of the member states of the Commission on the Status of Women, the officials of the Division for the Advancement of Women, the interagency committee on gender, and the representatives of nongovernmental organizations, there remain significant gaps in which United Nations organizations participate in "mainstreaming" gender. Those organizations most responsible for establishing the global norms of liberalization, such as the International Monetary Fund and the World Trade Organization, have remained the most distant from discussions of gender (Stienstra 1994, 138). This is also evident, as Judith Stiehm (this volume) highlights, in the area of peacekeeping, where there has been considerable resistance to the inclusion of women on peacekeeping missions. In the minds of many, it would seem that to include women would be to alter the norms around peacekeeping. Catherine Hoskyns (this volume) also highlights the resistance to the inclusion of women and gender and suggests that while the European Union has a long history of women-specific norms, insights from these and from feminist writings have been lacking in recent discussions around the development of the Amsterdam Treaty.

To understand global governance, we also need to consider factors outside the immediate process of developing and maintaining specific norms. For example, the norms affect different groups in different ways. Numerous feminist International Relations scholars suggest that we get a very different picture when we look at the effects of globalization on poor women of the South than if we look in general at the effects on all women. This suggests that norms are shaped by historical inequalities as well as local situations.

Norms also shift, evolve, and change over time. Different factors account for those changes at different times and locations. At this juncture in history, one of the most profound forces at work across the globe is the liberalization of the global economy. We can explore how it developed as a comprehensive norm, but we can also illustrate how it has molded the discourse and practices related to specific norms. Anne Sisson Runyan (this volume) suggests that this norm, or what she calls the neoliberal frame, has shaped the discourse related to women and gender, especially in the preparations in the ECE region for the Beijing conference and in discussions around the Social Summit. Global economic liberalization has also brought about significant, large-scale social transformation. This has propelled increased activity by social movements. Part of our discussion of norms needs to address the dynamic interaction between specific social movements and the comprehensive norm of liberalization, as Runyan (this volume) has done in outlining the alternative proposals and actions put forward by women's groups in response to the framing of the agenda in neoliberal terms. But the third set of forces necessary for understanding global governance is the role and actions of specific states. States with a leadership role or a strategic interest within the current world order will ensure that the comprehensive norms are maintained and enforced. In many ways, the United States has been at the forefront of the call for liberalization. Its strong, leading role in the current world order enables the United States to reaffirm the importance of this comprehensive norm while more specific norms are being developed.

Two examples illustrate some of these relationships between states, social movements, and other parts of global civil society in the development of norms. At the 1992 Rio Earth Summit, new norms and standards were established around the environment: what was considered acceptable and what was not acceptable for countries to do. For the first time, the United Nations allowed many NGOs without formal consultative status to participate. A groundswell of support for the Rio process was created through these NGOs, especially in their own communities over the two years of preparation for the conference. While many NGOs have criticized the resulting document, Agenda 21, for not going far enough, most felt that they had some stake in its successful implementation. In fact, many continued to participate in the evaluatory conference held five years later (although most were increasingly critical of government inactivity), even though it was clear that most governments had failed to meet the objectives that they had promised to implement in Rio. What accounts for that determination (or, some would say, naïveté)?

A similar situation exists in the women's movement. After a decade of commitments, thousands of women gathered in Nairobi in 1985 to participate in the third UN Conference on Women. Many worked on the resulting Nairobi *Forward-Looking Strategies* document committed to by governments. which was to motivate action for women's equality until the year 2000, as West (this volume) describes. Over the following ten years, the women's movement became more focused and sophisticated. By 1995, when governments called for a more focused and feasible set of commitments, women's NGOs participated in unprecedented numbers through the women's caucuses. Since the Fourth World Conference on Women in Beijing in 1995, women's NGOs have directed their attention to ensuring that the commitments made in Beijing will be implemented (WEDO 1996a). What accounts for their willingness to participate in the process that many would say can never meet their hopes or expectations?

Some would argue that these are simple examples of states co-opting NGOs for their own purposes. Indeed, states need the NGOs and the movements they represent in the development of norms and standards. The movements give the process of developing norms legitimacy, both nationally and internationally, and engagement with social movements also gives states access to the expertise within these movements. A growing number of activists are becoming state or United Nations officials or consultants, highlighting the greater fluidity between state and NGO boundaries, as D'Amico (this volume) illustrates. This increases the interconnections and mutual reliance between states and social movements.

Yet what we have here is more complex. Indeed, the states, through the institution of the United Nations, enabled NGOs to have greater participation than they have had in the past. For many NGOs this greater participation was equated with more "power" or influence in the process. The NGOs saw that they were necessary partners in the process. Not only did they provide significant contributions to the development of text, thus assisting many states that did not have sufficient resources to do the type of analysis required, but also they came to have a stake in the outcome of the conferences and in the implementation of commitments. Yet many NGOs overestimated their influence. They operated in a broader context that included the push and pull of other social forces, including transnational corporations and global finance. Cecelia Lynch (1998) suggests that those social movements that responded to globalization were able to challenge some of the economic and political practices associated with it. However, as a result of the disagreements between the movements about the role of social forces that are propelling globalization, they were unable to pursue common strategies against market liberalization.

When we consider global governance as the process of constructing and maintaining common norms and standards, our focus necessarily is no longer state centered. We recognize that states work together and with NGOs to develop and maintain these norms. But they also have dynamic relationships with other forces in the world order, including transnational capital and global finance. The relationships may be as obvious as the managing of International Monetary Fund resources through several international banks or giving investors, including corporations, the same rights as states under the draft Multilateral Agreement on Investment (MAI) being negotiated through the Organization for Economic Cooperation and Development (OECD) in 1997 and 1998. It is clear that corporations have been closely involved in drafting and negotiating the MAI, even though they are not recognized as formal participants. The increased participation of corporations and banks in global governance means a movement away from accountability to citizens (which is expected of representatives of democratic governments) and decreased opportunities for NGOs to participate effectively in decision making. Social movements have reconsidered their tactics in light of these changes to global governance.

But in most cases the role of transnational capital and finance is much more subtle than the obvious examples outlined above. The system of global governance has been re-created around one comprehensive norm, the liberalization and globalization of economies. In many ways, this norm has come to replace the "first principle," or comprehensive norm, of military security that guided the international community during the Cold War. Since the 1980s, states and international organizations have established their national and international priorities and structures to enhance and support globalization. This has entailed a massive process of restructuring by states, voluntary and imposed. When we consider the development of any other norms within global governance, we need to be aware of the background that this first principle gives.

The processes of restructuring have relied heavily on the existing unequal gender relations. At the local and national levels, women have disproportionately borne the burden of structural adjustment policies through the erosion of welfare states and processes of privatization, with a corresponding feminization of poverty (Marchand and Runyan forthcoming). At the international level, restructuring has intensified the gendered and racialized divisions of labor by relying for cheap labor on women of the South (Chang and Ling forthcoming). Restructuring has also challenged how workers are defined and the ways in which home-based workers can be incorporated into the global political economy, as Elisabeth Prügl (this volume) illustrates.

The comprehensive norm of liberalization and globalization has also shaped the ways in which social movements are able to respond. There has been some significant resistance to globalization (Lynch 1998) from NGOs and more particularly from women's NGOs and those concerned about the gendered nature of restructuring (Stienstra forthcoming; Kerr 1996). This has been evident in significant strategic alliances formed across social movements, especially in response to the United Nations conferences between 1992 and

1996. A transnational umbrella group, the International Forum on Globalization (IFG), has attempted to build alliances around globalization. Yet the resistance has been tempered, in large part by the NGOs' lack of access to processes in which relations between states and transnational capital and finance are developed and maintained. Thus their response is reactive rather than proactive. As Lynch notes, social movements have been unable to create new meanings or alternative political and economic practices that challenge the norms, although the movements have a continued importance in providing legitimacy for the norms and for the institutions developed to maintain the norms.

More specific norms are also highly gendered. As I have argued elsewhere (Stienstra 1994), the work of the League of Nations and United Nations on the status of women has reflected changing gender relations. But the ways that specific norms related to the status of women were institutionalized were shaped as well by the organizing work of women's movements. Gendered norms and feminist interpretations have emerged in the population movement, as Sandra Whitworth (1994) and Amy Higer (this volume) have illustrated. Recent women's activism in the area of human rights has met with success in illustrating how rights have been gendered and the need for change (Bunch and Reilly 1994; Miller this volume). Emek Uçarer (this volume) suggests that the lack of effective specific international norms around trafficking in women and children is the result of approaches that failed to combine responses to both migration and human rights activism. Erin Baines (this volume) argues that the United Nations High Commissioner on Refugees guidelines on refugee women and their implementation provide a specific gendered norm that required the support and interpretation made possible through cooperation with women's groups in Guatemala. In each of these cases states have recognized women's activism as legitimate only when they recognized that women were stakeholders or experts in these areas. But recognition that gender, not just women, was important has been a point of contention right up to the 1995 Beijing women's conference and remains marginal to most of the work of the United Nations.

Two areas that remain resistant to both feminist analysis and activism are the specific norms related to the economy and military security. While women's peace groups, such as the Women's International League for Peace and Freedom (Meyer this volume), have worked for the past century to enable women to be considered legitimate participants and provide women's perspectives on peace, very few of the specific norms that guide this area reflect their contributions. Women's movements have successfully initiated specific norms related to violence against women, as Jutta Joachim (this volume) and Mary K. Meyer (on CIM this volume) discuss. Yet their work has also had little impact on the international institutions related to military security. In the area of the economy, as discussed above, gender remains marginal. This is illustrated in the area of trade by Susan Joekes and Ann Weston (1994) and in the global political economy by Runyan, Prügl, and Stephanie Halleck Johnson (this volume). The practices, politics, and discourses related to military security and the economy ignore the gendered power relations upon which they are built and fail to recognize as legitimate those activists who seek to raise these issues.

The ecosystem of social movements, gender, and global governance is intertwined and complex. Yet we have begun to tease out some of the questions that need to be considered when we explore the development of norms within the world order. We have examined some of the ways in which social movements have become an active part of global civil society. We have highlighted some of the intertwined branches and limbs of the states, global governance, social movements, and gender. We have seen how comprehensive norms like economic globalization have shaped the ways in which the entire ecosystem can grow and develop. And we have seen the ways in which the roots of gender relations, with other power relations, feed all parts of the ecosystem. One final set of questions remains. Given the complexity of these relationships, when and how can social movements have an impact on global governance?

Some social movement theorists, such as Sidney Tarrow (1994) and Joachim (this volume) who translate social movement theory to the international level, suggest that social movements can be most effective when a political opportunity structure exists. An opportunity structure becomes available when there is "the opening up of access to participation, shifts in ruling alignments, the availability of influential allies, and cleavages within and among elites" (Tarrow 1994, 86). This provides the possibility for effective action by social movements. But it requires the mobilization of resources, whether those are money, community, or knowledge. This approach is particularly inviting for explanations of the success and failure of particular organizations' and movements' attempts to affect the actions of states. Indeed, in the context of specific norms within global governance, it may help to identify the particular context for the success or failure of a social movement's interventions. Yet this approach is unable to help identify some of the complexities at work in the development and maintenance of norms, such as the role of transnational capital and finance, and the place of gender, race, and class.

Using the insights of critical theory, we are reminded that there are no easy victories for social movements. They are working against the institutionalization of particular power relations. Unless the unequal power relations are changed, there will be no fundamental change to global governance. Yet states' efforts to create and maintain consensual global norms require the presence of social movements, especially for legitimacy. This creates opportunities for social movements to attempt to shape the discourse, structures, and policies that maintain the norms. It is likely that social movements will have more success in the development and maintenance of specific, rather than comprehensive, norms. They will be particularly effective when they are seen to be stakeholders or are able to create the perception that they are stakeholders; when they are seen to provide a necessary expertise; or when they can convince the broader public of the legitimacy of their alternatives. This requires that social movements work in coalitions with other parts of global civil society; find or create allies within international organizations; and work closely with, and provide support for, sympathetic states. It also requires that feminist activists work within social movements as well as bureaucracies, participating in and challenging government-sponsored meetings and reflecting on the construction and maintenance of specific and comprehensive norms. As several of the chapters in this book suggest, these strategies work particularly well in the development and maintenance of specific norms.

Social movements have much greater difficulty in effecting change in comprehensive norms. It is often the fond dream of critical theorists that social movements will be able to form the basis for a counterhegemony at the global level—providing alternative goals and institutions to those of the existing world order that could unite and mobilize the peoples of the world (see, e.g., Cox 1987, 403). These alternative goals and institutions will undermine the legitimacy needed for maintaining the comprehensive norms. But an individual movement will not be able to do this alone. Often the difficulty between social movements is that they have been unable to find ways to work effectively in coalitions even when they share common goals. The women's movements have provided at least one example of what it will take for social movements to work more effectively in coalition. Social movements must recognize and address their own diversities and the ways in which they are shaped by power relations. This will entail gaining knowledge about the world order and the underlying power relations from a wide variety of sources rather than only from a central position, recognizing and respecting that different histories and situations may require different strategies and tactics, and working to find shared goals in the complexities of these diversities. Using these goals as a basis for developing coalitions, the social movements will be more effective in providing alternative goals and institutions that will draw increasing numbers of people away from acceptance of the dominant norms and towards challenging and changing them.

Note

1. A critique of this approach can be found in Stienstra 1994.

Works Cited

Abzug, Bella. 1995. From Beijing to Tikkum Olam: The Jewish Woman's Role in Repairing the World. Remarks presented at conference held at Brandeis University, 7 May.

Adamson, Nancy, Linda Briskin, and Margaret McPhail. 1988. *Feminist Organizing for Change: The Contemporary Women's Movement in Canada.* Toronto: Oxford University Press.

Ahmed, Fauzia E. 1996. Beyond Beijing: Making Room for Feminist Men. *Sojourner: The Women's Forum* 22, no. 2: 18.

Al-Azhar Office of the Grand Imam Sheikh of Al-Azhar. 1995 (Rabi/Al-thani 1416 A.H.). Statement of the Islamic Research Academy Al-Azhar Al-Sharif. Al-Azhar: Africa Muslims Agency.

Alexander, Nancy. 1996. Gender Justice and the World Bank: Mapping Out a Journey for Engendering Change at the World Bank. Washington, D.C.: Development Bank Watchers' Project of Bread for the World Institute, September.

Allan, Virginia R., Margaret E. Galey, and Mildred E. Persinger. 1995. World Conference of International Women's Year. Pp. 29–44 in *Women, Politics, and the United Nations,* ed. Anne Winslow. Westport, Conn.: Greenwood Press.

Alonso, José Antonio. 1983. The Domestic Clothing Workers in the Mexican Metropolis and Their Relation to Dependent Capitalism. Pp. 161–72 in *Women, Men, and the International Division of Labor,* ed. June Nash and María Patricia Fernández-Kelly. Albany: State University of New York Press.

Alston, Philip. 1991. The International Covenant on Economic, Social, and Cultural Rights. Pp. 39–78 in *Manual on Human Rights Reporting.* Geneva: UNCHR/UNITAR. UN Doc. HR/PUB/91/1.

Amnesty International. 1998. *1998: A Wonderful Year for Women's Human Rights? The United Nations, Governments, and the Human Rights of Women.* New York: Amnesty International Publications.

———. 1995. *It's about Time: Human Rights Are Women's Rights.* New York: Amnesty International Publications.

Armstrong, Kenneth. 1996. Citizenship of the Union? Lessons from *Carvel* and the *Guardian. Modern Law Review* 59, no. 4: 582–88.

Association Démocratique des Femmes du Maroc. 1996. *Parallel Report of Moroccan NGOs on the Application of the Convention on Eliminating All Forms of Discrimination against Women.* December. On file with UNIFEM.

Azad, Nandini. 1996. Grassroots Women: A Response to Global Poverty: Statement by Grassroots Organizations Operating Together in Sisterhood. *Women's Studies Quarterly,* nos. 1 and 2: 107–9.

Baden, Sally, and Anne Marie Goetz. 1997. Who Needs [Sex] When You Can Have [Gender]? *Feminist Review* 56 (Summer): 3–25.

273

274   *Works Cited*

Ballantyne, Edith. 1989. The International Office. *Peace and Freedom* 49 (November/ December): 6–9.

———. 1986. A Message from Geneva. *Peace and Freedom* 46 (November/December): 2–3.

Barroso, Carmen. 1992. *The Impact and Future Directions of the Population Program.* Chicago: MacArthur Foundation.

Barry, Kathleen, Charlotte Bunch, and Shirley Castley, eds. 1984. *International Feminism: Networking against Female Sexual Slavery: Report of the Global Feminist Workshop to Organize against Traffic in Women, Rotterdam, The Netherlands, 6–15 April 1993.* New York: International Women's Tribune Center.

Basu, Amrita, ed. 1995. *The Challenge of Local Feminisms: Women's Movements in Global Perspective.* Boulder, Colo.: Westview Press.

Baxi, Upendra. 1996. "Global Neighborhood" and the "Universal Otherhood": Notes on the Report of the Commission on Global Governance. *Alternatives* 21: 525–49.

Beckman, Peter R., and Francine D'Amico. 1994. *Women, Gender, and World Politics: Perspectives, Policies, and Prospects.* Westport, Conn.: Bergin & Garvey/Greenwood.

Beckmann, David. 1991. Recent Experience and Emerging Trends. Pp. 134–54 in *Nongovernmental Organizations and the World Bank: Cooperation for Development,* ed. Samuel Paul and Arturo Israel. Washington, D.C.: World Bank.

Benería, Lourdes. 1992. The Mexican Debt Crisis: Restructuring in the Economy and the Household. Pp. 83–104 in *Unequal Burden: Economic Crises, Persistent Poverty, and Women's Work,* ed. Lourdes Benería and Shelley Feldman. Boulder, Colo.: Westview Press.

Benería, Lourdes, and Martha Roldán. 1987. *The Crossroads of Class and Gender: Industrial Subcontracting, and Household Dynamics in Mexico City.* Chicago: University of Chicago Press.

Bequele, Assefa. 1988. Homework: Why Should We Care? Pp. 35–45 in *Asian Subregional Tripartite Seminar on the Protection of Homeworkers: Proceedings,* by International Labor Organization. Geneva: ILO.

Berer, Marge. 1991. What Would a Feminist Population Policy Be Like? *Conscience* 12, no. 5: 1–5.

Berik, Günseli. 1987. *Women Carpet Weavers in Rural Turkey: Patterns of Employment, Earnings, and Status.* Geneva: International Labor Office.

Bernstein, Johannah. 1994. Cairo Highlights. *Earth Negotiations Bulletin* (Winnipeg) 6 (December): 1.

Best, Jaquie. 1993. Learning from the Guatemalan Women's Movement. University of British Columbia.

Bhatty, Zarina. 1981. *The Economic Role and Status of Women in the Beedi Industry in Allahabad, India.* Saarbrücken, Germany: Verlag Breitenbach.

Bonnerjea, Lucy. 1985. *Shaming the World: The Needs of Refugee Women.* London: Change.

Boris, Eileen, and Elisabeth Prügl, eds. 1996. *Homeworkers in Global Perspective: Invisible No More.* New York: Routledge.

Bowen, Jerilyn. 1992. A Fond Farewell. *Peace and Freedom* 52 (September/October): 26.

Bowring-Trenn, Ursula. 1986. Leadership and Support: How to Keep on Keeping On. *Peace and Freedom* 46 (July/August): 14–15.

Boyer, Robert. 1990. *The Regulation School: A Critical Introduction.* New York: Columbia University Press.

Brasileiro, Ana Maria, and Karen Judd. 1996. Can Women Change the World? Pp. 3–16 in *Women's Leadership in a Changing World,* ed. Ana Maria Brasileiro. New York: UNIFEM.

Bretherton, Charlotte. 1996. Gender and Environmental Change: Are Women the Key to Safeguarding the Planet? Pp. 99–110 in *The Environment and International Relations,* eds. John Vogler and Mark F. Imber. London: Routledge.

Bunch, Charlotte. Director, Center for Women's Global Leadership. 1995. Interview by Jutta Joachim. New Brunswick, N.J., November.

———. 1990. Women's Rights as Human Rights: Toward a Re-Vision of Human Rights. *Human Rights Quarterly* 12 (November): 486–500.

Bunch, Charlotte, and Samantha Frost. 1998. Women's Human Rights: An Introduction. In *1998 Global Campaign for Women's Human Rights: Take Action Kit.* New Brunswick, N.J.: Center for Women's Global Leadership, Rutgers University.

Bunch, Charlotte, and Niamh Reilly. 1994. *Demanding Accountability: The Global Campaign and Vienna Tribunal for Women's Human Rights.* New Brunswick, N.J.: Center for Women's Global Leadership, and New York: UNIFEM.

Buvinic, Mayra. 1997. Women in Poverty: A New Global Underclass. *Foreign Policy* 108: 38–53.

Bussey, Gertrude, and Margaret Tims. 1980. *Pioneers for Peace: Women's International League for Peace and Freedom, 1915–1965.* London: Allen & Unwin, 1965. Reprint WILPF British Section.

Byrnes, Andrew. 1989. The Other Human Rights Treaty Body: The Work of the Committee on the Elimination of Discrimination against Women. *Yale Journal of International Law* 14: 1–67.

Cagatay, Nilufer, Caren Grown, and Aida Santiago. 1986. Commentary: The Nairobi Women's Conference: Toward a Global Feminism? *Feminist Studies* 12 (2): 401–12.

Campaign Refuted. 1995. *Forum '95: The Independent Daily of the NGO Forum on Women, Beijing '95* 6 (September): 16.

Camus-Jacques, Geneviève. 1989. Refugee Women: The Forgotten Majority. Pp. 141–57 in *Refugees and International Relations,* ed. Gil Loescher and Laila Monahan.. Oxford: Oxford University Press.

Carillo, Roxanna, Director, Women's Human Rights Programme, UNIFEM. 1995. Interview by Jutta Joachim. New York, October.

Carlson, Allan. 1995. Women's Conference or Valkyries Ride Again? *Family in America* 9, no. 8: 1–7.

Castells, Manuel. 1997. *The Information Age: Economy, Society, and Culture. Vol. 2: The Power of Identity.* Malden, Mass.: Blackwell.

CEDAW: See United Nations Committee on the Elimination of Discrimination against Women.

Center for Women's Global Leadership. 1993. *International Campaign for Women's Human Rights, 1992–1993 Report.* New Brunswick, N.J.: Center for Women's Global Leadership.

———. 1992. *1991 Women's Leadership Institute Report: Women, Violence, and Human Rights.* New Brunswick: Center for Women's Global Leadership.

Chamberlain, Mariam K. 1996. A Review of Resource Volumes Prepared for the United Nations Fourth World Conference on Women. *Women's Studies Quarterly* 24, nos. 1 and 2: 290–98.

Chang, Kimberly, and L.H.M. Ling. Forthcoming. Globalization and Its Intimate Other: Filipina Domestic Workers in Hong Kong. In *Gender and Global Restructuring*, ed. Marianne Marchand and Anne Sisson Runyan.

Charlesworth, Hillary. 1996. Women as Sherpas: Are Global Summits Useful for Women? *Feminist Studies* 22, no. 3: 537–47.

Charlesworth, Hillary, Christine Chinkin, and Shelley Wright. 1996. Feminist Approaches to International Law. Pp. 256–86 in *International Rules: Approaches from International Law and International Relations*, ed. Robert J. Beck, Anthony Clark Arend, and Robert D. Vander Lugt. Oxford: Oxford University Press.

———. Feminist Approaches to International Law. *American Journal of International Law* 85: 613–45.

Chen, Lincoln. 1995. Population Policies and Human Rights. Talk given at Harvard University Law School, 11 March.

Chen, Martha Alter. 1996. Engendering World Conferences: The International Women's Movement and the UN. Pp. 139–55 in *NGOs, the UN, and Global Governance*, ed. Thomas G. Weiss and Leon Gordenker. Boulder, Colo.: Lynne Rienner.

Chryssochou, Dimitris N. 1994. Democracy and Symbiosis in the EU: Towards a Confederal Consociation. *West European Politics* 17, no. 4: 1–14.

Clapham, Andrew. 1997. Defining the Role of Non-Governmental Organizations. Draft paper prepared for conference, Enforcing International Human Rights Law: The Treaty System in the Twenty-first Century. Centre for Refugee Studies, York University, Toronto, Canada, 22–24 June.

Clark, John. 1995. The State, Popular Participation, and the Voluntary Sector. *World Development* 23 (April): 593–602.

———. 1991. *Democratizing Development: The Role of Voluntary Organizations*. West Hartford, Conn.: Kumarian.

Clement, Marilyn. U.S. Section Coordinator and Executive Director for U.S. Section WILPF. 1996. Telephone Interview by Mary K. Meyer. 20 August.

Cockburn, Cynthia. 1995. Strategies for Gender Democracy: Women and the European Social Dialogue. *Social Europe*, Supplement 4 (whole issue).

Cohen, Sue. 1995. Women's Perspectives on Social Solidarity in the EU: The Politics of Body, Space, and Presence. M.Sc. thesis. University of Bristol.

Cohen, Susan A. 1993. The Road from Rio to Cairo: Toward a Common Agenda. *International Family Planning Perspectives* 19, (June): 61–66.

Cohen, Susan A., and Cory I. Richards. 1994. The Cairo Consensus: Population, Development and Women. *Family Planning Perspectives* 26 (November/December): 272–77.

Committee on Women, Population, and the Environment (CWPE). 1992. Call for a New Approach. Available from Population and Development Program, Hampshire College.

Conferences Summarized: What was Accomplished? 1996. *Earth Times,* 30 June–14 July, 17.

CONGCOOP (Coordination of NGOs and Cooperatives for the Accompaniment of Population Affected by the Internal Armed Conflict). 1994–95. Women Refugees: Leading the Fight for Equality. *Reunion*, December 1994–January 1995.

Connell, R. W. 1995. *Masculinities*. Berkeley and Los Angeles: University of California Press.

Connors, Jane. 1997. Legal Aspects of Women as a Particular Social Group. *International Journal of Refugee Law* 9, Special Issue (Autumn): 114–28.

Cook, Rebecca J. 1995. Human Rights and Reproductive Self-Determination. *American University Law Review* 44 (April).

———. 1994a. State Accountability under the Convention on the Elimination of All Forms of Discrimination against Women. Pp. 228–56 in *The Human Rights of Women: National and International Perspectives,* ed. Rebecca J. Cook. Philadelphia: University of Pennsylvania Press.

———, ed. 1994b. *The Human Rights of Women: National and International Perspectives.* Philadelphia: University of Pennsylvania Press.

Copelon, Rhonda. 1995. Gendered War Crimes: Reconceptualizing Rape in Time of War. Pp. 197–214 in *Women's Rights, Human Rights,* ed. Julie Peters and Andrea Wolper. New York: Routledge.

Corral, Thais. 1996. Can Women Make a Difference? Experiences at the UN Conferences. *Political Environments: A Publication of the Committee on Women, Population, and the Environment,* no. 3 (Winter/Spring): 17.

Correa, Sonia. 1994. *Population and Reproductive Rights: Feminist Perspectives from the South.* London: Zed Books.

Correa, Sonia, Martha de la Fuente, Adrienne Germain, Loes Keysers, Bene Madungu, and Jacqueline Pitanguy. 1994. History and Process of Some Initiatives in Relation to the UN-ICPD to Be Held in Cairo. Available from the Women's Global Network on Reproductive Rights, Amsterdam.

Council of Europe. 1989. The Protection of Persons Working at Home. Strasbourg.

Cousins, Mel. 1994. Equal Treatment and Social Security. *European Law Review* 19, no. 2: 123–45.

Cox, Robert W. 1996a. The Global Political Economy and Social Choice. Pp. 191–208 in *Approaches to World Order,* by Robert W. Cox and Timothy J. Sinclair. Cambridge: Cambridge University Press.

———. 1996b. Gramsci, Hegemony, and International Relations: An Essay in Method [1983]. Pp. 124–43 in *Approaches to World Order,* by Robert W. Cox and Timothy Sinclair. Cambridge: Cambridge University Press.

———. 1996c. Labor and Hegemony. Pp. 420–70 in *Approaches to World Order,* by Robert W. Cox and Timothy Sinclair. Cambridge: Cambridge University Press.

———. 1996d. Social Forces, States, and World Orders: Beyond International Relations Theory. Pp. 85–123 in *Approaches to World Order,* by Robert W. Cox and Timothy Sinclair. Cambridge: Cambridge University Press.

———. 1996e. Towards a Posthegemonic Conceptualization of World Order: Reflections on the Relevancy of Ibn Khaldun. Pp. 144–73 in *Approaches to World Order,* by Robert W. Cox and Timothy J. Sinclair. Cambridge: Cambridge University Press.

———. 1987. *Production, Power, and World Order: Social Forces in the Making of History.* New York: Columbia University Press.

Crane, Barbara. 1993. International Population Institutions: Adaptation to a Changing World Order. Pp. 351–93 in *Institutions for the Earth: Sources of Effective International Environmental Protection,* ed. Peter M. Haas, Robert O. Keohane, and Marc A. Levy. Cambridge: MIT Press.

Crane, Barbara, and Stephen L. Isaacs. 1995. The Cairo Programme of Action: A New Framework for International Cooperation on Population and Development Issues. *Harvard International Law Journal* 36 (Spring): 295–306.

CSW: See United Nations Commission on the Status of Women.

Czech Republic. 1996. Intergovernmental Consultations: Minimum Standards for an Anti-Trafficking Legislation. Paper read at Expert Group of the Budapest Group, 2–3 May, Prague.

Daines, Victoria, and David Seddon. 1993. Confronting Austerity: Women's Responses to Economic Reform. Pp. 3–32 in *Women's Lives and Public Policy: The International Experience*, ed. Meredeth Turshen and Briavel Holcomb. Westport, Conn.: Praeger.

D'Amico, Francine. 1995. Women National Leaders. Pp. 15–30 in *Women in World Politics: An Introduction*, ed. Francine D'Amico and Peter R. Beckman. Westport, Conn.: Bergin & Garvey/Greenwood.

D'Amico, Francine, and Peter R. Beckman, eds. 1995. *Women in World Politics: An Introduction*. Westport, Conn.: Bergin & Garvey.

Danaher, Kevin, ed. 1994. *Fifty Years Is Enough: The Case against the World Bank and the International Monetary Fund*. Boston: South End Press.

Davar, Binaifer A. 1993. Rethinking Human Rights, Development, and Humanitarianism: A Gender Specific Response. Paper presented at Conference on Gender Issues and Refugees: Development Implications, 9–11 May, York University, Toronto.

David, Rina Jimenez. 1995. Global Government Here. *Forum '95: The Independent Daily of the NGO Forum on Women, Beijing '95*, 2 September, 3.

Davis, Angela. 1990. Racism, Birth Control, and Reproductive Rights. Pp. 15–26 in *From Abortion to Reproductive Freedom: Transforming a Movement*, ed. Marlene Gerber Fried. Boston: South End Press.

de Burca, Graine. 1996. The Quest for Legitimacy in the European Union. *Modern Law Review* 59, no. 3: 349–77.

de Cerraza, Olga, Oficina Nacional de la Mujer (ONMA). 1997. Interview by Erin K. Baines. Quetzaltenango, Guatemala, 4 June.

de Fonseka, Chandra. 1991. Alliance of Convenience, *Lok Niti* (Journal of the Asian NGO Coalition) 7, no. 2: 4–7.

Diamond, Irene, and Gloria Femen Orenstein, eds. 1990. *Reweaving the World: The Emergence of Ecofeminism*. San Francisco: Sierra Club Books.

Diamond, Larry, ed. 1993. *Political Culture and Democracy in Developing Countries*. Baltimore, Md.: Johns Hopkins University Press.

Dixon-Mueller, Ruth. 1993. *Population Policy, and Women's Rights: Transforming Reproductive Choice*. Westport, Conn.: Praeger.

Dominelli, Lena, and Tim Gollins. 1997. Men, Power, and Caring Relationships. *Sociological Review* 45, no. 3: 396–415.

Donini, Antonio. 1996. The Bureaucracy and the Free Spirits: Stagnation and Innovation in the Relationship between the UN and NGOs. Pp. 83–101 in *NGOs, the UN, and Global Governance*, ed. Thomas G. Weiss and Leon Gordenker. Boulder, Colo.: Lynne Rienner.

ECOSOC: See United Nations Economic and Social Council.

Eduards, Maud L. 1994. Women's Agency and Collective Action. *Women's Studies International Forum* 17, nos. 2/3: 181–86.

Elias, Robert, and Jennifer Turpin, eds. 1994. *Rethinking Peace*. Boulder, Colo.: Lynne Rienner.

Elman, Amy, ed. 1996. *Sexual Politics and the European Union*. Oxford: Berghahn.

Elshtain, Jean Bethke. 1995. Exporting Feminism. *Journal of International Affairs* 48 (Winter): 541–58.

Eluf, Luzia. 1992. A New Approach to Law Enforcement: The Special Women's Police Stations.

Pp. 199–212 in *Freedom from Violence: Women's Strategies from Around the World*, ed. M. Schuler. Washington, D.C.: Women, Law, and Development, OEF International.

Enloe, Cynthia. 1990a. *Bananas, Beaches, and Bases: Making Feminist Sense of International Politics*. Berkeley and Los Angeles: University of California Press.

———. 1990b. Feminists Thinking about War, Militarism, and Peace. Pp. 526–47 in *Analyzing Gender*, ed. Beth B. Hess and Myra M. Ferree. Newbury, Calif.: Sage.

European Union Commission. 1996a. *The Commission's Work Programme for 1997*. Brussels. (COM(96)507 final).

———. 1996b. *Communication from the Commission to the Council and the European Parliament on Trafficking in Women for the Purpose of Sexual Exploitation*. Brussels. COM(96) 567 final.

European Union Parliament. Committee on Civil Liberties and Internal Affairs. 1995. *Report on Trafficking in Human Beings*. Strasbourg. (PE 213.438/fin).

Evans, Gareth. 1993. *Cooperating for Peace*. St. Leonards, Australia: Allen & Unwin.

Faludi, Susan. 1991. *Backlash: The Undeclared War against American Women*. New York: Crown.

Farer, Tom, and Felice Gaer. 1993. The UN and Human Rights: At the End of the Beginning. Pp. 240–96 in *United Nations, Divided World*, ed. Adam Roberts and Benedict Kingsbury, 2d ed. Oxford: Clarendon Press.

Featherstone, Kevin. 1994. Jean Monnet and the "Democratic Deficit" in the EU. *Journal of Common Market Studies* 32, no. 2: 149–70.

Federal Republic of Germany, Ministry of Labor and Social Affairs. 1988. *Bundesarbeitsblatt* (Bonn) 10: 70.

———. 1985. *Bundesarbeitsblatt* (Bonn) 3: 133.

Fee, Elizabeth. 1983. Women and Health Care: A Comparison of Theories. Pp. 17–33 in *Women and Health: The Politics of Sex in Medicine*, ed. Elizabeth Fee. Farmingdale, N.Y.: Baywood Publishing.

Fee, Elizabeth, and Michael Wallace. 1979. The History and Politics of Birth Control: A Review Essay. *Feminist Studies* 5, no. 1 (Spring): 201–15.

Ferguson, Kathy E. 1990. Women, Feminism, and Development. Pp. 291–303 in *Women, International Development and Politics: The Bureaucratic Mire*, ed. Kathleen Staudt. Philadelphia: Temple University Press.

Finkle, Jason L., and C. Alison McIntosh. 1994. Introduction. In *The New Politics of Population: Conflict and Consensus in Family Planning*, ed. Jason L. Finkle and C. Alison McIntosh, Supplement to *Population and Development Review* 20: 3–34. New York: Population Council.

Forbes Martin, Susan, ed. 1992. *Refugee Women*. London: Zed Books.

Ford Foundation. 1991. *A Reproductive Health Strategy for the 1990s*. New York: Ford Foundation.

Foster, Catherine. 1989. *Women for All Seasons: The Story of the Women's International League for Peace and Freedom*. Athens: University of Georgia Press.

Fraser, Arvonne S. 1995. The Convention on the Elimination of All Forms of Discrimination against Women (The Women's Convention). Pp. 77–94 in *Women, Politics, and the United Nations*, ed. Anne Winslow. Westport, Conn.: Greenwood Press.

———. 1987. *The UN Decade for Women: Documents and Dialogue*. Boulder, Colo.: Westview Press.

Freeman, Jack. 1996. So Much Hope. So Much Hoopla. *Earth Times*, 30 June–14 July, 15.

Fröbel, Folker, Otto Kreye, and Jürgen Heinrichs. 1980. *The New International Division of Labour: Structural Unemployment in Industrialised Countries and Industrialisation in Developing Countries*. Translated by Pete Burgess. Cambridge: Cambridge University Press.

Galey, Margaret E. 1995a. Forerunners in Women's Quest for Partnership. Pp. 1–10 in *Women, Politics, and the United Nations*, ed. Anne Winslow. Westport, Conn.: Greenwood Press.

———. 1995b. Women Find a Place. Pp. 11–27 in *Women, Politics, and the United Nations*, ed. Anne Winslow. Westport, Conn.: Greenwood Press.

———. 1994. The United Nations and Women's Issues. Pp. 131–53 in *Women, Gender, and World Politics: Perspectives, Policies, and Prospects*, ed. Peter R. Beckman and Francine D'Amico. Westport, Conn.: Bergin & Garvey.

———. 1984. International Enforcement of Women's Rights. *Human Rights Quarterly* 6 (November): 463–90.

———. 1979. Promoting Nondiscrimination against Women: The UN Commission on the Status of Women. *International Studies Quarterly* 23 (June): 273–302.

Garcia, Sandra. 1995. On the Outside, Looking In. *Refugees II*. Available from http://www.webcom.com/hrin/july96/guatewom.html; Internet.

Garcia Hernandez, Guadelupe, and Natividad Garcia. 1996. Mamá Maquín Refugee Women: Participation and Organization. Pp. 258–67 in *Development and Diaspora: Gender and the Refugee Experience*, ed. Wenona. Giles, Helene Moussa, and Penny Van Esterik. Dundas, Ontario: Artemis Enterprises.

Germain, Adrienne. 1987. Reproductive Health and Dignity: Choices by Third World Women. Background Paper for the International Conference on Better Health for Women and Children through Family Planning, held in Nairobi, Kenya, 5–9 October 1987. New York: Population Council, August.

Germain, Adrienne, and Rachel Kyte. 1995. *The Cairo Consensus: The Right Agenda for the Right Time*. New York: International Women's Health Coalition.

Ghils, Paul. 1992. International Civil Society: International Non-Governmental Organizations in the International System. *International Social Science Journal* (August): 417–29.

Goetz, Anne Marie. 1991. Feminism and the Claim to Know: Contradictions in Feminist Approaches to Women in Development. Pp. 133–57 in *Gender and International Relations*, ed. Rebecca Grant and Kathleen Newland. Bloomington: Indiana University Press.

Gordenker, Leon, and Thomas Weiss. 1996. Pluralizing Global Governance: Analytical Approaches and Dimensions. Pp. 17–47 in *NGOs, the UN, and Global Governance*, ed. Thomas G. Weiss and Leon Gordenker. Boulder, Colo.: Lynne Rienner.

Gordon, Linda. 1983. *Women's Bodies, Women's Rights: A Social History of Birth Control in America*. New York: Penguin Books.

Gore, Jean, and Margaret Jacobs. 1989. Women Building a Common and Secure Future: A Report from WILPF's 24th International Congress. *Peace and Freedom* 49 (November/Dececember): 10.

Government of Chile, SERNAM (Servicio Nacional de la Mujer). 1992a. *Hagamos un nuevo trato* (Let's make a new contract). Santiago.

———. 1992b. *No mas violencia contra la mujer* (No more violence against women). Pamphlet. Santiago.

Gramsci, Antonio. 1971. *Selections from the Prison Notebooks of Antonio Gramsci*. Translated by Q. Hoare and G. Nowell Smith. New York: International Publishers.

Grant, Nicole J. 1992. *The Selling of Contraception: The Dalkon Shield Case, Sexuality, and Women's Autonomy*. Columbus: Ohio State University Press.

Greenwood, Justin, Jurgen R. Grote, and Karsten Ronit. 1992. *Organised Interests and the European Community*. London: Sage.

Gruhn, Isebill. 1996. NGOs in Partnership with the UN: A New Fix or a New Problem for African Development? Paper presented at the Ninth Annual Meeting of the Academic Council on the United Nations System (ACUNS), Turin, Italy, June.

Guan, Jian. 1996. Review of UN Reports. *Signs: Journal of Women in Culture and Society* 22, no. 1: 222–26.

Haas, Ernst B. 1968. *The Uniting of Europe*. Stanford, Calif.: Stanford University Press.

———. 1964. *Beyond the Nation-State*. Stanford, Calif.: Stanford University Press.

Habermas, Jürgen. 1992. Citizenship and National Identity: Some Reflections on the Future of Europe. *Praxis International* 12, no.1.

Hakim, Catherine. 1984. Homework and Outwork: National Estimates from Two Surveys. *Employment Gazette* 92 (January): 7–12.

Hale, Sylvia M. 1989. Using the Oppressor's Language in the Study of Women and Development. *Women and Language* 11, no. 2: 38–43.

Hallowes, Frances S. 1915. *Mothers of Men and Militarism*. London: Headly Brothers.

Harris, Adrienne, and Ynestra King, eds. 1989. *Rocking the Ship of State: Toward a Feminist Peace Politics*. Boulder, Colo.: Westview Press.

Hartmann, Betsy. 1987. *Reproductive Rights and Wrongs: The Global Politics of Population Control and Contraceptive Choice*. New York: Harper & Row.

Harvey, David. 1989. *The Condition of Postmodernity: An Enquiry into the Origins of Cultural Change*. Oxford: Basil Blackwell.

Hedetoft, Ulf. 1994. National Identities and European Integration "from Below": Bringing People Back In. *Journal of European Integration* 18, no.1: 1–28.

Heise Lori L. 1994 Violence Against Women: The Hidden Health Burden. With Jacqueline Pitanguy and Adrienne Germain. World Bank Discussion Papers. Washington, D. C.: World Bank.

Henkin, Louis, ed. 1981. *The International Bill of Rights: The International Covenant on Civil and Political Rights*. New York: Columbia University Press.

Hirsch, Michele. 1996. Plan of Action against Traffic in Women and Forced Prostitution. Strasbourg: Council of Europe. EG (96) 2w.

Hodgson, Dennis. 1991. The Ideological Origins of the Population Association of America. *Population and Development Review* 17, no. 1 (March): 1–33.

Hodgson, Dennis, and Susan Cotts Watkins. 1996. Population Controllers and Feminists: Strange Bedmates at Cairo? Paper presented at the Annual Meeting of the Population Association of America, May.

hooks, bell. 1981. *Ain't I a Woman? Black Women and Feminism*. Boston: South End Press.

Hopkins, Barbara. 1996. In Search of a New Economic Order: Women's Agenda for the Next Millennium. *Feminist Studies* 22, no. 3: 529–36.

Hopkinson, Alexandra. 1995. *Democracy and European Integration*. M.A. thesis, University of Kent.

Hoskyns, Catherine. 1996. *Integrating Gender: Women, Law and Politics in the European Union*. London: Verso.

———. 1991. The European Women's Lobby. *Feminist Review*, no. 38: 67–70.

Hsiung, Ping-Chun, and Yuk-Lin Wong. 1997. The Making of Chinese Women's Gender and National Identities: An Analysis of the Political Discourse Surrounding the 1995 World Conference on Women in Beijing. Paper presented at the 1997 American Sociological Association Conference, Toronto, Canada.

Human Rights Watch. 1995. *The Human Rights Watch Global Report on Women's Rights*. New York: Human Rights Watch.

Hurtado, Maria Elena. 1995. Forum Bag Sponsor Hit. *Forum '95: The Independent Daily of the NGO Forum on Women, Beijing '95*, 5 September, p. 5.

ILO Meeting of Experts on the Social Protection of Homeworkers. 1990. Geneva, 1–5 October. Notes of Elisabeth Prügl.

Indra, Doreen. 1987. Gender: A Key Dimension of the Refugee Experience. *Refuge* 6 (February): 3–5.

International Labour Organisation. 1996a. *International Labour Conference, 83rd Session: Provisional Record 10*. Geneva.

———. 1996b. *International Labour Conference, 83rd Session: Record of Proceedings*. Geneva.

———. 1996c. *International Labour Conference, 83rd Session: Report IV (2A): Home Work*. Geneva.

———. 1995a. *International Labour Conference, 82nd Session: Provisional Record 27*. Geneva.

———. 1995b. *International Labour Conference, 82nd Session: Report V (1): Home Work*. Geneva.

———. 1991. *Meeting of Experts on the Social Protection of Homeworkers: Documents*. Geneva.

International Organization for Migration. 1996a. Trafficking in Women to Austria for Sexual Exploitation. Geneva.

———. 1996b. Trafficking in Women from the Dominican Republic for Sexual Exploitation. Geneva.

———. 1996c. Trafficking of Women to the European Union: Characteristics, Trends, and Policy Issues. Paper presented at Conference on Trafficking in Women, 10–11 June, Vienna, Austria.

———. 1996d. Trafficking in Women for Sexual Exploitation to Italy. Geneva.

———. 1995. Migrant Trafficking: An Overview. Paper prseented at Seminar on Migrant Trafficking in Central America, 19–20 October, Panama City, Panama.

International Women's Health Coalition (IWHC) and Citizenship, Studies, Information, Action (CEPIA). 1994. *Reproductive Health and Justice: International Women's Conference for Cairo. Report*. New York: IWHC.

International Women's Tribune Center. 1996. Bringing Beijing Home: The Platform for Action and You. *Women's Studies International Forum* 24, nos. 1 and 2: 141–54.

Interview: Leila Khaled. 1980. *Spare Rib* 98 (September): 11–12.

Isis International. 1978. *Women and Health*. Special Issue of *Isis International Bulletin*, no. 7 (Spring).

Jacobson, Roberta. 1991. The Committee on the Elimination of Discrimination against

Women. Pp. 444–72 in *The United Nations and Human Rights: A Critical Appraisal,* ed. Philip Alston. New York: Oxford University Press.

Jahan, Rounaq. 1995. *The Elusive Agenda: Mainstreaming Women in Development.* London: Zed Press.

Jaquette, Jane S. 1997. Women in Power: From Tokenism to Critical Mass. *Foreign Policy* 108: 23–37.

———. 1995. Losing the Battle/Winning the War: International Politics, Women's Issues, and the 1980 Mid-Decade Conference. Pp. 45–59 in *Women, Politics and the United Nations,* ed. Anne Winslow. Westport, Conn.: Greenwood Press.

Jaquette, Jane S., and Kathleen A. Staudt. 1988. Politics, Population, and Gender: A Feminist Analysis of U.S. Population Policy. Pp. 214–33 in *The Political Interests of Gender: Developing Theory and Research with a Feminist Face,* ed. Kathleen B. Jones and Anna G. Jonasdottir. London: Sage Publications.

Jhabvala, Renana. 1994. Self-Employed Women's Association: Organising Women by Struggle and Development. Pp. 114–38 in *Dignity and Daily Bread: New Forms of Economic Organising Among Poor Women in the Third World and the First,* ed. Sheila Rowbotham and Swasti Mitter. London: Routledge.

Joekes, Susan, and Ann Weston. 1994. *Women and the New Trade Agenda.* New York: United Nations Development Fund for Women.

Joffe, Carole E. 1986. *The Regulation of Sexuality: Experiences of Family Planning Workers.* Philadelphia: Temple University Press.

Jurik, Nancy. 1998. Getting Away and Getting By: The Experiences of Self-Employed Homeworkers. *Work and Occupations* 25 (February): 7–35.

Kabeer, Naila, 1994. *Reversed Realities: Gender Hierarchies in Development Thought.* London: Verso.

Kakabadse, Yolanda, and Sarah Burns. 1994. Movers and Shapers: NGOs in International Affairs. *Development* 24, no. 4: 52–55.

Kalkar, Govind. 1992. "Stopping Violence against Women: Fifteen Years of Activism." Pp. 75–100 in *Freedom from Violence: Women's Struggles from Around the World,* ed. Margaret Schuler. Washington, D.C.: Women, Law, and Development, OEF International.

Kaplan, Gisela. 1992. *Contemporary Western European Feminism.* London: Allen & Unwin.

Kardam, Nüket. 1991. *Bringing Women In: Women's Issues in International Development Programs.* Boulder, Colo.: Lynne Rienner.

Kelly, Nancy. 1993. Assessing Gender-Based Persecution Claims. Paper presented at Conference on Gender Issues and Refugees: Development Implication. York University, Toronto, 9–11 May.

Kerr, Joanna. 1996. Transnational Resistance: Strategies to Alleviate the Impacts of Restructuring on Women. Pp. 243–60 in *Rethinking Restructuring: Gender and Change in Canada,* ed. Isabella Bakker. Toronto: University of Toronto Press.

———. 1994. Expert Group Meeting on Women and Global Restructuring, 20–22 June 1994, Ottawa, Canada: Final Report. Ottawa: North-South Institute.

Keysers, Loes. 1994. WGNRR Background Paper for Plenary Panels on Key Issues for Organizers for Reproductive Health and Justice. *Women's Global Network for Reproductive Rights Newsletter* (Amsterdam) 45 (24 January).

King, Ynestrra 1990. *What Is Ecofeminism?* New York: Ecofeminist Resources.

Kingdon, John W. 1984. *Agendas, Alternatives, and Public Policies.* Boston: Little, Brown.

Kratochwil, Friedrich, and John Gerard Ruggie. 1986. International Organization: A State of the Art on an Art of the State. *International Organization* 40: 753–75.

Kremenetzky, Mercedes, Specialist, Inter-American Commission of Women. 1997. Telephone interview by Mary K. Meyer. 10 March.

———. 1995. Interviews by Mary K. Meyer. Washington, D.C., 6, 7, and 11 July.

Kusterer, Ken. 1990. The Imminent Demise of Patriarchy. Pp. 239–55 in *Persistent Inequalities: Women and World Development*, ed. Irene Tinker. New York: Oxford University Press.

Kznaric, Roman. 1997. Guatemalan Returnees and the Dilemma of Political Mobilization. *Journal of Refugee Studies* 10, no. 1: 61–78.

Lambert, John. 1994. *Solidarity and Survival: A Vision for Europe*. Aldershot, Eng-land: Avebury.

Lazo, Lucita. 1996. Women's Empowerment in the Making: The Philippine Bid for Social Protection. pp. 259–71 in *Homeworkers in Global Perspective: Invisible No More*, ed. Eileen Boris and Elisabeth Prügl. New York: Routledge.

Lazo, Lucita, and Phanomwan Yoodee. 1993. Networking for Economic Empowerment: The Chiangmai Homenet. Pp. 31–70 in *From the Shadows to the Fore: Practical Actions for the Social Protection of Homeworkers in Thailand*, ed. Lucita Lazo. Bangkok: International Labour Organization.

Lee, Tanya. 1996. Unpublished Report on Beijing NGO Forum. Kunming, Yunnan: Yunnan University.

Lewis, Shelby. 1995. Black Women at the Founding Conference. Pp. 16–23 in *Black Women at the United Nations*, ed. Hanes Walton Jr. San Bernardino, Calif: Borgo Press.

Liddington, Jill. 1989. *The Long Road to Greenham: Feminism and Anti-Militarism in Britain since 1820*. London: Virago Press.

Linder, Marc. 1992. *Farewell to the Self-Employed: Deconstructing a Socioeconomic and Legal Solipsism*. New York: Greenwood Press.

Linton, Rhoda. 1989. Seneca Women's Peace Camp: Shapes of Things to Come. Pp. 239–61 in *Rocking the Ship of State: Toward a Feminist Peace Politics*, ed. Adrienne Harris and Ynestra King. Boulder, Colo.: Westview Press.

Lipietz, Alain. 1987. *Mirages and Miracles: The Crises of Global Fordism*. Trans. David Macey. London: Verso.

Lipschutz, Ronnie D. 1992. Reconstructing World Politics: The Emergence of Global Civil Society. *Millennium: Journal of International Studies* 21, no. 3: 389–420.

Lister, Ruth. 1997. *Citizenship: Feminist Perspectives*. Basingstoke, England: Macmillan.

Longhurst, Richard. 1982. Resource Allocation and the Sexual Division of Labor: A Case Study of a Moslem Hausa Village in Northern Nigeria. Pp. 95–117 in *Women and Development: The Sexual Division of Labor in Rural Societies*, ed. Lourdes Benería. New York: Praeger.

Lotherington, Ann Therese, and Anne Britt Flemmen. 1991. Negotiating Gender: The Case of the International Labour Organization, ILO. Pp. 273–307 in *Gender and Change in Developing Countries*, ed. Kristi Anne Stølen and Mariken Vaa. Oslo: Norwegian University Press.

Lovenduski, Joni. 1986. *Women and European Politics*. London: Wheatsheaf.

Lozano, Itziar. 1996. *Lecciones Aprendidas en el Trabajo con Mujeres Refugiados: El Caso de Chiapas*. Chiapas, Mexico: UNHCR.

Lubin, Carol Riegelman, and Anne Winslow. 1990. *Social Justice for Women: The International Labor Organization and Women.* Durham, N.C.: Duke University Press.

Lynch, Cecelia. 1998. Social Movements and the Problem of "Globalization." *Alternatives* 23, 3 (March): 149–73.

Maathai, Waangari. 1988. *The Green Belt Movement: Sharing the Approach and the Experience.* Nairobi, Kenya: Environmental Liaison Centre International.

Macdonald, Laura. 1994. Globalizing Civil Society: Interpreting International NGOs in Central America. *Millennium: Journal of International Studies* 23, no. 2: 267–85.

MacKinnon, Catherine. 1987. *Feminism Unmodified: Discourses on Life and Law.* Cambridge: Harvard University Press.

Macklin, Audrey. 1997. Gender-Based Persecution in Armed Conflict: Focus on Refugee and Internally Displaced Women. Paper presented at the UN Expert Group Meeting on Gender-Based Persecution, Toronto, 9–12 November.

Mair, Lucille Mathurin. 1986. Women: A Decade Is Time Enough. *Third World Quarterly* 8, no. 2: 583–93.

Malena, Carmen. World Bank Staff in the Human Resource Division. 1995. Interview by Irene Tinker, Washington, D.C., 24 March.

Mamá Maquín and CIAM (Women's Center for Research and Action). 1994. *From Refugees to Returnees: A Chronicle of Women Refugees' Organizing Experiences in Chiapas.* Comitan, Mexico: CIAM.

Maran, Rita. Forthcoming. Combatting Torture: The Role of Non-Governmental Organizations. In *The Evil That Men Do.* Stockholm: Swedish Institute of International Affairs.

Marchand, Marianne, and Anne Sisson Runyan, eds. Forthcoming. *Gender and Global Restructuring.*

Margolis, Diane Rothbard. 1993. Women's Movements around the World: Cross-Cultural Comparisons. *Gender and Society* 7, no. 3: 379–99.

Martin, Philip L. 1997. The Impacts of Immigration in Receiving Countries. Pp. 17–27 in *Immigration into Western Societies: Problems and Policies,* ed. Emek M. Uçarer and Donald J. Puchala. London: Pinter.

———. 1994. The United States: Benign Neglect toward Immigration. Pp. 13–36 in *Migration Policies: A Comparative Perspective,* ed. F. Heckmann and W. Bosswick. Bamberg, Germany: Europäisches Forum für Migrationsstudien.

Martin, Susan. 1980. *Breaking and Entering.* Berkeley and Los Angeles: University of California Press.

Mass, Bonnie. 1976. *Population Target: The Political Economy of Population Control in Latin America.* Brampton, Ontario: Charters Publishing.

McGlen, Nancy E., and Meredith Reid Sarkees. 1993. *Women in Foreign Policy: The Insiders.* New York: Routledge.

McIntosh, Alison, C., and Jason L. Finkle. 1995. The Cairo Conference on Population and Development. *Population and Development Review* 21, (June): 223–60.

McIntosh, Margaret, Alice K. Wong, Nilufer Cagatay and Ursula Funk, Helen I. Safa, Leila Ahmed, Dafna N. Izrawli, Krishna Ahooja-Patel, and Charlotte Bunch. 1981. Comments on Tinker's "A Feminist View of Copenhagen." *Signs: Journal of Women in Culture and Society* 6, no. 4: 771–90.

Meehan, Elizabeth. 1993. *Citizenship and the European Community.* London: Sage.

Melucci, Antonio. 1988. Social Movements and the Democratization of Everyday Life. Pp.

245–60 in *Civil Society and the State: New European Perspectives*, ed. John Keane. London: Verso.

Merchant, Carolyn. 1992. *Radical Ecology: The Search for a Livable World*. New York: Routledge.

————. 1980. *The Death of Nature: Women, Ecology, and the Scientific Revolution*. San Francisco: Harper & Row.

Mies, Maria. 1993. The Need for a New Vision: The Subsistence Perspective. Pp. 297–324 in *Ecofeminism*, ed. Maria Mies and Vandana Shiva. London: Zed Books.

————. 1982. *The Lace Makers of Narsapur: Indian Housewives Produce for the World Market*. London: Zed Press, 1982.

Miller, Carol. 1994. "Geneva—The Key to Equality": Inter-War Feminists and the League of Nations. *Women's History Review* 3, no. 2: 219–45.

Miller, Francesca. 1991. *Latin American Women and the Search for Social Justice*. Hanover, N.H.: University Press of New England.

Mitter, Swasti. 1994. On Organising Women in Casualised Work: A Global Overview. Pp. 14–52 in *Dignity and Daily Bread: New Forms of Economic Organising Among Poor Women in the Third World and the First*, ed. Sheila Rowbotham and Swasti Mitter. London: Routledge.

————. 1991. Computer-Aided Manufacturing and Women's Employment: A Global Critique of Post-Fordism. Pp. 53–65 in *Women, Work and Computerization: Understanding and Overcoming Bias in Work and Education*, ed. Inger V. Eriksson, Barbara A. Kitchenham, and Kea G. Tijdens. Amsterdam: North-Holland.

————. 1990. Homeworking: An Evaluation in a Global Context. Unpublished manuscript, prepared for the International Labor Organization.

————. 1986. *Common Fate, Common Bond: Women in the Global Economy*. London: Pluto Press.

Mohanty, Chadra Talpade. 1991. Under Western Eyes: Feminist Scholarship and Colonial Discourses. Pp. 51–80 in *Third World Women and the Politics of Feminism*, ed. Chandra Talpade Mohanty, Ann Russo, and Lourdes Torres. Bloomington and Indianapolis: Indiana University Press.

Moore, Carol V. 1996. Membership Report. *Peace and Freedom* 56 (April-June): 5.

Morel, Terry, UNHCR Mexico. 1998. E-mail exchange with Erin Baines, 13 January and 18 February.

Morgan, Robin. 1996. The UN Conference: Out of the Holy Brackets and into the Policy Mainstream. *Women's Studies Quarterly* 24, nos. 1 and 2: 77–83.

Morin, Ann Miller. 1995. *Her Excellency: An Oral History of American Women Ambassadors*. New York: Twayne.

Murfitt-Eller, C., Principal Specialist, Inter-American Commission of Women. 1995. Interview by Mary K. Meyer, Washington, D.C., 3 July.

Nash, June. 1993a. *Crafts in the World Market: The Impact of Global Exchange on Middle American Artisans*. Albany: State University of New York Press.

————. 1993b. Maya Household Production in the World Market: The Potters of Amatenango del Valle, Chiapas, Mexico. Pp. 127–53 in *Crafts in the World Market: The Impact of Global Exchange on Middle American Artisans*, ed. June Nash. Albany: State University of New York Press.

Nash, June, and Maria Patricia Fernandez-Kelly, eds. 1983. *Women, Men, and the International Division of Labor*. Albany: State University of New York Press.

Nelson, Paul. 1995. *The World Bank and NGOs: The Limits of Apolitical Development*. New York: St. Martin's Press.

Nicholls, Jill. 1980. United Nations Notices Women. *Spare Rib* 98 (September): 9–16.

Nordic Council of Ministers. 1995. *Gender Equality: The Nordic Model*. Copenhagen: Nordic Council of Ministers.

———. 1994. *Women and Men in the Nordic Countries*. Stockholm: Nordic Council of Ministers.

OECD: See Organization for Economic Cooperation and Development.

Oldfield, Sybil. 1989. *Women against the Iron Fist: Alternatives to Militarism, 1900–1989*. Cambridge: Basil Blackwell.

Olmstead, Mary S., Bernice Baer, Jean Joyce, and Georgiana M. Prince. 1984. *Women at State: An Inquiry into the Status of Women in the United States Department of State*. Washington, D.C.: Women's Research and Education Institute (WREI) of the Congressional Caucus for Women's Issues.

Organization of American States, Comisión Interamericana de Mujeres/Inter-American Commission of Women (CIM). 1995. *A Century of Struggle for Women's Rights in the Americas. CIM Achieving the Promise*. Washington, D.C.: OAS Office of Historical Research and *Americas Magazine* (April).

———. 1994. *Intergovernmental Meeting of Experts to Consider the Preliminary Draft Inter-American Convention on Women and Violence. Second Session: Preliminary Report of the Conclusions*. Washington, D.C. OEA/Ser.L/II.7.5/CIM/RECOVI/doc.36/93 corr.2.

———. 1993. *Intergovernmental Meeting of Experts to Consider the Preliminary Draft Inter-American Convention of Women and Violence. First Session: Progress Report*. Washington, D.C. OEA/Ser.L/II.7.5/CIM/RECOVI/doc.21/93.

———. 1992. *Historia de la Comision Interamericana de Mujeres (History of the Inter-American Commission of Women), 1928–1992*. Washington, D.C.

———. 1990. *Twenty-fifth Assembly of Delegates: Conclusions and Recommendations of the Inter-American Consultation on Women and Violence*. Washington, D.C. OEA/Ser.L/II.2.26/CIM/doc.23/92.

Organization of American States General Assembly. 1994. *Twenty-fourth Session: Inter-American Convention on the Prevention, Punishment, and Eradication of Violence against Women*. Washington, D.C.

Organization for Economic Cooperation and Development (OECD). 1979. *Equal Opportunities for Women*. Paris.

———. 1975. *The Role of Women in the Economy*. Paris.

Overholt, Catherine. 1996. Introducing a Gender Approach into UNHCR Programming. Geneva: Collaborative Action for Development.

Patton, Charlotte. 1995. Women and Power: The Nairobi Conference, 1985. Pp. 61–76 in *Women, Politics and the United Nations*, ed. Anne Winslow. Westport, Conn.: Greenwood Press.

Paul, Samuel, and Arturo Israel. 1991. *Nongovernmental Organizations and the World Bank: Cooperation for Development*. Washington, D.C.: World Bank.

288   *Works Cited*

People's Republic of China, State Council. 1994. *The Situation of Chinese Women.* Beijing: Information Office of the State Council.

Perera, Lakshmi. 1995. Women in Micro- and Small-Scale Enterprise Development in Sri Lanka. Pp. 101–16 in *Women in Micro- and Small-Scale Enterprise Development,* ed. Louise Dignard and José Havet. Boulder, Colo.: Westview Press.

Peterson, V. Spike. 1996. Shifting Ground(s): Epistemological and Territorial Remapping in the Context of Globalization(s). Pp. 11–28 in *Globalization: Theory and Practice,* ed. Eleonore Kofman and Gillian Young. New York: Pinter.

Pietilä, Hilkka, and Jeanne Vickers. 1994. *Making Women Matter: The Role of the United Nations,* 2d ed. London: Zed Books.

Pineda-Ofreneo, Rosalinda. 1990. Women and Work: Focus on Homework in the Philippines. *Review of Women's Studies* 1, no. 1: 42–55.

Platform for Action, United Nations Fourth World Conference on Women. 1996. *Women's Studies Quarterly* 24, nos. 1 and 2: 159–289.

Portes, Alejandro, and Saskia Sassen-Koob. 1987. Making It Underground: Comparative Material on the Informal Sector in Western Market Economies. *American Journal of Sociology* 93, no. 1 (July): 30–61.

President's Interagency Council on Women. 1997. *America's Commitment: Federal Programs Benefiting Women and New Initiatives as Follow-up to the UN Fourth World Conference on Women.* Washington, D.C.: White House.

———. 1996. *U.S. Follow-up to the U.N. Fourth World Conference on Women.* Washington, D.C.: White House.

Pritchard, Diana. 1996. The Legacy of Conflict: Refugee Repatriation and Reintegration in Central America. Pp. 103–34 in *Central America: Fragile Transition,* ed. Rachel Sieder. New York: St. Martin's Press.

Prügl, Elisabeth. Forthcoming. *The Global Construction of Gender: Home-Based Work in the Political Economy of the Twentieth Century.* New York: Columbia University Press.

Rao, Arati. 1996. Home-Word Bound: Women's Place in the Family of International Human Rights. *Global Governance* 2, no. 2: 241–60.

Raymond, Janice G. 1995. *Report to the Special Rapporteur on Violence against Women.* Amherst, Mass.: Coalition against Trafficking in Women.

Reanda, Laura. 1992. The Commission on the Status of Women. Pp. 265–303 in *The United Nations and Human Rights: A Critical Appraisal,* ed. Philip Alston. Oxford: Clarendon Press/Oxford University Press.

Reed, James. 1978. *The Birth Control Movement in American Society: From Public Vice to Private Virtue.* Princeton: Princeton University Press.

Renshaw, Laura Roper. 1994. Strengthening Civil Society: The Role of NGOs. *Development* 24, no. 4: 46–49.

Ritchey-Vance, Marion. 1996. Social Capital, Sustainability, and Working Democracy: New Yardsticks for Grassroots Development. *Grassroots Development* 20, no. 1: 2–9.

Rio Statement. 1994. Pp. 4–7 in *Reproductive Health and Justice: International Women's Health Conference for Cairo.* By the International Women's Health Coalition (IWHC) and Citizenship, Studies, Information, Action (CEPIA). New York: IWHC.

Roberts, Adam, and Benedict Kingsbury, eds. 1993. *United Nations, Divided World: The UN's Roles in International Relations,* 2d ed. Oxford: Clarendon Press.

Roberts, Bryan R. 1989. Employment Structure, Life Cycles, and Life Chances: Formal and

Informal Sectors in Guadalajara. Pp. 41–77 in *The Informal Economy: Studies in Advanced and Less Developed Countries*, ed. Alejandro Portes, Manuel Castells, and Lauren A. Benton. Baltimore, Md.: Johns Hopkins University Press.

Rochon, Thomas R. 1988. *Mobilizing for Peace: The Antinuclear Movements in Western Europe*. London: Adamantine Press.

Rogers, Barbara. 1980. *The Domestication of Women: Discrimination in Developing Societies*. London: St. Martin's Press.

Romany, Celina. 1994. State Responsibility Goes Private: A Feminist Critique of the Public/Private Distinction in International Human Rights Law. Pp. 85–115 in *The Human Rights of Women: National and International Perspectives*, ed. Rebecca J. Cook. Philadelphia: University of Pennsylvania Press.

Rose, Kalima. 1992. *Where Women Are Leaders: The SEWA Movement in India*. London: Zed Press.

Rose, Ruth, and Michel Grant. 1983. *Le travail à domicile dans l'industrie du vêtement au Québec*. Montréal: Université du Québec à Montréal.

Roseneil, Sasha. 1995. *Disarming Patriarchy: Feminism and Political Action at Greenham*. Philadelphia: Open University Press.

Ross, Loretta. 1994. Why Women of Color Can't Talk about Population. *Amicus* (Winter), 27–29.

Rowbotham, Sheila, and Swasti Mitter. 1994. *Dignity and Daily Bread: New Forms of Economic Organising among Poor Women in the Third World and the First*. London: Routledge.

Rowlands, Ian H. 1992. The International Politics of Environment and Development: The Post-UNCED Agenda. *Millennium* 21, no. 2: 215–17.

Rupp, Leila J. 1994. Constructing Internationalism: The Case of Transnational Women's Organizations, 1888–1945. *American Historical Review* 99 (December): 1571–1600.

Russell, Diana E. H., and Nicole Van de Ven, eds. 1976. *The Proceedings of the International Tribunal on Crimes against Women*. Milbrae: Les Femmes.

Ruzek, Sheryl. 1978. *The Women's Health Movement: Feminist Alternatives to Medical Control*. New York: Praeger.

Safa, Helen I., and Peggy Antrobus. 1992. Women and the Economic Crisis in the Caribbean. Pp. 49–82 in *Unequal Burden: Economic Crises, Persistent Poverty, and Women's Work*, ed. Lourdes Benería and Shelley Feldman. Boulder, Colo.: Westview Press.

Salvado, Luis Raul. 1988. *The Other Refugees: A Study of Non-Recognized Guatemalan Refugees in Chiapas, Mexico*. Washington D.C.: Center for Immigration Policy and Refugee Assistance, Georgetown University.

Samarasinghe, Vidyamali. 1993. The Last Frontier or a New Beginning? Women's Microenterprises in Sri Lanka. Pp. 30–44 in *Women at the Center: Development Issues and Practices for the 1990s*, ed. Gay Young, Vidyamali Samarasinghe, and Ken Kusterer. West Hartford, Conn.: Kumarian Press.

Sapiro, Virginia. 1994. *Women in American Society*. Mountain View, Calif.: Mayfield.

Sayavedra, Gloria H. 1997. *Lecciones aprendidas: Salud reproductiva para población refugiada*. Mexico: ACNUR, Sub-Oficina Comitán.

Schuler, Margaret. 1992. Violence against Women: An International Perspective. Pp. 1–48 in *Freedom from Violence: Women's Struggles from Around the World*, ed. Margaret Schuler. Washington, D.C.: Women, Law, and Development, OEF International.

Scott, Joan W. 1986. Gender: A Useful Category. *American Historical Review* 91 (December): 1053–75.

Scott, Joan W., Cora Kaplan, and Debra Keates, eds. 1997. *Transitions, Environments, Translations: Feminisms in International Politics.* New York: Routledge.

Seagar, Joni. 1997. *The State of Women in the World Atlas.* London: Penguin Books.

Seaman, Barbara. 1969. *The Doctor's Case against the Pill.* New York: Avon.

Sen, Amartya. 1990. Gender and Cooperative Conflicts. Pp. 123–49 in *Persistent Inequalities: Women and World Development,* ed. Irene Tinker. New York: Oxford.

Sen, Gita. 1995. The World Programme of Action: A New Paradigm for Population Policy. *Environment* 37 (January/February): 10.

———. 1994. Cairo from a Feminist Perspective. Talk given at the Harvard Center for Population and Development Studies, Cambridge, Mass., 7 November.

Sen, Gita, Adrienne Germain, and Lincoln C. Chen, eds. 1994. *Population Policies Reconsidered: Health, Empowerment, and Rights.* Boston: Harvard University Press.

Sen, Gita, and Caren Grown. 1985. *Development, Crises, and Alternative Visions: Third World Women's Perspective. A Report from DAWN: Development Alternatives with Women for a New Era.* New Delhi: DAWN.

Shallat, Lezak. 1993. Global Issues from an African Point of View. *Women's Health Journal* (April): 52–56.

Sharpless, John. 1995. World Population Growth, Family Planning, and American Foreign Policy. *Journal of Policy History* 7, no. 1, Special Issue: The Politics of Abortion and Birth Control in Historical Perspective: 72–102.

Shiva, Vandana. 1995. *Trading Our Lives Away: An Ecological and Gender Analysis of "Free Trade" and the WTO.* Penang, Malaysia, and New Delhi, India: Pesticide Action Network Asia and Pacific (PAN) and Research Foundation for Science, Technology and Natural Resource Policy.

———. 1990. Development as a New Project of Western Patriarchy. Pp. 189–200 in *Reweaving the World: The Emergence of Ecofeminism,* ed. Irene Diamond and Gloria Feman Orenstein. San Francisco: Sierra Club Books.

Shreir, Sally. 1988. *Women's Movements of the World: An International Directory and Reference Guide.* Harlow, England: Longman Group.

Sikkink, Kathryn. 1993. Human Rights, Principled Issue-Networks, and Sovereignty in Latin America. *International Organization* 47 (Summer): 411–41.

Sinding, Steven, Director, Population Sciences, Rockefeller Foundation. 1994. Interview by Amy Higer, New York, 23 November.

Singh, Andrea M., and Anita Kelles-Viitanen, eds. 1987. *Invisible Hands: Women in Home-Based Production.* New Delhi: Sage.

Singh, Negendra. 1993. The UN and the Development of International Law. Pp. 384–419 in *United Nations, Divided World,* 2d ed., ed. Adam Roberts and Benedict Kingsbury. Oxford: Clarendon Press.

Skrobanck, Siriporn. 1992. "Exotic, Subservient, and Trapped: Confronting Prostitution and Traffic in Women." Pp. 121–40 in *Freedom from Violence: Women's Struggles from Around the World,* ed. Margaret Schuler. Washington, D.C.: Women, Law, and Development, OEF International.

Smith-Ayala, Emilie. 1991. *The Granddaughters of Ixmucane: Guatemalan Women Speak.* Toronto, Canada: Women's Press.

Spalin, Elizabeth. 1992. Abortion, Speech, and the European Community. *Journal of Social Welfare and Family Law*: 17–32.

Spalter-Roth, Roberta, and Ronnee Schreiber. 1995. Outsider Issues and Insider Tactics: Strategic Tensions in the Women's Policy Network during the 1980s. Pp. 105–27 in *Feminist Organizations: Harvest of the New Women's Movement*, ed. Myra Marx Ferree and Patricia Yancey Martin. Philadelphia: Temple University Press.

Spelman, Elizabeth V. 1988. *Inessential Woman: Problems of Exclusion in Feminist Thought*. Boston: Beacon Press.

Spijkerboer, T. 1994. *Women and Refugee Status: Beyond the Public-Private Distinction*. The Hague: Emancipation Council.

Spivak, Gayatri Chakravorty. 1996. "Woman" as Theatre: United Nations Conference on Women, Beijing 1995. *Radical Philosophy* 75 (January/February): 2–4.

Spivek, Roberta. 1995. *Generations of Courage*. Philadelphia: WILPF U.S. Section.

Staggenborg, Suzanne. 1995. Can Feminist Organizations Be Effective? Pp. 339–55 in *Feminist Organizations: Harvest of the New Women's Movement*, ed. Myra Marx Ferree and Patricia Yancey Martin. Philadelphia: Temple University Press.

Statute of the International Criminal Tribunal for the Prosecution of Persons Responsible for Genocide and Other Serious Violations of International Humanitarian Law Committed in the Territory of Rwanda and Rwandan Citizens Responsible for Genocide and Other Such Violations Committed in the Territory of Neighboring States, between 1 January and 31 December 1994.

Statute of the International Tribunal for the Prosecution of Persons Responsible for Serious Violations of International Humanitarian Law Committed in the Territory of the Former Yugoslavia since 1991.

Stead, W. Edward, and Jean Garner Stead. 1992. *Management for a Small Planet: Strategic Decision-Making and the Environment*. Thousand Oaks, Calif.: Sage.

Sternbach, Nancy Saporta, Marysa Navarro-Aranguren, Patricia Chuchryk, and Sonia E. Alvarez. 1992. Feminisms in Latin America: From Bogotá to San Bernardo. *Signs: Journal of Women in Culture and Society* 17 (Winter): 393–434.

Stephenson, Carolyn. 1995. Women's International Nongovernmental Organizations at the United Nations. Pp. 135–53 in *Women, Politics, and the United Nations*, ed. Anne Winslow. Westport, Conn.: Greenwood Press.

Stevens, Doris. n.d. Doris Stevens' Removal from the Commission. Doris Stevens's Papers. Carton 3, vol. 113, pp. 1–33. Schlesinger Library. Radcliff College.

Stienstra, Deborah. Forthcoming. Dancing Resistance from Rio to Beijing: Transnational Women's Organizing and United Nations Conferences, 1992–1996. In *Gender and Global Restructuring*, ed. Marianne Marchand and Anne Sisson Runyan.

———. 1995. Organizing for Change: International Women's Movements and World Politics. Pp. 143–54 in *Women in World Politics: An Introduction*, ed. Francine D'Amico and Peter R. Beckman. Westport, Conn.: Bergin & Garvey.

———. 1994. *Women's Movements and International Organizations*. New York: St. Martin's Press.

Stienstra, Deborah, and W. J. Patrick Kellerman. 1998. Disposable Bodies: International Norms on Disability. Paper presented to the Annual Meeting of the International Studies Association, Minneapolis, 17–21 March.

Stiglmayer, Alexandra. 1992. *Mass Rape: The War against Women in Bosnia-Herzegovina.* Lincoln: University of Nebraska Press.

Storper, Michael, and Allen J. Scott. 1989. Work Organisation and Local Labour Markets in an Era of Flexible Production. World Employment Programme Research Working Paper no. 30. Geneva: International Labour Office.

Sullivan, Donna. 1998. *Integration of Women's Human Rights into the Work of the Special Rapporteurs.* New York: United Nations Development Fund for Women.

———, Director, Women in the Law Programme, International Human Rights Law Group. 1995a. Interview by Jutta Joachim. New York, October.

———. 1995b. The Public-Private Distinction in International Human Rights Law. Pp. 126–34 in *Women's Rights/Human Rights: International Feminist Perspectives,* ed. Julie Peters and Andrea Wolpers. New York: Routledge.

Sullivan, Kathleen. 1996. Constructing La Casa de la Mujer: The Guatemalan Refugee Women and the Midwives of Monja Blanca in El Porvenir Border Camp, Mexico. Pp. 268–79 in *Development and Diaspora: Gender and the Refugee Experience,* ed. Wenona Giles, Helene Moussa, and Penny Van Esterik. Dundas, Ontario: Artemis Enterprises.

Summerfield, Gale, and Irene Tinker, eds. 1997. Symposium: NGO Forum, United Nations' Fourth Conference on Women, 1995. *Review of Social Economy* 60, no.2 (Summer): 196–260.

Swenson, Norma. Founding member, Boston Women's Health Book Collective. 1994. Interview by Amy Higer, Somerville, Mass., 12 May.

Tarrow, Sidney. 1995. The Europe of Conflict: Reflections from a Social Movement Perspective. *West European Politics* 18, no. 2: 223–45.

———. 1994. *Power in Movement: Social Movements, Collective Action, and Politics.* Cambridge: Cambridge University Press.

Technology Links Forum to the UN and the World. 1995. *NGO Forum on Women '95 Bulletin,* December, p. 10.

Therien, Jean-Philippe, Michel Fortmann, and Guy Gosselin. 1996. The Organization of American States: Restructuring Inter-American Multilateralism. *Global Governance* 2, no. 2: 215–39.

Timothy, Kristen. 1995a. Equality for Women in the United Nations Secretariat. Pp. 117–32 in *Women, Politics, and the United Nations,* ed. Anne Winslow. Westport, Conn.: Greenwood Press.

———. 1995b. Women as Insiders: The Glass Ceiling at the United Nations. Pp. 85–94 in *Women in World Politics: An Introduction,* ed. Francine D'Amico and Peter R. Beckman. Westport, Conn.: Bergin & Garvey/Greenwood.

Tickner, J. Ann. 1997. You Just Don't Understand: Troubled Engagements between Feminists and IR Theorists. *International Studies Quarterly* 41 (December): 611–32

Tinker, Irene. Forthcoming. Women's Empowerment through Rights to Land and Housing. In *Women's Changing Rights to House and Land in China, Laos, and Vietnam,* ed. Irene Tinker and Gale Summerfield. Boulder, Colo.: Lynne Rienner.

———. 1997. *Street Foods: Urban Food and Employment in Developing Countries.* New York: Oxford University Press.

———. 1996. *Expectations of the Roles of Indigenous Nongovernmental Organizations for Sustainable Development and Democracy: Myth and Reality.* Berkeley: Institute for Urban and Regional Development (IURD), Working Paper no. 680.

————. 1993. Global Policies regarding Shelter for Women: Experiences of the UN Centre for Human Settlements. Pp. 23–32 in *Shelter, Women, and Development: First and Third World Perspectives*, ed. Hemalata Dandekar. Ann Arbor, Mich.: George Wahr.

————, ed. 1990. *Persistent Inequalities: Women and World Development.* New York: Oxford University Press.

————. 1983. Women in Development. Pp. 227–38 in *Women in Washington: Advocates for Public Policy*, ed. Irene Tinker. Beverly Hills, Calif.: Sage.

Tinker, Irene, and Michelle Bo Bramsen, eds. 1976. *Women and World Development.* New York: Praeger.

Tinker, Irene, and Jane S. Jaquette. 1987. UN Decade for Women: Its Impact and Legacy. *World Development* 15, no. 4: 419–24.

Torres Jimenez, Ruben. 1993. Women, Victims of Violence at Home. *Mexico Newspack* (24 October): 10. InterPress Service.

Toubia, Nahid. 1995. Female Genital Mutilation. Pp. 224–37 in *Women's Rights as Human Rights: International Feminist Perspectives*, ed. Julie Peters and Andrea Wolpers. New York: Routledge.

Tripp, Aili Mari. 1996. Urban Women's Movements and Political Liberalization in East Africa. Pp. 285–308 in *Courtyards, Markets, City Streets: Urban Women in Africa*, ed. Kathleen Sheldon. Boulder, Colo.: Westview Press.

————. 1992. The Impact of Crisis and Economic Reform on Women in Urban Tanzania. Pp. 159–80 in *Unequal Burden: Economic Crises, Persistent Poverty, and Women's Work*, ed. Lourdes Benería and Shelley Feldman. Boulder, Colo.: Westview Press.

UNHCR: See United Nations High Commissioner for Refugees.

UNHCR in the Americas. 1997. *Gender Newsletter* (UNHCR Americas Division), May.

United Nations. 1997. *Manual on Human Rights Reporting under Six Major International Instruments.* New York.

————. 1995a. *Fourth World Conference of Women: Report.* New York. A/CONF.177/20.

————. 1995b. *From Nairobi to Beijing: Second Review and Appraisal of the Implementation of the Nairobi Forward-Looking Strategies for the Advancement of Women: Report of the Secretary-General.* New York.

————. 1995c. *Women: Looking Beyond 2000.* New York.

————. 1995d. *World Summit for Social Development. Draft Declaration and Draft Programme of Action.* New York. A/CONF.166/L.1.

————. 1995e. *The World's Women 1995. Trends and Statistics.* New York.

————. 1995f. *Expert Group Meeting on the Development of Guidelines for the Integration of Gender Perspectives into the United Nations Activities and Programmes: Report.* New York. E/CN.4/1996/105.

————. 1994. *International Conference on Population and Development: Report.* New York. A/CONF.171/13.

————. 1993. *World Conference on Human Rights: Vienna Declaration and Programme of Action.* New York. A/Conf.157/24.

————. 1991a. *Women: Challenges to the Year 2000.* New York.

————. 1991b. *The World's Women 1970–1990: Trends and Statistics.* New York.

————. 1991c. *UNTAG in Namibia: A New Nation is Born.* New York.

————. 1990. *The Blue Helmets, A Review of United Nations Peacekeeping.* New York.

————. 1985. *World Conference to Review and Appraise the Achievements of the United*

Nations Decade for Women: Equality, Development, and Peace: Report. New York. A/CONF.116/Rev.1.

————. 1980. *World Conference of the United Nations Decade for Women: Equality, Development, and Peace: Report.* New York. A/Conf.94/35.

————. 1975. *World Conference of the International Women's Year: Report.* New York. A/Conf.66/34.

United Nations Branch for the Advancement of Women. 1986. *Expert Group Meeting on Violence Against Women in the Family with Special Emphasis on its Effects on Women: Report.* Vienna.

United Nations Commission on Human Rights. 1993. *49th Session: Report.* Geneva. E/1993/23.

United Nations Commission on the Status of Women. 1996a. *Follow-up to the Fourth World Conference on Women: Draft Resolution on Mainstreaming the Human Rights of Women.* Submitted by Australia, Canada, and Norway. Geneva. E/CN.6/1996/L.4.

————. 1996b. *Follow-up to the Fourth World Conference on Women: Draft Resolution on Traffic in Women and Girls.* Submitted by Fiji, Ghana, Nigeria, Philippines, and Thailand. Geneva. E/CN .6/1996/L.5.

————. 1996c. *Follow-up to the Fourth World Conference on Women: Draft Resolution on Violence Against Women Migration Workers.* Submitted by Fiji, Ghana, and Philippines. Geneva. E/CN.6/1996/L.7.

————. 1993. *37th Session: Report.* Vienna. E/CN.6/1993/18.

————. 1992a. *36th Session: Report.* Vienna. E/CN.6/1992/4.

————. 1992b. *Report of the Working Group on Violence Against Women: Preparation of a Declaration on Violence Against Women.* Vienna. E/CN.6/WG2/1992/L.2.

————. 1988. *32nd Session: Report.* Vienna. E/CN.6/1988/11/Rev.1.

————. 1984. *30th Session: Report.* Vienna. E/CN.6/1984/12.

United Nations Committee on the Elimination of Discrimination Against Women. 1997. *Reservations to the Convention on the Elimination of All Forms of Discrimination Against Women.* CEDAW/C/1997/4.

United Nations Department of Public Information. 1995 and 1996. *The United Nations and the Advancement of Women 1945–1996.* United Nations Blue Book Series, vol. 6. New York.

————. 1994. *United Nations Peace-Keeping Operations: Background Note.* New York. PS/DPI/15/Rev.6.

United Nations Development Programme. 1995. *Human Development Report 1995.* New York: Oxford University Press.

————. 1993. *Human Development Report.* New York: Oxford University Press.

United Nations Economic and Social Council. 1997. *Draft Agreed Conclusions. Coordination of Policies and Activities of the Specialized Agencies and Other Bodies of the UN System Related to the Following Theme: Mainstreaming a Gender Perspective into All Policies and Programmes in the United Nations System.* New York. E/1997/l.30.

————. 1996. Res. 1996/31.

————. 1994a. *Draft Regional Platform for Action: Women in a Changing World— Call for Action from an ECE Perspective.* New York. E/ECE/RW/HLM/L.3/Rev.1.

————. 1994b. *General Review of Arrangements for Consultations with Non-Governmental Organizations: Report of the Secretary General.* New York. E/AC.70/1994/5.

————. 1994c. *Working with Non-Governmental Organizations: Operational Activities for*

Development of the United Nations System with Non-Governmental Organizations and Governments at the Grass-Roots and National Levels: Note by the Secretary-General. New York. A/49/122; E/1994/44.

———. 1946a. *Resolution Establishing the Commission on Human Rights and the Subcommission on the Status of Women.* New York, 18 February. E/RES/5(1). Reprinted in United Nations Department of Public Information, *The United Nations and the Advancement of Women, 1945–1995,* UN Blue Book Series, vol. 6, doc. 3, pp. 99–100.

———. 1946b. *Resolution Establishing the Commission on the Status of Women (CSW).* New York, 21 June. E/RES/2/11. Reprinted in United Nations Department of Public Information, *The United Nations and the Advancement of Women, 1945–1995.* UN Blue Book Series, vol. 6, doc. 6, p. 102.

United Nations General Assembly. 1996. *Follow-up to the Fourth World Conference on Women and Full Implementation of the Beijing Declaration and the Platform for Action.* New York. 23 February. A/RES/50/203.

———. 1993a. *Adopting the Declaration on the Elimination of Violence against Women.* New York. A/RES/48/104.

———. 1993b. *Rape and Abuse of Women in the Former Yugoslavia.* New York. GA48/143.

———. 1990. *Improvement of the Status of Women in the Secretariat.* New York. 14 December. A/RES/45/125.

———. 1985. *Personnel Questions: Improvement of the Status of Women in the Secretariat.* New York. 18 December. A/RES/40/258 B.

———. 1946. *"'Open Letter to the Women of the World,'" read by Eleanor Roosevelt, representative of the delegation of the United States of America, to the first session of the General Assembly; and statements made by representatives on the participation of women in the work of the United Nations and the creation of a committee on the status of women (extract).* New York. 12 February. A/PV.29. Reprinted in United Nations Department of Public Information, *The United Nations and the Advancement of Women, 1945–1995,* UN Blue Book Series, vol. 6, doc. 2, pp. 93–98.

United Nations High Commissioner for Refugees. 1995a. *Conclusions on the International Protection of Refugees Adopted by the Executive Committee.* Geneva.

———. 1995b. *Sexual Violence against Refugees: Guidelines on Prevention and Response.* Geneva.

———. 1995c. *The State of the World's Refugees: In Search of Solutions.* Oxford: Oxford University Press.

———. 1993. *Report of the 18 May 1993 Joint Meeting of the Sub-Committee on Administrative and Financial Matters and the Subcommittee of the Whole on International Protection.* Geneva.

———. 1991a. *Guidelines on the Protection of Refugee Women.* Geneva.

———. 1991b. *UNHCR Policy on Refugee Women.* Geneva.

———. 1951. *Convention and Protocol Relating to the Status of Refugees.* Geneva.

United Nations International Trade Centre UNCTAD/GATT. 1994. *Contribution to the Regional Platform for Action—Europe: Integrating the Trade Dimension into Gender-Sensitive Sustainable Development Strategies and Programmes/Economies in Transition/A Regional Perspective.* For ECE High Level Regional Preparatory Meeting for the Fourth World Conference on Women, Vienna, Austria, 17–21 October.

United Nations Office of Public Information. 1977. *United Nations Special Observances and Conferences*. Reference Paper no. 15, New York.

United Nations Office of the Secretary-General. 1998a. Daily Press Briefing of Office of Spokesman for the Secretary-General. New York. 12 January.

———. 1998b. Press Release (9 March). New York. SG/SM/6480, WOM/1045.

———. 1998c. *Report of the Secretary-General on Improvement of the Status of Women in the Secretariat*. New York. E/CN.6/1998/8.

———. 1997a. *Advancement of Women: Improvement of the Status of Women in the Secretariat*. New York. A/52/408.

———. 1997b. Press Release, 27 August. SG/A/648.

———. 1995. *Peace: Women in International Decision-Making*. New York. E/CN.6/1995/12.

———. 1989. *Report of the Secretary General to the CSW on the First Review and Appraisal of the Implementation of the Nairobi Forward-Looking Strategies*. New York. E/CN.6/1990/5.

———. 1951. *Memorandum by the Secretary-General to the CSW on the Participation of Women in the Work of the United Nations*. New York. E/CN.6/167.

———. 1950. *Report of the Secretary-General to the CSW on the Participation of Women in the Work of the United Nations*. New York. E/CN.6/132.

United Nations Statistical Division. 1994. *Report of Statistical Compilation on Women in Peace-Keeping for the Second Issue of The World's Women: Trend and Statistics*. New York. DESIPA, STAT 321(a).

United Nations Treaty Series. 1981. Convention on the Elimination of All Forms of Discrimination against Women. *Treaties and International Agreements Registered or Filed or Reported with the Secretariat of the United Nations*, vol. 1249, no. 20378, p. 14.

———. 1951. Convention for the Suppression of the Traffic in Persons and of the Exploitation of the Prostitution of Others. *Treaties and International Agreements Registered or Filed or Reported with the Secretariat of the United Nations*, vol. 96, no. 1342, p. 270.

United States of America. 1984. *Policy Statement of the United States of America at the United Nations International Conference on Population*.

United States of America. Mission to the United Nations. 1993. Press Release, no. 63 (93), 11 May.

Vellacott, Jo. 1993. A Place for Pacifism and Transnationalism in Feminist Theory: The Early Work of the Women's International League for Peace and Freedom. *Women's History Review* 2, no. 1: 23–56.

Vienna NGO Forum. 1994. Vienna NGO Forum 94 Call to Action. Recommendations prepared for reading into the official record of the ECE Regional Preparatory Meeting for the Fourth World Conference for Women, Vienna, Austria, 17–21 October.

Violence in Ixcán Grande. 1997. *CERIGUA Weekly Briefs*, no. 18 (22 May).

Walby, Sylvia. 1994. Is Citizenship Gendered? *Sociology* 28, no. 2: 379–95.

Wali, Sima. 1995. Human Rights for Refugee and Displaced Women. Pp. 335–43 in *Women's Rights, Human Rights*, ed. Julie Peters and Andrea Wolper. New York: Routledge.

Walker, Millidge. 1996. *NGO Participation in a Corporatist State: The Example of Indonesia*. Berkeley, Calif.: Institute of Urban and Regional Development, Working Paper no. 673.

Wallace, William, and Julie Smith. 1995. Democracy or Technocracy? European Integration and the Problem of Popular Consent. *West European Politics* 18, no. 3: 135–57.

Walton, Hanes Jr. 1995. *Black Women at the United Nations: The Politics: A Theoretical Model, and the Documents*. San Bernardino, Calif.: Borgo Press.

Wang Zheng. 1996. A Historic Turning Point for the Women's Movement in China. *Signs: Journal of Women in Culture and Society* 22, no. 1 (Autumn): 192–99.

Ward, Kathryn, ed. 1990. *Women Workers and Global Restructuring*. Ithaca, N.Y.: ILR Press.

Warren, Karen J., ed. 1996. *Ecological Feminist Philosophies*. Bloomington: Indiana University Press.

———. 1994. *Ecological Feminism*. New York: Routledge.

WEDO: See Women's Environment and Development Organization.

Weiler, Joseph. 1992. After Maastricht: Community Legitimacy in Post-1992 Europe. Pp. 11–53 in *Singular Europe*, ed. William J. Adams. Ann Arbor: University of Michigan Press.

Weiss, Anita. 1992. *Within Walls: Life Histories of Working Women in the Old City of Lahore*. Boulder, Colo.: Westview Press.

Weiss, Thomas, and Leon Gordenker, eds. 1996a. *NGOs, the UN, and Global Governance*. With a foreword by Boutros Boutros-Ghali. Boulder, Colo.: Lynne Rienner.

———. 1996b. Pluralizing Global Governance: Analytical Approaches and Dimensions. Pp. 17–50 in *NGOs, the UN, and Global Governance*, ed. Thomas Weiss and Leon Gordenker. Boulder, Colo.: Lynne Rienner.

West, Lois. A. 1997. *Feminist Nationalism*. New York: Routledge.

———. 1980. U.N. Mid-Decade Conference for Women. *Off Our Backs* 10, no. 9: 2.

Whitworth, Sandra. 1994. *Feminism and International Relations: Towards a Political Economy of Gender in Interstate and Non-Governmental Institutions*. New York: St. Martin's Press.

WHO and IWHC. See World Health Organization.

WIDE, NAC, Alt-WID, CRIAW. 1994. Wealth of Nations—Poverty of Women. Paper presented at the Globalization of the Economy and Economic Justice for Women workshop at the NGO Forum of the ECE Regional Preparatory Meeting for the Fourth World Conference for Women, Vienna, Austria, 13–15 October.

Wilkins, Richard G. 1996. Bias, Error, and Duplicity: The UN and Domestic Law. *World and I*, December, 287–305.

Willetts, Peter. 1996. From Stockholm to Rio and Beyond: The Impact of the Environmental Movement on the UN's Consultative Arrangements for NGOs. *Review of International Studies* 22 (January): 57–80.

———. 1989. The Pattern of Conferences. Pp. 35–72 in *Global Issues in the United Nations' Framework*, ed. Paul Taylor and A. J. R. Groom. New York: St. Martin's Press.

———. 1982. Pressure Groups as Transnational Actors. Pp. 1–27 in *Pressure Groups in the International System: The Transnational Relations of Issue-Oriented Non-Governmental Organizations*, ed. Peter Willetts7. New York: St. Martin's Press.

Winslow, Anne. 1995a. Specialized Agencies and the World Bank. Pp. 155–75 in *Women Politics, and the United Nations*, ed. Anne Winslow. Westport, Conn.: Greenwood.

———, ed. 1995b. *Women, Politics, and the United Nations*. Westport, Conn: Greenwood Press.

Wiseberg, Laurie S. 1996. "Resolution 1296 Revised: A Done Deal on Consultative Status—Not Ideal but a Major Improvement." *Human Rights Tribune* 3 (August–September): 7–11.

Wolf, Diane, ed. 1996. *Feminist Dilemmas in Fieldwork*. Boulder, Colo.: Westview Press.

298   *Works Cited*

Women's Caucus. 1994. The Women's Caucus at the ICPD: Recommendations on Bracketed Text in the Draft Programme of Action of the ICPD. New York: Women's Environment and Development Organization (WEDO).

Women's Commission for Refugee Women and Children (WCRWC). 1992. *We Have a Voice and We Can Speak.* Delegation to Central America.

Women's Environment and Development Organization (WEDO). 1996a. *Beyond Promises: Governments in Motion One Year after the Beijing Women's Conference.* New York.

———. 1996b. *First Steps: What Has Happened since Beijing.* New York.

———. n.d [1996?]. *A Brief Analysis of the UN Fourth World Conference on Women Beijing Declaration and Platform for Action.* New York.

———. 1994. Fact Sheet. New York.

———. 1991. *Official Report of the World Women's Congress for a Healthy Planet, Miami, Fla.* New York.

Women's Global Alliance for Development Alternatives. 1995. Women Reclaim the Market: August 1995 Draft Report of Roundtable and Slide Show, NGO Forum, World Summit for Social Development, Copenhagen, 9 March. Brussels: WIDE.

Women's Global Network on Reproductive Rights (WGNRR). 1993. The Women's Alliance and the Women's Global Network for Reproductive Rights. *WGNRR Newsletter* (Amsterdam) (April-June): 43–49.

Women's Studies: A World View. 1996. *Women's Studies Quarterly* 24, nos. 1–2: 299–464.

A World Full of Activists: Reports from WILPF Sections. 1989. *Peace and Freedom* 49 (November/December): 19.

World Health Organization/Special Programme of Research, Development and Research Training in Human Reproduction (WHO/HRP) and International Women's Health Coalition (IWHC). 1991. Creating Common Ground: Women's Perspectives on the Selection and Introduction of Fertility Regulation Technologies. Report of a Meeting between Women's Health Advocates and Scientists. Geneva.

Wright, Shelley. 1993. Human Rights and Women's Rights: An Analysis of the United Nations Convention on the Elimination of All Forms of Discrimination against Women. Pp. 75–88 in *Human Rights in the Twenty-first Century: A Global Challenge*, ed. Kathleen Mahoney and Peter Mahoney. Dordrecht, The Netherlands: Martinus Nijhoff/Kluwer.

Yanco, Jennifer, and Gabriela Canepa, Director of International Programs and Member, respectively, of the Boston Women's Health Collective. 1994. Interview by Amy Higer, 7 February.

Yayasan Pengembangan Pedesaan. 1993. Grassroots Organizing of Homeworkers: The Gondang Experiment. Pp. 59–74 in *From the Shadows to the Fore: Practical Actions for the Social Protection of Homeworkers in Indonesia*, ed. Lucita Lazo. Bangkok: International Labour Organization.

Zalewski, Marysia. 1998. Women, Gender, and International Relations Ten Years On: "To Return as a Woman and Be Heard." Paper presented at the 1998 Millennium Conference, 13–14 September, London.

Appendix

The United Nations System

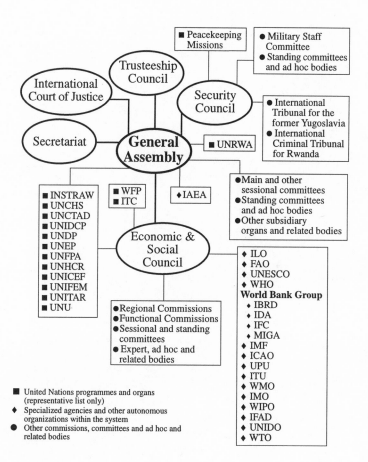

Index

Page references followed by *t* indicate material found in tables.

301

About the Contributors

ERIN K. BAINES is a Ph.D. candidate in the Department of Political Science at Dalhousie University in Halifax, Nova Scotia. She is currently completing her thesis, "Protecting Refugee Women: Recognizing Gender-Related Persecution," with support from the Social Sciences and Humanities Council as well as a Killiam Fellowship. She volunteers for Project Accompaniment Canada, which has led her to Guatemala on a number of occasions to work with refugee and displaced populations.

FRANCINE D'AMICO, Ph.D., is coeditor of *Gender Camouflage: Women and the U.S. Military* (New York University Press 1998), *Women in World Politics: An Introduction* (Bergin & Garvey 1995). and *Women, Gender, and World Politics: Perspectives, Policies, and Prospects* (Bergin & Garvey 1994). She has taught courses on international politics, law, and organizations at Ithaca College, Hobart and William Smith Colleges, and Cornell University, and she has served as an officer of the Feminist Theory and Gender Studies Section of the International Studies Association.

AMY J. HIGER is a visiting assistant professor at Rutgers University. She received her M.A. from American University and her Ph.D. in 1997 from Brandeis University, where she wrote her dissertation, "The International Women's Health Movement and Population Policy."

CATHERINE HOSKYNS is Jean Monnet Professor of European Studies at Coventry University in the United Kingdom. She is the author of *Integrating Gender: Women, Law, and Politics* (Verso 1996). She is currently working on issues of transnational democracy as these apply in the European Union.

JUTTA JOACHIM holds an M.A. in international studies from the University of South Carolina and has recently completed her Ph.D. in the Department of Political Science at the University of Wisconsin–Madison. The title of her dissertation is "The UN, Agenda-Setting, and NGOs: Violence against Women and Reproductive Rights and Health."

STEPHANIE HALLOCK JOHNSON completed her Ph.D. at the Graduate

313

School of International Studies at the University of Miami. Her dissertation explores the connections between ecofeminist thought and International Relations theory. She is currently an adjunct instructor of political science at Barry University and serves as director of communications for the South Florida Veterans Affairs Foundation for Research and Education.

MARY K. MEYER is associate professor of political science at Eckerd College, where she teaches courses in International Relations and Latin American politics. She has published articles on Latin American diplomacy and the Inter-American Commission of Women and is currently doing research on women and gender politics in the Northern Ireland peace process.

ALICE M. MILLER directs the Women's Rights Advocacy Program of the International Human Rights Law Group based in Washington, D.C. She completed her undergraduate work in 1979 at Radcliffe College, Harvard University, and her J.D. in 1985 at the University of Washington.

ELISABETH PRÜGL is assistant professor of international relations at Florida International University. She is the author of *The Global Construction of Gender: Home-Based Work in the Political Economy of the Twentieth Century* (Columbia University Press forthcoming) and coeditor of *Homeworkers in Global Perspective: Invisible No More* (Routledge 1996). Her current research focuses on constructions of citizenship in the European Union and the intersection of gender theory and constructivism.

ANNE SISSON RUNYAN is director of women's studies and associate professor of political science at Wright State University. She has published widely in the area of gender and international relations, including coauthoring (with V. Spike Peterson) *Global Gender Issues* (Westview Press 1993, 2d ed. forthcoming). She is currently coediting (with Marianne Marchand) a volume on gender and global restructuring.

JUDITH HICKS STIEHM is a professor of political science at Florida International University. She is the author of *Nonviolent Power: Active and Passive Resistance in America* (Heath 1972), *Bring Me Men and Women: Mandated Change in the U.S. Air Force Academy* (University of California Press 1981), and *Arms and the Enlisted Woman* (Temple University Press 1989). She edited *It's Our Military Too!* (Temple University Press 1996) and is working on a book on the U.S. War Colleges.

DEBORAH STIENSTRA teaches politics at the University of Winnipeg and is an activist especially around post-Beijing issues. She has written two books, *Women's Movements and International Organizations* (St. Martin's 1994) and, with Barbara Roberts, *Strategies for the Year 2000: A Woman's Handbook* (Fernwood 1995). She has also written articles on prostitution and international law, gender and foreign policy, global organizing using the Internet, and international norms on disability.

IRENE TINKER, professor emerita, University of California, Berkeley, is a committed activist who has worked alternatively for universities and nonprofit organizations, including the American Association for the Advancement of Science and the Equity Policy Center, which she founded in 1978. She has held leadership roles in a dozen women's organizations, documented in *Women in Washington: Advocates for Public Policy* (Sage 1994); run for state office; and represented many groups at United Nations meetings and conferences. Recent publications include *Street Foods: Urban Food and Employment in Developing Countries* (Oxford University Press 1997) and *Women's Changing Rights to House and Land in China, Laos, and Vietnam* (Lynne Rienner forthcoming).

EMEK M. UÇARER is assistant professor of international relations at Bucknell University. Her Ph.D. is from the University of South Carolina, and her dissertation focused on the harmonization of asylum policies in the European Union. She is coeditor, with Donald J. Puchala, of *Immigration into Western Societies: Problems and Policies* (Pinter 1997).

LOIS A. WEST is associate professor of sociology and women's studies at Florida International University. She has a Ph.D. in sociology from the University of California, Berkeley, and an M.A. in women's studies from George Washington University. She is author of *Militant Labor in the Philippines* (Temple University Press 1997) and editor of *Feminist Nationalism* (Routledge 1997).